ANNUAL EDITIONS

Education 10/11

Thirty-Seventh Edition

EDITOR

Dr. Rebecca B. Evers
Winthrop University

Dr. Rebecca Evers, an associate professor in the Center for Pedagogy at the Richard W. Riley College of Education, attended Illinois College to earn a BA in English education in 1966, an MA in the Rehabilitation Teaching of the Adult Blind from Western Michigan University in 1969, and an EdD in special education at Northern Illinois University in 1994. She is actively involved in researching methods to determine and assess the quality of teacher candidate's dispositions. Her primary focus is dispositions for providing equitable access to learning for students with disabilities and other exceptional needs.

ANNUAL EDITIONS: EDUCATION, THIRTY-SEVENTH EDITION

Published by McGraw-Hill, a business unit of The McGraw-Hill Companies, Inc., 1221 Avenue of the Americas, New York, NY 10020. Copyright © 2010 by The McGraw-Hill Companies, Inc. All rights reserved. Previous edition(s) 1972–2008. No part of this publication may be reproduced or distributed in any form or by any means, or stored in a database or retrieval system, without the prior written consent of The McGraw-Hill Companies, Inc., including, but not limited to, in any network or other electronic storage or transmission, or broadcast for distance learning.

Some ancillaries, including electronic and print components, may not be available to customers outside the United States.

Annual Editions® is a registered trademark of The McGraw-Hill Companies, Inc.

Annual Editions is published by the **Contemporary Learning Series** group within the McGraw-Hill Higher Education division.

1 2 3 4 5 6 7 8 9 0 QPD/QPD 0 9

ISBN 978–0–07–813585–9
MHID 0–07–813585–0
ISSN 0272–5010

Managing Editor: *Larry Loeppke*
Senior Production Manager: *Faye Schilling*
Developmental Editor: *Dave Welsh*
Editorial Coordinator: *Mary Foust*
Editorial Assistant: *Cindy Hedley*
Production Service Assistant: *Rita Hingtgen*
Permissions Coordinator: *DeAnna Dausener*
Senior Marketing Manager: *Julie Keck*
Marketing Communications Specialist: *Mary Klein*
Marketing Coordinator: *Alice Link*
Project Manager: *Joyce Watters*
Design Specialist: *Tara McDermott*
Production Supervisor: *Sue Culbertson*
Cover Graphics: *Kristine Jubeck*

Compositor: Laserwords Private Limited
Cover Image: © Comstock Images/Alamy (inset); © Comstock/Corbis (background)

Library in Congress Cataloging-in-Publication Data
Main entry under title: Annual Editions: Education. 2010/2011.
 1. Education—Periodicals. I. Evers, Rebecca B., *comp.* II. Title: Education.
658'.05

www.mhhe.com

Editors/Academic Advisory Board

Members of the Academic Advisory Board are instrumental in the final selection of articles for each edition of ANNUAL EDITIONS. Their review of articles for content, level, and appropriateness provides critical direction to the editors and staff. We think that you will find their careful consideration well reflected in this volume.

ANNUAL EDITIONS: Education 10/11
37th Edition

EDITOR

Dr. Rebecca B. Evers
Winthrop University

Editors/Academic Advisory Board continued

Preface

In publishing ANNUAL EDITIONS we recognize the enormous role played by the magazines, newspapers, and journals of the public press in providing current, first-rate educational information in a broad spectrum of interest areas. Many of these articles are appropriate for students, researchers, and professionals seeking accurate, current material to help bridge the gap between principles and theories and the real world. These articles, however, become more useful for study when those of lasting value are carefully collected, organized, indexed, and reproduced in a low-cost format, which provides easy and permanent access when the material is needed. That is the role played by ANNUAL EDITIONS.

We face a myriad of quandaries in our schools today, not unfamiliar in our history as a nation, divided and not easily resolved. On the one hand, we are to have "highly qualified teachers"; on the other hand, we leave it to state politicians and the local school authorities as to what constitutes "highly qualified teachers." This is a typical enigmatic dilemma in the history of U.S. education. If we are not to leave any student behind, really and sincerely, can we come to grips with what it means to have a "highly qualified teacher"?

Issues regarding the purposes of education as well as the appropriate methods of educating have been debated throughout all generations of literate human culture. This is because the meaning of the word "educated" shifts within ideological realms of thought and cultural belief systems. There will always be debates over the purposes and the ends of "education" as they are understood in any time or place. This is because each generation must continuously reconstruct the definition of "education" based upon its understanding of "justice," "fairness," and "equity" in human relations, and each generation must locate and position its understanding of social justice and personal responsibility to our children and youth. All of this occurs as the United States continues to experience fundamentally important demographic shifts in its cultural makeup.

We must decide what knowledge is of most worth and what basic skills and information each child needs to know. We must face this question once and for all; it is a duty, if we are disciplined persons interested in the well-being of our children and adolescents. We have before us a great qualitative challenge, our response to which may determine the fate of future generations of our society.

The technological breakthroughs now developing in the information sciences are having an amazing impact on how people learn. The rates of change in how we learn and how we obtain information is already increasing at a very rapid pace that will assuredly continue.

The public conversation on the purposes and future directions of education is lively as ever. Alternative visions and voices regarding the broad social aims of schools and the preparation of teachers continue to be presented.

Annual Editions: Education 10/11 attempts to reflect current mainstream as well as alternative visions as to what education ought to be. Equity issues regarding what constitutes equal treatment of students in the schools continue to be addressed. This year's edition contains articles on important issues facing educators and students. We present articles discussing the issues of educating students who do not speak English as a native language, students who have disabilities, and students who may not wish to pursue a four-year postsecondary education. If we desire "highly qualified" teachers, should we also ask that our teacher have a prescribed set of dispositions for teaching? Concerns that we have unfilled teaching positions and educators who leave teaching within their first five-years are addressed in several articles. We include authors who express the desire that the curriculum should include themes of democracy, altruism, and patriotism.

In assembling this volume, we make every effort to stay in touch with movements in educational studies and with the social forces at work in schools. Members of the advisory board contribute valuable insights, and the production and editorial staffs at the publisher, McGraw-Hill Contemporary Learning Series, coordinate our efforts.

The readings in *Annual Editions: Education 10/11* explore the social and academic goals of education, the current conditions of the nation's educational systems, the teaching profession, and the future of U.S. education. In addition, these selections address the issues of change and the moral and ethical foundations of schooling. As always, we would like you to help us improve this volume. Please rate the material in this edition on the postage-paid *article rating form* provided at the back of this book and send it to us. We care about what you think. Give us the public feedback that we need.

Rebecca B. Evers
Editor

Contents

Preface   *v*

Correlation Guide   *xii*

Topic Guide   *xiii*

Internet References   *xv*

UNIT 1
Assessment and Research: Do They Inform Our Teaching Practices?

Unit Overview   **xviii**

1. **Where Have All the Strong Poets Gone?,** Alan C. Jones,
Phi Delta Kappan, April 2007

   The author makes a telling metaphorical point regarding where we are in the current debate about the restructuring or renewal of American schooling. We stand on the shoulders of intellectual giants. Where have they gone? What have we forgotten?   **2**

2. **Proficiency for All?,** Dave Moscinski, *American School Board Journal,*
November 2007

   A school superintendent suggests ten strategies for living with and using the No Child Left Behind Act to improve the educational opportunities for all students in all grades.   **5**

3. **Bridging the Gap between Research and Practice: What's Good, What's Bad, and How Can One Be Sure?,** Stephen H. Davis, *Phi Delta Kappan,* April 2007

   This is an insightful introduction for teachers as to what is "good" for the students' learning in schools. The author attempts to bridge the gap between educational theory and practice. The language clarity gap between academic scholars in education and classroom teachers in schools is well described.   **7**

4. **Learning to Love Assessment,** Carol Ann Tomlinson,
Educational Leadership, December 2008

   As a novice teacher, the author was apprehensive about how to assess her students. She describes her journey from fearing assessment to using informative assessment to improve her teaching and student learning.   **15**

5. **The Case for and against Homework,** Robert J. Marzano and
Debra J. Pickering, *Educational Leadership,* March 2007

   The value of homework has been a perennial topic for teachers, administrators, and parents. The authors urge readers to reconsider the importance of homework as a powerful instructional tool when used correctly. They offer suggestions for using homework as a positive tool for all involved.   **19**

UNIT 2
Reformatting Our Schools

Unit Overview   **24**

6. **Assessing Applied Skills,** Joe DiMartino and Andrea Castaneda,
Educational Leadership, April 2007

   The authors discuss the use of applied skills in school learning. They advocate very useful skill development courses/technics for students that will improve their performance in schools. They describe examples of how authentic, individualized "project" approaches to schooling can optimize student learning and performance.   **27**

The concepts in bold italics are developed in the article. For further expansion, please refer to the Topic Guide.

7. **From the Mouths of Middle-Schoolers: Important Changes for High School and College,** William J. Bushaw, *Phi Delta Kappan,* November 2007

As politicians and educators debated about the educational system, one voice was missing—the students' voice. This report supplies that missing voice, as middle-schoolers tell us what they think about schools and the training they receive. **30**

8. **Industrial Arts: Call It What You Want, the Need Still Exists,** James Howlett, *Phi Delta Kappan,* March 2008

Who will fill the industrial jobs in the 21st century? The author is concerned that schools are not graduating enough skilled students for the jobs that will be left vacant when the baby-boomers leave the workforce. This may cause a serious issue for our manufacturing industry, as well the for the service and construction industries. **33**

9. **High Schools Have Got It Bad for Higher Ed—And That Ain't Good,** Rona Wilensky, *Phi Delta Kappan,* December 2007

In this article the author discusses the skewing of high school courses toward the college-bound students. She explains how this creates a watered-down curriculum for the non-college-bound students. Finally, she offers a discussion of what should be the focus of high school in the 21st century. **36**

10. **All Our Students Thinking,** Nel Noddings, *Educational Leadership,* February 2008

This is a thoughtful piece about teaching our students to think at all levels rather than merely making them memorize facts. As our world is changing, all citizens, whether employed in blue, pink, or white collar jobs, must be life-long learners who can think independently and solve problems effectively. **44**

UNIT 3
Addressing Diversity in Your School

Unit Overview **48**

11. **As Diversity Grows, So Must We,** Gary R. Howard, *Educational Leadership,* March 2007

The author addresses the issue of cultural diversity in schools with good insight and understanding of the demographic changes in schools. He suggests five phases of professional development to educators for assisting students to adjust to the changing social phenomenon. **50**

12. **African American Parents: Improving Connections with Their Child's Educational Environment,** Regina R. Brandon, *Intervention in School and Clinic,* November 2007

In this article, the author explains why parents don't interact with their child's school. The author offers suggestions for improving the rate of parental interaction with schools. These suggestions may also be used to improve interaction among parents from different cultures. **54**

13. **The Myth of the "Culture of Poverty",** Paul Gorski, *Educational Leadership,* April 2008

Gorski explains how we came to believe that a culture of poverty exists. He examines a set of false stereotypes that recent research has proven to be false. Another point is that teachers who believe in the stereotypes are in danger of engaging in classism. The author finishes with a list of actions teachers to promote equality and equity in their schools. **59**

14. **Becoming Adept at Code-Switching,** Rebecca S. Wheeler, *Educational Leadership,* April 2008

Students who do not hear or speak Standard English in their community need a teacher who understands the need to teach code-switching. The author offers suggestions with examples to teachers who teach students from diverse cultural and linguistic backgrounds. **63**

The concepts in bold italics are developed in the article. For further expansion, please refer to the Topic Guide.

15. **Overcoming Lethargy in Gifted and Talented Education with Contract Activity Packages: I'm Choosing to Learn!,** Janet Caraisco, *The Clearing House,* July/August 2007

The author suggests the use of contract activity packages, which target learning preferences. Her research suggests a significant improvement in positive attitude for learning science. Sufficient information is given in this article for teachers to reproduce these results. 66

16. **Mother Goose Teaches on the Wild Side: Motivating At-Risk Mexican and Chicano Youngsters via a Multicultural Curriculum,** Martha Casas, *Multicultural Review,* Winter 2006

This article is about a teacher who became a college professor and returned to the middle school where she once taught to research a multicultural curriculum to students enrolled in the alternative education program. She presents research-based teaching methods with a "wild side" to students who were hard to reach. 71

17. **Celebrating Diversity through Explorations of Arab Children's Literature,** Tami Al-Hazza and Bob Lucking, *Childhood Education,* Spring 2007

According to these authors, recent national and global events have dramatically changed global perceptions of Arab culture and religious practices with negative stereotypes. They wish to help teachers and families find literature that will accurately depict the cultural norms of the Arab world. 80

18. **Books That Portray Characters with Disabilities: A Top 25 List for Children and Young Adults,** Mary Anne Prater and Tina Taylor Dyches, *Teaching Exceptional Children,* March/April 2008

Teachers and parents will find this list of books very helpful in teaching children about their siblings or classmates with disabilities. Further, the books also offer role models for all children. Be sure to review the authors' guidelines for book selection to help you find additional books. 84

UNIT 4
Preparing Teachers to Teach All Students in All Schools

Unit Overview 90

19. **Reluctant Teachers, Reluctant Learners,** Julie Landsman, Tiffany Moore, and Robert Simmons, *Educational Leadership,* March 2008

These authors suggested a primary reason for reluctant students is teachers who are reluctant to authentically engage with students who do not look, act, or talk like the teacher. They discuss how and why this happens. Finally, they offer suggestions that teachers can use immediately to prevent or change the possibly that their actions are affecting student learning and behavior. 92

20. **Musing: A Way to Inform and Inspire Pedagogy through Self-Reflection,** Jane Moore and Vickie Fields Whitfield, *Reading Teacher,* April 2008

In order to deal with the social and educational issues facing teachers, these authors suggest that teachers engage in self-reflection. Musing allows teachers to grow and defend their teaching practices. After explaining the reasons to reflect and three levels of reflection, they offer questions to guide personal musings. 96

21. **Why Teacher Networks (Can) Work,** Tricia Niesz, *Phi Delta Kappan,* April 2007

The author discusses the concept of teacher networks and how they work. "Communities of practice" where teachers form communities or networks to engage in learning from shared dialogue about professional practice is endorsed. Teacher candidates and novice teachers will find the suggestions helpful as they begin their own careers. 99

The concepts in bold italics are developed in the article. For further expansion, please refer to the Topic Guide.

UNIT 5
Cornerstones to Learning: Reading and Math

Unit Overview   **104**

22. **Response to Intervention (RTI): What Teachers of Reading Need to Know,** Eric M. Mesmer and Heidi Anne E. Mesmer, *The Reading Teacher,* December 2008/January 2009

    Educational law, Individuals with Disabilities Education Act, introduced Response to Intervention (RTI) as a method for establishing eligibility for special education services. These authors explain the five-step process. A vignette of a real student provides an example of teacher duties and responsibilities when implementing RTI.   **106**

23. **You Should Read This Book!,** Jennifer Hartley, *Educational Leadership,* March 2008

    The previous article suggests that we drop everything and just read, but how do we do that? The author of this article, a teacher, shares her multi-trial process to developing a sustained silent reading program in her classroom. Teachers and parents will be able to use her information to support students.   **115**

24. **Getting Children In2Books: Engagement in Authentic Reading, Writing, and Thinking,** William H. Teale et al., *Phi Delta Kappan,* March 2007

    Combining reading, writing, and thinking, the authors suggest a program to motivate students to generalize and use authentic high order thinking, and composing and comprehension skills across the curriculum. In other words, they encourage the students to use the skills that are considered vital for adulthood.   **118**

25. **Using Literature Circles with English Language Learners at the Middle Level,** Pamela J. Farris, Pamela A. Nelson, and Susan L'Ailler, *Middle School Journal,* March 2007

    Reading activities in classrooms can be a bewildering experience for students who are ELL. These authors explain how they encouraged reading in students with literature circles. These methods are also well suited to be used by students with exceptional needs.   **122**

26. **Losing the Fear of Sharing Control: Starting a Reading Workshop,** Lesley Roessing, *Middle School Journal,* January 2007

    Does a teacher's need to control the classroom discourage student learning? As one teacher answered that question, she explained how she traded total control for student's choice. Using shared readings, book club communities, individual reading workshops, and written student responses, this teacher makes a change in her classes from hating to read to loving to read.   **126**

27. **Nine Ways to Catch Kids Up,** Marilyn Burns, *Educational Leadership,* November 2007

    Burns asks and answers the question of how to help floundering students with nine intervention strategies. Then she describes three times when intervention can be valuable for students; while the class is learning, before the class has learned, and after the class has learned.   **132**

28. **The Classroom That Math Built: Encouraging Young Mathematicians to Pose Problems,** Ann H. Wallace, Deborah Abbott, and Renee McAlhaney Blary, *Young Children,* September 2007

    Giving students the freedom to pose their own math problems is the primary focus of this article. The example of a practicing teacher and her methods for engaging students in posing math problems will allow readers to understand how to implement these teaching methods in their own classes.   **137**

The concepts in bold italics are developed in the article. For further expansion, please refer to the Topic Guide.

UNIT 6
Rethinking Behavior Management: Getting the Behavior You Want and Need to Teach Effectively

Unit Overview   **142**

29. **Tackling a Problematic Behavior Management Issue: Teachers' Intervention in Childhood Bullying Problems,** Laura M. Crothers and Jered B. Kolbert, *Intervention in School and Clinic,* January 2008

The issue of bullying has been highlighted by the recent violent events caused by persons who were bullied by their peers. These authors suggest that bullying is a classroom management issue and offer eight strategies to address bullying behaviors. Teachers at all grades levels will find these strategies helpful.   **144**

30. **The Under-Appreciated Role of Humiliation in the Middle School,** Nancy Frey and Douglas Fisher, *Middle School Journal,* January 2008

Many of us can think back to bad days in middle school; of the humiliation as peers laughed at us or called us names. The authors discuss the long-term effects of humiliation on young adolescents and strategies for reducing that humiliation.   **152**

31. **The Power of Our Words,** Paula Denton, *Educational Leadership,* September 2008

While bullying by peers can have a negative impact on a person's life so can the words spoken by teachers. Denton uses examples of teacher language that can negatively shape students' thoughts, feelings, and experiences. Finally, Denton suggests five guiding principles for using positive language.   **160**

32. **Marketing Civility,** Michael Stiles and Ben Tyson, *American School Board,* March 2008

These authors cite data from a study of bullying in a suburban high school that indicate bullying is not just an urban school issue. They suggest six school-wide efforts that can change a school's climate.   **163**

33. **Classwide Interventions: Effective Instruction Makes a Difference,** Maureen A. Conroy et al., *Teaching Exceptional Children,* June/July 2008

Two case studies, one of a classroom that works and one that has challenges, anchor this article. The authors posit that there are six universal classroom tools for effective instruction that when used will positively and preventively reduce behavior problems.   **165**

34. **Developing Effective Behavior Intervention Plans: Suggestions for School Personnel,** Kim Killu, *Intervention in School and Clinic,* January 2008

Inclusive classrooms may have students with persistent behavior problems. Also, federal law requires that students in IEPs also be included in Behavior Intervention Plans (BIPs). Teachers will find this article on assessing and planning interventions helpful, as they strive to manage persistent behavior problems that are resistant to typical management strategies.   **172**

UNIT 7
Creating Caring Communities of Learners

Unit Overview   **182**

35. **Becoming Citizens of the World,** Vivien Stewart, *Educational Leadership,* April 2007

The author addresses the issue of the vision of American education as she addresses the worldwide vision of what education can become in a multicultural world. She presents the concept of "global competence" and predicts what American high school graduates will be able to do. She argues that all of us must have a vision of what we wish to achieve.   **184**

The concepts in bold italics are developed in the article. For further expansion, please refer to the Topic Guide.

36. **Democracy and Education: Empowering Students to Make Sense of Their World,** William H. Garrison, *Phi Delta Kappan,* January 2008

The author makes a case for empowering students with freedom and personal responsibility for their learning. He asserts that democratic social institutions are produced when persons have the freedom to learn from experiences, build on the experiences, and use this knowledge to direct future experiences.   **189**

37. **Thinking about Patriotism,** Joel Westheimer, *Educational Leadership,* February 2008

Are we teaching our students to be member of a truly democratic society? This author asserts that we are not doing this, but rather teaching disconnected facts that do not help our students to understand the quintessential American experiences of struggle for a better society.   **191**

38. **What Is Personalization?,** James W. Keefe, *Phi Delta Kappan,* November 2007

Keefe notes that the concept of a personalized education has been around for 40 years, but has never been more important than the present. The discussion offered in this article explains clearly what is meant by personalization and offers examples of how teachers have achieved it.   **195**

39. **Cultivating Optimism in the Classroom,** Richard Sagor, *Educational Leadership,* March 2008

One reason students drop out of school is that they do not see any reason to invest time and energy in something that does not have meaning for lives. Sagor recommends strategies and actions for educators to use to build student optimism, thereby creating a culture in which they will put forth their best efforts.   **200**

Test-Your-Knowledge Form   **204**
Article Rating Form   **205**

The concepts in bold italics are developed in the article. For further expansion, please refer to the Topic Guide.

Correlation Guide

The *Annual Editions* series provides students with convenient, inexpensive access to current, carefully selected articles from the public press. **Annual Editions: Education 10/11** is an easy-to-use reader that presents articles on important topics such as *assessment and research, new school trends, the effects and challenges of diversity and poverty,* and many more. For more information on *Annual Editions* and other *McGraw-Hill Contemporary Learning Series* titles, visit www.mhhe.com/cls.

This convenient guide matches the units in **Annual Editions: Education 10/11** with the corresponding chapters in three of our best-selling McGraw-Hill Education textbooks by Tozer et al., Nelson et al., and Spring.

Annual Editions: Education 10/11	School and Society: Historical and Contemporary Perspectives, 6/e by Tozer et al.	Critical Issues in Education: Dialogues and Dialectics, 7/e by Nelson et al.	American Education, 14/e by Spring
Unit 1: Assessment and Research: Do They Inform Our Teaching Practices?	**Chapter 7:** National School Reform: The Early Cold War Era	**Chapter 14:** Standardized Testing: Restrict or Expand	**Chapter 7:** Power and Control at State and National Levels: Political Party Platforms, High- Stakes Testing, and School Violence
Unit 2: Reformatting Our Schools	**Chapter 7:** National School Reform: The Early Cold War Era **Chapter 11:** Differentiated Schooling, Labor Market Preparation and Contemporary School Reform	**Chapter 10:** The Academic Achievement Gap: Old Remedies or New **Chapter 11:** Values/Character Education: Traditional or Liberational **Chapter 13:** Technology and Learning: Enabling or Subverting	**Chapter 1:** The History and Goals of Public Schooling
Unit 3: Addressing Diversity in Your School	**Chapter 4:** Diversity and Equity: Schooling and African Americans **Chapter 5:** Social Diversity and Differentiated Schooling: The Progressive Era **Chapter 6:** Diversity and Equity: Schooling and American Indians **Chapter 8:** Diversity and Equity Schooling Girls and Women **Chapter 12:** Diversity and Equity Today: Defining the Challenge	**Chapter 12:** Multicultural Education: Democratic or Divisive	**Chapter 2:** Education and Equality of Opportunity **Chapter 3:** Equality of Educational Opportunity: Race, Gender, and Special Needs **Chapter 4:** Student Diversity **Chapter 5:** Multicultural and Multilingual Education
Unit 4: Preparing Teachers to Teach All Students in All Schools	**Chapter 1:** Introduction: Understanding School and Society **Chapter 2:** Liberty and Literacy: The Jeffersonian Era **Chapter 3:** School as a Public Institution: The Common-School Era **Chapter 7:** National School Reform: The Early Cold War Era **Chapter 9:** Liberty and Literacy Today: Contemporary Perspectives **Chapter 11:** Differentiated Schooling, Labor Market Preparation and Contemporary School Reform	**Chapter 18:** Inclusion and Mainstreaming: Common or Special Education **Chapter 17:** Academic Freedom: Teacher Rights or Responsibilities	**Chapter 8:** The Profession of Teaching
Unit 5: Cornerstones to Learning: Reading and Math			
Unit 6: Rethinking Behavior Management: Getting the Behavior You Want and Need to Teach Effectively		**Chapter 15:** Discipline and Justice: Zero Tolerance or Discretion **Chapter 19:** Violence in Schools: School Treatable or Beyond School Control	
Unit 7: Creating Caring Communities of Learners	**Chapter 1:** Introduction: Understanding School and Society **Chapter 4:** Diversity and Equity: Schooling and African Americans **Chapter 5:** Social Diversity and Differentiated Schooling: The Progressive Era **Chapter 6:** Diversity and Equity: Schooling and American Indians **Chapter 8:** Diversity and Equity Schooling Girls and Women **Chapter 11:** Differentiated Schooling, Labor Market Preparation, and Contemporary School Reform: The Post-Cold War Era	**Chapter 12:** Multicultural Education: Democratic or Divisive **Chapter 18:** Inclusion and Mainstreaming: Common or Special Education	**Chapter 1:** The History and Goals of Public Schooling **Chapter 2:** Education and Equality of Opportunity **Chapter 3:** Equality of Educational Opportunity: Race, Gender, and Special Needs **Chapter 4:** Student Diversity **Chapter 5:** Multicultural and Multilingual Education

Topic Guide

This topic guide suggests how the selections in this book relate to the subjects covered in your course. You may want to use the topics listed on these pages to search the Web more easily.

On the following pages a number of Web sites have been gathered specifically for this book. They are arranged to reflect the units of this Annual Editions reader. You can link to these sites by going to *http://www.mhcls.com.*

All the articles that relate to each topic are listed below the bold-faced term.

Authentic learning
8. Industrial Arts: Call It What You Want, the Need Still Exists
15. Overcoming Lethargy in Gifted and Talented Education with Contract Activity Packages: I'm Choosing to Learn!
24. Getting Children In2Books: Engagement in Authentic Reading, Writing, and Thinking
25. Using Literature Circles with English Language Learners at the Middle Level

African Americans
12. African American Parents: Improving Connections with Their Child's Educational Environment

Applied skills
6. Assessing Applied Skills
8. Industrial Arts: Call It What You Want, the Need Still Exists

Assessment and research
1. Where Have All the Strong Poets Gone?
2. Proficiency for All?
3. Bridging the Gap between Research and Practice: What's Good, What's Bad, and How Can One Be Sure?
4. Learning to Love Assessment
5. The Case for and against Homework
6. Assessing Applied Skills

Behavior management
29. Tackling a Problematic Behavior Management Issue: Teachers' Intervention in Childhood Bullying Problems
34. Developing Effective Behavior Intervention Plans: Suggestions for School Personnel

Bullying
29. Tackling a Problematic Behavior Management Issue: Teachers' Intervention in Childhood Bullying Problems

Caring communities of learners
35. Becoming Citizens of the World
36. Democracy and Education: Empowering Students to Make Sense of Their World
37. Thinking about Patriotism

Critical thinking skills
9. High Schools Have Got It Bad for Higher Ed—And That Ain't Good

Cultural diversity
11. As Diversity Grows, So Must We
12. African American Parents: Improving Connections with Their Child's Educational Environment
14. Becoming Adept at Code-Switching

Democracy
36. Democracy and Education: Empowering Students to Make Sense of Their World
37. Thinking about Patriotism

Disability
18. Books That Portray Characters with Disabilities: A Top 25 List for Children and Young Adults
33. Classwide Interventions: Effective Instruction Makes a Difference

Discipline
29. Tackling a Problematic Behavior Management Issue: Teachers' Intervention in Childhood Bullying Problems
34. Developing Effective Behavior Intervention Plans: Suggestions for School Personnel

Diversity
11. As Diversity Grows, So Must We
12. African American Parents: Improving Connections with Their Child's Educational Environment
13. The Myth of the "Culture of Poverty"
14. Becoming Adept at Code-Switching
15. Overcoming Lethargy in Gifted and Talented Education with Contract Activity Packages: I'm Choosing to Learn!
16. Mother Goose Teaches on the Wild Side: Motivating At-Risk Mexican and Chicano Youngsters via a Multicultural Curriculum
17. Celebrating Diversity through Explorations of Arab Children's Literature
18. Books That Portray Characters with Disabilities: A Top 25 List for Children and Young Adults
19. Reluctant Teachers, Reluctant Learners

Educating our workforce
6. Assessing Applied Skills
7. From the Mouths of Middle-Schoolers: Important Changes for High School and College
8. Industrial Arts: Call It What You Want, the Need Still Exists

English language learners
14. Becoming Adept at Code-Switching
25. Using Literature Circles with English Language Learners at the Middle Level

Families
12. African American Parents: Improving Connections with Their Child's Educational Environment
13. The Myth of the "Culture of Poverty"

Gifted and talented
15. Overcoming Lethargy in Gifted and Talented Education with Contract Activity Packages: I'm Choosing to Learn!

Inclusion
15. Overcoming Lethargy in Gifted and Talented Education with Contract Activity Packages: I'm Choosing to Learn!
18. Books That Portray Characters with Disabilities: A Top 25 List for Children and Young Adults

Literacy

23. You Should Read This Book!
24. Getting Children In2Books: Engagement in Authentic Reading, Writing, and Thinking
25. Using Literature Circles with English Language Learners at the Middle Level
26. Losing the Fear of Sharing Control: Starting a Reading Workshop

Middle school students

7. From the Mouths of Middle-Schoolers: Important Changes for High School and College
26. Losing the Fear of Sharing Control: Starting a Reading Workshop
30. The Under-Appreciated Role of Humiliation in the Middle School

Morality and values in education

37. Thinking about Patriotism

Multicultural education

11. As Diversity Grows, So Must We
12. African American Parents: Improving Connections with Their Child's Educational Environment
14. Becoming Adept at Code-Switching
16. Mother Goose Teaches on the Wild Side: Motivating At-Risk Mexican and Chicano Youngsters via a Multicultural Curriculum
17. Celebrating Diversity through Explorations of Arab Children's Literature

No child left behind

2. Proficiency for All?

Patriotism

37. Thinking about Patriotism

Preparing teachers to teach all students

15. Overcoming Lethargy in Gifted and Talented Education with Contract Activity Packages: I'm Choosing to Learn!
16. Mother Goose Teaches on the Wild Side: Motivating At-Risk Mexican and Chicano Youngsters via a Multicultural Curriculum
19. Reluctant Teachers, Reluctant Learners
21. Why Teacher Networks (Can) Work

Race and education

12. African American Parents: Improving Connections with Their Child's Educational Environment

Reformatting our schools

6. Assessing Applied Skills
7. From the Mouths of Middle-Schoolers: Important Changes for High School and College
8. Industrial Arts: Call It What You Want, the Need Still Exists
9. High Schools Have Got It Bad for Higher Ed—And That Ain't Good
10. All Our Students Thinking

Real world relevance in schools

8. Industrial Arts: Call It What You Want, the Need Still Exists
9. High Schools Have Got It Bad for Higher Ed—And That Ain't Good
10. All Our Students Thinking

Research

3. Bridging the Gap between Research and Practice: What's Good, What's Bad, and How Can One Be Sure?

Rethinking education

1. Where Have All the Strong Poets Gone?
6. Assessing Applied Skills
7. From the Mouths of Middle-Schoolers: Important Changes for High School and College

Secondary education

6. Assessing Applied Skills
8. Industrial Arts: Call It What You Want, the Need Still Exists
9. High Schools Have Got It Bad for Higher Ed—And That Ain't Good

Special education

18. Books That Portray Characters with Disabilities: A Top 25 List for Children and Young Adults
29. Tackling a Problematic Behavior Management Issue: Teachers' Intervention in Childhood Bullying Problems
34. Developing Effective Behavior Intervention Plans: Suggestions for School Personnel

Teacher networks

21. Why Teacher Networks (Can) Work

Vision and hope

35. Becoming Citizens of the World
36. Democracy and Education: Empowering Students to Make Sense of Their World
39. Cultivating Optimism in the Classroom

Internet References

The following Internet sites have been selected to support the articles found in this reader. These sites were available at the time of publication. However, because websites often change their structure and content, the information listed may no longer be available. We invite you to visit *http://www.mhcls.com* for easy access to these sites.

Annual Editions: Education 10/11

General Sources

Education Week on the Web
http://www.edweek.org

At this Education Week home page, you will be able to open its archives, read special reports on education, keep up on current events in education, look for job opportunities, and access articles relevant to educators today.

Educational Resources Information Center
http://www.eric.ed.gov

This invaluable site provides links to all ERIC sites: clearinghouses, support components, and publishers of ERIC materials. You can search the ERIC database, find out what is new, and ask questions about ERIC.

National Education Association
http://www.nea.org

Something about virtually every education-related topic can be accessed via this site of the 2.3-million-strong National Education Association.

National Parent Information Network/ERIC
http://npin.org

This is a clearinghouse of information on elementary and early childhood education as well as urban education. Browse through its links for information for parents and for people who work with parents.

U.S. Department of Education
http://www.ed.gov

Explore this government site for examination of institutional aspects of multicultural education. National goals, projects, grants, and other educational programs are listed here as well as many links to teacher services and resources.

UNIT 1: Assessment and Research: Do They Inform Our Teaching Practices?

North Central Regional Educational Laboratory
http://www.ncrel.org/sdrs/areas/issues/methods/assment/as700.htm

This Web page provides information about the changing role of assessment and the reasons why we must change how we assess student learning. The hyperlinks take you to additional information on a variety of assessment topics as well as illustrative cases.

The National Center for Educational Statistics (NCES)
http://nces.ed.gov

The Center is located within the U.S. Department of Education and the Institute for Education Sciences. They are the primary federal agency for collecting and analyzing data related to education. You will be able to find information on a wide variety of educational issues, such as demographics, the National Report Card, private schools, and links to additional government documents.

Wrightslaw
http://www.wrightslaw.com/advoc/articles/tests_measurements.html

Peter and Pamela Wright founded this website for parents and teachers who work with students who have disabilities. However, all teachers will find their explanation of tests and measurements, statistics, and how to understand test scores very informative.

U.S. Department of Education: No Child Left Behind
http://www.ed.gov/nclb/landing.jhtml

This government site allows you to explore all aspects of NCLB. There are links to proposals for the reauthorization of the bill. You can see your states scores and progress toward its goals. Be sure to check the link to teaching resources.

Unit 2: Reformatting Our Schools

The Bill & Melinda Gates Foundation
http://www.gatesfoundation.org/topics/Pages/high-schools.aspx

The Gates Foundation provides grants and donations to schools. Visit this website to learn how they are working to improve educational opportunities across the country.

What Works Clearinghouse
http://ies.ed.gov/ncee/wwc

The Clearinghouse is a source for programs with scientific evidence that they work. You are able to create a summary of the research findings on a topic such as beginning reading and then read summaries of the research on all of the reviewed programs.

The Center for Comprehensive School Reform and Improvement
http://www.centerforcsri.org

Information about research-based strategies and assistance for schools wishing to make positive changes is available on this U.S. Department of Education–sponsored website. You can search the data base by topic, listen to podcasts, and view videos to learn how schools are working to reform the educational experience for students.

Council of the Great City Schools
http://www.cgcs.org

The Council mission is to improve the education of urban students. It offers articles and reports on topics of interest to teachers in urban schools.

The Annenberg Institute
http://www.annenberginstitute.org

The Annenberg Institute at Brown University is focused on reform in urban schools. Check out its products, which includes access to its journal, *Voices in Urban Education* as well as downloads of reports and its newsletter.

The Center for Social Organization of Schools
http://web.jhu.edu/CSOS.index.html

The Center is housed at Johns Hopkins University where researcher and school districts are collaborating on a variety of reform projects. You can read reports on efforts to improve early learning, middle and secondary school learning, and the graduation gap.

Internet References

Unit 3: Addressing Diversity in Your School

The National Coalition for Parent Involvement in Education (NCPIE)
http://www.ncpie.org

On this website you will find information and ideas about research, programs, and policies to increase family involvement in education. You will find access to resources, tools, and legislative updates to assist you in promoting parent and family involvement in their child's education.

New Horizons for Learning
http://www.newhorizons.org/

This site has many resources for teachers who work with diverse students. The topics addressed by the group are news from the neuroscience, teaching strategies, student voices, lifelong learning, and special needs. Resources include articles to read online, lists of additional recommended reading, and related links.

National Association for Multicultural Education (NAME)
http://www.nameorg.org/index.html

NAME is a professional organization for persons interested in multicultural education. However, there are many resources available for nonmember teachers in its Resource Center.

Everything ESL
http://www.everythingesl.net/

You will find everything at this website! This veteran teacher offers lesson plans ready to use, teaching tips, discussion topics where you can ask questions and read teaching tips from other teachers, and links to additional resources.

The National Research Center on the Gifted and Talented
http://www.gifted.uconn.edu/nrcgt/

Learn about research-based models, read articles, and link to organizations for students who are gifted/talented on this website.

Circle of Inclusion
http://circleofinclusion.org/

Educators who work with young children will find the resources on this website useful. You will find information about inclusion and accommodations strategies, augmentative communication, and downloadable forms.

Special Education Law Blog
http://specialedlaw.blogs.com/

Charlie Fox, an attorney specializing in Special Education, blogs on a wide variety of topics relating to teaching, living with, and working with persons who have disabilities.

LD Online
http://www.ldonline.org/

LD OnLine is a national educational service of WETA-TV, the PBS station in Washington, DC, in partnership with seven leading special education professional organizations. Topics of interest to both teachers and parents include resources for teaching and living with persons who have LD, including opportunities to ask questions of leading experts in the field.

Council for Exceptional Children (CEC)
http://www.cec.sped.org/

CEC is the largest professional organization devoted to teaching students with exceptional needs, including gifted and talented. You will find information about membership, research-based practices, conferences at state and national levels, and news of policy and advocacy.

Unit 4: Preparing Teachers to Teach All Students in All Schools

The Teacher's Network
http://teachers.net/

The Teacher's Network will connect you to a variety of networks, by state, grade level, subject, and more. Also you will find teacher blogs, chat rooms, lesson plans, articles, and much, much more.

MiddleWeb's The First Days of School
http://www.middleweb.com/1stDResources.html

This website is devoted to supporting middle school teachers with all things middle school. The homepage provides links to articles about classroom management strategies and preparation for the first days of school.

Teachers First
http://www.teachersfirst.com

Teachers First offers resources for free professional development; allows users to post questions for other educators to answer; and includes lesson plans, units, and web resources for teaching.

Donors Choose
http://www.donorschoose.org/

Need something for your classroom or a project, but need the funds? This website was developed in 2000 to help teachers in low-income schools purchase the items their school districts cannot supply. You will find complete instructions and other useful tips on the website. Then find your state on the state locator and write up your proposal.

Edutopia
http://www.edutopia.org

One method for bringing the real world into the classroom is project-based learning. This website has many video examples and articles about how teachers are integrating the real world into their teaching.

Unit 5: Cornerstones to Learning: Reading and Math

Literature Circles Resource Center
http://www.litcircles.org

The comprehensive website will help you start a literature circle in your classroom. Begin with the link to *How to use this site.*

Teacher Scholastic: Meet the Expert
http://teacher.scholastic.com/professional/readexpert/laurarobb.htm

Although this reading workshop is developed with middle schoolers, it can be used at most grade levels. To find out more about reading workshops, click on the links in the left column.

The Literacy Web
http://www.literacy.uconn.edu/index.htm

The University of Connecticut sponsors this website devoted to literacy. You will find many useful resources for teaching reading to all students. If you are interested in teaching English Language Learners, go to Literacy Topics page and scroll down to find link to ESL/EFL.

The National Council of Teachers of English (NCTE)
http://www.ncte.org/collections/secell

NCTE provides teaching strategies for supporting language learning for students who are not native English speakers. In addition, it provides information about other resources and professional readings.

Internet References

Read, Write, Think
http://www.readwritethink.org/

This resource-rich website is sponsored by the International Reading Association and National Council of Teachers of English. You can find lesson plans, student materials, and Web resources for teaching language and reading.

National Council of Teachers of Mathematics
http://www.nctm.org

The National Council of Teachers of Mathematics (NCTM) has a resource-rich website for any teacher who wants professional development, suggestions for teaching, or is interested in attending conferences and workshops. Membership in this professional organization offers opportunities to network with teachers who share an interest in mathematics.

Unit 6: Rethinking Behavior Management: Getting the Behavior You Want and Need to Teach Effectively

The OSEP Technical Assistance Center of Positive Behavior Interventions & Supports (PBIS)
http://www.pbis.org/school/what_is_swpbs.aspx

Positive Behavior Interventions & Supports is being used across the country as behavior management system. This website provides a comprehensive overview of this method used to change inappropriate behaviors and teach positive social behaviors. You can find this information by clicking on the link, School-Wide PBS.

Bully OnLine
http://www.bullyonline.org/

Need to know more about bullying? This is the place to go. One reason you may want to visit this website is that it discusses all of the places where children and teens can be bullied and offer suggestions for helping victims outside school.

Teaching Tolerance
http://www.tolerance.org/

Teaching Tolerance offers a two-part series on *The ABCs of Classroom Management.* The first part offers articles and videos on Democratic Classroom, Positive Behavior, and Authentic Relationships. Part two covers Engaging Curriculum, Being Culturally Responsive, and Motivation.

National Education Association: Classroom Management
http://www.nea.org/tools/ClassroomManagement.html

Need a quick tip to solve a management problem? This website has many of them.

Teacher Vision
http://www.teachervision.fen.com/

Once at the homepage, look for the link to Class Management for information about topics for positive behavior management; lesson planning advice, and other topics of interest to all teachers.

Center for Safe and Responsible Internet Use
http://www.cskcst.com

As more and more children have unsupervised access to the Internet, cyberbullying has risen. Teachers can raise awareness in their students. You will find the link to cyberBullying at the top of the home page, then scroll down for articles, a poster, and informational guides for students and parents.

Unit 7: Creating Caring Communities of Learners

Association for Supervision and Curriculum Development (ASCD)
http://www.ascd.org

Educators for Social Responsibility International (ESR)
http://www.esrnational.org/

ESR offers an online Teacher Center where you can find lesson plans for building a caring community. Under the NEWS link you will find information about helping students cope with a variety of crisis situations. Also, you can sign up for a free E-newsletter and register for free access to other resources.

Coalition of Essential Schools
http://www.essentialschools.org/

The Coalition is about creating and sustaining personalized, equitable, and intellectually challenging schools. While you will have access to many resources on this website, if you register, you can participate in blogs and discussions online.

The Forum for Education and Democracy
http://www.forumforeducation.org/index.php

Leaders in education contribute to this forum's blog. Under the Resources heading you will find articles, research reports, books, and additional links.

Institute for Democracy in Education
http://www.ohiou.edu/ide/index.htm

You will find links to websites, books, and journal articles regarding teaching and creating democratic students.

UNIT 1

Assessment and Research: Do They Inform Our Teaching Practices?

Unit Selections

1. **Where Have All the Strong Poets Gone?,** Alan C. Jones
2. **Proficiency for All?,** Dave Moscinski
3. **Bridging the Gap between Research and Practice: What's Good, What's Bad, and How Can One Be Sure?,** Stephen H. Davis
4. **Learning to Love Assessment,** Carol Ann Tomlinson
5. **The Case for and against Homework,** Robert J. Marzano and Debra J. Pickering

Key Points to Consider

- Why should we be cautious every time we accept a new teaching idea or innovation?

- What are the positive actions that are being taken by teachers and administrators with respect to the requirements of NCLB and assessment?

- What are the reasons behind the stand for and against homework and what are your personal views regarding homework?

- Why is understanding and using educational research important for teachers who plan for and instruct students?

Student Website
www.mhcls.com

Internet References

North Central Regional Educational Laboratory
http://www.ncrel.org/sdrs/areas/issues/methods/assment/as700.htm
The National Center for Educational Statistics (NCES)
http://nces.ed.gov
Wrightslaw
http://www.wrightslaw.com/advoc/articles/tests_measurements.html
U.S. Department of Education: No Child Left Behind
http://www.ed.gov/nclb/landing.jhtml

We are all familiar with testing and assessment. Every reader of this text has been through years of education that included hundreds of tests and other types of assessment. Assessment has been and certainly will always be part of the educational experience of teachers and students, just as it has been since ancient Greek and Roman schools. We even have examples of testing standards or standardized administration of assessments in Jesuit schools of the 1600s. Teachers have always held students accountable for learning; school administrators held teachers accountable for teaching; and communities held the administrators accountable for school achievement. However, I have never met a student who honestly liked to take tests; every time I elected to cancel a test in one of my college courses, the class rose in a deafening cheer. This dislike of tests on the part of students who become teachers can lead to teachers who do not like to give tests. Teachers like to teach, teachers want to teach, and many of us cannot think of any other occupation that would suit us, but most of us do not like to test. Yet, we must assess if we want to be better teachers. This is the primary reason to assess: to know what students have learned and just as importantly, what they have not learned, and to know if the methods and materials we used or provided were helpful, and finally, to know what to do next. Assessments give us the data we need to reflect upon our teaching practices and the learning experiences of our students.

Certainly, reflecting and planning for instruction are the most important reasons to assess students. In recent years, organizations and agencies outside the field of education have become interested in what is happening in schools. They are particularly interested in the progress of students who are achieving at substantially low levels, such as groups of students who are minorities, disadvantaged, or disabled. We hear advocates of standardized testing speak of using test scores to improve impoverished schools and remove ineffective teachers. This rise in interest for minority groups has a major impact on education and can be seen in the passage of laws that have implications for assessment of students in these minority groups. Prior to the 1990s, the primary purposes of assessment were to assign grades to individual students for administrative purposes, such as grade promotion, or to predict a person's ability to compete in college classes, such as the SAT or ACT exams. However, in the 1990s the development of Goals 2000 introduced a new dimension to assessment: accountability. A decade later, the passage of No Child Left Behind (NCLB) changed assessment from a teacher responsibility to a state responsibility.

But do statewide standardized assessments answer the question of what our children need to learn to be citizens in this multicultural, ever-evolving world and also be caring, nurturing parents and knowledgeable employees? Do teachers and school administrators use the results of assessments in the most effective way? Does the state and district implementation of NCLB really help us meet student needs, improve student learning, or make lasting reforms? Why *should* we assess student learning?

In addition to using assessment data, we can use what we know from the educational thinkers. In this arena, members of think tanks, researchers, and university professors from colleges

© Liquidlibrary/Jupiterimages

of education recommend that public school personnel use research-based or evidence-based teaching methods and curriculum. This recommendation is even written into both NCLB and Individuals with Disabilities Education Improvement Act-2004 (IDEIA-04). Across the country, teachers and administrators look for experts to inform and advise their teaching practices. But who should earn our trust and respect? What do we do when faced with conflicting views from researchers?© Comstock/PictureQuest

The articles in this section offer diverse outlooks on educational assessment and research. First, we consider recent reforms that Alan Jones sees as punitive to classroom teachers and school administrators. He calls for us to listen to leaders such as Kozol who find fault with the implementation of NCLB and to follow the educational leadership offered by Dewey, Counts, and Freire. In another article on research, Stephen Davis notes that, in the era of high-stakes accountability and standards-based instructions, our decisions must be based on empirical research. Educators must be able to bridge that gap between research and practice to find the best ways to meet student needs. However, he also cautions us to think carefully about what is good or bad research and offers suggestions to help us tell the difference. Finally, the last article illustrates how two respected educators can look at research and reach two different conclusions about the use of homework. There are important lessons to be learned from both authors about refraining from rushing to make reforms, unless those reforms are based on sound research.

We have included two articles that discuss how two educators turn assessment into a *silk purse*. These two educators used standardized and teacher-made assessments to their advantage to improve student learning. The stories of a superintendent who embraced the heart of NCLB to work for proficiency of all students and the teacher who learned to love assessment because she came to understand its true purpose illustrate how assessment might be used to improve education.

Taken together, this set of articles offers us an opportunity to think critically about how we can use both educational research and assessment practices and data to inform our teaching practices.

Where Have All the Strong Poets Gone?

The approaches that are being touted as ways to improve our poorest schools are themselves impoverished, Mr. Jones finds. He urges educators to take a stand against the current policies and to muster the imagination to devise true solutions.

ALAN C. JONES

Jonathan Kozol's latest book, The *Shame of the Nation,* documents the landscapes of the two education systems in America. One system is located in the suburbs, where mostly white students sit in classrooms with teachers who possess the content knowledge to construct engaging lessons that accurately reflect the content and structure of the discipline that they teach. The breadth and depth of the curriculum in these suburban schools provide students with the knowledge and skills to do well in postsecondary settings. In addition, these suburban schools have sprawling campuses that possess all the accoutrements of Ivy League universities—a high-quality library, computer labs with the latest technology, state-of-the-art science labs, and a rich variety of support services that will enhance the social and emotional development of young people.

At the same time that white suburban students are being prepared to become the future bosses in our country, African American and Hispanic students sit in classrooms with young, inexperienced teachers whose minimal training in their content areas leaves them with little ability to construct lessons that will adequately prepare students for postsecondary schooling. Instead of being offered engaging lessons that reflect state-of-the-art approaches to curriculum and instruction, students in our urban and rural areas are subjected to an instructional program that Kozol calls "a test-preparation boot camp." Inductees in this boot camp are expected to listen to scripted lessons, complete practice test-preparation exercises, and take an endless stream of tests. The facilities in these "boot camps" are as deplorable as the instructional program. Students sit in classrooms without windows, go to bathrooms that do not function, and work in labs without chemicals or specimens.

Why has the resegregation of our nation's schools into two systems—one poor and urban and one well-off and suburban—remained unnoticed by the public and our policy makers? The parents of poor urban students do not possess the political or economic capital to generate outrage at, or sometimes even awareness of, the dilapidated buildings and dead-end curriculum that their children are subjected to every day. Suburban parents,

who do possess the political and economic power to call attention to the deplorable conditions in our urban schools, remain silent simply because they have the schools they want. White suburban schools, especially the elite white suburban schools, have it all—why talk of funding formulas and social policies that would require wealthier parents to share the resources that are currently being lavished on their children?

As for state and national policy makers, they have diverted attention away from the deep political, social, and economic forces that have conspired to segregate our schools, our neighborhoods, and the futures of our children by using the high-sounding rhetoric of equal educational opportunities for all children—"all children can learn" and "no child left behind"—and the vocabulary of business accountability measures—test, inspect, and reconstitute. The relentless use of a vocabulary of equality married to a whole host of school accountability measures has proven to be a potent strategy for dodging the thorny policy issues that might actually develop the conditions that "no child left behind" was meant to achieve—equal-funding formulas, scattered site housing, universal health care, and a high-quality child-care system. The cruelty of this policy shell game is to punish the schools that serve the poor and voiceless in our society and to reward the schools that serve the wealthiest and most powerful.

Education consultants, professors of education, school administrators, and state and national educational leaders have stood by in silence or have actively supported punitive strategies for holding students, teachers, and school administrators responsible for student achievement.

In an era of "greed is good," I can well understand why state and national policy makers and their suburban constituencies have adopted a vocabulary and an ideology that mask gross inequalities in our nation's schools. Sadly, the general tenor of our nation appears to have forsaken the social justice concerns and the civil rights movement that motivated our young people during the Sixties for a "gated-community" mentality that aggressively fights any encroachment on the rights and privileges that wealth and power have bestowed on their sons and daughters.

However, what I do not understand is why our nation's professional education organizations and the academic community not only have remained silent about the conditions, the facilities, the pedagogy, and the curriculum that urban children are subjected to on a daily basis, but have supported and pursued accountability measures that can only worsen the educational futures of urban youths. A brief visit to an education convention or an urban school, or a cursory look at a popular education journal, would quickly confirm how the education establishment in our country has all but surrendered the high ground of the ideals expressed in *Brown v. Board of Education*. Rather than pursue policies, curricula, and instructional strategies that would provide all children with rich instructional environments, education consultants, professors of education, school administrators, and state and national educational leaders have stood by in silence or have actively supported punitive strategies for holding students, teachers, and school administrators responsible for student achievement. Even worse, many have promoted "how to" approaches for implementing accountability measures that straitjacket teachers and systematically destroy whatever self-esteem urban children bring when they enter the schoolhouse doors.

What we need in today's educational climate are school leaders in the tradition of John Dewey, George Counts, and Paulo Freire who possess the intellectual power and rhetorical skill to make everything in the field of education look new and to change the way the public and educators look at schools. Richard Rorty refers to such individuals as "strong poets." By strong poet, Rorty does not mean literally a poet; he means individuals who possess the imagination to create a new story about what teaching and learning should look like in our urban schools and who have the courage to develop an oppositional vocabulary that critiques the motives and the consequences of wealth and power.

What message and course of action should our Strong Professors of Education be pursuing in a country that has all but accepted a school system segregated by race and income? Strong Professors of Education should be using their classrooms, the educational media, and their research interests to identify and provide a rationale for curricular approaches and pedagogical techniques that are not harmful to urban young people and to expose the gross inequities that now exist in our public school systems. Strong Deans of Education should use their authority to voice opposition to accreditation measures and policy initiatives that intensify punitive accountability measures and that continue to promote inequalities in how we fund our schools. Both Strong Professors of Education and Strong Deans of Education should be teaching, writing, and creating courses of study that not only provide best practice in the field of teaching and learning for urban youths but also provide future teachers

with methods and forums to study and discuss the relationship between the most vexing problems of our time—racism, poverty, sexism, violence, prejudice—and the routines of institutional schooling that historically have hidden and perpetuated these injustices.

Most important, Strong Poets in the academy must refocus the public's attention on the real causes of poor achievement in our urban school systems. For too long the academy has allowed policy makers to shift attention away from the effects that racism and poverty have on urban schools and onto bogus accountability measures—data-driven schools, retention, high-stakes testing—that have no effect on the long-term achievement of urban school children but that do great harm to the social and emotional well-being of these same children. Race and poverty have never been neutral when it comes to schooling—the academy must stop treating race and poverty as silent variables in urban school achievement.

Each year in our urban school systems we lose a generation of young people who have the potential to become productive citizens in our country. The substandard physical and educational condition of our urban schools remains tragically out of sight and out of mind for most Americans.

What should our Strong School Administrators be doing in the urban schools they lead? First, school administrators must have the courage and skill to become Strong Educational Leaders. It is dishonest for school administrators to portray themselves as "pawns" in the hands of powerful political interests and then disappear behind the curtain of the management functions of their job while the children in their schools languish in crumbling facilities and "drill and kill" classrooms. School administrators will always have control over the important allocation of time, resources, and instructional approaches in the buildings they lead. Strong Educational Leaders exercise that control in a way that provides teachers in their buildings with the time, the resources, and the instructional skills to make differences in the way urban young people read, write, compute, and think.

As with medical doctors, Strong Educational Leaders should first "do no harm." Many of the current accountability measures—retention policies, special education placements, suspensions and expulsions, remedial services of all kinds—are destructive to the intellects and souls of urban youths. Strong Educational Leaders should be actively opposing these policies and making every effort to ameliorate institutional policies and accountability measures that are hurtful to urban young people.

Strong Educational Leaders need a strong understanding of the theories, ideas, and practices that govern teaching and learning in our schools. Much of the destructiveness of current "comprehensive reform proposals" occurs because there is no one in a leadership capacity who is mediating the effects of pure theory on young people's learning. No theory of learning—no matter how "scientific"—should be unleashed in a learning environment without reformulating the components of that theory to be sensitive to the social context of the school. The important process of reformulating theories that enter a school can be accomplished only by school administrators who are knowledgeable about the ideas that underlie a particular school reform proposal.

Each year in our urban school systems we lose a generation of young people who have the potential to become productive citizens in our country. The substandard physical and educational condition of our urban schools remains tragically out of sight and out of mind for most Americans. However, professional educators are morally bound to provide a voice for those students and teachers who go to crumbling and debilitating schools.

Strong Poets, as Rorty describes them, possess a message that deflates accepted ways of seeing the world and, most important, the courage to voice the message in hostile settings. We, as professional educators, do possess the strong messages about what needs to be done in urban schools. What we are missing is the courage.

ALAN C. JONES is an assistant professor in the Saint Xavier University School of Education, Chicago, Illinois.

Proficiency for All?

A superintendent reflects on how he learned to stop complaining and love NCLB.

DAVE MOSCINSKI

As superintendent in a small, rural Wisconsin district, I initially did not like the No Child Left Behind Act. I called it a federal attempt to privatize public education with subgroup goals that were statistically impossible to attain. I thought it was a payback to education companies that supported the party in power. I thought it carried an awfully large stick with an awfully small carrot.

With time, however, I examined NCLB's basic tenet of proficiency for all, and, with the exception of the allowable exemption for a small percentage of special needs students, asked, "What's so bad about that?"

I encouraged the Shiocton school board to set achievement goals equal to the upper 10 percent of all districts in the state. Over time, we had moved from being in the upper 60 percent to the upper 30 percent of districts. Good, but to get into the top 10 percent, we had to have 100 percent proficiency in some areas. So we developed a back door accommodation to NCLB because, ultimately, we wanted the same thing—reading and math proficiency for all students.

Shiocton, dubbed the sauerkraut capital of the world, has some advantages. A bedroom community for commuters from Green Bay and the Fox Cities, Shiocton has about a quarter of its 830 students receiving free and reduced-price lunch. We receive more state aid than other districts in the area because much of our land is state- and county-owned for public hunting, but federal aid accounts for only 1 percent of our total budget.

That said, there are many things you can learn from the process we undertook for our district. Here are my top 10 lessons for helping you reach the goal of proficiency for all.

- **Start with the school board.** Shiocton's dramatic increase in student proficiency is the result of a multistep plan to improve student achievement that began with our board of education. Our board has a "no excuses" belief system and an ongoing dedication to improvement that mirrors other districts cited in the Iowa Association of School Board's Lighthouse Study.

  The study concluded that, in high-achieving districts, the board-superintendent team and district staff "consistently expressed an 'elevating' view of students. Students were viewed as emerging and flexible and the school's job

was seen as releasing each student's potential. The social or economic conditions of homes and the community were seen as challenges in the quest to help all students succeed. 'This is a place for all kids to excel.'"

The elevated level of expectancy is seen at Shiocton when you enter the main building. Above the front door is the school motto: "Shiocton Schools—Where Excellence Is Expected."

- **Advertise the goal.** With the board's expectations leading the way, we put our achievement goal—all students at proficiency and our schools among the best in the state—in writing and advertised it to the staff and public at large. The goal was publicized in the district newsletter. Goal certificates were printed and distributed to every classroom for posting.

- **Establish baseline data.** Where are you starting in your quest to grow student achievement? Look at your data—we used *SchoolFacts* from the Taxpayers Alliance—and determine what it will take to meet the No Child Left Behind mandate. No matter what your scores, accept where you are and pledge to grow from there.

- **Align your curriculum with the standards.** The next step is to take time and effort to make sure your district curriculum is aligned to state standards. Some people criticize this effort as "teaching to the test," but it is what teachers do every day. Teachers test what they teach.

  "Teaching to the test" is a valid criticism for norm-referenced standardized tests that are not related to a district's curriculum. These tests offer a series of questions or tasks that gradually increase in difficulty and divide students into groups based on their ability to respond to items completely unrelated to what they have been taught. Criterion referenced tests evaluate student performance based on specific criteria from curricular standards. It is perfectly all right to test what students have been taught in the classroom.

- **Use data to improve instruction.** Shiocton uses the Measures of Academic Progress (MAPS) assessment system developed by the Northwest Evaluation Association. MAPS is administered twice annually at the second- through eighth-grade levels to set individual learning goals for each student. Goals are aligned with the state standards, which in turn are evaluated by the Wisconsin Knowledge and Concepts Examination (WKCE), our state test.

MAPS is a computerized adaptive assessment program that provides teachers with information they need to improve teaching and learning. Results also are used to select students who will participate in the AutoSkill's Academy of Reading and Academy of Math, the individualized, computer-based instructional programs with built-in reward systems. These academies can occur in summer school or in classes that add to the regular instructional program.

- **Make sure curriculum is taught.** This is where supervision and evaluation come into play. Principals, through their classroom observations of teachers, must see that the curriculum standards are taught in the classroom. Some districts have teacher lesson plans that list the standard that each lesson addresses. In smaller rural districts, which are the most common in Wisconsin, often one or two teachers at each grade are responsible for ensuring that the curriculum alignment is in place. This ensures that the link from teaching to learning to evaluation is the most direct.

- **Eliminate defeatist thinking.** This type of thinking is most commonly seen in a deceptively positive form. Somewhere along the line a class gets a reputation as particularly bright or good. It usually starts in kindergarten and is passed along through conversations in the teacher's lounge. Good test scores are attributed to this "good class" status as if classroom instruction was a nonexistent variable.

This is defeatist thinking because it sets up the excuse that less-than-proficient performance in other classes is somehow the students' fault and not the result of an inappropriate curriculum, poor instructional methods, or low teacher expectations.

A reverse example of this occurred in Shiocton, where we had an eighth-grade math class that made a top score on the WKCE. The class had a reputation in middle school as being a good, bright group. But when we went back and looked at their results, the class had only average test scores four years earlier. The students had been influenced by good teaching combined with a self-fulfilling prophecy, an educational Pygmalion Effect.

The concept can be summarized in these key principles:

- We form certain expectations of people or events.
- We communicate those expectations with various cues.
- Children tend to respond by adjusting their behavior to match the cues.

The result is that the original expectation becomes true. This creates a circle of self-fulfilling prophecies. We must believe the best will happen for students because anything less sells them short.

- **Motivate the students.** Make sure students are rested, well fed, and primed to do their best. Enlist parents to help children do well. Emphasize to students that we know they will do well because they are knowledgeable and capable. Provide extrinsic motivators at the appropriate grade levels. Shiocton's 10th-graders are exempted from end-of-year exams if they test at proficient or advanced levels.

- **Celebrate success.** Let the public and staff members know about your progress. If your scores are not moving in the right direction, let the public know that, too, and tell it what you plan to do about it in the next year. All this directs focus on student learning and how we can provide it in the most efficient manner.

- **Provide marginal students with direct instruction targeted at achieving proficiency.** This is the most important recommendation of all. Wisconsin students are tested in the fall and results are reported the following spring. The cycle repeats itself the next fall. Little can be done in the meantime to grow the skills of students whose scores are minimal or basic. This situation can be remedied by using computer assisted reteaching programs to individualize instruction to students.

Those are my top 10. As Shiocton continues its significant experiment to see if proficiency for all is indeed attainable, some grades in some schools and some schools in some districts already reach this goal of top proficiency. We want to do it for all students in all grades in our district.

DAVE MOSCINSKI (dmoscins@shiocton.k12.wi.us) is the district administrator for the School District of Shiocton.

Bridging the Gap between Research and Practice

What's Good, What's Bad, and How Can One Be Sure?

Mr. Davis, a professor, advises readers of this article who are practitioners not to trust everything he and his colleagues have to say about schools. Then he explains why and offers helpful tips that will allow teachers and administrators to make their own judgments about what they can profitably apply from educational research.

STEPHEN H. DAVIS

We have to live today by what truth we can get today and be ready tomorrow to call it falsehood.

—William James

I teach at a large research university and deeply appreciate the opportunities I have to help shape the careers of aspiring school leaders and, in some ways, the institution of public education itself. As expected of professors in universities like mine, I have written quite a bit and conducted several research studies that I hope have made a reasonable contribution to my field. But I often wonder how much of what I've written has actually made a difference in the lives of school practitioners. For that matter, I wonder how much of what is thought about and produced by scholars and researchers actually affects the way administrators and teachers behave in schools. And most important of all, I wonder how practitioners learn to judge the quality of research and determine what research to pay attention to and what to ignore. These questions are crucial, especially now that the mandates of No Child Left Behind and the standards and accountability movement are pressuring American public schools to use research-based programs.

Feedback from the field suggests that a gap between research and practice persists while bridges between them remain tenuous and unsteady. It appears that comparatively little of what is written and thought about by scholars and policy makers actually has any appreciable impact on classrooms or drives durable systemwide reform efforts. In their acclaimed book on school reform, *Tinkering Toward Utopia*, Larry Cuban and David Tyack trace the long and often confounding history of reform efforts in American public schools.[1] They argue that, despite decades of reform initiatives and millions of dollars spent in the pursuit of educational innovation, the fundamental tenets of effective educational practice have changed very little.

Of course, not all reform efforts have been research-based, and not all good research is lost in the trickledown journey between the halls of academe and Ms. Doe's third-grade classroom. But enough of value is lost to raise suspicions about the relevance of the work of researchers and the vitality of the relationship between researchers and public school practitioners.

For decades, public schools in America have been awash in waves of reform that have emerged from a slippery mélange of empirical research studies, politically formulated mandates, and locally derived best-practice initiatives. Most have been well intentioned, many have been misguided, and some have come to schools without careful regard for hard evidence or with distorted claims of causality. Unfortunately, some of what has made it into Ms. Doe's classroom may not represent the best research, nor has it necessarily been applied with fidelity to the scientifically supportable findings from which it was derived. A close look at how research findings relating to such topics as heterogeneous classrooms, mainstreaming of special-needs students, social promotion, bilingual education, and instructional methods are actually applied in public school classrooms reveals numerous variations based on local policies and politics, management philosophies, school culture, student characteristics, levels of teachers' skill, and available resources.

But today, now that public schools have entered an era of high-stakes accountability and standards-based instruction in which decisions about educational programs and activities are expected to be closely aligned with empirical research and evidentiary data, it can be argued that scholars and practitioners must redouble their efforts to bridge the gap between theory and practice.[2] Unfortunately, conversations about the reform du jour usually overlook any questions of how to tell the difference between good research and not-so-good research or between the attributes of research in the abstract and research as it may apply to a particular school district, school, or classroom. Perhaps most important, even research of the highest quality may never make its way into public school classrooms simply because the pipeline through which important academic discoveries travel to schools and classrooms is inconsistent, inchoate, and often tainted by the political process used to craft education policy.

For example, critics maintain that the death of bilingual instruction in California public schools in the 1990s was more the product of ill-informed public sentiment and partisan politics than of a serious and balanced investigation of empirical research on how children who are not native speakers of English learn a new language. The fact is that bilingual education came under heavy fire because of its costs, the expected growth of new financial burdens, the paucity of basic research in the field, the lack of qualified teachers, and its real or supposed lack of success.[3]

As a former superintendent, principal, personnel director, and high school teacher, I can't count the times that I've heard fellow administrators and teachers begin a conversation about the qualities of a particular educational program or instructional method with the phrase "The research says." It is always uttered as if the mere declaration, in and of itself, contains sufficient gravity to forestall further dissent or discussion. The problem, of course, is that most school administrators and teachers are not sophisticated consumers of research. Nor are many college professors, for that matter. Practitioners, especially, take far too much for granted and often exaggerate the importance of mediocre research, attempt to generalize qualitative research findings, and frequently misapply research findings derived from one sample population to different populations. Most people (scholars included) also tend to pay greater attention to research studies that confirm their deeply held beliefs and assumptions than to studies that challenge their sensibilities.[4]

So how can practitioners learn to become better consumers of scholarly research? Short of conscripting teachers and administrators into doctoral-level courses in research methods and short of reassigning all education professors to a team-teaching stint with Ms. Doe, I offer some thoughts and suggestions that may help to inform practitioners about the factors that influence the quality and evaluation of educational research. In the process, I hope to reduce the distance between the worlds of practitioners and academics.

The Arrogance of Academe

To begin, school leaders should never completely trust what people like me have to say about schools. I'm serious. Take what we professors have to say with a grain of salt. I know, most of you are thinking that I must have had a particularly bad day at the office. But, truth be told, I'm one of "them." By them, I mean professors and researchers who ply their trade from the rarefied air of the ivory tower. What we have to tell you about schools simply can't be fully trusted. Here's why:

1. Many of us have simply lost touch with the day-to-day complexity of human interactions in schools. As a result, too many of us begin to think about schooling and the behaviors of people who work and study in schools as abstractions, as plots on a regression line, or as categorical representations of patterned activity. Too many of us have buffered ourselves and our work from the subtleties, nuances, and untidiness of human behavior in schools. Academic myopia can cloud our ability to appreciate on a visceral level what life in schools is really like and, more important, the extent to which grand ideas generated from our research actually stick to the ribs of school reform efforts.

Recently, I spent some time on the campus of a large suburban high school, leading a scheduled state accreditation review process. Over the years, I've volunteered for "accreditation duty" numerous times and have visited many schools. Each experience has enriched my understanding of how schools in the U.S. work. Yet each experience also underscores my growing sense of disconnection from the real people who populate schools, from the turbulent rhythm of school life, and from the logic of school operations (i.e., the relationship between events, situations, and objects and the inevitable consequences of their interaction). I spent the better part of 19 years teaching and leading in public schools, but I am incrementally losing touch. And I know I can't be alone in this. Imagine a scholar who has never worked in the school system and whose only contacts have been narrowly tailored to the needs of his or her particular research interests. Academic pedigrees and good intentions notwithstanding, would you trust what this person has to say about schools?

> **In my nationally acclaimed school of education, I am the *only* professor who has been a principal or superintendent of a large, comprehensive public school or school district.**

Here's a sobering fact: in my nationally acclaimed school of education, I am the *only* professor who has been a principal or superintendent of a large, comprehensive public school or school district. Only a modest number of faculty members have actually taught in public schools, and, for those who have, many years have passed since their public school teaching days. Yet several colleagues are deeply involved in researching, teaching, and consulting on topics related to the leadership, governance, and redesign of schools. For many of my colleagues, their understanding about life in schools is based on their exposure to the literature, their own particular strand of research, episodic campus visits, or the anecdotal reports of those who work in schools. A rough parallel might be a physician whose knowledge of the inner workings of the human body was derived primarily from examining the pictures in Gray's *Anatomy* and supplemented by occasional visits to the operating room viewing theater. A great deal is lost when "book learnin'" forms the primary source of a person's expertise.

My colleagues here and in similar universities across the country are unquestionably accomplished scholars with brilliant minds, and the best of them often generate new thoughts and ideas that ought to be carefully considered by practitioners. But should practitioners completely trust what they have to say about schools?

2. Academics often write for the wrong audience. As a group, academics gain notoriety, respect, and career advancement not from their ability to reach out to the "grunts on the front lines" but from their ability to impress their peers. Young professors don't acquire tenure by writing for trade journals, and associate professors who aspire to become full professors don't make the leap by publishing books based on literature reviews or philosophical musings about best practices in schools. Rather, we write for one another, while adhering to the strictures of academic scholarship. In the process, we often fail to adequately capture or even acknowledge the nuanced qualities of schooling. Granted, every so often, seeds of wisdom escape this incestuous process to take root in the terra firma of schools, but not necessarily through the intentional efforts of their originators. As a result, practitioners are justifiably suspicious about the relevance of scholarly research. A review of several widely read education journals is more likely to reveal articles written by practitioners for practitioners than articles written by academics for practitioners.

A big piece of the communication gap is in the language used by scholars. The language we speak is different from that spoken by common folk. For example, a school administrator or teacher not schooled in the lexicon of statistics (and most aren't) would probably find the following statement from a recently published article in *Educational Administration Quarterly* nearly incomprehensible: "Multilevel modeling provides a framework in which researchers can place explanatory variables at their correct level of the data hierarchy." Here's another brain buster from the same journal: "Organizations do not appear ex nihilo but instead emerge within an existing sociopolitical context. How this context interacts with organizational factors to initiate normative structure is poorly understood." Poorly understood? Why am I not surprised?

The language gap between researchers and practitioners is underscored by the following quote from Carolyn Riehl and her colleagues: "Research should be accessible to its community. Educational administration professors are often frustrated by the fact that many students find the language of research off-putting. But in fact, much of the research is written in language and terms that make it inaccessible to many of the people it is intended to reach."[5]

Conscientious scholars can and should write to be understood. Education experts such as Diane Ravitch, Michael Fullan, Michael Kirst, Larry Cuban, and Linda Darling-Hammond are among the most prominent and respected scholars in their fields. Yet they have mastered the craft of communicating complex ideas in ways that can be understood by practitioners without compromising the sophistication of their scholarship.

A group discussion at a recent faculty meeting shows the low regard accorded to scholars who write for practitioners. The work of a promising candidate for a tenure-track faculty position was under close scrutiny at the meeting. The candidate had amassed an impressive array of published articles in reference journals reporting the results of her extensive body of empirical research. However, one transgression nearly derailed her candidacy: she was in the finishing stages of writing a book intended for the parents of public school children, not for scholars. The fact that the book was written well and filled a void did little to assuage the prickly indignation expressed by some senior faculty members.

3. Academics frequently use "hit and run" tactics. We are harvesters of data and rarely stay very long in one place. Although some scholars do indeed conduct long-term and penetrating studies of their subjects and environments, far too many of us rely on ex post facto analyses of behaviors or events that occurred at a single time. As a result, what we often present are snapshots of events that fail to capture the patterns, routines, trends, or rhythms that represent organizational life or individual behavior.

Scholars often fail to consider the synergistic properties of organizational activities in schools or take account of the unanticipated effects of subtle relationships. We tend to focus instead on relatively narrow dimensions of human activity and thinly sliced representations of organizational or leadership behavior. Unfortunately, researchers who operate this way can engender feelings of mistrust and suspicion about their motives, a situation that impedes free and forthright dialogue with practitioners. Seasoned practitioners tacitly understand the holistic properties of schools, and they are loath to give much credibility to scholars with narrowly framed research agendas.

4. Academics can be an arrogant bunch. Swathed in egos plumped up by the untouchable status that comes with lifetime tenure, academics love to pontificate to the masses with unshakable certainty of the righteousness of their beliefs. Their messages are often interpreted as "We're basically smarter than most of you, and therefore we know more than you do." Do they really? The corridor of history is littered with discarded bodies of work that were at the time of their invention considered to be on the cutting edge of scholarly research. Practitioners should listen carefully to what we have to say, but always assume a critical stance. They need to ask themselves whether an idea will work in their school or district, given the unique needs and characteristics of the students, teachers, and community members. They need to decide whether the idea aligns with common sense, and they need to remember that, just because it's new, it doesn't mean it's necessarily better.

5. Not all research is good research. You'd be surprised at the quantity of poorly supported information presented in the guise of empirical research that has made its way to the front lines of public schools. The literature is rife with half-truths, popular myths, contradictions, poorly designed studies, misinterpreted findings, and conclusions soaked in the personal biases and deeply held assumptions of researchers.[6]

I am reminded of the body of research relating to the field of organizational leadership. Thirty years ago, the literature commonly portrayed successful leaders as charismatic and heroic figures. They were men (most often) who possessed the requisite ambition, vision, drive, and know-how to steer their organizations toward desirable ends. Today, prominent authors like Thomas Sergiovanni and Linda Lambert portray a very different model of leadership that depicts successful leaders as humble servants and moral stewards who are transformational, inspirational, and skilled in the ability to facilitate collaboration, common vision, a sense of community, and shared values.[7] What proof do we have about the effectiveness of either model? Do more recent models of leadership result in better student learning? How can practitioners make sense of the contradictory "evidence" about effective leadership?

Perhaps a better example of how research myths can permeate the collective mentality of educators is the emergent theory that large comprehensive high schools are no longer the most effective vehicle for educating teens. The dominant argument is that large schools are impersonal and overly bureaucratic and too easily alienate students—particularly those who are at risk or come from underrepresented ethnic groups. To "fix" this problem, school districts across the country have begun to convert large high schools into smaller learning communities. Such efforts are under way in the inner cities, in the suburbs, and even in some rural communities—despite the fact that the idea was originally intended as a way to advance the academic achievement and graduation rates of low-income urban youths. In an unexpected move, the Bill & Melinda Gates Foundation, benefactor to more than 1,600 small-school conversion programs, recently toned down its energetic support for the concept, maintaining that perhaps a more important strategy would be to focus on improving the instructional practices of teachers.

On its face, the logic of creating smaller schools is compelling: greater faculty empowerment in school governance and decision making, increased personalization for students, less pressure on students to conform to large-group norms, less exposure to disruptive behaviors, improved feelings of identification with the school, better response time in meeting individual needs, increased flexibility of program and personnel policies, more frequent opportunities for faculty collaboration, and better monitoring of individual student progress.

Attractive in theory, but does it really work? Moreover, is the model necessarily superior to more traditionally structured comprehensive schools? In some environments, it certainly is; in others, not necessarily. Should models of conversion to small schools become a universal template for high school reform? Consider the potential tradeoffs: fewer elective and specialty courses, reduction in the breadth and scope of staff expertise, fewer opportunities for extracurricular and athletic participation, increased intra- and extra-organizational competition for resources, limited access to specialized instructional facilities like science labs, and an increase in the likelihood of policy drift within school districts (i.e., departures from common values, goals, and quality indicators). Moreover, do the assumptions that underlie the logic of small schools necessarily apply evenly to all communities, all students, and all socioeconomic groups? Do teachers actually teach differently in small schools than they do in larger schools? Are these differences large enough to foster better student learning? Is the curriculum offered to students in small schools appreciably better than the curriculum commonly offered in larger schools? Does increased personalization always result in better student academic achievement? Will the "treatment" effects of small school conversions justify the costs in all school settings (e.g., for upper-income suburban students as opposed to lower-income urban students)? What will the consequences be for those students who are already doing well in large comprehensive school settings?

These and many other questions remain largely unanswered and should give pause to practitioners who might otherwise interpret the recent outpouring of favorable literature on the subject as proof positive of the approach's universal efficacy. According to a recent study by Barbara Schneider, Adam Wysse, and Vanessa Keesler of Michigan State University, there's consensus in the field that it's not simply going smaller, it's what you do and how you teach in those smaller settings that matter most.[8] A recent report published by the National Association of Secondary School Principals concludes by stating, "Implementing small learning communities will not, in and of itself, increase student achievement. It may help to do so, but the studies do not provide conclusive evidence on this point."[9]

Some research, of course, is simply crummy, regardless of the topic under scrutiny. For example, it is not uncommon for authors to overstate the importance of their findings. In other cases, authors have been known to highlight findings that agree with their deeply held values and assumptions while downplaying the importance of contradictory findings. It is also not unheard of for authors to use weak or inappropriate statistical measures, to use self-designed surveys and questionnaires that are unreliable and lack validity, or to generalize findings derived from nonrandomized samples or from qualitative data.

I am reminded of the highly controversial (and by many accounts slippery) findings of Richard Herrnstein and Charles Murray, described in *The Bell Curve*, in which the authors maintained that intelligence is both inheritable and differentiated by race. Or the book *The End of Racism*, in which Dinesh D'Souza claimed that racism is no longer an important factor in American life and that the government must therefore cease to legislate issues on a racial basis.[10]

How can practitioners uninitiated in the finer points of research design distinguish between the good, the bad, and the just plain ugly? One way to start is to read research published in reputable journals (usually referenced). For example, in the field of educational leadership, practitioners could rely on such journals as *Educational Administration Quarterly*, the *Journal of School Leadership*, and the *Journal of Educational Administration*. Other examples of reputable journals in education include *Educational Researcher, Harvard Educational Review*, and the *American Journal of Education*. Another way is for practitioners to become proficient by learning the fundamentals of research design from credible experts like John Creswell or Michael Patton. And yet a third way is to read more than one article on a particular subject and then compare and contrast methods, findings, and conclusions. Look for common threads, discrepant information, and citations of supporting work throughout the text. However, regardless of how good one becomes at this, always keep in mind that even the best research can be wrong for a particular school district, school, or classroom.

Quantitative or Qualitative: Which Is Better?

Thirty years ago, reputable research in the field of education was normally quantitative in design. The predominant research method was to distribute surveys to randomly selected samples of targeted subjects and to conduct statistical comparisons of numerical datasets. In fact, most scholars in education considered qualitative research methods to be "soft," lacking in methodological rigor, and of limited value with regard to the study of large populations. It was widely—and not altogether unreasonably—believed that qualitative research was susceptible to researcher bias and the generation of unsubstantiated and highly subjective data based largely on self-reported perceptions and experiences. The question of how one can reliably extrapolate useful information from a qualitative study and confidently apply the findings to large numbers of schools and children continues to be at the center of the debate.[11]

> **Many contemporary scholars maintain that good qualitative research has equaled, if not exceeded, quantitative research in status, relevance, and methodological rigor.**

However, much has changed. In many universities today, the popularity and frequency of qualitative research in education overshadow the traditional emphasis on quantitative studies. Many contemporary scholars maintain that good qualitative research has equaled, if not exceeded, quantitative research in status, relevance, and methodological rigor. In essence, over the past quarter century, education scholars came to the realization that most surveys and statistical analyses failed to capture the fine-grained qualities of schooling. Yes, well-designed quantitative studies allowed for generalizing findings to larger populations, but legitimate concerns arose regarding the ability of such research to effectively capture the nuances of human interactions and program effects, differences in environmental contexts, and depth of understanding. Today, the focus is on finding patterns of behavior, documenting through thick descriptions, and seeking deeper meaning rather than higher levels of statistical significance.

Despite the rise in the popularity of qualitative research, a pronounced shift has recently occurred in national policy. In 2001 the No Child Left Behind Act refocused the national agenda of educational researchers on studies that can be classified as "scientifically based." To determine whether a study is scientifically based, NCLB offered the following standards:

- The research involves the application of rigorous, systematic, and objective procedures to obtain reliable and valid knowledge.
- The research employs empirical methods that draw on observation or experiment.
- The research employs rigorous data analyses adequate to test stated hypotheses and justify general conclusions.
- The research problems and data are evaluated using experimental or quasi-experimental methods.

The question of whether qualitative research can be considered scientifically based according to these standards is the center of a vigorous debate among scholars and policy makers.[12] And the jury is still out. So that brings us back to the question of what is better, quantitative or qualitative research? Perhaps the question shouldn't rest on the notion of what is better, but what is most relevant to practitioners in the field.

Here's my take on the matter. Since practitioners deal mostly with the day-to-day intimacies and idiosyncratic behaviors of children and colleagues, they are best served by research findings that can help them build technical competence and strategies for managing other people. Statistical analyses and numerical data can fail to provide the fine-grained insights needed to complete a full portrait of how schools work and how learning occurs in nuanced environments. Therefore, well-devised qualitative research (e.g., ethnographic studies, case studies, phenomenologies, grounded theories, and other descriptive narratives) is most likely to resonate with practitioners—and especially with practitioners not well trained in the fundamentals of statistical research (i.e., the vast majority).

Once again, however, I must caution that, regardless of the research design or methods used, the results should always be reviewed with a critical eye.

Practitioners Are Part of the Problem

Of course, practitioners also contribute to the persistent gap between research and its application in practice. The items that follow are several errors in thinking about research, truth, and knowledge that are commonly made by practitioners.

1. The seductive power of silver bullets and gurus. Besieged by the unremitting turbulence of daily activities in schools, practitioners favor technical solutions and "quick fixes" and have little patience (or time) for more abstract or nuanced research about schools and students. They want to know what works and how to go about fixing things. The problem is that there are no silver bullets. What works in one setting or with a particular group of people will inevitably play out differently (subtly or significantly) in different settings or with different people. Practitioners are wise to examine scientifically based research, but always with the understanding that, in the education business, "one size rarely fits all."

Practitioners also love gurus. Gurus offer us visions, wisdom, and certainty. Gurus exist in many forms. They can be thought leaders, authors, consultants, professors, politicians, or practitioners. They come wrapped in a veil of magic and often possess a personal magnetism that draws people into their sphere. In general, gurus influence others through the power of their personalities and their ideas.

Thirty years ago, I attended a seminar conducted by Werner Erhard (born John Paul Rosenberg), the spiritual leader of the New Age self-help group EST. It was held at the Cow Palace in Daly City, California. Over ten thousand people sat transfixed for several hours while Erhard spoke extemporaneously about existentialism, self-empowerment, and the meaning of life. Although I recall very little about the content of his talk, I vividly remember his charisma. Through the power of his mesmerizing personality, Erhard virtually ate up the stage. For all I cared, he could have been speaking about the finer points of Etruscan pottery. For thousands of devotees, he was a guru exemplar. Whether his ideas were right or wrong, I don't know. But he certainly had an impassioned point of view and the ability to convince others of the truth of his beliefs. He was later convicted of tax evasion and suspected of spousal abuse—but that's a different story.

Let me share another story to illustrate how the power of a scientifically based idea can cause practitioners in search of silver bullets and enamored by gurus to misapply the idea in practice. At about the same time, in the mid-1970s, UCLA professor Madeline Hunter championed what was to become a wildly popular model for planning and assessing teaching. Referred to as the Seven Step Lesson Plan, Hunter's "direct instruction" model (which she assembled from several research studies) quickly became the silver bullet that administrators and teacher trainers across the nation craved.

Unfortunately, too many school districts and administrators used the model as a rigid template for judging the quality of teaching. By her own admission, Hunter recognized the model's limits and repeatedly cautioned practitioners not to apply it too rigidly. After all, not every lesson necessarily required the application of all seven steps. Nevertheless, teacher evaluation protocols, rating forms, and staff development programs that framed teaching exclusively in terms of these seven steps popped up in districts across the country.[13]

As a young high school administrator in a district that used Hunter's model religiously, I fervently applied the framework with each teacher whom I was responsible for evaluating. A highly popular veteran teacher, Richard Loftus, was my very first victim. Loftus was an economics teacher who loved to lecture. In fact, that's just about all he ever did. Nevertheless, he did it exceptionally well, and the students relished it. Over the years, many of Loftus' former students who went on to college reported that his course more than adequately prepared them for college-level economics. Moreover, on the economics Advanced Placement exam, most of Loftus' students outperformed students across the state. In hindsight, either he had an incredible run of brilliant students, or he was doing something right in the classroom.

During my first observation of Loftus in action, I sat in the back of the classroom, armed with a Seven Step Lesson Plan checklist. At the end of the lesson, he had failed to employ even one of the seven steps. However, his lecture was lively, creative, and informative. Students were taking notes and were highly attentive. During the post-lesson conference, I informed Loftus that his rating for the lesson was unsatisfactory and that he needed to improve in all seven areas. Without uttering a word in his defense, he abruptly stormed out of my office and slammed the door. He rarely spoke with me again. Although Loftus wasn't much of a "scientist" in his approach to teaching, he was an exceptional "artist," a quality that was completely overlooked by the rigid application of the district's evaluation protocol.

Gurus aren't all bad. In fact, some are the real deal. They're often smart, experienced, and wise. But who are the modern-day gurus—Tom Peters, Bill Gates, Maya Angelou, Hillary Clinton, Al Gore, Margaret Wheatley, the Dalai Lama? The answer is: all of them and none of them. It depends on one's point of view, the context, and situational factors. Not one, however, possesses a "silver bullet."

One last comment about gurus: gurus are gurus not always because they challenge us to think differently, but often because what they offer resonates with our existing values and beliefs. So we must pick and choose among them and sort out the relevant from the irrelevant, the meaningful from the nonsensical, and we must always maintain an underlying sense of skepticism about what we (and they) really know.[14]

2. Exaggerated attributions of causality and misconceptions about chance. Practitioners are prone to overestimate the effects of particular reforms and underestimate the probability of randomness. According to Daniel Kahneman and Amos Tversky, "People often make extreme predictions on the basis of information whose reliability and predictive validity are known to be low."[15] Promising new programs and practices that generate improvements in student learning and performance are often credited with "causing" the desired outcomes. However, educating children can't be reduced to a set of universal truths, skills, or strategies. Education is as much art as it is science.[16]

No reform, no method, no pedagogical approach can completely control for the inevitable and infinite variations of human behavior and their effects on learning. As a result, it is almost impossible to provide irrefutable proof that a particular educational approach acts as the sole causal agent in changed behavior. One must also consider how other factors, such as peer influences, teacher dispositions and skills, physical and emotional status of the child, family influences, the Hawthorne Effect, and so on, may contribute to observed or measured changes. According to a nationally distributed school reform research briefing, "It is important to have high ambitions and reasonable expectations about the results that reforms can produce. Careful evaluations of reform efforts seldom find large and dramatic effects."[17]

3. Presumed associations. Practitioners often assume that, because an empirically supported principle of human behavior or learning or an innovative program or practice seems to work in one setting or context, it will apply just as well in different settings. But is this a safe assumption? For example, will a reading program that works well for a certain group of inner-city minority students elicit comparable levels of growth from minority students in middle-income suburban settings? Will a successful approach to developing English-language skills with immigrant Asian children from developed countries work equally well with immigrant Hispanic children from developing countries? Is the widely held principle that homogeneous grouping of students is bad for learning (and most certainly bad education policy) true in all situations? Will children in homogeneous groups always fail to learn as effectively or as much as children in heterogeneous groups? Will zero tolerance discipline policies reduce campus violence with equal effect in lower-income inner-city schools and middle-class suburban schools? Do the strategies used to encourage school involvement with highly educated parents in white-collar professions work equally well with less-educated blue-collar parents? Does the elimination of social promotion practices in schools stimulate low-achieving students to perform better?

The answer to these and many other questions like them is, "Sometimes yes, and sometimes no." However, one thing is certain: just because an empirically supported practice works well in one context doesn't mean that it will work equally well in other contexts (similar or otherwise). Neither does it mean that the positive effects of a research-based reform will be equally sustainable over the long term from one setting to the next.

4. Wishful thinking. Under the press for sustained improvement in student achievement, educators are generally eager to see new educational interventions succeed. They are far too busy with the day-to-day tasks of managing schools and classrooms to waste time on unproven or weak strategies. So when they do invest themselves in promoting change, it's not uncommon for them to be optimistic that their efforts will pay off.

Take, for example, the tragic case of a charismatic superintendent from a large suburban school district in Northern California. In an effort to improve academic achievement and reduce the dropout rates among poor minority students, he devised a highly innovative and expensive magnet school plan. At the time (the late 1980s), magnet schools had gained considerable popularity across the nation's urban school districts. They were seen as a way to distribute students more evenly across socioeconomic boundaries, pique students' intrinsic motivation, and provide intra-district choice. So eager were the superintendent and the school board to implement the plan that they based several critical decisions about resource allocation on their expectations of supplemental funding from both private and public sources. Tragically, the funding sources never materialized, and the school district went into state receivership, after posting a budget deficit of more than $28 million. The superintendent lost his job, but he was able to repeat this scurrilous feat in two more school districts before his eventual retirement.[18]

The point is that wishful thinking clouds good judgment. When we want something bad enough, it's easy to throw caution to the wind while ignoring disconfirming evidence and common sense.

5. Generalizing from nonrandom and small samples. Jaime Escalante was, in the minds of many educators, a miracle worker. A passionate and creative high school math teacher born in Bolivia, Escalante gained notoriety in the 1980s for his legendary ability to take low-income, under-achieving minority students at Garfield High School in Los Angeles and transform them into Advanced Placement calculus savants through his magical approach to teaching. He was the subject of the popular movie *Stand and Deliver*, which idealized his exploits and understated the years of work it took to cultivate the math skills of a select group of carefully groomed students. Escalante became a hero to legions of administrators and teachers. Yet, despite countless efforts by inner-city teachers across the country to replicate his instructional success, few have matched or sustained Escalante's track record of success.[19] Why is that?

For one thing, Escalante's methods were applied to very small samples of students. He didn't teach in 10 schools, or a hundred, or a thousand. He taught in one school in Los Angeles and one in Sacramento. And, over the course of his career, not all students succeeded on the Advanced Placement exams. Then, too, Escalante was Escalante. The qualities and behaviors that make a successful teacher are far more complex than the instructional methods used in the classroom. Granted, we all learned a great deal from Escalante about passion, focused instruction, and the application of math concepts to real-world problems. But we also know that the sample of students whom he taught over the years was not necessarily representative of all students in all schools and certainly not large enough to confidently generalize the qualities of his teaching to all teachers who work in high-minority schools in the nation's cities.

The moral of the story is that what works in Ms. Doe's classroom may or may not work in yours. There is no way to reliably predict success. However, what works in the classrooms of a thousand randomly selected Ms. Does is far more likely to work in yours as well.

6. Generalizing from perceptions and self-reported data. Much of the qualitative and quantitative research today depicts self-reported experiences, judgments, and perceptions of reality. Understanding what, how, and why particular individuals think or behave the way that they do by asking them can be quite interesting and useful. Well-written narrative accounts of self-reported data can be fascinating, very persuasive, and authoritative in tone. Such accounts, however, cannot and should not be generalized to large groups.

There are three particularly pernicious aspects of self-reported information: fallible memories, biased mental models, and narrow frames of reference. Let's start with memory. Memories are imperfect. They are distorted by time, lack of use, new stimuli, and emotions. Vivid as a memory might be, it is never objective and always represents an individual's subjective account of reality and truth.[20] Granted, memories are often all a researcher has to go on, but at best they represent approximations of past events.

Self-reported data are deeply influenced by an individual's mental models. In plain language, a mental model represents a person's world view, assumptions, beliefs, and core values. As first explained by psychologist Kenneth Craik in the early 1940s, the mind constructs "small-scale models" of reality that it uses to anticipate events. Mental models can be constructed from perception, imagination, or the comprehension of discourse. Like memories, mental models are unique to individuals and never fully represent objective truth. The way we think and feel about the world shapes our interpretation of events past, present, and future.

Finally, an individual's ability to frame situations and problems from multiple perspectives bears upon the credibility of that individual's interpretation of events. Narrow-minded people see the world through a singular lens and often fail to empathize with others' perspectives or feelings. They also fail to consider alternative explanations of the truth or reality.[21] Some critics of the war in Iraq contend that the current U.S. Administration failed to consider or anticipate the social and political dynamics of the post-Saddam Iraq through multiple frames of reference. As a result, the depth and breadth of the insurgency has greatly exceeded prewar expectations.[22]

To correct for the distortions of memory, mental models, and framing, competent researchers look for corroborating evidence. They evaluate self-reported information in light of the narrative explanations of others, confirming or disconfirming documentation, and observation. Without such careful craftsmanship, self-reported data should always be treated with caution and never extrapolated to explain the behaviors, perceptions, values, or beliefs of large groups.

Credible Evidence: What to Attend to and What to Ignore

I'd like to conclude by revisiting the question of what practitioners should attend to and what they should ignore. First, practitioners must consider empirical research as encyclopedic rather than plenary. In education, even the most credible research is subject to differing interpretations and rarely depicts the final word or an indisputable truth. Good research is a road map and rarely a destination.

Second, useful evidence can come in many forms. Obviously, a well-designed research study provides the most credible form of evidence about what works in schools. But whether the research is qualitative or quantitative in form is less important than its relevance to problems of practice. And the most important issue for practitioners is not the broad relevance of research to the field, but the relevance of research findings to particular contexts and circumstances. For example, research about developing charter schools as vehicles for improving academic achievement among low-income urban minority youths probably won't provide much relevant information to those who want to develop charter schools in middle- and upper-income suburban environments. Likewise, attempts to apply empirically supported strategies for teaching reading to underachieving children from low socioeconomic family backgrounds are likely to be less effective in stimulating the reading skills of underachieving children from higher socioeconomic backgrounds. Stated simply, context matters.

Third, don't dismiss the usefulness of anecdotal evidence. Firsthand accounts of what works and what doesn't are important sources of information. At the very least, such accounts can (and should) provoke inquiry into the research literature. Corroborating the anecdotal evidence with reports from several expert practitioners and from the research literature, of course, is more credible than simply relying on individual anecdotal accounts. However, the intriguing potential of anecdotal evidence is that it can stimulate experimentation and innovation. Since silver bullets are extremely rare in the education business, practitioners must rely on modest experiments and incremental "wins." They must understand that making progress in the education of children is rarely linear and more often recursive, episodic, and even idiosyncratic. Practitioners must develop a "nose" for possibilities, imaginative strategies, and potential pathways that may lead to improved educational practice. The findings of published research alone probably won't get you to the promised land.

Finally, trust your gut. If an empirically tested strategy or program doesn't feel right for your school or district, it probably isn't right. Intuition can be a useful barometer for judging when to slow down and search for additional information. Let common sense be your guide. A recent study of 92 school principals revealed that the principals frequently used their intuition when making important decisions. Most important, the study also revealed that, even though intuitively derived decisions didn't always turn out well, the principals always regretted it when they failed to follow their gut.[23]

Notes

1. Larry Cuban and David Tyack, *Tinkering Toward Utopia: A Century of Public School Reform* (Cambridge, Mass.: Harvard University Press, 1998).

2. Frances Lawrenz, Douglas Huffman, and Bethann Lavoie, "Implementing and Sustaining Standards-Based Curriculum Reform," *NASSP Bulletin*, June 2005, pp. 2–17.

3. James Crawford, Stephen Krashen, and Haeyoung Kim, "Anti-Bilingual Initiatives: Confusing in Any Language," Hispanic Link News Service, 29 March 1998.

4. Jeffrey Pfeffer and Robert I. Sutton, *Hard Facts, Dangerous Half-Truths, and Total Nonsense: Profiting from Evidence-Based Management* (Cambridge, Mass.: Harvard Business School Press, 2006).

5. Carolyn Riehl et al., "Reconceptualizing Research and Scholarship in Educational Administration: Learning to Know, Knowing to Do, Doing to Learn," *Educational Administration Quarterly*, vol. 36, 2000, p. 405.

6. Pfeffer and Sutton, op. cit.

7. Thomas J. Sergiovanni, *Moral Leadership: Getting to the Heart of School Improvement* (Hoboken, N.J.: Wiley, 1996); and Linda Lambert, *Leadership Capacity for Lasting School Improvement* (Alexandria, Va.: Association for Supervision and Curriculum Development, 2003).

8. Deborah Viadero, "Study Questions Push for Smaller High Schools," *Education Week*, 6 June 2006, pp. 12–13.

9. Janet Quint, "Research-Based Lessons for High School Reform: Findings from Three Models," *Principal's Research Review*, vol. 1, no. 3, 2006, pp. 1–8.

10. Richard Herrnstein and Charles Murray, *The Bell Curve: Intelligence and Class Structure in American Life* (New York: Simon & Schuster, 1994); and Dinesh D'Souza, *The End of Racism: Principles for a Multiracial Society* (New York: Simon & Schuster, 1996).

11. Gavriel Solomon, "Transcending the Qualitative-Quantitative Debate: The Analytic and Systemic Approaches to Educational Research," *Educational Researcher*, August/September 1991, pp. 10–18.

12. Margaret Eisenhart and Lisa Towne, "Contestation and Change in National Policy on 'Scientifically Based' Education Research," *Educational Researcher*, October 2003, pp. 31–38.

13. Patricia Wolfe, "What the 'Seven-Step Lesson Plan' Isn't," *Educational Leadership*, February 1987, pp. 70–71.

14. Pfeffer and Sutton, op. cit.

15. Daniel Kahneman and Amos Tversky, "Intuitive Prediction: Biases and Corrective Procedures," in Daniel Kahneman, Paul Slovic, and Amos Tversky, eds., *Judgment Under Uncertainty: Heuristics and Biases* (Cambridge: Cambridge University Press, 1982), p. 417.

16. N. L. Gage, *The Scientific Basis of the Art of Teaching* (New York: Teachers College Press, 1978).

17. Quint, p. 7.

18. Lisa Snell, "Scandals Prevalent in Public Schools" (commentary), Reason Foundation, 2004, available at www.reason.org/commentaries/snell_20040601b.shtml.

19. Jay Mathews, *Escalante: The Best Teacher in America* (New York: Holt, 1989).

20. Antonio R. Damasio, *Descartes' Error: Emotion, Reason, and the Human Brain* (1994; rpt. New York: Penguin, 2005).

21. Lee G. Bolman and Terrence E. Deal, *Reframing Organizations: Artistry, Choice, and Leadership*, 3rd ed. (New York: Wiley, 2003).

22. Larry J. Diamond, *Squandered Victory: The American Occupation and Bungled Effort to Bring Democracy to Iraq* (New York: Holt, 2005).

23. Stephen H. Davis and Patricia B. Davis, *The Intuitive Dimensions of Administrative Decision Making* (Lanham, Md.: Scarecrow Education, 2003).

STEPHEN H. DAVIS is an associate professor in the School of Education, Stanford University, Stanford, Calif.

From *Phi Delta Kappan*, by Stephen H. Davis, April 2007, pp. 569–578. Copyright © 2007 by Phi Delta Kappan. Reprinted by permission of the publisher and Stephen H. Davis.

Learning to Love Assessment

From judging performance to guiding students to shaping instruction to informing learning, coming to grips with informative assessment is one insightful journey.

CAROL ANN TOMLINSON

When I was a young teacher—young both in years and in understanding of the profession I had entered—I nonetheless went about my work as though I comprehended its various elements. I immediately set out to arrange furniture, put up bulletin boards, make lesson plans, assign homework, give tests, compute grades, and distribute report cards as though I knew what I was doing.

I had not set out to be a teacher, and so I had not really studied education in any meaningful way. I had not student taught. Had I done those things, however, I am not convinced that my evolution as a teacher would have been remarkably different. In either case, my long apprenticeship as a student (Lortie, 1975) would likely have dominated any more recent knowledge I might have acquired about what it means to be a teacher. I simply "played school" in the same way that young children "play house"—by mimicking what we think the adults around us do.

The one element I knew I was unprepared to confront was classroom management. Consequently, that's the element that garnered most of my attention during my early teaching years. The element to which I gave least attention was assessment. In truth, I didn't even know the word *assessment* for a good number of years. I simply knew I was supposed to give tests and grades. I didn't much like tests in those years. It was difficult for me to move beyond their judgmental aspect. They made kids nervous. They made me nervous. With no understanding of the role of assessment in a dynamic and success-oriented classroom, I initially ignored assessment when I could and did it when I had to.

Now, more than three decades into the teaching career I never intended to have, it's difficult for me to remember exactly when I had the legion of insights that have contributed to my growth as an educator. I do know, however, that those insights are the milestones that mark my evolution from seeing teaching as a job to seeing teaching as a science-informed art that has become a passion.

Following are 10 understandings about classroom assessment that sometimes gradually and sometimes suddenly illuminated my work. I am not finished with the insights yet because I am not finished with my work as a teacher or learner. I present the understandings in something like the order they unfolded in my thinking.

The formulation of one insight generally prepared the way for the next. Now, of course, they are seamless, interconnected, and interdependent. But they did not come to me that way. Over time and taken together, the understandings make me an advocate of *informative assessment*—a concept that initially played no conscious role in my work as a teacher.

Understanding 1. Informative assessment isn't just about tests.

Initially I thought about assessment as test giving. Over time, I became aware of students who did poorly on tests but who showed other evidence of learning. They solved problems well, contributed to discussions, generated rich ideas, drew sketches to illustrate, and role-played. When they wanted to communicate, they always found a way. I began to realize that when I gave students multiple ways to express learning or gave them a say in how they could show what they knew, more students were engaged. More to the point, more students were learning.

Although I still had a shallow sense of the possibilities of assessment, I did at least begin to try in multiple ways to let kids show what they knew. I used more authentic products as well as tests to gain a sense of student understanding. I began to realize that when one form of assessment was ineffective for a student, it did not necessarily indicate a lack of student success but could, in fact, represent a poor fit between the student and the method through which I was trying to make the student communicate. I studied students to see what forms of assessment worked for them and to be sure I never settled for a single assessment as an adequate representation of what a student knew.

Understanding 2. Informative assessment really isn't about the grade book.

At about the same time that Understanding 1 emerged in my thinking, I began to sense that filling a grade book was both less interesting and less useful than trying to figure out what individual students knew, understood, or could do. My thinking was shifting from assessment as judging students to assessment as guiding students. I was beginning to think about student accomplishment more than about student ranking (Wiggins, 1993).

Giving students feedback seemed to be more productive than giving them grades. If I carefully and consistently gave them feedback about their work, I felt more like a teacher than a warden. I felt more respectful of the students and their possibilities (Wiggins, 1993). I began to understand the difference between teaching for success and "gotcha" teaching and to sense the crucial role of informative assessment in the former.

Understanding 3. Informative assessment isn't always formal.

I also became conscious of the fact that some of the most valuable insights I gleaned about students came from moments or events that I'd never associated with assessment. When I read in a student's journal that his parents were divorcing, I understood why he was disengaged in class. I got a clear picture of one student's misunderstanding when I walked around as students worked and saw a diagram she made to represent how she understood the concept we were discussing. I could figure out how to help a student be more successful in small groups when I took the time to study systematically, but from a distance, what he did to make groups grow impatient with him.

Assessment, then, was more than "tests plus other formats." Informative assessment could occur any time I went in search of information about a student. In fact, it could occur when I was not actively searching but was merely conscious of what was happening around me.

I began to talk in more purposeful ways with students as they entered and left the classroom. I began to carry around a clipboard on which I took notes about students. I developed a filing system that enabled me to easily store and retrieve information about students as individuals and learners. I was more focused in moving around the room to spot-check student work in progress for particular proficiencies. I began to sense that virtually all student products and interactions can serve as informative assessment because I, as a teacher, have the power to use them that way.

Understanding 4. Informative assessment isn't separate from the curriculum.

Early in my teaching, I made lesson plans. Later on, I made unit plans. In neither time frame did I see assessment as a part of the curriculum design process. As is the case with many teachers, I planned what I would teach, taught it, and then created assessments. The assessments were largely derived from what had transpired during a segment of lessons and ultimately what had transpired during a unit of study. It was a while before I understood what Wiggins and McTighe (1998) call *backward design*.

That evolution came in three stages for me. First, I began to understand the imperative of laying out precisely what mattered most for students to know and be able to do—but also what they should understand—as a result of our work together. Then I began to discover that many of my lessons had been only loosely coupled to learning goals. I'd sometimes (often?) been teaching in response to what my students liked rather than in response to crucial learning goals. I understood the need to make certain that my teaching was a consistent match for what students needed to know, understand, and be able to do at the end of a unit. Finally, I began to realize that if I wanted to teach for success, my assessments had to be absolutely aligned with the knowledge, understanding, and skill I'd designated as essential learning outcomes. There was a glimmer of recognition in my work that assessment was a part of—not apart from—curriculum design.

Understanding 5. Informative assessment isn't about "after."

I came to understand that assessments that came at the end of a unit—although important manifestations of student knowledge, understanding, and skill—were less useful to me as a teacher than were assessments that occurred during a unit of study. By the time I gave and graded a final assessment, we were already moving on to a new topic or unit. There was only a limited amount I could do at that stage with information that revealed to me that some students fell short of mastering essential outcomes—or that others had likely been bored senseless by instruction that focused on outcomes they had mastered long before the unit had begun. When I studied student work in the course of a unit, however, I could do many things to support or extend student learning. I began to be a devotee of *formative assessment*, although I did not know that term for many years.

It took time before I understood the crucial role of preassessment or diagnostic assessment in teaching. Likely the insight was the product of the embarrassment of realizing that a student had no idea what I was talking about because he or she lacked vocabulary I assumed every 7th grader knew or of having a student answer a question in class early in a unit that made it clear he already knew more about the topic at hand than I was planning to teach. At that point, I began to check early in the year to see whether students could read the textbook, how well they could produce expository writing, what their spelling level was, and so on. I began systematically to use preassessments before a unit started to see where students stood in regard to prerequisite and upcoming knowledge, understanding, and skills.

Understanding 6. Informative assessment isn't an end in itself.

I slowly came to realize that the most useful assessment practices would shape how I taught. I began to explore and appreciate two potent principles of informative assessment. First, the greatest power of assessment information lies in its capacity to help me see how to be a better teacher. If I know what students are and are not grasping at a given moment in a sequence of study, I know how to plan our time better. I know when to reteach, when to move ahead, and when to explain or demonstrate something in another way. Informative assessment is not an end in itself, but the beginning of better instruction.

Understanding 7. Informative assessment isn't separate from instruction.

A second and related understanding hovered around my sense that assessment should teach me how to be a better teacher. Whether I liked it or not, informative assessment always demonstrated to me that my students' knowledge, understanding, and skill were emerging along different time continuums and at different depths. It became excruciatingly clear that my brilliant teaching was not equally brilliant for everyone in my classes. In other words, informative assessment helped me solidify a need for differentiation. As Lorna Earl (2003) notes, if teachers know a precise learning destination and consistently check to see where students are relative to that destination, differentiation isn't just an option; it's the logical next step in teaching. Informative assessment made it clear—at first, painfully so—that if I meant for every student to succeed, I was going to have to teach with both singular and group needs in mind.

If I meant for every student to succeed, I was going to have to teach with both singular and group needs in mind.

Understanding 8. Informative assessment isn't just about student readiness.

Initially, my emergent sense of the power of assessment to improve my teaching focused on student readiness. At the time, I was teaching in a school with a bimodal population—lots of students were three or more years behind grade level or three or more years above grade level, with almost no students in between. Addressing that expansive gap in student readiness was a daily challenge. I was coming to realize the role of informative assessment in ensuring that students worked as often as possible at appropriate levels of challenge (Earl, 2003).

Only later was I aware of the potential role of assessment in determining what students cared about and how they learned. When I could attach what I was teaching to what students cared about, they learned more readily and more durably. When I could give them options about how to learn and express what they knew, learning improved. I realized I could pursue insights about student interests and preferred modes of learning, just as I had about their readiness needs.

I began to use surveys to determine student interests, hunt for clues about their individual and shared passions, and take notes on who learned better alone and who learned better in small groups. I began to ask students to write to me about which instructional approaches were working for them and which were not. I was coming to understand that learning is multidimensional and that assessment could help me understand learners as multidimensional as well.

Understanding 9. Informative assessment isn't just about finding weaknesses.

As my sense of the elasticity of assessment developed, so did my sense of the wisdom of using assessment to accentuate student positives rather than negatives. With readiness-based assessments, I had most often been on the hunt for what students didn't know, couldn't do, or didn't understand. Using assessment to focus on student interests and learning preferences illustrated for me the power of emphasizing what works for students.

When I saw "positive space" in students and reflected that to them, the results were stunningly different from when I reported on their "negative space." It gave students something to build on—a sense of possibility. I began to spend at least as much time gathering assessment information on what students *could* do as on what they couldn't. That, in turn, helped me develop a

conviction that each student in my classes brought strengths to our work and that it was my job to bring those strengths to the surface so that all of us could benefit.

Understanding 10. Informative assessment isn't just for the teacher.

Up to this point, much of my thinking was about the teacher—about me, my class, my work, my growth. The first nine understandings about assessment were, in fact, crucial to my development. But it was the 10th understanding that revolutionized what happened in the classrooms I shared with my students. I finally began to grasp that teaching requires a plural pronoun. The best teaching is never so much about *me* as about *us*. I began to see my students as full partners in their success.

Informative assessment is not an end in itself, but the beginning of better instruction.

My sense of the role of assessment necessarily shifted. I was a better teacher—but more to the point, my students were better learners—when assessment helped all of us push learning forward (Earl, 2003). When students clearly understood our learning objectives, knew precisely what success would look like, understood how each assignment contributed to their success, could articulate the role of assessment in ensuring their success, and understood that their work correlated with their needs, they developed a sense of self-efficacy that was powerful in their lives as learners. Over time, as I developed, my students got better at self-monitoring, self-managing, and self-modifying (Costa & Kallick, 2004). They developed an internal locus of control that caused them to work hard rather than to rely on luck or the teacher's good will (Stiggins, 2000).

Assessing Wisely

Lorna Earl (2003) distinguishes between assessment *of* learning, assessment *for* learning, and assessment *as* learning. In many ways, my growth as a teacher slowly and imperfectly followed that progression. I began by seeing assessment as judging performance, then as informing teaching, and finally as informing learning. In reality, all those perspectives play a role in effective teaching. The key is where we place the emphasis.

Certainly a teacher and his or her students need to know who reaches (and exceeds) important learning targets—thus summative assessment, or assessment *of* learning, has a place in teaching. Robust learning generally requires robust teaching, and both diagnostic and formative assessments, or assessments *for* learning, are catalysts for better teaching. In the end, however, when assessment is seen *as* learning—for students as well as for teachers—it becomes most informative and generative for students and teachers alike.

References

Costa, A., & Kallick, B. (2004). *Assessment strategies for self-directed learning*. Thousand Oaks, CA: Corwin.

Earl, L. (2003). Assessment as learning: Using classroom assessment to maximize student learning. Thousand Oaks, CA: Corwin.

Lortie, D. (1975). *Schoolteacher: A sociological study*. Chicago: University of Chicago Press.

Stiggins, R. (2000). *Student-involved classroom assessment* (3rd ed.). Upper Saddle River, NJ: Prentice-Hall.

Wiggins, G. (1993). Assessing student performance: Exploring the purpose and limits of testing. San Francisco: Jossey-Bass.

Wiggins, G., & McTighe, J. (1998). *Understanding by design*. Alexandria, VA: Association for Supervision and Curriculum Development.

CAROL ANN TOMLINSON is Professor of Educational Leadership, Foundation, and Policy at the University of Virginia in Charlottesville; cat3y@virginia.edu.

From *Educational Leadership*, December 2008, pp. 8–13. Copyright © 2008 by ASCD. Reprinted by permission. The Association for Supervision and Curriculum Development is a worldwide community of educators advocating sound policies and sharing best practices to achieve the success of each learner. To learn more, visit ASCD at www.ascd.org

The Case for and against Homework

**Teachers should not abandon homework.
Instead, they should improve its instructional quality.**

ROBERT J. MARZANO AND DEBRA J. PICKERING

Homework has been a perennial topic of debate in education, and attitudes toward it have been cyclical (Gill & Schlossman, 2000). Throughout the first few decades of the 20th century, educators commonly believed that homework helped create disciplined minds. By 1940, growing concern that homework interfered with other home activities sparked a reaction against it. This trend was reversed in the late 1950s when the Soviets' launch of *Sputnik* led to concern that U.S. education lacked rigor; schools viewed more rigorous homework as a partial solution to the problem. By 1980, the trend had reversed again, with some learning theorists claiming that homework could be detrimental to students' mental health. Since then, impassioned arguments for and against homework have continued to proliferate.

We now stand at an interesting intersection in the evolution of the homework debate. Arguments against homework are becoming louder and more popular, as evidenced by several recent books as well as an editorial in *Time* magazine (Wallis, 2006) that presented these arguments as truth without much discussion of alternative perspectives. At the same time, a number of studies have provided growing evidence of the usefulness of homework when employed effectively.

The Case for Homework

Homework is typically defined as any tasks "assigned to students by school teachers that are meant to be carried out during nonschool hours" (Cooper, 1989a, p. 7). A number of synthesis studies have been conducted on homework, spanning a broad range of methodologies and levels of specificity (see Figure 1). Some are quite general and mix the results from experimental studies with correlational studies.

**Arguments against homework are
becoming louder and more popular.**

Two meta-analyses by Cooper and colleagues (Cooper, 1989a; Cooper, Robinson, & Patall, 2006) are the most comprehensive and rigorous. The 1989 meta-analysis reviewed research dating as far back as the 1930s; the 2006 study reviewed research from 1987 to 2003. Commenting on studies that attempted to examine the causal relationship between homework and student achievement by comparing experimental (homework) and control (no homework) groups, Cooper, Robinson, and Patall (2006) noted,

> With only rare exceptions, the relationship between the amount of homework students do and their achievement outcomes was found to be positive and statistically significant. Therefore, we think it would not be imprudent, based on the evidence in hand, to conclude that doing homework causes improved academic achievement. (p. 48)

The Case against Homework

Although the research support for homework is compelling, the case against homework is popular. *The End of Homework: How Homework Disrupts Families, Overburdens Children, and Limits Learning* by Kralovec and Buell (2000), considered by many to be the first high-profile attack on homework, asserted that homework contributes to a corporate-style, competitive U.S. culture that overvalues work to the detriment of personal and familial well-being. The authors focused particularly on the harm to economically disadvantaged students, who are unintentionally penalized because their environments often make it almost impossible to complete assignments at home. The authors called for people to unite against homework and to lobby for an extended school day instead.

A similar call for action came from Bennett and Kalish (2006) in *The Case Against Homework: How Homework Is Hurting Our Children and What We Can Do About It*. These authors criticized both the quantity and quality of homework. They provided evidence that too much homework harms students' health and family time, and they asserted that teachers are not well trained in how to assign homework. The authors suggested that individuals and parent groups should insist that teachers reduce the amount of homework, design

Synthesis Study	Focus	Number of Effect Sizes	Average	Percentile Gains
Graue, Weinstein, & Walberg, 1983[1]	General effects of homework	29	.49	19
Bloom, 1984	General effects of homework	—	.30	12
Paschal Weinstein, & Walberg, 1984[2]	Homework versus no homework	47	.28	11
Cooper, 1989a	Homework versus no homework	20	.21	8
Hattie, 1992; Fraser, Walberg, Welch, & Hattie, 1987	General effects of homework	110	.43	17
Walberg, 1999	With teacher comments	2	.88	31
Walberg, 1999	Graded	5	.78	28
Cooper, Robinson, & Patall, 2006	Homework versus no homework	6	.60	23

Figure 1 Synthesis studies on homework.

Note: This figure describes the eight major research syntheses on the effects of homework published from 1983 to 2006 that provide the basis for the analysis in this article. The "Number of Effect Sizes" column includes results from experimental/control group studies only.

1 Reported in Fraser, Walberg, Welch, & Hattie, 1987.
2 Reported in Kavale, 1988.

more valuable assignments, and avoid homework altogether over breaks and holidays.

In a third book, *The Homework Myth: Why Our Kids Get Too Much of a Bad Thing* (2006a), Kohn took direct aim at the research on homework. In this book and in a recent article in *Phi Delta Kappan* (2006b), he became quite personal in his condemnation of researchers. For example, referring to Harris Cooper, the lead author of the two leading meta-analyses on homework, Kohn noted,

> A careful reading of Cooper's own studies . . . reveals further examples of his determination to massage the numbers until they yield somcthing—anything—on which to construct a defense of homework for younger children. (2006a, p. 84)

He also attacked a section on homework in our book *Classroom Instruction that Works* (Marzano, Pickering, & Pollock, 2001).

Kohn concluded that research fails to demonstrate homework's effectiveness as an instructional tool and recommended changing the "default state" from an expectation that homework *will* be assigned to an expectation that homework *will not* be assigned. According to Kohn, teachers should only assign homework when they can justify that the assignments are "beneficial" (2006a, p. 166)—ideally involving students in activities appropriate for the home, such as performing an experiment in the kitchen, cooking, doing crossword puzzles with the family, watching good TV shows, or reading. Finally, Kohn urged teachers to involve students in deciding what homework, and how much, they should do.

Some of Kohn's recommendations have merit. For example, it makes good sense to only assign homework that is beneficial to student learning instead of assigning homework as a matter of policy. Many of those who conduct research on homework explicitly or implicitly recommend this practice. However, his misunderstanding or misrepresentation of the research sends the inaccurate message that research does not support homework. As Figure 1 indicates, homework has decades of research

supporting its effective use. Kohn's allegations that researchers are trying to mislead practitioners and the general public are unfounded and detract from a useful debate on effective practice.[1]

The Dangers of Ignoring the Research

Certainly, inappropriate homework may produce little or no benefit—it may even decrease student achievement. All three of the books criticizing homework provide compelling anecdotes to this effect. Schools should strengthen their policies to ensure that teachers use homework properly.

If a district or school discards homework altogether, however, it will be throwing away a powerful instructional tool. Cooper and colleagues' (2006) comparison of homework with no homework indicates that the average student in a class in which appropriate homework was assigned would score 23 percentile points higher on tests of the knowledge addressed in that class than the average student in a class in which homework was not assigned.

Perhaps the most important advantage of homework is that it can enhance achievement by extending learning beyond the school day. This characteristic is important because U.S. students spend much less time studying academic content than students in other countries do. A 1994 report examined the amount of time U.S. students spend studying core academic subjects compared with students in other countries that typically outperform the United States academically, such as Japan, Germany, and France. The study found that "students abroad are required to work on demanding subject matter at least twice as long" as are U.S. students (National Education Commission on Time and Learning, 1994, p. 25).

To drop the use of homework, then, a school or district would be obliged to identify a practice that produces a similar effect within the confines of the school day without taking away or diminishing the benefits of other academic activities—no easy accomplishment. A better approach is to ensure that teachers use homework effectively. To enact effective homework policies, however, schools and districts must address the following issues.

Grade Level

Although teachers across the K–12 spectrum commonly assign homework, research has produced no clear-cut consensus on the benefits of homework at the early elementary grade levels. In his early meta-analysis, Cooper (1989a) reported the following effect sizes (p. 71):

Grades 4–6: ES = .15 (Percentile gain = 6)
Grades 7–9: ES = .31 (Percentile gain = 12)
Grades 10–12: ES = .64 (Percentile gain = 24)

The pattern clearly indicates that homework has smaller effects at lower grade levels. Even so, Cooper (1989b) still recommended homework for elementary students because

homework for young children should help them develop good study habits, foster positive attitudes toward school, and communicate to students the idea that learning takes work at home as well as at school. (p. 90)

The Cooper, Robinson, and Patall (2006) meta-analysis found the same pattern of stronger relationships at the secondary level but also identified a number of studies at grades 2, 3, and 4 demonstrating positive effects for homework. In *The Battle over Homework* (2007), Cooper noted that homework should have different purposes at different grade levels:

- For students in the *earliest grades*, it should foster positive attitudes, habits, and character traits; permit appropriate parent involvement; and reinforce learning of simple skills introduced in class.
- For students in *upper elementary grades*, it should play a more direct role in fostering improved school achievement.
- In *6th grade and beyond*, it should play an important role in improving standardized test scores and grades.

Time Spent on Homework

One of the more contentious issues in the homework debate is the amount of time students should spend on homework. The Cooper synthesis (1989a) reported that for junior high school students, the benefits increased as time increased, up to 1 to 2 hours of homework a night, and then decreased. The Cooper, Robinson, and Patall (2006) study reported similar findings: 7 to 12 hours of homework per week produced the largest effect size for 12th grade students. The researchers suggested that for 12th graders the optimum amount of homework might lie between 1.5 and 2.5 hours per night, but they cautioned that no hard-and-fast rules are warranted. Still, researchers have offered various recommendations. For example, Good and

Brophy (2003) cautioned that teachers must take care not to assign too much homework. They suggested that

homework must be realistic in length and difficulty given the students' abilities to work independently. Thus, 5 to 10 minutes per subject might be appropriate for 4th graders, whereas 30 to 60 minutes might be appropriate for college-bound high school students. (p. 394)

Cooper, Robinson, and Patall (2006) also issued a strong warning about too much homework:

Even for these oldest students, too much homework may diminish its effectiveness or even become counterproductive. (p 53)

Cooper (2007) suggested that research findings support the common "10-minute rule" (p. 92), which states that all daily homework assignments combined should take about as long to complete as 10 minutes multiplied by the student's grade level. He added that when required reading is included as a type of homework, the 10-minute rule might be increased to 15 minutes.

Focusing on the amount of time students spend on homework, however, may miss the point. A significant proportion of the research on homework indicates that the positive effects of homework relate to the amount of homework that the student completes rather than the amount of time spent on homework or the amount of homework actually assigned. Thus, simply assigning homework may not produce the desired effect—in fact, ill-structured homework might even have a negative effect on student achievement. Teachers must carefully plan and assign homework in a way that maximizes the potential for student success (see Research-Based Homework Guidelines).

Parent Involvement

Another question regarding homework is the extent to which schools should involve parents. Some studies have reported minimal positive effects or even negative effects for parental involvement. In addition, many parents report that they feel unprepared to help their children with homework and that their efforts to help frequently cause stress (see Balli, 1998; Corno, 1996; Hoover-Dempsey, Bassler, & Burow, 1995; Perkins & Milgram, 1996).

Epstein and colleagues conducted a series of studies to identify the conditions under which parental involvement enhances homework (Epstein, 2001; Epstein & Becker, 1982; Van Voorhis, 2003). They recommended *interactive* homework in which

- Parents receive clear guidelines spelling out their role.
- Teachers do not expect parents to act as experts regarding content or to attempt to teach the content.
- Parents ask questions that help students clarify and summarize what they have learned.

Good and Brophy (2003) provided the following recommendations regarding parent involvement:

Especially useful for parent-child relations purposes are assignments calling for students to show or explain their written work or other products completed at school to their parents and get their reactions (Epstein, 2001; Epstein, Simon, & Salinas, 1997) or to interview their parents to develop information about parental experiences or opinions relating to topics studied in social studies (Alleman & Brophy, 1998). Such assignments cause students and their parents or other family members to become engaged in conversations that relate to the academic curriculum and thus extend the students' learning. Furthermore, because these are likely to be genuine conversations rather than more formally structured teaching/learning tasks, both parents and children are likely to experience them as enjoyable rather than threatening. (p. 395)

Going Beyond the Research

Although research has established the overall viability of homework as a tool to enhance student achievement, for the most part the research does not provide recommendations that are specific enough to help busy practitioners. This is the nature of research—it errs on the side of assuming that something does not work until substantial evidence establishes that it does. The research community takes a long time to formulate firm conclusions on the basis of research. Homework is a perfect example: Figure 1 includes synthesis studies that go back as far as 60 years, yet all that research translates to a handful of recommendations articulated at a very general level.

In addition, research in a specific area, such as homework, sometimes contradicts research in related areas. For example, Cooper (2007) recommended on the basis of 60-plus years of homework research that teachers should not comment on or grade every homework assignment. But practitioners might draw a different conclusion from the research on providing feedback to students, which has found that providing "feedback coupled with remediation" (Hattie, 1992) or feedback on "test-like events" in the form of explanations to students (Bangert-Drowns, Kulik, Kulik, & Morgan, 1991) positively affects achievement.

Riehl (2006) pointed out the similarity between education research and medical research. She commented,

> When reported in the popular media, medical research often appears as a blunt instrument, able to obliterate skeptics or opponents by the force of its evidence and arguments. . . . Yet repeated visits to the medical journals themselves can leave a much different impression. The serious medical journals convey the sense that medical research is an ongoing conversation and quest, punctuated occasionally by important findings that can and should alter practice, but more often characterized by continuing investigations. These investigations, taken cumulatively, can inform the work of practitioners who are building their own local knowledge bases on medical care. (pp. 27–28)

Research-Based Homework Guidelines

Research provides strong evidence that, when used appropriately, homework benefits student achievement. To make sure that homework is appropriate, teachers should follow these guidelines:

- Assign purposeful homework. Legitimate purposes for homework include introducing new content, practicing a skill or process that students can do independently but not fluently, elaborating on information that has been addressed in class to deepen students' knowledge, and providing opportunities for students to explore topics of their own interest.
- Design homework to maximize the chances that students will complete it. For example, ensure that homework is at the appropriate level of difficulty. Students should be able to complete homework assignments independently with relatively high success rates, but they should still find the assignments challenging enough to be interesting.
- Involve parents in appropriate ways (for example, as a sounding board to help students summarize what they learned from the homework) without requiring parents to act as teachers or to police students' homework completion.
- Carefully monitor the amount of homework assigned so that it is appropriate to students' age levels and does not take too much time away from other home activities.

If relying solely on research is problematic, what are busy practitioners to do? The answer is certainly not to wait until research "proves" that a practice is effective. Instead, educators should combine research-based generalizations, research from related areas, and their own professional judgment based on firsthand experience to develop specific practices and make adjustments as necessary. Like medical practitioners, education practitioners must develop their own "local knowledge base" on homework and all other aspects of teaching. Educators can develop the most effective practices by observing changes in the achievement of the students with whom they work every day.

If a district or school discards homework altogether, it will be throwing away a powerful instructional tool.

Note

1. For a more detailed response to Kohn's views on homework, see Marzano & Pickering (2007) and Marzano & Pickering (in press).

References

Balli, S. J. (1998). When mom and dad help: Student reflections on parent involvement with homework. *Journal of Research and Development in Education, 31*(3), 142–148.

Bangert-Drowns, R. L., Kulik, C. C., Kulik, J. A., & Morgan, M. (1991). The instructional effects of feedback in test-like events. *Review of Educational Research, 61*(2), 213–238.

Bennett, S., & Kalish, N. (2006). *The case against homework: How homework is hurting our children and what we can do about it.* New York: Crown.

Bloom, B. S. (1984). The search for methods of group instruction as effective as one-to-one tutoring. *Educational Leadership, 41*(8), 4–18.

Cooper, H. (1989a). *Homework.* White Plains, NY: Longman.

Cooper, H. (1989b). Synthesis of research on homework. *Educational Leadership, 47*(3), 85–91.

Cooper, H. (2007). *The battle over homework* (3rd ed.). Thousand Oaks, CA: Corwin Press.

Cooper, H., Robinson, J. C., & Patall, E. A. (2006). Does homework improve academic achievement? A synthesis of research, 1987–2003. *Review of Educational Research, 76*(1), 1–62.

Corno, L. (1996). Homework is a complicated thing. *Educational Researcher, 25*(8), 27–30.

Epstein, J. (2001). *School, family, and community partnerships: Preparing educators and improving schools.* Boulder, CO: Westview.

Epstein, J. L., & Becker, H. J. (1982). Teachers' reported practices of parent involvement: Problems and possibilities. *Elementary School Journal, 83*, 103–113.

Fraser, B. J., Walberg, H. J., Welch, W. W., & Hattie, J. A. (1987). Synthesis of educational productivity research [Special issue]. *International Journal of Educational Research, 11*(2), 145–252.

Gill, B. P., & Schlossman, S. L. (2000). The lost cause of homework reform. *American Journal of Education, 109*, 27–62.

Good, T. L., & Brophy, J. E. (2003). *Looking in classrooms* (9th ed.). Boston: Allyn & Bacon.

Graue, M. E., Weinstein, T., & Walberg, H. J. (1983). School-based home instruction and learning: A quantitative synthesis. *Journal of Educational Research, 76*, 351–360.

Hattie, J. A. (1992). Measuring the effects of schooling. *Australian Journal of Education, 36*(1), 5–13.

Hoover-Dempsey, K. V., Bassler, O. C., & Burow, R. (1995). Parents' reported involvement in students' homework: Strategies and practices. *The Elementary School Journal, 95*(5), 435–450.

Kavale, K. A. (1988). Using meta-analyses to answer the question: What are the important influences on school learning? *School Psychology Review, 17*(4), 644–650.

Kohn, A. (2006a). *The homework myth: Why our kids get too much of a bad thing.* Cambridge, MA: Da Capo Press.

Kohn, A. (2006b). Abusing research: The study of homework and other examples. *Phi Delta Kappan, 88*(1), 9–22.

Kralovec, E., & Buell, J. (2000). *The end of homework: How homework disrupts families, overburdens children, and limits learning.* Boston: Beacon.

Marzano, R. J., & Pickering, D. J. (2007). Response to Kohn's allegations. Centennial, CO: Marzano & Associates. Available: http://marzanoandassociates.com/documents/KohnResponse.pdf

Marzano, R. J., & Pickering, D. J. (in press). Errors and allegations about research on homework. *Phi Delta Kappan.*

Marzano, R. J., Pickering, D. J., & Pollock, J. E. (2001). *Classroom instruction that works: Research-based strategies for increasing student achievement.* Alexandria, VA: ASCD.

National Education Commission on Time and Learning (1994). *Prisoners of time.* Washington, DC: U.S. Department of Education.

Paschal, R. A., Weinstein, T., & Walberg, H. J. (1984). The effects of homework on learning: A quantitative synthesis. *Journal of Educational Research, 78*, 97–104.

Perkins, P. G., & Milgram, R. B. (1996). Parental involvement in homework: A double-edge sword. *International Journal of Adolescence and Youth, 6*(3), 195–203.

Riehl, C. (2006). Feeling better: A comparison of medical research and education research. *Educational Researcher, 35*(5), 24–29.

Van Voorhis, F. (2003). Interactive homework in middle school: Effects on family involvement and science achievement. *Journal of Educational Research, 96*, 323–338.

Walberg, H. J. (1999). Productive teaching. In H. C. Waxman & H. J. Walberg (Eds.), *New directions for teaching practice research* (pp. 75–104). Berkeley, CA: McCutchen.

Wallis, C. (2006). Viewpoint: The myth about homework. *Time, 168*(10), 57.

ROBERT J. MARZANO is a Senior Scholar at Mid-Continent Research for Education and Learning in Aurora, Colorado; an Associate Professor at Cardinal Stritch University in Milwaukee, Wisconsin; and President of Marzano & Associates consulting firm in Centennial, Colorado; robertjmarzano@aol.com. **DEBRA J. PICKERING** is a private consultant and Director of Staff Development in Littleton Public Schools, Littleton, Colorado; djplearn@hotmail.com.

UNIT 2
Reformatting Our Schools

Unit Selections

6. **Assessing Applied Skills,** Joe DiMartino and Andrea Castaneda
7. **From the Mouths of Middle-Schoolers: Important Changes for High School and College,** William J. Bushaw
8. **Industrial Arts: Call It What You Want, the Need Still Exists,** James Howlett
9. **High Schools Have Got It Bad for Higher Ed—And That Ain't Good,** Rona Wilensky
10. **All Our Students Thinking,** Nel Noddings

Key Points to Consider

- What are the important issues in the school reform debate?

- Why should we consider how students view their educational experience?

- What should teachers do to ensure that all students have a successful experience?

- What are the critical issues included in the discussion about the purpose of school?

- What should we be teaching our students?

- Can we teach children the skills required for the real world and critical thinking?

Student Website
www.mhcls.com

Internet References

The Bill & Melinda Gates Foundation
http://www.gatesfoundation.org/topics/Pages/high-schools.aspx

What Works Clearinghouse
http://ies.ed.gov/ncee/wwc/

The Center for Comprehensive School Reform and Improvement
http://www.centerforcsri.org

Council of the Great City Schools
http://www.cgcs.org

The Annenberg Institute
http://www.annenberginstitute.org

The Center for Social Organization of Schools
http://web.jhu.edu/CSOS.index.html

As school districts have implemented "No Child Left Behind" (NCLB) legislation, they have restructured the schools to emphasize core content proficiency. In other words, the emphasis has been on preparing students to meet college entrance requirements. We are left to decide the equity issues involved. We are also left to answer the most fundamental question of all: What constitutes a "well-educated high school graduate"? What educational background should the person have? We are a democratic society, committed to the free education of all our citizens, but are we accomplishing that goal? Under the Clinton administration, Goals 2000 were established under the *Educate America Act*. Two of these goals are important to the discussion of what constitutes a well-educated graduate. First, are we keeping students in school? Second, are they prepared with the necessary skills that will enable them to participate in a global economy?

Goal 2 states that "The high school graduation rate will increase to at least 90 percent" (U.S. Department of Education, n.d.). The data indicate that we have not reached this goal and are far from achieving it. While there is some disagreement on the exact percentages, most researchers agree that we have not reached the goal of 90 percent. For example, Heckman and LaFontaine (2008) note regarding the graduation rates in the United States that the minority graduation rates are still substantially below the rates for non-Hispanic whites, and the decline in high school graduation is greater for males than it is for females.

Goal 5 states that "Every adult American will be literate and will possess the knowledge and skills necessary to compete in a global economy and exercise the rights and responsibilities of citizenship" (U. S. Department of Education, n.d.). Educators have acknowledged that high school graduates get more satisfactory jobs, are happier in their job choices, and earn higher salaries than non-graduates. Heckman and LaFontaine (2008) note that the decline in high school graduation since 1970 (for cohorts born after 1950) has flattened growth in the skill level of the U.S. workforce. We must, at the very least, confront the dropout problem to increase the skill levels of the future workforce. We must also consider how high schools that respond only to higher education demands may be ignoring the needs of the nation at large for a skilled workforce that can compete in a global market. Bridgeland, Dilulio, and Morrison (2006) found in a survey of dropouts that 47 percent reported that a major reason why they left school was that the classes were not interesting. We must consider that by simply preparing students to attend traditional four-year institutions we may be ignoring their interests and desires and thus alienating them.

Each of the articles in this unit relates to the tension involved in reconceiving how educational development should proceed in response to all the dramatic social and economic changes in society. In their article, DiMartino and Castaneda suggest that the very structure of our schools, where the Carnegie unit is used, may not be suitable for 21st-century schools. They suggest that our national obsession with core content proficiency is distracting us from teaching the skills that students need for success in the real world. They offer solutions and examples for assessing the applied skills needed in the real world. The focus of Bushaw's article is on one group we rarely have an opportunity to hear from in this debate about school reform, the student body. This author offers an insight through an article that expresses the thoughts of middle schoolers. These students give us a clear picture of their personal expectations and hopes for high school. Another voice of concern is Howlett, who writes about the industrial and technical education courses being taught in high schools. Much of his concern is based on the number of baby boomers who will retire in the coming years, approximately 70 million, but workforce reports estimate that we will only have about 40 million new workers to replace them. Is it the responsibility of schools to train workers? Shouldn't we be more concerned about making sure that every child who wants to go to college will be prepared for it? How might we support both these seemingly competing ideas? Wilensky believes that school personnel who decide the curriculum and course offerings are overly influenced by college entrance requirements. She is concerned that we are missing an opportunity to reform education for the new demands of the globalized economy of the United States and the interdependent world. In addition, she explains that she sees the emphasis on college prep courses as further stratifying our schools into classes of students who do well in academic tasks and those who do not. Often these differences fall along racial and socioeconomic lines and cause further racial and class strife. Her ideas and solutions are worthy of consideration and debate by those who are concerned about school reform. And in the final article, Noddings states that she is concerned about the intellectual development of all students, in particular about their ability to think. She suggests that all teachers, regardless of their content area or grade level, can and should promote critical thinking in intellectually challenging ways. These articles add to the debate on school reform and the responsibilities of educators to meet the needs of their community.

As we consider reformatting the educational system of the United States, we must engage in an intensively reflective and analytical effort. Further, we must give considerable contemplation and forethought to the consequences, because our actions will shape not only the students' futures, but also the future of our country, as a member of the global community.

Prospective teachers are being encouraged to question their own individual educational experiences as they read the articles presented in this section. All of us must acknowledge that our values affect both our ideas about curriculum and what we believe is the purpose of educating others. This is vitally important when engaging in a dialogue that will either help or hinder students' ability to meet graduation requirements and be successful in adult living and work settings. The economic and demographic changes in the last decade and those that will occur in the future necessitate a fundamental reconceptualization of how schools ought to respond to the many social and economic environments in which they are located. How can schools, for instance, reflect the needs of and respond to the diverse group of students they serve while meeting the needs of our democratic society?

References

Bridgeland, J. M., Dilulio, J. J., & Morrison, K. B. (2006). The Silent Epidemic: Perspectives of High School Dropouts. Bill & Melinda Gates Foundation. Retrieved on 28 May 2008 from http://www.gatesfoundation.org/UnitedStates/Education/TransformingHighSchools.

Heckman, J. T. & LaFontaine, P. A. (2008) The Declining American High School Graduation Rate: Evidence, Sources, and Consequences: Research Summary 2008. National Bureau of Economic Research. Retrieved on 28 May 2008 from http://www.nber.org/reporter/2008number1/heckman.html.

U. S. Department of Education. Summary of Goals 2000: Educate America Act. Author. Retrieved on 28 May 2008 from http://www.ed.gov/legislation/GOALS2000/TheAct/sec102.html.

Assessing Applied Skills

The Carnegie unit, awarding course credit for seat time, is working against efforts to teach and test 21st century workforce skills.

JOE DIMARTINO AND ANDREA CASTANEDA

"The future workforce is here—and it is woefully ill-prepared for the demands of today's (and tomorrow's) workplace" (Casner-Lotto & Barrington, 2006, p. 9).

This was the stark conclusion of a study conducted by the Partnership for 21st Century Skills and three other organizations that surveyed 400 employers across the United States about the workforce readiness of recent high school and college graduates. The respondents indicated that the skills new job entrants *most* need for success in the workplace—oral and written communication, time management, critical thinking, problem solving, personal accountability, and the ability to work effectively with others—are the areas in which graduates are *least* prepared.

In other words, the United States' national obsession with core content proficiency is distracting us from teaching the skills that all graduates need for success. From Massachusetts to Texas to California, we are not testing, and therefore not teaching, the applied skills that employers most need and want. These applied skills often drop below the radar of standardized assessment. They can be observed and assessed, however, through another model: authentic assessment. This model, advocated by a committed core of education heavy hitters (Darling-Hammond, Rustique-Forrester, & Pecheone, 2005; Herman, 1997; Wiggins, 1990), could redirect high school instruction toward a more balanced approach—one that recognizes the need to address *both* core content knowledge and applied skills.

Authentic assessments require students to use prior knowledge, recent learning, and relevant skills to solve realistic, complex problems. For example, students may conduct senior projects in which they choose a topic, work with a community mentor, prepare a research paper, and exhibit their final product to a panel of evaluators. Another type of authentic assessment is a portfolio that represents a student's best work during the four years of high school, demonstrating that the student has met rigorous applied learning standards.

Although not without its critics, authentic assessment has been shown to have a measurable positive effect on instruction (Berryman & Russel, 2001; Herman, 1997). During the last decade, research projects in Kentucky, Vermont, California, and Maryland have described how performance assessments at the secondary level have provided an effective lever for changing teacher instructional practices to include a greater emphasis on analysis, communication, meaningful problem solving, and writing for a variety of purposes. As one teacher commented,

> [Portfolio] exercises push me to question instructional choices, to look back critically at what's worked and what hasn't and to try to figure out why. The students' portfolios give me their most significant moments as learners. Inevitably, they become a site of inquiry, reflection, and change. (Tierney, Fenner, Herter, Simpson, & Wiser, 1998)

Authentic assessments provide a vehicle for teaching and testing student skills that we know employers value, such as effective self-management, communication, and problem solving. But although authentic assessments offer a bevy of instructional benefits, their widespread implementation has been stifled by one of the most insidious and powerful forces in U.S. high schools: the Carnegie unit.

Unhappy Bedfellows

More than a century ago, during the first U.S. wave of standardization, the Carnegie Foundation for the Advancement of Teaching proposed a system to standardize high school credits by assigning one unit of value to a subject taught one hour a day, five days a week, for one school year. Since then, the Carnegie unit has admirably performed its singular purpose: transforming the ambiguities of education into a clear set of inputs, outputs, and calculations. Seat time yields credits; credits yield a diploma.

During the last 20 years, the Carnegie unit has come under widespread criticism. In fact, it was disowned by its family when the Carnegie Foundation's then-president, Ernest Boyer, "officially declare[d] the Carnegie unit obsolete" (Boyer, 1993). But despite its increasingly unwelcome and counterproductive place in U.S. high schools, the Carnegie unit persists because it has successfully taken control of the most intransigent elements of these schools: scheduling, grading, staffing, higher education admissions, and the four-year sequenced curriculum.

The Carnegie unit and authentic assessment are unhappy bedfellows. A seven-period school day can be neatly divided into disciplines and tidily equated with Carnegie units, but it cripples the most prevalent forms of authentic assessment. Teaching and assessing through senior projects, exhibitions, portfolios, and capstone projects require multidisciplinary, extended learning time that collides with a seven-period day or even a 4x4 block schedule. To integrate authentic assessment and the prevailing Carnegie unit system, administrators and teachers must perform instructional and logistical gymnastics to address difficult questions: Is a student project worth "credits"? If so, how many? What core content areas should long-term student projects count toward? How does student performance on authentic assessments fit into classroom grades—or do such assessments render letter grades obsolete? How do we create transcripts that reflect student proficiency on authentic assessments, and will colleges and universities accept them? These questions, and the time and effort required to answer them, aren't about pedagogy or even about education. They are about compliance with an anachronistic system that schools seem reluctant to retire.

Authentic assessments provide a vehicle for teaching and testing student skills that we know employers value.

Unfortunately, for the foreseeable future, the Carnegie unit is likely to persist as the structuring principle of U.S. high schools. Within these staid parameters, however, educators have found ways to use authentic instruction and assessment to create well-rounded students. These innovators use, adapt, and in some cases subvert the Carnegie unit system in an effort to transform their students into prepared graduates.

Organizing Curriculum around Applied Skills

The MET School in Providence, Rhode Island, has been the subject of enormous interest and debate. The MET is a career and technical school with a reputation for serving students who haven't succeeded in traditional high schools. The MET fosters critical and creative thinking through internships and other independent projects and organizes its entire curriculum into applied skill sets: empirical reasoning, quantitative reasoning, communication, social reasoning, and personal qualities. These areas neatly overlap with the most-needed skills identified by the Partnership for 21st Century Skills study.

The MET's approach to instruction reverses the typical paradigm. Instead of attempting to embed applied learning opportunities within core content instruction, the MET embeds core content instruction into project-based learning. Student projects, one a semester for each student, dominate teaching and learning. In one such project, a group of six students and their community mentor examined the role of education in producing citizens and democracies. As part of the project, the group took an 18-day trip to Nicaragua, where students explored the history of Nicaragua, attended lectures at the country's national university, visited local schools, and met with teachers.

At the end of each semester, students present their project to a panel of peers, teachers, and community members. The panel's evaluation is combined with classroom assessments to yield a snapshot of student proficiency and growth.

The MET school doesn't award grades. Rather, it measures student growth through a dialogic process. First, students, teachers, and family members meet to establish individual learning goals. These goals form the basis for all the formal and informal assessments during the semester. The culminating authentic, project-based assessment demonstrates how the student has met—or exceeded—his or her personal goals. To meet the requirements of postsecondary admissions departments, the MET translates student projects into "credits" to create a standard high school transcript.

Although this approach to assessment is unconventional and, for many, uncomfortable, the proof is in the pudding. The MET posts some of the highest student-achievement and college-acceptance scores in Rhode Island, while educating "hard-to-reach" students.

Ensuring Rigorous Assessment

Some educators have expressed concern that authentic pedagogy is too subjective and may result in student work that is not rigorous. At Federal Hocking High School in Stewart, Ohio, teachers have developed rigorous authentic assessments. Federal Hocking, a small rural school serving approximately 400 students, began working to implement more authentic pedagogy in 1992. Since then, the school has reduced the number of required course credits to 14 to make room in the schedule for required senior projects and portfolio assessments.

Federal Hocking has identified a set of desired outcomes for students that are similar to those identified by the Partnership for 21st Century Skills. The school emphasizes crucial "soft" skills, such as self-confidence, self-motivation, resilience, and adaptability. Students take courses during 9th and 10th grades that start them on the road to developing these skills and that also deliver the content more typical of the high school curriculum. During their final two years of high school, students have interdisciplinary opportunities to develop and demonstrate competency. For example, students complete a graduation portfolio consisting of three elements:

- The *career readiness folio* includes an up-to-date résumé, a college or job application, two recent reference letters, and a personal reflection on the student's readiness to take on the world after high school.

We need a system for measuring and recording student learning that values, rather than ignores, applied skills.

- The *democratic citizenship folio* includes evidence of active citizenship in the school or the greater community (including taking a stand on an issue in public that is based on evidence), as well as a reflection on the student's readiness to take on the role of citizen.
- The *skills for lifelong learning folio* includes artifacts of the student's best work in writing, math, and science; an artifact of best work in another discipline or area of interest; a bibliography of books read over the student's four years of high school; and a reflection on who the student is as a learner.

Another example of a rigorous, authentic assignment at Federal Hocking is the senior project that all students must complete for graduation. Students choose a topic that interests them, conduct research, create a product (not just a research paper), and exhibit their work to an audience that goes beyond the teacher. In preparation for their project exhibition, students are responsible for setting up the room, arranging for the attendance of an approved community member to provide feedback, sending reminders to committee members, providing visual aids, preparing presentation tools, and wearing appropriate dress.

Senior projects give students the opportunity to produce rigorous work in an area of individual interest. For example, one student researched the Underground Railroad and produced a set of maps showing how escaped slaves moved through the local area; the student presented these maps to teachers as an instructional resource. One student who was interested in sports built a ropes course that gym classes at the school regularly use. Another student explored the use of dragons in fantasy and myth, comparing Eastern and Western depictions. The student's final paper and presentation included slides and photos of dragons through the eyes of writers and illustrators.

The staff has created rubrics for both formative and summative assessment of all aspects of both the senior project and the graduation portfolio. The criteria incorporated into the rubrics emphasize skills that the school has identified as important for success after graduation. For example, students are evaluated on how well their presentation shows they have developed career flexibility, the awareness and participation required of a democratic citizen, and the qualities of a lifelong learner. They must use their portfolio and written reflections to illustrate their presentation. They are also evaluated on their presentation skills, organization, and preparation (Wood, 2005).

To ensure that these authentic assessments are used appropriately and result in rigorous student achievement, Federal Hocking High School provides intensive staff development in assessment. For example, the school has sent teams of teachers to visit other schools using authentic assessment and then used discussion protocols to look at student work and discuss appropriate assessment (Wood, 2005).

Federal Hocking High School's emphasis on authentic assessment has produced improvements in attendance, graduation rates, and state assessment scores. The school earned the Ohio Department of Education's recognition as an effective high school on the basis of its standardized test scores. But even more impressive, in the decade since the school moved from conventional assessment to authentic assessment, the college-going rate for its graduates has risen from 20 percent to over 70 percent.

Eliminating the Carnegie Unit

In 2005, New Hampshire became the first state to formally eliminate the Carnegie unit. The New Hampshire Board of Education has directed every school district in the state to design and implement a competency-based system that will allow students to earn credits—and diplomas—through a process ungoverned by the 120-hour Carnegie unit requirement. This new system moves authentic assessment from the trunk of the car to the driver's seat, where it will now serve as the predominant mechanism for awarding student credit both in and out of the classroom.

Within the broad scope of local control, New Hampshire's new education regulations contain a small but crucial set of established parameters. First, districts must identify core competencies and establish authentic assessments to evaluate student mastery of those competencies for every high school course. Second, districts must provide the state department of education with evidence that they've established and implemented a competency assessment system that is grounded in appropriate local and national standards. If they address these two requirements, districts will be largely free to change or retain virtually any of the structuring and scheduling elements typical of secondary education.

The skills new job entrants *most* need for success in the workplace are the areas in which graduates are *least* prepared.

Few school districts in New Hampshire are ready to tackle these daunting challenges immediately; many are moving forward cautiously, creating limited and carefully defined approaches to authentic teaching and assessment. A significant number of administrators, however, have welcomed the new policy as the long-absent lever that will force real, lasting, schoolwide improvement. These leaders, most of whom have been working to develop authentic assessments for years, are beginning to implement new and varied methods for awarding students academic credit.

A Small but Significant Change

Moving toward more authentic assessment doesn't require a large-scale curricular overhaul. Like all change, it can begin with incremental steps—student-led conferences and periodic oral presentations, for example. Even schools or districts that lack the time, resources, or political will to undertake bold reforms can implement one small but important strategy: Reduce the number of Carnegie units required for graduation, and redirect that instructional time toward more authentic instruction and assessment.

This strategy runs in direct opposition to the widespread assumption that requiring more Carnegie units will yield a more rigorous high school experience. But the Partnership for 21st Century Skills study and the innovations visible in schools and districts across the United States challenge this assumption.

If we want our high schools to prepare students with the applied skills that they need for success in any postsecondary venture, we need a system for measuring and recording student learning that values, rather than ignores, these skills. It isn't surprising that employers are disappointed when recent graduates arrive to work late and sit, unengaged, waiting patiently for the workday to end. It isn't surprising that many young workers believe their only job is to be physically present while remaining intellectually absent. It isn't surprising that so many recent high school graduates lack the ability and will to tackle unexpected problems. We maintain a secondary school system whose design systematically encourages precisely these behaviors. Until we can find ways, both large and small, to buck the Carnegie unit and the assessments that serve it, we will continue producing unprepared graduates.

References

Berryman, L., & Russel, D. R. (2001). Portfolios across the curriculum: Whole school assessment in Kentucky. *The English Journal, 90*(6), 76–83.

Boyer, E. (1993, March). *In search of community*. Presentation at the ASCD Annual Conference, Washington, DC.

Casner-Lotto, J., & Barrington, L. (2006). *Are they really ready to work? Employers' perspectives on the basic knowledge and applied skills of new entrants to the 21st century U.S. workforce,* p.9: Conference Board, Corporate Voices for Working Families, Partnership for 21st Century Skills, and Society for Human Resource Management.

Darling-Hammond, L., Rustique-Forrester, E., & Pecheone, R. (2005). *Multiple measures approaches to high school graduation.* Stanford, CA: School Redesign Network at Stanford University.

Herman, J. (1997). Assessing new assessments: Do they measure up? *Theory into Practice, 36*(4), 196–204.

Tierney, R., Fenner, L., Herter, R., Simpson, C. S., & Wiser, B. (1998). Portfolios: Assumptions, tensions, and possibilities. *Theory and Research into Practice, 33*(4), 474–486.

Wiggins, G. (1990). The case for authentic assessment. *Practical Assessment, Research, and Evaluation, 2*(2). Available: http://pareonline.net.

Wood, G. (2005). *Time to learn: How to create high schools that serve all students.* Portsmouth, NH: Heinemann.

Joe DiMartino is President, Center for Secondary School Redesign, WestWarwick, Rhode Island; Joedimartino@cssr.us. **Andrea Castaneda** is School Improvement and Planning Officer, Providence School District, Rhode Island.

From the Mouths of Middle-Schoolers
Important Changes for High School and College

What can we learn from middle-schoolers about reforming our high schools and colleges? More than you might guess, according to Mr. Bushaw.

WILLIAM J. BUSHAW

We may believe that middle school students are flaky. And why wouldn't we think that? They're undergoing hormonal changes, they sometimes exhibit defiance, and they're not good at accepting advice. Yet, when we took the trouble to ask, we found their opinions about their current school activities and about their preparation for success in high school and college to be thoughtful and enlightening. What's more, their opinions confirm for me that some emerging high school reforms are taking us in the right direction.

Three highly regarded organizations, the National Association of Secondary School Principals (NASSP), Phi Delta Kappa (PDK) International, and the Lumina Foundation for Education, undertook an important project to collect the opinions of middle school students using a scientific polling process.

The idea to poll middle school students took shape at a meeting in Washington, D.C., when Gerald Tirozzi, executive director of the NASSP, and I talked about school reform. Opinions range widely on this topic. The Republicans say one thing, the Democrats suggest other solutions. Educators offer different ideas, and parents are vocal with their own opinions. At some point—we can't remember who said it first—one of us suggested that there was a voice missing from the conversation: the voice of students—in particular, middle school students. What do the middle school students think about their schools and the preparation they receive for further schooling and for success in life?

A Method to Our Madness

Having raised these questions, we set about answering them. And while the project loomed large, the three sponsoring organizations had some experience in working at this scale, so we undertook the following steps to learn more about the opinions of middle school students.

1. *Establishing goals.* First, we needed to be clear about why we would undertake the daunting task of polling middle school students, and we identified four goals:

- to bring the voice of middle-level students to the forefront of the national dialogue on school reform;
- to draw the attention of policy makers and the public to the importance of effective schooling for students in the middle grades;
- to inform educators about the strengths and weaknesses of middle-level schooling, as seen through the eyes of the students; and
- to provide a roadmap for the changes needed to improve middle-level education.

2. *Identifying prior research.* We checked to determine if anyone else had polled middle school students about their schooling, with a focus on instructional rather than behavioral issues. We didn't find any data of this kind from polls of 12- and 13-year-olds.

3. *Developing questions.* Knowing that we wanted to cluster our questions, we identified six broad topic areas: 1) testing, 2) No Child Left Behind, 3) the curriculum, 4) teachers and teaching, 5) preparation for high school and college, and 6) current school experiences. The question-development process was iterative, with extensive involvement by the staffs of PDK, NASSP, and the Lumina Foundation. We presented a draft set of questions to the members of an NASSP advisory committee who were middle-level administrators and made further refinements as a result of their suggestions.

4. *Conducting the poll.* The three partners needed a highly reputable polling organization with experience in youth polling. We turned to Harris Interactive, one of the most experienced market research companies and one with considerable experience in the youth market. Using a state-of-the-art polling model, Harris gave us access to a sample of middle school students who had received their parents' or guardians' permission to participate.

The draft questions were forwarded to scientists at Harris, and they suggested important changes to minimize question bias. Harris also provided the appropriate questions to establish the sample's demographics and tested the questions with a representative student panel before suggesting final edits.

Then Harris conducted the poll, using the Harris Poll Online database, supplemented by a sample obtained from Survey Sampling, Inc. Polling began on 14 February 2007 and concluded on 5 March 2007. Qualified respondents were U.S. residents in grades 7 or 8. In total, 1,814 middle-level students successfully completed the survey. Gender, grade level, race/ethnicity, parents' highest level of education, geographic region, and urbanicity were weighted to align the sample with their actual proportions in the population. The sampling error for the total sample was +/-3.3 percentage points.

5. *Analyzing the results.* The poll yielded a range of findings, many expected and some surprising. Among the areas addressed were standardized and classroom testing, the helpfulness of teachers, how students act toward one another, the amount of homework assigned, and the ways in which schools involve students in decision making. I encourage readers to explore these findings in detail at www.pdkintl.org/ms_poll/ms_poll.htm.

NASSP, PDK, and the Lumina Foundation created a summary of the results, titled *A Voice from the Middle: Highlights of the 2007 NASSP/PDK Middle School Student Poll*. In August 2007, a copy of this summary was mailed to every middle school and high school principal in the United States.

I wish to focus here on one finding in particular that was highlighted in the summary but not extensively explored: the views of middle school students on their preparation for success in their current school, in high school, and in postsecondary settings. These views are generally strongly positive, but they are not necessarily in line with the reality of what is happening in many American high schools today.

Ready for High School and College?

Middle school students are optimistic, both about their current school situation and about their academic future. Ninety percent of the students polled felt that they were very or somewhat prepared to succeed in their current middle school, and 84% felt that they were very or somewhat prepared to succeed in high school (see Figure 1). Further, 61% felt that their writing, math, and reading skills were strong enough for them to be successful in high school, while only 9% said that they weren't strong enough, and 30% said they weren't sure.

Students also understood the rigors they will face in high school. Ninety-one percent felt that high school work would be very or somewhat difficult, and 87% felt that it was very or somewhat important for high school students to take math all four years. While middle school students predicted that good behavior was the best way to fit in while attending high school, doing well in class followed closely behind. Finally, 93% said there was *no chance* that they would drop out of high school and not graduate, and 92% indicated that they would definitely or probably attend college.

So these seventh- and eighth-grade students are confident that they are well prepared to succeed in their current school, and they understand that high school will be more challenging but still feel confident about meeting the tougher requirements of high school. Finally, a large percentage of them are also confident that they will attend college.

Yet we know that the high school dropout rate is significantly higher than the sum of the 6% of our student sample who felt that there was "some chance" that they might not graduate and the 1% who said that there was a "good chance" that they would drop out. While high school dropout data are hotly contested, the estimates range from about 17% to about 25%, depending upon the definition of a dropout and the dataset used for analysis. And what about the 92% who said they will definitely or probably attend college? Actual postsecondary attendance rates hover around 66% for students in the first year after they graduate from high school. So why would we observe such a large discrepancy (see Figure 2) between what students tell us about their plans and the actual data?

When I shared this inconsistency with adults, not one person responded with the observation that, while our students want to graduate from high school and attend college, we must be doing something wrong in high schools to dissuade or prevent them from attaining these goals. In fact, the reaction was quite the opposite. In almost every case, adults reacted with comments like "These students have yet to face real-world challenges," or "Wait until they get to high school. They will finally realize that they are not college material."

The High School Mission to Sort and Select

It's easy to dismiss the opinions of 12- and 13-year-olds. But what if we don't? What if we accept that the overwhelming majority of middle school students really do have lofty goals and that, if these goals are not being met, then we are doing something wrong in our high schools? What could that possibly be?

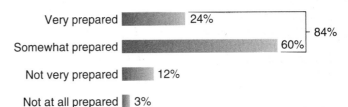

Figure 1 How well prepared do you think you will be to succeed in high school?

I believe that the problem is rooted in a long-standing but increasingly antiquated mission of the American high school: namely, that it is the high school's responsibility to offer a program of study geared to *sorting* students according to their grades in a variety of classes. Academically successful high school students are encouraged to attend college; their less-successful peers are enrolled in less-challenging courses that lead to jobs requiring only a high school diploma. This approach is referred to as the "sort and select" mission. Hidden within it is the requirement that, in order for some students to be selected for college, other students must be *de*selected. These are the students who fail or at least do poorly in some of their work.

Let's think about high school reform in light of the opinions expressed by the middle school students in the current poll. Is it conceivable that American high schools could offer a challenging course of study for all students without intentionally and systematically failing some of them? I think so. But it will mean abandoning the long-accepted dichotomy between college preparation and work preparation.

We need to replace the "sort and select" mission with the unifying goal of preparing all students for meaningful postsecondary career opportunities that are linked to their interests. And students' interests might lie in working with their hands, working with other people, working in an environment of constantly changing ideas, or working in a career that follows carefully established patterns. All of these areas include a variety of occupations that require more or less education. Within each area, some occupations require extensive college instruction beyond high school, while others in the same area require an associate's degree or a technical certificate or license.

As we shift our focus to a unifying theme centered on the successful preparation of all students for postsecondary career opportunities, we need to decide how college attendance fits into this equation. If we listen to our middle school students, preparation for college becomes the default setting for all students. But I think there is an important consideration that we often overlook when we think about preparing all students for college: we need to accept a definition of college that more honestly reflects current college attendance patterns.

What Is College?

Most Americans equate college with a four-year, full-time continuous program started immediately after completing high school and resulting in a bachelor's degree within six years. However, in the last 40 years, college has become something very different for large percentages of Americans.

For many young people today, going to college means attending a community college, often part time, while continuing to work full time. Some students earn an associate's degree and proceed more or less directly to a bachelor's degree. Others complete postsecondary coursework that leads to a license or certificate that advances them in their chosen career. And while college attendance was once considered a typical activity only for those in their twenties, immediately following high school, large percentages of Americans now enroll in college at all stages of their adult lives. What's more, our conventional understanding of college has expanded even more with the proliferation of courses and degree programs offered over the Internet.

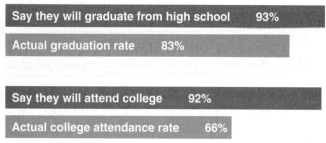

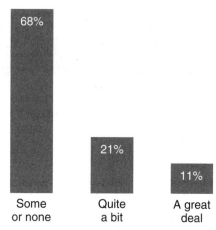

Figure 2 Middle-Schoolers' Optimism Doesn't Always Pan Out.

Sources: Actual graduation rate: Lawrence Mishel and Joydeep Roy, "Accurately Assessing High School Graduation Rates," *Phi Delta Kappan*, December 2006, pp. 287–92. Actual college attendance rate: U.S. Bureau of Labor Statistics, "College Enrollment and Work Activity of 2006 High School Graduates," Economic News Release, 26 April 2007.

Figure 3 How much information do you have about how to choose the high school courses that will prepare you to attend college?

Where Do We Go from Here?

Fortunately, there are many excellent programs offered in high schools throughout the U.S. that already attempt to address the important issues raised by our middle school students. Several of these programs are highlighted in two publications from the NASSP: *Breaking Ranks II* and *Breaking Ranks in the Middle*. Here are my suggestions for five activities on which we should focus our efforts.

1. *Accept that we can challenge high school students without systematically failing some.* This notion will be difficult to embrace, for it eliminates the long-standing practice of preparing students for an either/or future: attend college immediately or join the work force immediately. Adopting this inclusive goal requires that we focus on unique definitions of student success. Success for some students will depend on their interest and competency in literature and writing, while for others success will come from high degrees of interest and competency in the arts or in technical areas. The immediate reaction of many Americans to such proposals will be that this initiative will make high schools less rigorous. That is by no means the intent. In fact, this suggestion highlights the need to have all high school students meet higher standards, but not necessarily the same standards.

2. *Eliminate the sink-or-swim transition from middle school to high school.* The ninth grade, in particular, represents a weak link in the chain of schooling where students sometimes begin to disengage from their schools and so place themselves in danger of dropping out. Recognizing that ninth-grade students have high failure rates, many high schools now offer new programs designed to help all ninth-graders succeed in making the difficult transition from middle school to high school.

3. *Partner with parents and guardians in providing students with more information about their postsecondary options starting in middle school.* Our polling data revealed that students know very little about the courses they need to take to prepare them for college (see Figure 3). Indeed, only 32% said they have a great deal or quite a bit of information about selecting high school classes that will prepare them for college. Even more troubling, middle school students who earn low grades or whose parents have less education have even less information about what is required of them to graduate from high school and feel less prepared to succeed once they get there. Many high schools are addressing this "information gap" by offering ninth-grade classes that outline which high school courses are required for college entrance.

4. *Support programs that reduce the financial burdens that prevent low-income students from attending or completing college.* In our poll, 92% of the students who said there is a chance they might not attend college said the reason was that it "costs too much." Students who want to go to college and are adequately prepared to do so should not be denied the opportunity because of financial concerns. Policy makers should consider: 1) increasing the amount of need-based funding, such as Pell Grants, that is available to lower-income students; 2) supporting greater access to low-interest student loans; and 3) evaluating the cost-effectiveness and academic soundness of such ways of delivering postsecondary education as aligning community college curricula with university requirements so that students can complete their freshman and sophomore years in a lower-cost setting before transferring to a four-year campus.

5. *Help students in middle schools and high schools to better understand their interests and relate them to a program of study leading to a postsecondary experience.* This practice is already occurring in many high schools that have adopted the career-pathways approach to categorizing classes and helping students create their high school experience. This approach does not pigeonhole students into skills for a single job, as the traditional vocational education model sometimes did. Instead, the focus is squarely on helping students recognize lifelong occupational interests.

We asked. They answered. Now how do we act upon the opinions of these middle school students?

They tell us that they are prepared for high school, that they plan to graduate, and that they plan to attend college. Let's not dismiss their aspirations because they're too young to have experienced the "real world." Let's leverage this optimism to accomplish what we know is important for our nation's future: offering outstanding educational opportunities to as many of our young Americans as possible. Let's discontinue the systematic practice of identifying successful and unsuccessful high school students so that we can learn which ones deserve college and which ones don't. Let's redirect our efforts to preparing all students for some kind of postsecondary learning in keeping with our new definition of college. This is what our middle school students say they want, and this is what our nation needs.

WILLIAM J. BUSHAW is executive director of Phi Delta Kappa International, Bloomington, Ind.

Industrial Arts

Call It What You Want, the Need Still Exists

Teaching "technological literacy" at the expense of hands-on skills training is wrong for the students, wrong for the economy, and wrong for the nation, Mr. Howlett argues.

JAMES HOWLETT

We clearly have a division of thinking within the education community. Unfortunately, that division is within the disciplines that have devoted themselves to the task of passing on to the next generation the body of knowledge that has been the hallmark of progress for the "industrialized" world. Len Litowitz and Scott Warner—and apparently the entire International Technology Education Association (ITEA)—assert that "technology education" has taken over the teaching of industrial arts. Perhaps.

Litowitz and Warner summarize the history of vocational education and argue that industrial arts education is no longer necessary. Their goal of "developing technologically literate citizens" is admirable, and it is obvious that much time and thought have been devoted to the conceptualization of "technology education." What is missing from the decision to provide students with a program to ensure "technological literacy" at the expense of skills training is the research and accompanying data to justify the changes. This is a philosophical decision based on an effort to divine the future.

The ITEA *Standards for Technological Literacy* advocate that "all students in K-12 can become technologically literate and should be given the opportunity to do so." How is that to be done? Litowitz and Warner talk extensively about "contemporary technology education curricula," but no course titles are offered. Let us assume for the moment that we have a class titled "Power Mechanics," in which we have incorporated the concepts of applying Science, Technology, Engineering, and Math (STEM). Litowitz and Warner suggest three questions that might be asked in a technology education course to explore various sides of contemporary issues: "Do robots in industry really eliminate more jobs than they create? Are hybrid vehicles really better for the environment than gasoline-powered vehicles? Is the use of more nuclear power generation desirable or even inevitable?" Ask these questions of most high school students—even in the best of circumstances—and you will be greeted with a wave of apathy. In the arena of high school electives, the survival of a class depends on having a "hook"—something that ignites immediate interest, something that grabs students' attention and holds it for 36 weeks. These questions do not.

On curricular matters, Litowitz and Warner claim that vocational education "focuses on trade preparation, whereas technology education is broader" in its content and intended audience. I'm not sure how they arrive at this conclusion. Most vocational education teachers rely on federal funding to stay current with industry and to purchase equipment, and one of the requirements of the Carl D. Perkins Career and Technical Improvement Act of 2006 is that the curriculum must "teach all aspects of the industry." A tall order, indeed, but surely not a narrow one. Moreover, I am confused by their reference to a "contemporary computer-aided drafting course." Is there any other kind? I have taught CAD (computer-assisted design) classes since the mid-1980s, and the beauty of teaching CAD is that students can be challenged to apply all their knowledge in new ways. Notice the word "apply." All good high school industrial technology/arts teachers look for opportunities to expand their skills training with mind-stretching activities.

Certainly, "contemporary technology education curricula serve to enhance the development of such core subjects as mathematics, science, and reading by adding variety, relevance, and purpose to a student's academic program of study." Good stuff! That is precisely the point of the original article. It was an affirmation, a restatement of the content and rigor taught in today's courses that remain the core of industrial technology/arts: Wood, Metals/Machines, Auto, Drafting, and Welding. Where then lies the basis of their criticism? It seems to be in the method of delivery. If "industrial arts" is passé and no longer relevant in the education system, then are we to believe that "hands-on skills training" is no longer needed in the K-12 curriculum? If that is what they mean, they are wrong! Wrong for our students and wrong for the economy of the nation.

The Economic Costs

In *The 2010 Meltdown*, Edward Gordon notes that "70 million baby boomers, some highly skilled, will exit the work force in the next 18 years, with only 40 million workers coming in. . . . Throughout the entire economy," he continues, "the United States lacks adequate numbers of appropriately skilled workers to support high standards in personal or professional services, or properly maintain the physical and technological infrastructure upon which everyone relies and takes for granted. . . . The U.S. Bureau of Labor Statistics (BLS) predicts that in 2010 the economy will support about 167 million jobs, but the population will be able to fill only 157 million of them."[1]

As an example of what our economy needs, I cite a recent news release that quotes by Robert Balgenorth, president of the State Building and Construction Trades Council of California: "To keep pace with growing construction demands and to replace workers who will retire, California will need to produce about 30,000 skilled construction workers per year from now until 2014, according to Employment Development Department projections. That need is likely to continue far into the future."[2] And this is just construction. A review by the U.S. Department of Labor reveals a comparable shortage of skilled workers in all the areas traditionally taught in the "old industrial arts" classes.

By itself, "contemporary technology education" will not fill the need for skilled workers.

By itself, "contemporary technology education" will not fill this need. As Dan Walters, syndicated columnist for the *Sacramento Bee*, wrote:

Manufacturing, construction, auto repair jobs, and dozens of other industries are feeling the . . . pinch of hiring and retaining sufficient trained workers. There is, however, a larger context to the problem. . . . The state has sorely neglected vocational education in the popular, if wrongheaded, drive to direct every high school student into college, even though no more than a fifth of high school graduates will, in fact, obtain four-year degrees. A recent survey by the Public Policy Institute of California found that nearly two-thirds of Californians believe that someone must have a college education to succeed, which is patently wrong, as the highly paid technical and blue-collar jobs now going begging attest. Politicians and the education establishment feed that canard through policies that elevate college preparation above all other considerations. . . .

At the same time, however, California is losing millions of potential replacements for those aging baby boom workers by allowing nearly a third of high school students to drop out without obtaining diplomas.[3]

Bill Milliken founded Communities in Schools, a nonprofit organization, to help kids stay in school. His research shows that kids have five needs that must be met before they will learn and grow. One of those needs is "a marketable skill to use upon graduation."[4]

Costs to Students

California schools have embarked on a narrow path of "A-G requirements" (University of California admission requirements) as mandatory for all high school students. Discussions with the vast majority of counselors and teachers indicate that those who work with high school students do not agree with this approach. Alas, it is a top-down decision, with test scores once again driving curricular changes that will prove to be detrimental. Since 1980, California has seen the loss of over 80% of its industrial arts/technology classes, and its high school dropout rate has risen as well.

Deputy Superintendent Patrick Ainsworth of the California state department of education says that the dropout rate for secondary students enrolled in 2004–05 was roughly 30%. However, for those students taking a sequence of courses in career/technical education—*skill classes*—the rate of graduation was 84%. Just 16% dropped out. A study done by James Kulik noted that high-risk students are eight to 10 times less likely to drop out in the 11th and 12th grades if they enroll in a career/technical program rather than in a general program. Relevant data compiled by GetREAL, an organization of manufacturing and other businesses, show career/technical education courses, teachers, and enrollments have declined by more than 20% in the decade since 1997, while "non-graduates" have increased by 25%.[5] In short, as career/technical education courses disappear, the dropout rate rises. And the problem is larger in absolute terms than it appears because over that same decade the total number of students increased.

What many of these students want is a skill, a skill that at the end of high school will enable them to begin a career that will support a car, a spouse, and perhaps a family. Achieving "technological literacy" does not necessarily pay the bills.

High dropout rates have another side that is not often discussed. Dolores Carr, district attorney for Santa Clara County, California, is concerned about high school dropouts and states her point clearly:

Recent research from the California Dropout Research Project shows that dropouts are more likely to end up in jail or on welfare, at great expense to themselves and others. And because they tend to earn less, they will pay fewer taxes over the course of a lifetime. In fact, researchers calculate that California suffers more than $46 billion in economic losses from the 120,000 20-year-olds each year who have not completed high school, including $12 billion from increased crime alone. Fight crime by fighting [the] high school dropout rate.[6]

Looking to the Future

In 2006 the California Industrial Technology Educators Association (CITEA) adopted the following statement:

Career-Technical Education is organized educational programs offering sequences of courses directly related to preparing individuals for employment in current or emerging occupations requiring other than a baccalaureate or advanced degree.

These work force preparation programs include subjects in industrial and technology education, business education, agriculture, medical occupations, etc. They provide a variety of instructional strategies including competency-based applied learning that contributes to an individual's occupation-specific skills, higher-order reasoning, problem solving skills, and academic knowledge necessary for economic independence as a productive and contributing member of society and prepare participants for both post-secondary education and employment.

The essential test of whether or not a course of study is Career-Technical Education is found in whether or not the course provides entry-level preparation for a career that is essentially technical in nature, and that does not require a post secondary or advanced degree.[7]

From middle school through high school, students need not only the opportunity to explore a variety of trade skills but also the opportunity to learn a skill well. It is in the teaching of these skills that a wise teacher incorporates those STEM elements that are appropriate. We need to staunch the dropout hemorrhage and provide students with an entry to a career that can be the basis of further education. The CITEA definition above uses language that is inclusive, student-focused, and drawn primarily from the federal definition. Educators need to be equally inclusive in their thinking.

Notes

1. Edward E. Gordon, *The 2010 Meltdown: Solving the Impending Jobs Crisis* (Westport, Conn.: Praeger, 2005), p. 37.
2. Robert L. Balgenorth, president, State Building and Construction Trades Council of California, available at www.citea.org. Click on resources.
3. Dan Walters, "Health Care Triple Whammy," *Sacramento Bee*, 6 November 2007.
4. William E. Milliken, "What Do Kids Need Before They Graduate?," www.cisnet.org/media/news.asp?ID=2292, 31 March 2005.
5. GetREAL, "Relevance in Education and Learning," press release, 12 November 2007; more information is available at www.getrealca.com.
6. Dolores Carr, "Fight Crime by Fighting High School Dropout Rate," *San Jose Mercury News*, 3 October 2007.
7. Available at www.citea.org. Click on resources.

JAMES HOWLETT is a past president of the California Industrial and Technology Education Association Foundation, Diamond Springs, Calif.

High Schools Have Got It Bad for Higher Ed—And That Ain't Good

Will every child entering kindergarten eventually become a college professor? Of course not. Then why, Ms. Wilensky asks, is our entire education system geared toward preparing the few who will pursue academic careers? She finds the answer in the inordinate influence of college entrance requirements on K-12 schooling, an influence sustained by the values of our society's dominant culture.

RONA WILENSKY

In the last few years, education reformers have been proposing that high school graduation requirements align with the requirements for college entrance and that high schools organize themselves to ensure that all of their graduates are successful in college, without remediation, if they choose to attend. This strategy takes today's colleges and universities as the given of our education system and implies that the educational problems in need of major reform are to be found in the K-12 sector.

But recent research shows there is reason to be highly skeptical of this view. Colleges fail to graduate large numbers of the students they enroll,[1] and recent data on the literacy of college students in their last year of school indicate that only 31% of them are proficient, compared to 15% of all adults.[2] In the face of such data, we should not assume that the structures, practices, and expectations of colleges and universities are sacred.

I want to put forward here the view that colleges and universities are a major part of the educational problem we need to solve and, more specifically, that they exercise a detrimental effect on other elements of the system through the powerful influence exerted by traditional college entrance requirements. This is by no means the only problem facing our education system, but I suggest that, if we fail to deal with it, we cannot hope to truly prepare all our students for the 21st century.

If, as I will argue below, it is the hyper-academic focus of college entrance requirements that leads to the success of only a few, the outright failure of others, and the low achievement of many in our K-12 system, then further tightening the alignment between colleges and public schooling can only make things worse. And by keeping our attention focused on what has seemed to work in the past rather than on what is needed

for the future, we run the further risk of missing a current political opportunity to actually remake the landscape of education in a way that will prepare students for the new demands of the globalized economy and interdependent world.

I begin by looking at the way that the entire K-12 system is skewed toward meeting the needs of those students headed for selective colleges and universities and the way less successful students are funneled into watered-down versions of a college-preparatory curriculum. Next I explore the origin of the college entrance requirements that have been driving this system and examine how the K-12 focus on skills that lead to success in college, coupled with the political influence of powerful parents, contributes significantly to the very failures that we want to remedy.

Finally, I conclude by offering some suggestions for a way forward, though not a prescriptive plan. My goal is to widen the lens of reform to bring attention to the ways in which higher education is a part of the problem of the K-12 system and so needs to be a part of the solution. Only when we have identified all the elements of the system that produces our current reality, and only when all the players in that system own their responsibility and begin to look at ways to change, will it be possible to educate all our children for the complex, challenging, and dynamic future we know they are facing.

The Tail Is Wagging the Dog

Much of K-12 education is structured to pursue one goal that is rarely mentioned: the preparation of some students for admission to selective colleges. If you doubt this, visit any community in the United States when the local school board is asked to consider changes in scheduling, curriculum, school calendar, class rank, selection of valedictorian, or graduation requirements that might affect the curriculum vitae of that community's highest-performing students. What you will see is an outpouring of political muscle orchestrated by the wealthiest and most politically influential parents, who usually succeed in demanding that nothing be altered that might put their children at a disadvantage when applying to the prestigious college of their choice or to the honors program of their state's flagship university. And these politically active parents have got it right: the current system gets its "best" students into the "best" colleges, and changing elements of the K-12 system without changing the ways students get admitted to colleges, especially selective colleges, will indeed affect who wins and who loses that competitive race.

Significantly, the standards set by the admission requirements of the relatively small number of selective colleges and universities influence every high school in the nation. To their credit, there is not a rural, suburban, or urban school that wants to deny even one of its students the opportunity to reach the highest academic opportunities offered by this country. Nor is there one underachieving high school in any community that wants to admit that it is not in the business of preparing at least some students for the possibility of grabbing the brass ring of acceptance at a selective college. To make such an admission would call into question any school's educational credibility. As a result, whether a school serves a great many high-achieving students or only a few, almost every high school dances to the same tune by making sure that it offers at least one set of classes that aspire to prepare some students for admission to the "best" schools.

On the face of it, this doesn't look like a bad thing. But in what follows I consider how this focus on the preparation of top students for elite schools might in fact be a significant source of academic failure—or at least educational mediocrity—for all the other students.[3]

Just as high schools take cues from the most selective colleges, their middle and elementary feeder schools take cues from them. The schools serving grades K-8 organize themselves to make sure that they offer the classes that teach their "best" students the prerequisite knowledge and skills for success in advanced high school courses.

Given the ways in which all the parts interconnect, the college entrance requirements for highly competitive schools work their way through the nation's education system so that their influence is felt even on what kindergarten classrooms expect children to know and be able to do when they walk in the door. We may laugh at those infamous East Coast parents who, upon hearing the news of a positive pregnancy test, put their prospective child on the wait list for a highly regarded pre-school. But, as we laugh on the outside, on the inside, parents in almost every middle- or upper-class family are asking themselves if they are doing all they could do to increase their child's chance of qualifying for one of the "top" schools. In these moments of unease, we show that we truly understand the ways in which the educational pipeline functions to funnel the expectations of selective colleges down to the first schools that our children enter.

The most obvious way in which high schools are designed as pipelines to selective colleges is that they offer a curriculum that matches the familiar college entrance requirements: four years of English/language arts; three to four years of math, at least through trigonometry and preferably through calculus; three to four years of laboratory-based sciences, recognizable as biology, chemistry, and physics; three years of social studies; a range of offerings in foreign languages; and an array of "electives."

The second way in which high schools serve as pipelines is through the actual structure of these classes. There is little variation across the country in what high-quality advanced high school classes look like. They focus on close readings of academic texts (using both primary and secondary sources), developing the skills for writing academic research papers and literary analyses, mastering levels of mathematics and science needed for prospective math and science majors, memorizing large bodies of knowledge in all subject areas, and studying the vocabulary and grammar of world languages without necessarily acquiring the ability to speak them. Because it is targeted at preparing students for entrance to the most selective colleges, this pattern of education is widely accepted as the "gold standard" of the college-preparatory curriculum against which all other curricula (and all other entrance requirements) are measured. Under pressure from politically active, ambitious parents, this curriculum is attempted (although not always achieved) in every school district in the country, if not in every high school.

How College-Preparatory Tracking Works

Prior to 1983, the year *A Nation at Risk* was released, this "gold standard" curriculum (be it the real thing or the fool's gold version described below as the "more" curriculum) was called the academic track, and it coexisted with the commercial/business, vocational/technical, and general tracks that served students who did not "choose" or were not "qualified for" the academic track.

But *A Nation at Risk* recommended a new approach to schooling and called for increased graduation requirements in academic subjects for all students. More recently, reformers have also promoted "higher academic standards" under the banner of "college readiness for all" with the result that high schools offer courses with academic, college-preparatory titles to virtually all students. Ironically, since little has changed in the prekindergarten experiences of students, in the quality of teaching, or in the strategies that schools use for engaging the full range of students in academic study, the result of imposing higher graduation requirements that focus almost exclusively on academics has become simply a new form of school tracking.

Generally speaking, contemporary high schools no longer offer vocational, commercial/business, general, and academic tracks, although many districts still provide career and technical education centers at other sites in their communities. Nevertheless, despite the call for high standards for all students, powerful curricular distinctions within high schools still exist and still serve to sort students. These distinctions are now expressed in such designations as Advanced Placement (AP) or International Baccalaureate (IB) courses, accelerated or honors courses, regular courses, and basic courses.

Courses with similar titles—but in different "tracks"—differ in the topics covered, in the depth with which those topics are covered, in the pedagogy of the teachers, in the activities of the classroom, and in the assessments given. Perhaps the most obvious way courses differ is in the "rigor" of the academic tasks expected of the students. A simple rule of thumb is that the lower the track, the lower its goal on Bloom's taxonomy. That taxonomy begins with knowledge and increases in "rigor" through the subsequent levels of understanding, application, analysis, synthesis, and evaluation. At the highest levels, "students extend and refine their acquired knowledge to be able to use that knowledge automatically and routinely to analyze and solve problems and create unique solutions."[4]

High-end courses, at their best, are designed to develop higher-order thinking skills, sophisticated communication skills, and an appreciation for the complexity of a given subject. However, the unfortunate reality is that many advanced classes just feature "more"—more reading, more assignments, more topics, and more homework (since it is a rare teacher of an advanced class who doesn't think its necessary hallmark is at least one hour of nightly homework, regardless of educational merit). In these "more" classes, it is up to the students to *bring to* the classroom higher-order thinking skills, sophisticated communication skills, and an appreciation for the complexity of the subject. If they do not come equipped with these skills, they are unlikely to acquire them in "more" classrooms.

At the other end of the academic spectrum are the basic classes, which we must acknowledge as an educational disgrace. Content is drastically simplified, and teaching focuses on the acquisition and simple understanding of knowledge, rather than on its application and assimilation. Assessments emphasize rote recall. Perversely, to the extent that these academic requirements compromise intensive career and technical education programs, they can leave those at the "low" end of the system worse off than before. With neither the academic skills needed for four-year college success nor the technical skills needed for other postsecondary options, many students are caught between a rock and a hard place.[5]

Regular-track classes, which are pitched somewhere between the basic and the advanced classes, are currently caught in a squeeze. On one side, as the acceptance rates to selective colleges have plummeted, larger numbers of ambitious students have signed up for either the honors/accelerated classes or the AP/IB classes. As a result, regular classes have lost more and more of their "stronger" students. On the other side, high schools are feeling pressure to place English-language learners and special education students in mainstream environments. The result is that the distinctions between basic and regular classes are becoming less and less clear.

Students who wish to compete academically for entrance to selective colleges are thus faced with a painful choice. Regular classes have become more like basic classes, and so they are often neither interesting nor challenging. Meanwhile, accelerated classes can be overwhelming with their obsessive focus on

"more." Those students who take all or most of their academics as advanced courses can choose two of the following three options: 1) doing all their own schoolwork at a high level of quality, 2) getting adequate sleep, or 3) participating in extracurricular activities. Many of the students who choose options 2 and 3 over option 1 will not master the content or skills they are supposed to acquire in the advanced classes they attend.[6]

Two recent studies reflect on the efficacy of this system and show that, while most high school students are taking more academic courses, they do not appear to be acquiring the hoped-for outcomes:

- A 2007 report from the National Assessment of Educational Progress shows that, while 68% of students in 2005 were taking a standard curriculum or better (intended to prepare them for college) compared to 40% in 1990, the share of students who were proficient in reading dropped from 40% to 35% during that same time period.[7]
- A 2007 study by ACT showed that, while taking the right number of courses with the appropriate academic titles is better than not doing so, it is insufficient to guarantee that students will graduate ready for college. The study found that 75% of ACT-tested 2006 high school graduates who took a core curriculum were *not* prepared to take at least one credit-bearing entry-level college course and earn a course grade of C or better. To guarantee that they were prepared, students generally needed to take a number of courses beyond the minimum core.[8]

Faced with this evidence, what is to be done? Do we stick with the same game plan and try to figure out how to inject more rigor into the regular- and basic-track academic courses that are filling students' schedules but not teaching them college-preparatory skills? Or do we look for an alternative to the dictates of the traditional college-preparatory curriculum? Before addressing this question, it would be helpful to look more closely at what college-preparatory programs are supposed to be preparing students for and to consider whether college, as we know it, is as worthwhile as has been assumed.

What Is College Prep? Does It Make Any Sense?

It is self-evident that the goal of college entrance requirements is to outline a precollegiate course of study that will allow entering students to succeed at the college curriculum. But what is the college curriculum, and where does *it* come from?

I want to address this question by referring to those same selective colleges mentioned above in my discussion of the high school curriculum. The expectations of selective colleges for the preparation of high school students, which serve as the standard for the highest track of high school course offerings, also serve as the standard for college offerings. And just as most other high school tracks are attenuated versions of the accelerated high school track, the curricular offerings and expectations at most nonselective colleges are attenuated versions of the offerings at selective schools. While there may be many programs or even entire schools that do things differently, it is still the case that the majority of four-year colleges have an almost exclusively academic focus. Let me tease out here what having an "academic" focus actually means.

The essence of academic freedom (and the tenure that protects it) is that professors decide what should be taught in their classes. College faculty members, in general, do not take direction from students, parents, government, business, or the public. And many university administrators tear their hair out over the fact that faculty members do not take much direction from them either.

So what influences professors' notions of what they teach and therefore of what they expect incoming students to know and be able to do? The short answer is that their curricular ideas come from their own college experiences, from the view of their discipline transmitted through their graduate programs, and from the tenure process, which further adjudicates what is worthy of attention in a discipline. Thus the world of higher education is highly self-referential. What is taught and expected of students today is most strongly influenced by what was taught in the past, by those within the academy who train and induct its new members, and by the peer-review processes of academic journals and publishers. The fastest way to get insight into this culture is to look more closely at graduate school, that crucial link between a high-achieving undergraduate and an aspiring assistant professor.[9]

Most people enter graduate school because they want to continue studies that engaged them as undergraduates.[10] Typically, these students have been at the top of their classes in both high school and college. They like to read, write, and debate about academic issues. They enjoy analyzing, synthesizing, and evaluating facts and theories, and, significantly, they want to do this kind of work for the rest of their lives. They may also feel a calling to inspire in others a passion for learning about their subject.

Graduate students are expected to master one particular discipline, develop highly specialized interests in particular subareas of research, and address the findings of that research to a very small circle of others in their field. The explicit values of these programs are disciplinary research, as well as dialogue and argument within the academy. Graduate school is explicitly designed as preparation for advancing academic frontiers, not as a way to educate the broader public. Often, teaching undergraduates is seen as the price academics pay to continue being part of the academy.

This focus on academic concerns is strengthened by the tenure-granting process, which gives higher priority to the publication of articles and books written for scholars than to effective teaching or service within the academic community. This is especially true at the most competitive colleges and universities. Those who ultimately make it through this process are the ones who make decisions about curriculum and entrance requirements.[11]

So here's the answer: the selective college curriculum, which shapes college entrance requirements, which, as we have seen, shape all of K-12 education (and even preschools), is devised by a very small group of people (tenured and near-tenured faculty) whose focus is on theories and abstractions, analysis and synthesis, library or laboratory research, exegetical reading, and painstakingly careful writing about topics that typically don't have direct application outside the academy.

What is taught in the college curriculum generally reflects these dispositions and interests. Introductory courses are often intended to prepare students for the major, and courses in the major are mostly designed around issues that are salient within the academy. Students who are highly successful in these college courses are often encouraged to consider graduate school in order to become academics themselves. Whether this curriculum is of interest or use to most students is rarely the point, and rarely is general interest a criterion in the design of the collegiate course of study.

The reason for looking so closely at this tightly knit academic culture is to uncover what lies beneath the surface of the academic focus of public education. Unwittingly, we have built a universal public education system aimed at a college curriculum whose unspoken, but underlying, rationale is the selection and training of prospective college professors and academic researchers, who constitute approximately 1% of the labor force.[12] Everyone in this system—whether a college graduate or a college dropout, a high school graduate or a high school dropout, an engaged student or a disenfranchised one—spends most of his or her educational time and energy on tasks shaped by these implicit purposes.

It is obvious that, were these purposes and connections to be made explicit, there would not be the widespread support that there is today for the way we do either K-12 or postsecondary education. But these systems have developed and expanded without much conscious public attention. We have not previously asked, because we didn't need to, if there is any alignment between the ways of schools and colleges on the one hand and the needs of students and society on the other.

Prior to World War II, when only a tiny fraction of the population attended college, it was more obvious that colleges were in the business of educating their students for professions with a mostly academic bent. When only a small fraction of the population graduated from college, it seemed appropriate, or at least not harmful, that the curriculum focused on the narrow academic preparation deemed essential to the training of professors, researchers, school teachers, clerics, lawyers, and librarians.

After the war, higher education grew exponentially, fed first by returning GIs in the 1940s and next by their prosperous children, the baby boomers of the 1960s. With the U.S. economy dominating the world and providing decent jobs for those with and without education, there was no need to look closely at the match between the learning that was at the center of schools and colleges and the learning that was needed by society.

But globalization, which has been affecting the American economy since at least the 1970s, has changed all that. When work can be relocated around the world and the skills of labor are paramount, when our future well-being depends on effective and productive relationships with people who are culturally distinct from us, and when the pace of change is absolutely dizzying, it becomes essential to ask if the hyper-academic focus that has characterized the curricula of colleges and universities throughout their 500-year history is working for the benefit of the whole society.

How Does a Narrow Academic Focus Produce Failure?

To understand the full impact of this hyper-academic focus, there are two interrelated strands to keep in mind. First, we have a school system that, under pressure from politically powerful parents, maximizes the readiness of a small number of its students to compete with students from across the country for admission to highly selective colleges and universities. Second, we have a system that, in the name of school reform, has extended and wants to further extend the academic focus of these students to almost everyone else.

The public school saga begins on the first day of kindergarten when a whole range of students show up for school. But of course the tale really begins long before that. For complex reasons, success at academic tasks is deeply connected to what happens before school attendance begins. The research is unequivocal: children's readiness for the schooling system we have created is strongly influenced by all their prekindergarten experiences, beginning with the prenatal health and level of education of their mothers and going on to include their access to good nutrition and ongoing health care; physical and emotional safety; verbal, visual, and auditory stimulation and interaction; recreational and enrichment opportunities; and high-quality child care and preschool.

While research has also shown that access to teaching of exceptionally high quality can partially compensate for insufficient prekindergarten preparation for academic tasks, this seemingly hopeful finding is really scant consolation. No school system, not even the best, is currently able to guarantee that all its students have consistent access to that quality of instruction. And the very neighborhoods that have the fewest resources to prepare their students for academic success at the prekindergarten level will be least likely to have access to high-quality teaching for their students. I am, of course, talking about communities made up of low-income families, people of color, and recent immigrants.

Entering students also differ in terms of their potential strengths and weaknesses across the range of varied intelligences that humans possess, as well as in the interests and affinities that influence where they focus their attention. These separate, yet intertwining, strands of endowment and environment mean that some children come to school much more ready for meeting its expectations than others.

Students from all these backgrounds arrive at the kindergarten door, and there they encounter a system of "schooling" that is remarkably consistent even across all the disparate communities of the U.S.[13] One of the most important features of this "schooling" is a pervasive institutional bias toward tuning the curriculum so that those who are to become the "best" students are prepared for all the subsequent academic expectations they will meet. A second feature is that, in general, schools have little or no capacity to compensate for the differential readiness for school of the students who show up at the door.

The result of the encounter between this system of schooling and the diverse array of students who arrive at school is that, in general, schools work well for students with some or all of the following characteristics: they are verbally fluent, have had middle- or upper-class prekindergarten experiences, are female, and are willing to follow school rules. Conversely, schools do not work well, in general, for students who have some or all of these characteristics: they are less compliant, are male, are students of color, are learning English, and have personal strengths that are not in the domains of mainstream verbal ability and abstract analysis (math).

How, we must ask ourselves, does this situation actually come to be? For surely it wasn't planned to be so.

First, students get different curricula based on the differences that they bring to the school. The fact that they are not all ready to do the same thing when they enroll, combined with explicit or implicit pressure from the parents of better-prepared students, leads schools to work with students in groupings based on their early facility in the core academic skills of reading and math. This is the easiest and one of the most familiar (although not the best) of all schooling strategies. Not surprisingly, these groupings tend to be highly correlated with class, race, language spoken at home, and, because of the bias of schools toward a narrow definition of "good" behavior (e.g., sit still, work quietly), gender. What is most wrong with these groupings is that, in almost all cases, they actually teach students different material at significantly different levels of rigor. Over time, the cumulative effect makes it difficult, if not impossible, for students to switch from low to high groups.

Second, students who are less privileged, less academically talented, and less compliant quickly realize that they are less valued at school. To compensate, many develop behaviors that protect their sense of self but make it unlikely that they will engage enough to learn even the limited material they are offered.

The behaviors we see among these students include acting out, shutting down, or finding ways to not even attend. They stop trying so that their lack of success can be attributed to their behavior, not their ability. As a result, they do not practice and master the habits that characterize successful students: paying attention, taking notes, studying, doing homework—in short, engaging. Needless to say, these defensive strategies, which may succeed in protecting a child's sense of self, are ultimately self-defeating. Students who behave in these ways are unlikely to catch up or succeed in schooling.

These patterns are often exacerbated for students of color who encounter pervasive, if not conscious or intentional, racism as well as low expectations from teachers who are almost always from the dominant culture. The alienation and consequent school failure of these students is one of the most profound challenges facing public education.

Many undesirable student behaviors would not exist if we didn't have schooling as we know it. Ironically, teachers perceive these behaviors as inherent in the child, not as reactions to the patterns of schooling itself. As a result, schools simply respond to resistant, unskilled students in time-honored ways: they punish them, push them out, place them in special education, or offer them a watered-down education in which the material is simplified, the pace is slowed down, and the expectations are insultingly low. Voilà! We produce legions of students who "choose not to take" or do not "qualify for" rigorous academic course work at the high school level.

Is There a Way Out?

Students are likely to be successful at the academic tasks valued by the current patterns of schooling if they have any or all of the following characteristics: their prekindergarten years followed the pattern typically associated with dominant-culture, middle- and upper-class households; they work diligently and over many years at all school tasks, regardless of whether they have an interest in them, see their merit, or regard school as a place they themselves belong; or they "naturally" possess unusually strong verbal and mathematical abilities.

While students with these characteristics come from every kind of background, the intense stratification of the United States by race and class means that there are some consistent patterns to the academic success of students. Middle- and upper-class white students are privileged by the congruence between their backgrounds and the demands of schooling (although if they do not work at school tasks they are unlikely to become well educated, and only those with family connections will gain access to selective schools). Many Asian students benefit academically, although not necessarily personally, from the value that their cultures place on sustained effort in academic settings, even in the absence of other kinds of cultural congruence. And talented students whose backgrounds are African American, Latino, and Native American will be welcomed into the fold of school success and mentored accordingly because their achievement appears to validate the colorblindness of the system.

Of course, there are many successes and failures that cross these generalizations for a wide range of reasons based in community, family, or school circumstances that deviate from the sociological averages. More general patterns, such as the growing personal and financial instability of middle-class families, on the one hand, and the small but growing number of middle- and upper-class families of color on the other, also mean that race and class do not fully determine any given student's future. But the "academic sorting hat" nevertheless disenfranchises vast numbers of students, including all those who refuse, consciously or unconsciously, to play the game because of the way it is rigged.

The unrelenting focus on academics, as traditionally taught, helps to produce the very failure that many reformers want to redress with an even greater emphasis on traditional academics. We could follow these reformers' suggestions and attempt to keep the current focus on narrowly drawn academic learning. However, it would be possible to broaden the number and types of students who succeed at this curriculum only by 1) significantly improving the quality of instruction across all schools in all communities and 2) dramatically reducing the out-of-school inequalities among students. It is obvious that these steps would require not only tremendous effort and resources, but also a level of commitment to public education that this country has not yet witnessed.

Such changes, were they enacted, could result in significantly larger numbers of students who genuinely possess academic skills. But unless we change the purpose of schooling from a focus on decontextualized academic learning to the explicit teaching of the knowledge and skills needed to solve complex, undefined, and value-laden problems collaboratively in a continually changing world, we will fall short of the stated goal of all reformers: to prepare all students for leadership and success in the global economy and society.

There is an emerging consensus that a new set of skills is necessary for the 21st century. Howard Gardner speaks of the *Five Minds for the Future*. The report *Tough Choices or Tough Times* focuses on the creative work that the authors see as the best hope for the American economy in a global marketplace. Daniel Pink talks about *A Whole New Mind*. And the Partnership for 21st Century Skills outlines a comprehensive list of what will be needed to protect the American way of life. The common theme of these works is a focus on creativity, ethics, collaboration, cultural competency, and other intra- and interpersonal skills that fall outside the traditional academic framework.

There is agreement among these authors that these skills and dispositions should be integrated throughout the education system, from preschool programming through postsecondary degrees. What few say out loud, however, is that these new skills cannot simply be added to the existing curriculum. Research by John Kendall and Robert Marzano at McREL (Mid-continent Research for Education and Learning) has already conclusively demonstrated that there isn't enough time in the 13 years of public schooling to reach all the academic knowledge and skill benchmarks that have emerged out of the standards movement.[14] There certainly isn't time to also teach another whole set of skills that by their nature require extensive practice and coaching. If we are to make sure these new skills are learned, we really will have to transform the entire enterprise, including the graduate-level studies whose influence works its way throughout the whole system.

What is equally interesting about this new list of skills is that it includes capacities and dispositions that are less closely connected to the values of the dominant culture and the middle class than are the narrowly drawn academic skills privileged by the current system. For example, the skills of communication, collaboration, leadership, cross-cultural competency, and creativity, to name a few, characterize many young people in immigrant communities and communities of color. Were schools to actively value the varied ways in which these skills could be manifested and link genuinely important academic learning to them, a far wider range of students could succeed in school.[15]

The International Center for Leadership in Education, headed by Willard Daggett, has a framework for thinking about the K-12 curriculum that does just this by focusing on a combination of what it calls "rigor and relevance." More recently, the group has explicitly recognized the importance of relationships—between teachers and students and among students—as key ingredients in making this curriculum successful.

When rigor, relevance, and relationships are integrated, the focus of school tasks shifts from the acquisition and manipulation of knowledge for its own sake to solving real-world problems. When such problem-based learning is the center of the curriculum, there is a genuine context for the development of collaboration, leadership, innovation, communication, and other crucial nonacademic skills. In such a curriculum, less content is covered, but what is covered is actually learned.

The same cannot usually be said for the traditional academic curriculum, which teaches massive amounts of content in a way that seems guaranteed to go in one ear and out the other. (Do you remember what a glyceride is, the reasons for the War of 1812, or the formula for the area of a rhombus?) In a world where knowledge is being made available and created at exponential rates, it makes paramount sense for teaching to focus on its selective acquisition, evaluation, and application. No one can learn it all.

As promising as such an approach might be, an important theme of this article is that no such reform will be enacted if it conflicts with the perceived self-interest of powerful parents of academically strong students or if it leads to reduced college acceptance rates for any group of students. This means that the changes suggested above, or similar ones proposed by others, will never take hold if they are not embraced by higher education and especially by the most selective colleges and universities.

This political reality was not lost on the Progressive Education Association (PEA), when in the early 1930s it designed its famous Eight-Year Study to examine the impact of significant high school reform on college performance. Before lining up high schools willing to revamp their programs to align more closely with its agenda of more democratic schooling, the PEA enlisted the support of top colleges and secured their agreement to offer admission to students from the participating high schools with nontraditional profiles.[16]

We must take a page from the PEA playbook and include higher education in the reform of the whole system, preschool through graduate study. Only now the issue is not the willingness of selective schools to accept applications from a handful of nontraditional high schools, which is something they have already embraced. The issue today is a far-reaching, clear-eyed, no-holds-barred look at what we want and need colleges and universities to teach, how they should teach it, and how they fit into a complex web of postsecondary options. Because these institutions are the gatekeepers of this society's most important credential, their core values and practices must be thoroughly reexamined to see if they are truly aligned with the needs of the society.

Conclusion

Current public school reformers assume that higher education and its practices are a fixed component of the system. But as I have tried to show, until we explicitly move away from an education system driven by the traditional culture of the ivory tower—and currently embodied in the culture and admissions processes of colleges and universities—we will continue to reproduce a K-12 education system that sorts students by a narrow academic metric, depriving most young people of an education that would benefit them and the world at large. To continue to exempt higher education from the scrutiny recommended here is to perhaps lose our best—and maybe last—chance to remain competitive in the global market and become a more open and inclusive society at home.

There may well be a place for the academic skills prized by professors in selective colleges and universities in a redesigned P-20 system.[17] For my part, I deeply value many elements of a traditional liberal arts education. But if we are to remain a democratic society within a dynamic, complex, and interdependent world, we can no longer afford to conflate preparation for a high-quality liberal arts education, which is probably a choice of relatively few students, with the acquisition of scarce tickets to prestigious schools linked to the top of our political and economic pyramid. Using hyper-academic competence as the narrow gateway to worldly success has prevented our education system from meeting the needs of a great many of our students. To break free of this distorting influence, we must reimagine the purposes and structures of postsecondary education. Only when we have done so will it be possible to create a system that truly meets the learning needs of all our students.

Notes

1. James Hunt, Jr., and Thomas Tierney, *American Higher Education: How Does It Measure Up for the 21st Century?* (San Jose, Calif.: National Center for Public Policy and Higher Education, May 2006).

2. American Institutes for Research, "The National Survey of America's College Students," www.air.org/news/documents/collegeliteracyfactsheet.htm; and Mark Schneider, "Commissioner's Remarks," 2003 National Assessment of Adult Literacy (NAAL) Results, National Center for Education Statistics, 15 December 2005.

3. Of course, there are schools, both public and private, that do things quite differently. While they may explicitly adopt an unconventional educational philosophy, they nevertheless spend an inordinate amount of time and energy justifying it and showing that their students, too, get admitted to the "best" colleges and universities, albeit by being exceptions that prove the rule. I know this is true. I lead one of these schools.

4. *Rigor and Relevance Handbook* (Rexford, N.Y.: International Center for Leadership in Education, 2002), p. 3.

5. See James Rosenbaum, *Beyond College for All: Career Paths for the Forgotten Half* (New York: American Sociological Association Rose Series in Sociology, Russell Sage Foundation, 2001).

6. A small proportion of students will not conform to the homework demands of these accelerated classes but will nonetheless engage deeply with the material and often go on to earn high scores on AP or IB exams.

7. Diana Jean Schemo, "Grades Rise, but Reading Skills Do Not," *New York Times*, 23 February 2007.

8. *Rigor at Risk: Reaffirming Quality in the High School Core Curriculum* (Iowa City: ACT, 2007), announced in *Activity*, Spring 2007, www.act.org/activity/spring2007/rigor.html.

9. Significantly, there is a common culture across graduate schools that, not surprisingly, takes its cue from the top-ranked university departments. These top-ranked departments train most of the professors for selective colleges and universities, but they also prepare many of the professors who teach in nonselective colleges and universities. Their norms and

expectations are emulated by their less-competitive peers, who aspire to rise in the academic rankings that are used to sort graduate schools as much as undergraduate colleges.

10. There are others who enter graduate school to earn a credential that will give them a competitive advantage in the nonacademic job market. Unfortunately, few graduate programs offer such students an alternative to the training designed to prepare future professors.

11. While some professors, some disciplines, and even some institutions pride themselves on doing applied research, the way this work is executed and the level of preparation required to engage in it mean that it is more closely connected to the norms of pure research than to the ways that knowledge is applied in nonacademic settings.

12. Bureau of Labor Statistics, "Occupational Employment Projections to 2014," *Monthly Labor Review*, November 2005.

13. The Pianta study is the most recent to document how much more elementary schools are alike than different. See Robert C. Pianta et al., "Teaching: Opportunities to Learn in America's Elementary Classrooms," *Science*, 30 March 2007, pp. 1795–96.

14. John S. Kendall and Robert J. Marzano, *Content Knowledge: A Compendium of Standards and Benchmarks for K-12 Education* (Aurora, Colo.: Mid-continent Research for Education and Learning, 2004).

15. For an in-depth discussion of this issue, see Geneva Gay, *Culturally Responsive Teaching: Theory, Research, Practice* (New York: Teachers College Press, 2000).

16. Wilford Aikin, *The Story of the Eight-Year Study, with Conclusions and Recommendations* (New York: Harper & Brothers, 1942). An interesting side note is that the study found that high school reform, in general, did not harm college performance and that the more extensive a high school's reform, the higher the performance of its graduates in college.

17. P-20 is a current acronym intended to reflect a focus that ranges from preschool (P) through graduate school (grade 20).

RONA WILENSKY is the founding principal of New Vista High School, an innovative public high school of choice in Boulder, Colo. She can be reached at Rona.Wilensky@bvsd.org.

All Our Students Thinking

Any subject—be it physics, art, or auto repair—can promote critical thinking as long as teachers teach in intellectually challenging ways.

Nel Noddings

One stated aim of almost all schools today is to promote critical thinking. But how do we teach critical thinking? What do we mean by *thinking*?

In an earlier issue on the whole child (September 2005), *Educational Leadership* made it clear that education is rightly considered a multipurpose enterprise. Schools should encourage the development of all aspects of whole persons: their intellectual, moral, social, aesthetic, emotional, physical, and spiritual capacities. In this issue, I am primarily concerned with intellectual development, in particular, with teaching students to think. However, as we address this important aim, we need to ask how it fits with other important aims, how our choice of specific goals and objectives may affect the aim of thinking, and whether current practices enhance or impede this aim.

Thinking and Intellect

Writers often distinguish among such thinking categories as critical thinking, reflective thinking, creative thinking, and higher-order thinking. Here, I consider thinking as the sort of mental activity that uses facts to plan, order, and work toward an end; seeks meaning or an explanation; is self-reflective; and uses reason to question claims and make judgments. This seems to be what most teachers have in mind when they talk about thinking.

For centuries, many people have assumed that the study of certain subjects—such as algebra, Latin, and physics—has a desirable effect on the development of intellect. These subjects, it was thought, develop the mind, much as physical activity develops the muscles. John Dewey (1933/1971) rejected this view, writing, "It is desirable to expel . . . the notion that some subjects are inherently 'intellectual,' and hence possessed of an almost magical power to train the faculty of thought" (p. 46). Dewey argued, on the contrary, that

> any subject, from Greek to cooking, and from drawing to mathematics, is intellectual, if intellectual at all, not in its fixed inner structure, but in its function—in its power to start and direct significant inquiry and reflection. What geometry does for one, the manipulation of laboratory

apparatus, the mastery of a musical composition, or the conduct of a business affair, may do for another. (pp. 46–47)

More recently, Mike Rose has shown convincingly not only that thinking is required in physical work (2005), but also that nonacademic subjects can be taught in intellectually challenging ways (1995). We do our students and society a disservice when we suppose that there is no intellectual worth in such subjects as homemaking, parenting, getting along with others, living with plants and animals, and understanding advertising and propaganda (Noddings, 2005, 2006). The point is to appreciate the topics that matter in real life and encourage thinking in each area. This is not accomplished by first teaching everyone algebra—thus developing mental muscle—and *then* applying that muscle to everyday matters.

Nor is it accomplished by simply adding thinking to the set of objectives for each disciplinary course. More than 20 years ago, educators and policymakers advocated greater emphasis on thinking as an aim of education. Commenting on this popular demand, Matthew Lipman (1991), one of the founders of the modern Philosophy for Children movement, remarked,

> School administrators are calling for ways of "infusing thinking into the curriculum," apparently on the understanding that thinking can be added to the existing courses of studies as easily as we add vitamins to our diet. (p. 2)

But thinking cannot be formulated as a lesson objective—as something to teach, learn, and evaluate on Thursday morning. How, then, do we go about it?

Learning as Exploration

A few years ago, I watched a teenager whom I'll call Margie struggle with courses that discouraged thinking. In her U.S. history course, students were required to learn a list of facts for each unit of study. Margie had to memorize a set of 40 responses (names, places, and dates) for the unit on the American Revolutionary War and the postwar period. Conscientiously, she memorized the material and got a good grade on the test. When I talked with her, however, it was clear that she had not been asked to think and would soon forget the memorized facts. None of it meant anything to her; passing the test was her only objective.

Suppose, instead, that the teacher had asked students to consider such questions as these:

- What happened to the Tories during and after the war?
- Why was Thomas Paine honored as a hero for his tract *Common Sense* but reviled for his book *The Age of Reason*?
- Why might we be surprised (and dismayed) that John Adams signed the Alien and Sedition Acts?

Such questions would encourage students to read, write, argue, and consider the implications for current political life—all important aims of education. How many Tories left the United States? Where did they go? Where do refugees go today? Discussing the question on Thomas Paine could lead to a critical discussion of both nationalism and religion centered on Paine's statement, "My country is the world; my religion is to do good." Who reviled Paine and why? After reading biographical material on John Adams, students might indeed be amazed that he signed the Alien and Sedition Acts. What lesson might we take from this story about the effects of fear and distrust on even highly intelligent people?

Algebra for Some

When I first met with Margie, she was taking algebra. Looking through her textbook, I thought the course would be wonderful. The textbook was loaded with real-world applications and exercises that invited genuine thinking. But the teacher did not assign even one of these exercises. Not one! The following year, in geometry, Margie was never asked to do a proof. These algebra and geometry classes were composed of kids who, had they had a choice in the matter, would not have chosen courses in academic mathematics. Today, in the name of equality of opportunity, we force nearly all students into courses called Algebra and Geometry, but the courses often do not deserve their names because they lack genuine intellectual content. This practice is little short of pedagogical fraud. Many of Margie's classmates (and Margie, too) would have been better served by good career and technical education courses that would challenge them to think about the world of work for which they were preparing.

I am not suggesting that we go back to a system in which students are tested, sorted, and assigned either to academic courses or dead-end tracks in which they are treated with neglect, sometimes even with contempt. But the present practice of forcing everyone into academic courses is not working well. We would do better to design excellent career and technical education courses—very like the job-oriented programs provided in two-year colleges—and allow students to choose their own course of study. Students should not be forced into or excluded from academic courses, but they should be able to choose a nonacademic program with pride and confidence. Such programs are available in many Western countries, such as Germany and the Scandinavian countries. Programs like these might offer courses to prepare machinists, film technicians,

office managers, retail salespersons, food preparation and service workers, mechanics, and other skilled workers. Recent studies have shown that the United States actually has an oversupply of engineers and scientists but badly needs workers with high technical skills (Monastersky, 2007).

We can give students opportunities to think well in any course we offer, provided the students are interested in the subjects discussed. Algebra can be taught thoughtfully or stupidly. So can drafting, cooking, or parenting. The key is to give students opportunities to think and to make an effort to connect one subject area to other subject areas in the curriculum and to everyday life.

Consider the ongoing debate over popular science versus "real science." Many critics scorn popular science courses (for a powerful criticism of the critics, see Windschitl, 2006). They would prefer to enroll all students in science courses that would prepare them—through emphasis on vocabulary and abstract concepts—for the next science course. According to this view, practical or popular science has little value and should certainly not carry credits toward college preparation. But intelligent, well-educated nonscientists depend on popular (or popularized) science for a lifetime of essential information. Nonscientists like myself cannot run our own experiments and verify everything that comes through the science pipeline. Instead, we read widely and consider the credentials of those making various claims. High school courses should prepare not only future specialists but also all students for membership in this circle of thoughtful readers.

Deference to the formal disciplines sometimes actually impedes student thinking. A few years ago, it was recommended that math courses should teach students how to think like a mathematician. In science courses, they were to think like a scientist; in history, like a historian, and so on. But aside from the possibility that there may be more than one way to think like a mathematician, education efforts might better be aimed at showing students how to use mathematics to think about their own purposes. For example, carpenters don't need to think like mathematicians, but they do need to think about and use mathematics in their work.

Modeling Open-Ended Thinking

It may be useful, however, for students to see and hear their teachers thinking as mathematicians, historians, or artists. When I was studying for my master's degree in mathematics, I had one professor who frequently came to class unprepared. His fumbling about was often annoying; he wasted time. But sometimes his lack of preparedness led to eye-opening episodes. He would share aloud his thinking, working his way through a problem. Sometimes he would stop short and say, "This isn't going to work," and he'd explain why it wouldn't work. At other times, he'd say, "Ah, look, we're going great! What should we do next?" He modeled mathematical thinking for us, and I found it quite wonderful. The process was messy, uneven, time-consuming, and thrilling. That's the way real thinking is.

I am not recommending that teachers come to class unprepared, but we should at least occasionally tackle problems or ideas that we have not worked out beforehand. In doing so, we model thinking and demonstrate both the obstacles that we encounter and our successes.

Too often, we state beforehand exactly what we will teach and exactly what our students should know or do as a result. This is the right approach for some objectives. There is a place for automatic response in student learning; we do want students to carry out some operations automatically, without thinking. That sort of skill frees us to think about the real problems on which we should concentrate.

In today's schools, however, too much of what we teach is cast in terms of specific objectives or standards. Margie was told the 40 things she was expected to know about the American Revolutionary War. Some educators even argue that it is only fair to tell students exactly what they must know or do. But such full disclosure may foreclose learning to think. Thinking involves planning, ordering, creating structural outlines, deciding what is important, and reflecting on one's own activity. If all this is done for students—CliffsNotes for everything—they may pass tests on material they have memorized, but they will not learn to think, and they will quickly forget most of the memorized material.

Encouraging Teachers to Think

Our focus thus far has been on students. But what about teachers? Are they encouraged to think? Unfortunately, many teachers are told what topics to teach and how to teach them. In too many cases, they are even compelled to use scripted lessons. Ready-made lessons should be available for teachers who want to use them or for special purposes, but professional teachers should be allowed—even encouraged—to use their professional judgment in planning lessons and sequences of lessons.

If teachers want to teach students to think, they must think about what they themselves are doing. Critics both inside and outside the United States have characterized the U.S. curriculum as "a mile wide and an inch deep." The pressure to cover mandated material can lead to hasty and superficial instruction that favors correct responses to multiple-choice questions over thinking. Countless teachers have told me that they can't spend time on real-life applications of mathematics or the kinds of questions I suggested for Margie's history class. If they were to do so, they tell me, they wouldn't get through the required curriculum. But what is the point of getting through a huge body of material if students will soon forget it? How can we claim to educate our students if they do not acquire the intellectual habits of mind associated with thinking?

Teachers should also be willing to think critically about education theory and about what we might call education propaganda. Slogans are mouthed freely in education circles, and too few teachers challenge them (Noddings, 2007). For example, it is easy and politically correct to say, "All children can learn," but what does that mean? Can all children learn, say, algebra? If we answer a qualified *no* to this, are we demeaning the ability of some children (perhaps many), or might our answer be a respectful recognition that children differ and exhibit a wide range of talents and needs?

What Competing Really Means

Even if we believe that all children can learn algebra, we too seldom ask the question, Why should they? When we do ask it, the answer is usually that we live in an information age and that if students (and the United States) are to compete in a worldwide economy, they must know far more mathematics than previous generations did. We need, they say, more college-educated citizens.

Is this true? The information world is certainly growing, but in addition to its own growth, it has generated an enormous service world, and people in this world should also learn to think. The Bureau of Labor Statistics provides charts showing that, of the 10 occupations with the most openings in the next decade, only one or two require a college education. Occupations such as food preparation and service worker, retail salesperson, customer service representative, cashier, office clerk, and laborer and material mover will employ about five times more people than the computer/high-tech fields requiring a college education (see www.bls.gov/emp/home.htm for employment projections). No matter what we do in schools, most of our high school graduates will work at such jobs.

We live in an interdependent society, and one of our education aims is to prepare students for democratic citizenship. As part of that task, we should help students develop an appreciation for the wide range of essential work that must be done in our complex society. In the future, not everyone will need to have a traditional college education to experience occupational success, although postsecondary education or training will frequently enhance that success. Rather, occupational success will require flexibility, a willingness to continue learning, an ability to work in teams, patience and skill in problem solving, intellectual and personal honesty, and a well-developed capacity to think. Success in personal life requires many of the same qualities.

Even for those who go on to college and postgraduate education, the intellectual demands of the future are moving away from a narrow disciplinary emphasis. The biologist E. O. Wilson (2006) has commented on the new demands:

> The trajectory of world events suggests that educated people should be far better able than before to address the great issues courageously and analytically by undertaking a traverse of disciplines. We are into the age of synthesis, with a real empirical bite to it. Therefore, *sapere aude*. Dare to think on your own. (p. 137)

That's good advice for both teachers and students.

References

Dewey, J. (1933/1971). *How we think.* Chicago: Henry Regnery. (Original work published 1933)

Lipman, M. (1991). *Thinking in education.* Cambridge, UK: Cambridge University Press.

Monastersky, R. (2007, November 16). Researchers dispute notion that America lacks scientists and engineers. *The Chronicle of Higher Education, 54*(12), A14–15.

Noddings, N. (2005). *The challenge to care in schools* (2nd ed.). New York: Teachers College Press.

Noddings, N. (2006). *Critical lessons: What our schools should teach*. New York: Cambridge University Press.

Noddings, N. (2007). *When school reform goes wrong*. New York: Teachers College Press.

Rose, M. (1995). Possible lives: *The promise of public education in America*. Boston: Houghton Mifflin.

Rose, M. (2005). *The mind at work: Valuing the intelligence of the American worker*. New York: Penguin.

Wilson, E. O. (2006). *The creation: An appeal to save life on earth*. New York: Norton.

Windschitl, M. (2006). Why we can't talk to one another about science education reform. *Phi Delta Kappan, 87*(5), 348–355.

NEL NODDINGS is Lee L. Jacks Professor of Education, Emerita, at Stanford University, Stanford, California; noddings@stanford.edu.

UNIT 3

Addressing Diversity in Your School

Unit Selections

11. **As Diversity Grows, So Must We,** Gary R. Howard
12. **African American Parents: Improving Connections with Their Child's Educational Environment,** Regina R. Brandon
13. **The Myth of the "Culture of Poverty",** Paul Gorski
14. **Becoming Adept at Code-Switching,** Rebecca S. Wheeler
15. **Overcoming Lethargy in Gifted and Talented Education with Contract Activity Packages: I'm Choosing to Learn!,** Janet Caraisco
16. **Mother Goose Teaches on the Wild Side: Motivating At-Risk Mexican and Chicano Youngsters via a Multicultural Curriculum,** Martha Casas
17. **Celebrating Diversity through Explorations of Arab Children's Literature,** Tami Al-Hazza and Bob Lucking
18. **Books That Portray Characters with Disabilities: A Top 25 List for Children and Young Adults,** Mary Anne Prater and Tina Taylor Dyches

Key Points to Consider

- What are the challenges faced in schools due to diversity and poverty?

- What are the positive effects of diversity in our schools?

- Why might teaching code-switching be helpful to students who are both ELLs and African Americans?

- Could content activity packages be used with other student populations? What implications might this have for classroom teachers?

- How will you incorporate the suggestions given in this selection of articles into your teaching practice?

Student Website
www.mhcls.com

Internet References

The National Coalition for Parent Involvement in Education (NCPIE)
   http://www.ncpie.org
New Horizons for Learning
   http://www.newhorizons.org/
National Association for Multicultural Education (NAME)
   http://www.nameorg.org/index.html
Everything ESL
   http://www.everythingesl.net/

The concepts of culture and diversity encompass all of life ways, customs, traditions, and institutions that people develop as they create and experience their history and identity as a community. In the United States, very different cultures coexist within the civic framework of a shared constitutional tradition that guarantees equality before the law. So, many people are united as one nation by our constitutional heritage. Some of us are proud to say that we are a nation of immigrants. We are becoming more multicultural with every passing decade. Each of us is identified by our culture, language, and other socioeconomic factors in our society. However, as educators we have a unique opportunity. We are given the role to encourage and educate our diverse learners. The articles in this unit reflect upon all the concerns mentioned above.

The problem of high levels of poverty in urban and rural areas of our country is of great concern to U.S. educators. One in four American children does not have all of his or her basic needs met and lives under conditions of poverty. Almost one in three lives in a single-parent home, which in itself is no disadvantage, but under conditions of poverty, it often is. Children living in poverty are in crisis if their basic health and social needs are not adequately met, and their educational development can be affected by crises in their personal lives. We must teach and support these students and their families, even when it appears that they are not fully interested in their education. As a teacher, you may not have much control over the factors that shape the lives of our students. However, you can establish a classroom that is a place of care and nurture for your students; that is multicultural-friendly, equitable, and free from bigotry. A place where diverse students are not just tolerated but are wanted, welcomed, and accepted. A respect for all children and their capacity is the baseline for good teaching. Students must feel significant and cared for by all members of the classroom. Our diverse children should be exposed to an academically challenging curriculum that expects much from them and equips them for the real world.

Schools have an obligation not only to individual students, but to their families as well. Sometimes teachers engage in the classist idea that families are uncaring, uninformed, distracted, or too disorganized to offer educational and behavioral support to their children. What is missing here is a thoughtful teacher who understands that caregivers may have valid reasons for their lack of involvement such as physical health, other responsibilities, or a job where each missed hour means missed pay. In addition, the negative feelings caregivers have due to their experience in school, where they were made to feel self-conscious or distrustful, may color the opinion they have of the teachers of their children. Understanding what families and caregivers want and working with them will go a long way to build better relationships between teachers and families. We have a body of research that attests that families offer a valuable context for learning and can reduce the dissonance of differing expectations between school and home.

The articles in this unit address all of the issues mentioned above. Howard's article is about the rapid demographic growth affecting schools and how to meet those challenges with a five-phase plan of professional development for teachers. Brandon offers us suggestions for improving connections with families from diverse cultural backgrounds. He outlines the factors that can impact parental participation and suggests actions to improve home-school communication and interactions. Gorski contends that there is no such thing as a *culture of poverty*. He addresses four stereotypes that may create inequality in how teachers respond to, work with, and teach students from impoverished circumstances. Most important, he

© Jose Luis Pelaez Inc/Blend Images/Getty Images

concludes with a list of actions teachers and others can take to address classism and end inequity. Casas shares her research-in-action with at-risk Mexican and Chicano students, many of whom had been recently released from a juvenile detention center. She notes the rise in student achievement when they were fully engaged in their own learning used multicultural materials and lessons were linked to their real-life experiences. Wheeler summarizes research that suggests teachers are not trained to understand the linguistic differences that exist in urban African Americans' daily language. This lack of understanding can cause teachers to think these students have reading and writing deficits. She presents a set of strategies to build on the informal language structures students already know and lead them to accurate use of Standard English. Al-Hazza and Lucking note that since the 9/11 attack, and other incidents world-wide, there have been shifts in our view of Arabs. These authors give us a brief overview of the culture, mores, and traditional literature. One may be surprised by the similarities to our own cultural traditions and beliefs. This is the point of their work. To help our students overcome fears and anxiety they may have when encountering persons of Arab descent we could consider using the suggestions and books offered here.

Diversity includes students who learn differently from their typical same-age peers. Two of the articles in this section address the needs of these students; gifted and talented students need to be challenged and engaged, and students with disabilities need to be understood to be appreciated by and gain acceptance from peers. Caraisco's article explains how to use contract activity packages to challenge the gifted and talented. Caraisco provides an overview of the literature on the gifted, and notes that gifted and talented learners prefer to learn via independent study. She designed and conducted a study to use the contract activity package (CAP) with students; the findings were positive.

When prospective teachers ask me, "What do I tell the other children about Joey's disability?" I always tell them to ask the school librarian to buy books that realistically portray students with disabilities in a variety of situations and use these in their teaching. In their article, Prater and Dyches have constructed a list of award-winning books that include both text content and pictures about children and youth with disabilities. Teachers and parents will find these books well written, with positive examples of students with disabilities, and teachers will find them useful for teaching their students how others live with disabilities.

As Diversity Grows, So Must We

Schools that experience rapid demographic shifts can meet the challenge by implementing five phases of professional development.

Gary R. Howard

Many school districts nationwide are experiencing rapid growth in the number of students of color, culturally and linguistically diverse students, and students from low-income families. From my work with education leaders in some of these diversity-enhanced school districts, I know they are places of vibrant opportunity—places that call us to meaningful and exciting work. In these "welcome-to-America" schools, the global community shows up in our classrooms every day, inviting us—even requiring us—to grow as we learn from and with our students and their families.

The Need for Growth

All is not well, however, in these rapidly transitioning schools. Some teachers, administrators, and parents view their schools' increasing diversity as a problem rather than an opportunity For example, in a school district on the West Coast where the number of Latino students has quadrupled in the past 10 years, a teacher recently asked me, "Why are they sending these kids to our school?" In another district outside New York City—where the student population was once predominantly rich, white, and Jewish but is now about 90 percent low-income kids of color, mostly from the Caribbean and Latin America—a principal remarked in one workshop, "These kids don't value education, and their parents aren't helping either. They don't seem to care about their children's future." In a school district near Minneapolis with a rapidly increasing black population, a white parent remarked, "Students who are coming here now don't have much respect for authority. That's why we have so many discipline problems."

Diversity-enhanced schools are places of vibrant opportunity—places that call us as educators to meaningful and exciting work.

Other educators and parents, although less negative, still feel uneasy about their schools' new demographics. In a high school outside Washington, D.C., where the Latino immigrant population is increasing rapidly, a teacher told me that he was disappointed in himself for not feeling comfortable engaging his students in a discussion of immigration issues, a hot topic in the community in spring 2006. "I knew the kids needed to talk, but I just couldn't go there." And a black teacher who taught French successfully for many years in predominantly white suburban schools told me recently, "When I first found myself teaching classes of mostly black kids, I went home frustrated every night because I knew I wasn't getting through to them, and they were giving me a hard time. It only started getting better when I finally figured out that I had to re-examine everything I was doing."

This teacher has it right. As educators in rapidly transitioning schools, we need to reexamine everything we're doing. Continuing with business as usual will mean failure or mediocrity for too many of our students, as the data related to racial, cultural, linguistic, and economic achievement gaps demonstrate (National Center for Education Statistics, 2005). Rapidly changing demographics demand that we engage in a vigorous, ongoing, and systemic process of professional development to prepare all educators in the school to function effectively in a highly diverse environment.

Many education leaders in diversity-enhanced schools are moving beyond blame and befuddlement and working to transform themselves and their schools to serve all their students well. From observing and collaborating with them, I have learned that this transformative work proceeds best in five phases: (1) building trust, (2) engaging personal culture, (3) confronting issues of social dominance and social justice, (4) transforming instructional practices, and (5) engaging the entire school community.

Phase 1: Building Trust

Ninety percent of U.S. public school teachers are white; most grew up and attended school in middle-class, English-speaking, predominantly white communities and received their teacher preparation in predominantly white colleges and universities (Gay, Dingus, & Jackson, 2003). Thus, many white educators simply have not acquired the experiential and education background that would prepare them for the growing diversity of their students (Ladson-Billings, 2002; Vavrus, 2002).

The first priority in the trust phase is to acknowledge this challenge in a positive, inclusive, and honest way. School leaders should base initial discussions on the following assumptions:

- Inequities in diverse schools are not, for the most part, a function of intentional discrimination.
- Educators of *all* racial and cultural groups need to develop new competencies and pedagogies to successfully engage our changing populations.
- White teachers have their own cultural connections and unique personal narratives that are legitimate aspects of the overall mix of school diversity.

School leaders should also model for their colleagues inclusive and non-judgmental discussion, reflection, and engagement strategies that teachers can use to establish positive learning communities in their classrooms.

For example, school leaders in the Apple Valley Unified School District in Southern California, where racial, cultural, and linguistic diversity is rapidly increasing, have invested considerable time and resources in creating a climate of openness and trust. They recently implemented four days of intensive work with teams from each school, including principals, teacher leaders, union representatives, parents, clergy, business leaders, and community activists from the NAACP and other organizations.

One essential outcome in this initial phase of the conversation is to establish that racial, cultural, and economic differences are real—and that they make a difference in education outcomes. Said one Apple Valley participant, "I have become aware that the issue of race needs to be dealt with, not minimized." Said another, "I need to move beyond being color-blind." A second key outcome is to establish the need for a personal and professional journey toward greater awareness. As an Apple Valley educator noted, "There were a lot of different stories and viewpoints shared at this inservice, but the one thing we can agree on is that everyone needs to improve in certain areas." A third key outcome in the trust phase is to demonstrate that difficult topics can be discussed in an environment that is honest, safe, and productive. One Apple Valley teacher commented, "We were able to talk about all of the issues and not worry about being politically correct."

Through this work, Apple Valley educators and community leaders established a climate of constructive collaboration that can be directed toward addressing the district's new challenges. From the perspective of the school superintendent, "This is a conversation our community is not used to having, so we had to build a positive climate before moving to the harder questions of action."

Phase 2: Engaging Personal Culture

Change has to start with educators before it can realistically begin to take place with students. The central aim of the second phase of the work is building educators' *cultural competence*—their ability to form authentic and effective relationships across differences.

Young people, particularly those from historically marginalized groups, have sensitive antennae for authenticity I recently asked a group of racially and culturally diverse high school students to name the teachers in their school who really cared about them, respected them, and enjoyed getting to know them as people. Forty students pooling their answers could name only 10 teachers from a faculty of 120, which may be one reason this high school has a 50 percent dropout rate for students of color.

Aronson and Steele's (2005) work on stereotype threat demonstrates that intellectual performance, rather than being a fixed and constant quality, is quite fragile and can vary greatly depending on the social and interpersonal context of learning. In repeated studies, these researchers found that three factors have a major effect on students' motivation and performance: their feelings of belonging, their trust in the people around them, and their belief that teachers value their intellectual competence. This research suggests that the capacity of adults in the school to form trusting relationships with and supportive learning environments for their students can greatly influence achievement outcomes.

Leaders in the Metropolitan School District of Lawrence Township, outside Indianapolis, have taken this perspective seriously. Clear data showed gaps among ethnic groups in achievement, participation in higher-level courses, discipline referrals, and dropout rates. In response, district

teachers and administrators engaged in a vigorous and ongoing process of self-examination and personal growth related to cultural competence.

Central-office and building administrators started with themselves. Along with selected teachers from each school, they engaged in a multiyear program of shared reading, reflective conversations, professional development activities, and joint planning to increase their own and their colleagues' levels of cultural competence. They studied and practiced Margaret Wheatley's (2002) principles of conversation, with particular emphasis on her admonitions to expect things to be messy and to be willing to be disturbed. They designed their own Socratic seminars using chapters from *We Can't Teach What We Don't Know* (Howard, 2006) and used the stages of personal identity development model from that book as a foundation for ongoing reflective conversations about their own journeys toward cultural competence.

As this work among leaders began to be applied in various school buildings, one principal observed, "We are talking about things that we were afraid to talk about before—like our own prejudices and the biases in some of our curriculum materials." In another school, educators' discussions led to a decision to move parent-teacher conferences out of the school building and into the apartment complexes where their black and Latino students live.

Phase 3: Confronting Social Dominance and Social Justice

When we look at school outcome data, the history of racism, classism, and exclusion in the United States stares us in the face. Systems of privilege and preference often create enclaves of exclusivity in schools, in which certain demographic groups are served well while others languish in failure or mediocrity. As diversity grows in rapidly transitioning school districts, demographic gaps become increasingly apparent.

Educators of *all* racial and cultural groups need to develop new competencies and pedagogies to successfully engage our changing populations.

In phase three, educators directly confront the current and historical inequities that affect education. The central purpose of this phase is to construct a compelling narrative of social justice that will inform, inspire, and sustain educators in their work, without falling into the rhetoric of shame and blame. School leaders and teachers engage in a lively conversation about race, class, gender, sexual orientation, immigration, and other dimensions of diversity and social dominance. David Koyama, principal of a diversity-enhanced elementary school outside Seattle, said, "One of my most important functions as a school leader is to transform political jargon like 'no child left behind' into a moral imperative that inspires teachers to work toward justice, not mere compliance."

Unraveling social dominance takes courage—the kind of courage shown by the central office and school leadership team in the Roseville Area School District outside the twin cities of Minneapolis and St. Paul. Roseville is in the midst of a rapid demographic shift. As we approached this phase of the work, I asked Roseville leaders to examine how issues of privilege, power, and dominance might be functioning in their schools to shape educators' assumptions and beliefs about students and create inequitable outcomes.

One of the workshop activities engaged participants in a forced-choice simulation requiring them to choose which aspects of their identity they would give up or deny for the sake of personal survival in a hostile environment. Choosing from such identities as race, ethnicity, language, religion, values, and vocation, many white educators were quick to give up race. Among the Roseville administrative team, which is 95 percent white, the one white principal who chose to keep his racial identity during the simulation said during the debriefing discussion, "I seriously challenge my white colleagues who so easily gave up their race. I think if we are honest with ourselves, few would choose to lose the privilege and power that come with being white in the United States."

As an outgrowth of the authentic and sometimes contentious conversations that emerged from this and other activities, several core leaders and the superintendent identified a need to craft a strong Equity Vision statement for the district. The Equity Vision now headlines all opening-of-school events each year and is publicly displayed in district offices and schools. It reads,

> Roseville Area Schools is committed to ensuring an equitable and respectful educational experience for every student, family, and staff member, regardless of race, gender, sexual orientation, socioeconomic status, ability, home or first language, religion, national origin, or age.

As a result of the increased consciousness about issues of dominance and social justice, several schools have formed Equity Teams of teachers and students, and an Equity Parent Group has begun to meet. The district is looking seriously at how many students from dominant and subordinate groups are in its gifted and AP classes and is conscientiously working for more balance.

Like Roseville, other diversity-enhanced districts must establish clear public markers that unambiguously state, "This is who we are, this is what we believe, and this is what we will do." Any approach to school reform that does not honestly engage issues of power, privilege, and social dominance is naive, ungrounded in history, and unlikely to yield the deep changes needed to make schools more inclusive and equitable.

Phase 4: Transforming Instructional Practices

In this phase, schools assess and, where necessary, transform the way they carry out instruction to become more responsive to diversity. For teachers, this means examining pedagogy and curriculum, as well as expectations and interaction patterns with students. It means looking honestly at outcome data and creating new strategies designed to serve the students whom current instruction is not reaching. For school leaders, this often means facing the limits of their own knowledge and skills and becoming colearners with teachers to find ways to transform classroom practices.

As educators in rapidly transitioning schools, we need to reexamine everything we're doing.

In Loudoun County Public Schools, outside Washington, D.C., teachers and school leaders are taking this work seriously. One of the fastest-growing school systems in the United States, Loudoun County is experiencing rapid increases in racial, cultural, linguistic, and economic diversity on its eastern edge, closer to the city, while remaining more monocultural to the west. Six of Loudoun's most diverse schools have formed leadership teams to promote the following essential elements of culturally responsive teaching (CRT):

- Forming authentic and caring relationships with students.
- Using curriculum that honors each student's culture and life experience.
- Shifting instructional strategies to meet the diverse learning needs of students.
- Communicating respect for each student's intelligence.
- Holding consistent and high expectations for all learners. (Gay, 2000; Ladson-Billings, 1994; McKinley, 2005; Shade, Kelly, & Oberg, 1997)

CRT teams vary in size and membership but usually include principals, assistant principals, counselors, lead teachers, specialists, and, in some cases, parents. In addition to engaging deeply in the phases outlined above, these teams have begun to work with their broader school faculties to transform instruction. At Loudoun County's Sugarland Elementary, teacher members of the CRT team have designed student-based action research projects. They selected individual students from their most academically challenged demographic groups and then used the principles of CRT to plan new interventions to engage these students and track their progress.

In one action research project, a 5th grade teacher focused on a Latino student, an English language learner who "couldn't put two sentences together, let alone write the five-paragraph essay that is required to pass our 5th grade assessment." The teacher's first reaction was to ask, "How was this student allowed to slip by all these years without learning anything beyond 2nd grade writing skills?" When the teacher launched her CRT project, however, her perspective became more proactive. She realized that she couldn't just deliver the 5th grade curriculum—she had to meet this student where he was. She built a personal connection with the student, learned about his family culture and interests (a fascination with monkeys was a major access point), and used this relationship to reinforce his academic development. The student responded to her high expectations and passed his 5th grade writing assessment. And after missing its No Child Left Behind compliance goals in past years, Sugarland recently achieved adequate yearly progress for all subgroups in its highly diverse student population.

This phase requires a crucial paradigm shift, in which teachers and other school professionals stop blaming students and their families for gaps in academic achievement. Instead of pointing fingers, educators in Loudoun schools are placing their energies where they will have the most impact—in changing their *own* attitudes, beliefs, expectations, and practices. I frequently ask teachers and school leaders, "Of all the many factors that determine school success for our students, where can we as educators have the most influence?" After educators participate in the work outlined here, the answer is always, "Changing ourselves."

Phase 5: Engaging the Entire School Community

Changing demographics have profound implications for all levels and functions of the school system. To create welcoming and equitable learning environments for diverse students and their families, school leaders must engage the entire school community.

Leaders in the East Ramapo Central School District in New York State have committed themselves to just such a systemwide initiative. The school district, which lies across the Tappan Zee Bridge from New York City, has experienced a dramatic shift in student population in the past 15 years as low-income Haitian, Jamaican, Dominican, Latino, and black families from the city have moved into the community and middle-class white families have, unfortunately but predictably, fled to private schools or other less diverse districts.

In the midst of this demographic revolution, East Ramapo's broad-based diversity initiative has engaged all groups and constituencies in the school district community, not just teachers and administrators. For example, the district has provided workshops to help classified employees acknowledge their powerful role in setting a welcoming tone and creating an inclusive climate for students, parents, and colleagues in school offices, lunchrooms, hallways, and on the playground. For bus drivers, this work has meant gaining cultural competence skills for managing their immense safety responsibilities while communicating clearly and compassionately across many languages and cultures on their buses.

In one session that I led with school secretaries, we worked through their confusion and frustration related to all the diverse languages being spoken in the school offices and, in some cases, their feelings of anger and resentment about the demographic changes that had taken place in "their" schools. Asked what they learned from the session, participants commented, "I saw the frustration people can have, especially if they are from another country." "We all basically have the same feelings about family, pride in our culture, and the importance of getting along." "I learned from white people that they can also sometimes feel like a minority."

In addition to these sessions, East Ramapo has created learning opportunities for school board members, parents, students, counselors, and special education classroom assistants. The district has convened regular community forums focusing on student achievement and creating conversations across many diverse cultures. White parents who have kept their children in the public schools because they see the value of diversity in their education have been significant participants in these conversations.

As a result of East Ramapo's efforts, the achievement gaps in test scores along ethnic and economic lines have significantly narrowed. In the six years since the district consciously began implementing the professional development model discussed here, the pass rate for black and Hispanic students combined on the New York State elementary language arts test increased from 43 percent in 2000 to 54 percent in 2006; on the math test, the pass rate increased from 40 percent to 61 percent. During that same period, the gap between black and Hispanic students (combined) and white and Asian students (combined) decreased by 6 percentage points in language arts and 23 percentage points in math. The achievement gap between low-income elementary students and the general population decreased by 10 points in language arts and 6 points in math—results that are particularly impressive, given that the proportion of economically disadvantaged students grew from 51 percent in 2000 to 72 percent in 2006.

A Journey toward Awareness

Professional development for creating inclusive, equitable, and excellent schools is a long-term process. The school districts described here are at various stages in the process. Everyone involved would agree that the work is messier and more complex than can be communicated in this brief overview. However, one central leadership commitment is clear in all of these rapidly transitioning districts: When diversity comes to town, we are all challenged to grow.

References

Aronson, J., & Steele, C. M. (2005). Stereotypes and the fragility of human competence, motivation, and self-concept. In C. Dweck & E. Elliot (Eds.), *Handbook of competence and motivation* (pp. 436–456). New York: Guilford.

Gay, G. (2000). *Culturally responsive teaching: Theory, research, and practice.* New York: Teachers College Press.

Gay, G., Dingus, J. E., & Jackson, C. W. (2003, July). *The presence and performance of teachers of color in the profession.* Unpublished report prepared for the National Collaborative on Diversity in the Teaching Force, Washington, DC.

Howard, G. (2006). *We can't teach what we don't know: White teachers in multiracial schools* (2nd ed.). New York: Teachers College Press.

Ladson-Billings, G. (1994). *The dreamkeepers: Successful teachers of African American students.* San Francisco: Jossey-Bass.

Ladson-Billings, G. (2002). *Crossing over to Canaan: The journey of new teachers in diverse classrooms.* San Francisco: Jossey-Bass.

McKinley, J. H. (2005, March). *Culturally responsive teaching and learning.* Paper presented at the Annual State Conference of the Washington Alliance of Black School Educators, Bellevue, WA.

National Center for Education Statistics. (2005). *The nations report card.* Washington, DC: Author.

Shade, B. J., Kelly, C., & Oberg, M. (1997). *Creating culturally responsive classrooms.* Washington, DC: American Psychological Association.

Vavrus, M. (2002). *Transforming the multicultural education of teachers: Theory, research and practice.* New York: Teachers College Press.

Wheatley, M. (2002). *Turning to one another: Simple conversations to restore hope to the future.* San Francisco: Barrett-Koehler.

GARY R. HOWARD is Founder and President of the REACH Center for Multicultural Education in Seattle (www.reachctr.org); 206-634-2073; garyhoward@earthlink.net. He is the author of *We Can't Teach What We Don't Know: White Teachers, Multiracial Schools* (Teachers College Press, 2nd ed., 2006).

From *Educational Leadership,* March 2007, pp. 16–22. Copyright © 2007 by ASCD. Reprinted by permission. The Association for Supervision and Curriculum Development is a worldwide community of educators advocating sound policies and sharing best practices to achieve the success of each learner. To learn more, visit ASCD at www.ascd.org.

African American Parents

Improving Connections with Their Child's Educational Environment

REGINA R. BRANDON

Despite the known advantages of parental involvement in education, weak connections still exist between African American parents and their child's school. Parental involvement has many positive benefits for students; the most important is that it enhances students' academic and social achievement. When parents and educators do not develop positive partnerships, they can develop negative attitudes about each other, which often results in low parental participation. Educators must be aware of the factors that influence parental involvement so that they can develop strategies for open communication with parents and strengthen school–family connections.

The role parents play in their child's educational development has many positive possibilities, including enhancing academic and social success (Pena, 2000). Parental involvement in education also benefits teachers and parents themselves (Trotman, 2001). When parents actively take part in their child's schooling, positive family– school–community relationships develop (Feuerstein, 2000). However, many parents work long hours, have more than one job, and participate in multiple responsibilities that may limit their participation in their child's education (Coots, 1998; Pena, 2000; Smalley & Reyes-Blanes, 2001). Because of these factors, parents often do not meet educators' expectations for school participation and connection, resulting in educator criticism of parents (Bloom, 2001).

Despite the many known advantages to parental involvement, research indicates that weak connections exist between African American parents and the educational system (Davis, Brown, Bantz, & Manno, 2002; Thompson, 2003b). Many of these parents encounter personal, cultural, and structural barriers that may cause them to be isolated or alienated from the school system (Trotman, 2001).

This isolation or alienation can result in a lack of participation in children's education—whether or not the children have disabilities—and can prove to be detrimental to children (Bempechat, 1992). African American parents of children who have disabilities repeatedly express frustration and anger at polices they believe prevent them from participating in their children's education (Davis, Brown, Bantz, & Manno, 2002).

According to the U.S. *Census Report 2000*, 36.4 million (i.e., 12.9% of the population) identified themselves as African American. This group of citizens increased in numbers faster than did the total population between 1990 and 2000 (i.e., 4.7 million, or a 15% increase from 1990 to 2000) and made up 20.1% of the school-age population nationally. Thus, decreasing the isolation felt by and increasing the connection with education professionals for African American parents in regard to their children's schooling must be one of the major focuses of education today (Smalley & Reyes-Blanes, 2001).

Parent Isolation

Parents' isolation from or lack of connection with their child's school means that they feel out of place, experience real and perceived discrimination, and have a sense of estrangement when interacting with educators (Bempechat, 1992). This isolation may cause parents to express a sense of fear, depression, and even school phobia (Epstein, 1995). Because of this lack of connection, parents may be suspicious of the educational institution and confuse teaching with learning, grade advancement with education, and a diploma with competence (Epstein, 1996). Several factors have been identified that may influence parental participation in the school environment (see Table 1).

Research has also addressed the role that educator behavior plays in the lack of connection between African American parents and the educational system. Findings indicate that educators often show a lack of respect for different parenting styles, which results in parents' belief that their power is being undermined (Lareau, 1987; Thompson, 2003a). Lack of respect on the part of educators can be a direct result of their lack of preparation or experience in working with people who differ from them (e.g., linguistically, culturally, economically, ethnically; Thompson, 2003b). That is to say, most teachers lack the education and experiences to prepare them to work with African American parents. The gap created between African American parents and non–African American educators often leads to parents' feelings of isolation from their child's education (Calabrese, 1989; Scott-Jones, 1987).

Table 1 Factors Impacting Parental Participation

Factor	Description
Cultural and linguistic diversity	• Differences between the culture and/or language of the home and the school may lead to parental isolation. • School customs, expectations, and experiences often do not reflect the backgrounds of the neighborhood families (Calabrese, 1990). • Some parents do not participate in school activities because they believe it is the school's sole responsibility to educate their child (Epstein, 1996).
Economics	• Parents living in poverty are less likely to become involved in their child's education then are middle- and upper-class parents (Coots, 1998). • Parents' economic status is more likely to affect school-based involvement than home-based involvement (Coots, 1998; McDermott & Rothenberg, 2001). • Parents living in poverty often express doubts about their own educational abilities and abdicate the education of their child to the teacher (Sojourner & Kushner, 1997). • Parents living in poverty often are focused on the immediate needs of their family and do not have time to assist their child in school (Smalley & Reyes-Blanes, 2001). • Some teachers believe that families of low income do not value education and assume the parents do not have anything to contribute to the education of their children (Bloom, 2001).
Family composition	• Schools with a high population of single parents often experience less parental involvement. • There is decreased school involvement and support from the noncustodial parent in single-parent families (Bloom, 2001).
Parental educational level	• Parental educational level can have a direct impact on parent participation; the higher the educational level, the greater the participation (Epstein, 1995).
School communication	• Often, a weak communication system exists among the school, African American families, and the community (Morris, 1999; Thompson, 2003b).
Interaction with teachers	• Educators have equated parental involvement with parental value of education and have assumed that low involvement reflects a lack of parental interest in a child's education; thus, educators have not proactively interacted with parents (Thompson, 2003b; Trotman, 2001). • Educator misconceptions that parents are disinterested in their child's education results in educators' not encouraging parents to participate in school (Bloom, 2001).
Interaction with the school	• African American parents have experienced institutional barriers (e.g., personal, cultural, and structural; negative teacher and administration attitudes) that keep them from actively participating in their child's education (Thompson, 2003a).
School success of children	• Many African American parents see their child attending under-resourced and overcrowded schools (Brown, 2003) and believe that this has a direct impact on their child's educational achievement (Epstein, 1996).
Personal constraints	• Personal factors involve (a) lack of time, (b) lack of transportation, (c) lack of child care, (d) scheduling conflicts, and (e) lack of understanding of educational jargon (Coots, 1998; Harry, 1992; Pena, 2000; Smalley & Reyes-Blanes, 2001). • Parents' own negative school experiences can result in their feeling intimidated by the educational system (Thompson, 2003b).

Consequences of African American Parent Isolation

The research on parental participation has drawn attention to the relatively low and declining involvement of African American parents in the education of their children in both special and general education (Pena, 2000; Rao, 2000; Thompson, 2003a; Thompson, 2003b; Winters, 1994). This lack of involvement can have detrimental effects on children and youth. The lack of interaction between educators and parents can lead to a high dropout rate, a high rate of student suspension, low student motivation, and a high rate of placement in special education programs for students with mental retardation and emotional disabilities (Calabrese, 1990; Harrison & Mitylene, 1995).

African American parents have indicated that they want to be involved in their child's education (Adelman, 1994), yet they

Table 2 School–Home Communication

Suggestion	Implementation
Establish a schoolwide communication system that serves as a consistent and predictable communication resource for parents.	• Daily individual student report cards • Weekly or biweekly phone calls or e-mails, depending on parents' access to a computer • Monthly newsletters concerning school activities and happenings
Develop a parent handbook that addresses questions commonly asked by parents.	• Handbooks specific to each classroom or program • School handbook that covers school policy, requirements, and the yearly calendar
Provide parents with a calendar of parent conferences at the beginning of the year as well as an outline of a typical parent conference.	• Include (a) purpose of the conference, (b) faculty/staff who will attend, (c) length of the typical conference (important for parents who take time off work), (d) suggested questions for parents to ask, and (e) items to bring
Be polite.	• Though this may seem like common sense, cultural groups may have different communication customs that should be followed. For example, African American family members should always be addressed formally (e.g., Mrs. Jones, Mr. Daniel, Dr. Smith) until an individual is asked to call them by a different name.
Be aware of the different methods through which people communicate.	• Educators should reflect on their own beliefs as to how parents "should" communicate and evaluate whether or not these beliefs negatively affect their relationship with parents.
Explore the use of technology as a communication tool.	• The digital divide still exists, so it is important to explore parental access to. technology prior to using it as a communication tool. However, e-mail, a school Web site, and online chats may facilitate communication with parents who have difficulty coming to school in person.

also noted a weak connection with the school (Morris, 1999). This lack of connection results in low parental participation and a belief among educators that parents lack interest in and do not value their child's education (Thompson, 2003b; Trotman, 2001). Thus, both parties continue the cycle of uninvolvement—parents retreat and educators do not engage the parents. Only through proactive engagement and communication with parents can educators increase the likelihood of parental involvement (Johnson, 1990) and thus increase the educational attainment of the students who reside within their care (Lynn, 1997; Mapp, 1997; Thompson 2003b).

Increasing the Connection with the Educational Environment

Studies have indicated that children whose parents are involved in their formal education benefit from this involvement (Bempechat, 1992; Comer & Haynes, 1991; Hill & Craft, 2003). These benefits include (a) higher grades and test scores, (b) long-term academic achievement, (c) positive attitudes and behaviors, (d) success-

ful school programs, (e) higher completion rates, and (f) effective schools. Recent research indicates that all parents want their children to achieve academically (Thompson, 2003b). Overall, parents indicate that they want to be involved in their child's education (Smrekar & Cohen-Vogel, 2001). Sometimes, however, they simply do not know where or how to begin. Often, parents are intimidated by the educational system and feel that educators do not welcome them into the system (Sojourner & Kushner, 1997). Given the documented isolation of African American parents, educators must develop methods to include reluctant parents in their child's education (Hill & Craft, 2003). The ultimate goal is to create a strong connection between school educators and administrators and African American parents.

School–Home Communication

Frequently, a weak connection exists among schools, African American families, and communities (Morris, 1999). Too often, these relationships are characterized by the failure of schools to actively involve African American families and communities. This can result in a breakdown in the communication system

Table 3 Interaction with the School and Educators

Suggestion	Implementation
Solicit from parents the problems they encounter around the issue of school participation.	• Create a questionnaire that asks about work schedules that conflict with parent conferences, transportation issues, child care issues, etc. Work within the school setting to address identified issues (e.g., scheduling of meetings, child care provided during parent conferences).
Collect information from parents about their perceptions of the racial climate of the school.	• Create a questionnaire that focuses on the inclusion of diversity in all facets of the school environment (e.g., bulletin boards, assemblies), instructional techniques, and school discipline policies and practice.
Establish school committees run by parents that provide a vehicle for parents to offer input and establish social networks of support with other parents.	• The committee should meet regularly with the principal and other educators at the school. • Suggestions should be implemented and be apparent to parents and educators.
Establish parent and educator interaction/ communication training modules.	• Parent modules should be scheduled at times convenient to parents (as identified by a schoolwide survey), or offered through a school Web site. • Educator modules should be conducted during professional development time or through a school Web site.

between parents and professionals (Thompson, 2003b) and in negative attitudes on the part of both parties (Epstein, 1996; Thompson, 2003a).

Educators must take a proactive role in establishing an open communication system between parents and the school setting to establish a strong connection (Johnson, 1990). This system should solicit parent participation in a manner that facilitates parental ownership of the school (Epstein, 1996) and increases parents' understanding of how they can be involved. Although each school is unique, the goal for educators is to understand parents' communications and work to address those needs (see Table 2).

Interaction with the School and Educators

When parents, educators, and administrators do not develop partnerships, they often develop negative attitudes about one another (Epstein, 1996; Thompson, 2003a). As a result, parents may choose not to participate in their child's school, and educators may feel frustrated because of low parent participation. To alleviate this cycle, researchers have suggested that schools develop structured systems to involve parents and provide a continuous training program for parents, teachers, and administrators in interaction and communication skills (Nicholson, Evans, Tellier-Robinson, & Aviles, 2001). Often, schools do not have a structured system in place for developing connections with parents and facilitating parent ownership of the school. Conversely, parents and educators often do not possess the skills necessary to

communicate and develop connections with people who differ from them (e.g., ethnically, economically, educationally). Active encouragement of parental participation provides one method of enhancing parent connection to the school. Specialized communication/connection training can provide educators and parents the skills necessary to begin an open and honest dialogue and thus positively influence children's educational attainment (Lynn, 1997; Mapp, 1997; Thompson, 2003b). The ultimate goal is to increase parental involvement and decrease the isolation often felt by African American parents (see Table 3).

Conclusion

A major focus of educational policies in the United States is on closing the gap that exists in educational opportunities for all students (Reglin, King, Losike-Sedimo, & Ketterer, 2003). Researchers have suggested that parental involvement in children's education is one issue that influences this gap (Calabrese, 1989; Davis, Brown, Bantz, & Manno, 2002; Harry, 1992; Scott-Jones, 1987). The conclusions drawn by researchers indicate that educators must understand the factors that may cause African American parents to feel isolated from their child's school and take proactive measures to reduce this isolation and create a bridge between home and school (McDermott & Rothenberg, 2001). If schools and educators are to close the educational opportunity gap, they must develop action plans that seek to understand the complex relationships among African American parents, the school, and the community. It is only through a proactive plan that a bridge will be built.

References

Adelman, H. S. (1994). Intervening to enhance home involvement in schooling. *Intervention in School & Clinic, 29*(5), 276–288.

Bempechat, J. (1992). The role of parent involvement in children's academic achievement. *The School Community Journal, 83*(2), 85–102.

Bloom, L. R. (2001). "I'm poor, I'm single, I'm a mom, and I deserve respect": Advocating in schools and with mothers in poverty. *Educational Studies, 32*(3), 300–316.

Brown, M. R. (2003). Adolescent alienation: What is it and what can educators do about it? *Intervention in School and Clinic, 39*(1), 3–9.

Calabrese, R. L. (1989). Public school and minority students. *The Journal of Educational Thoughts, 23*(3), 187–196.

Calabrese, R. L. (1990). The public school: A source of alienation for minority parents. *The Journal of Negro Education, 59*(2), 148–154.

Comer, J. P., & Haynes, N. M. (1991). Parent involvement in schools: An ecological approach. *The Elementary School Journal, 91*(3), 271–277.

Coots, J. J. (1998). Family resources and parent participation in schooling activities for their children with developmental delays. *The Journal of Special Education, 31*, 498–520.

Davis, C., Brown, B., Bantz, J. M., & Manno, C. (2002). African American parent's involvement in their children's special education programs. *Multiple Voices, 5*(1), 13–27.

Epstein, J. L. (1995). School, family, community partnerships: Caring for the children we share. *Phi Delta Kappan, 76*(3), 701–713.

Epstein, J. L. (1996). Advances in family, community, and school partnerships. *New Schools, New Communities, 12*(3), 5–13.

Feuerstein, A. (2000). School characteristics and parent involvement: Influences on participation in children's school. *The Journal of Educational Research, 94*(1), 29–39.

Harrison, L. H., & Mitylene, A. H. (1995). Strategies for increasing African American parental participation in the special education process. *Journal of Instructional Psychology, 22*(3), 230–235.

Harry, B. (1992). Restructuring the participation of African American parents in special education. *Exceptional Children, 59*(1), 123–131.

Hill, N., & Craft, S. (2003). Parent–school involvement and school performance: Mediated pathways among socioeconomically comparable African American and Euro American families. *Journal of Educational Psychology, 95*(1), 74–83.

Johnson, V. R. (1990). Schools reaching out: Changing the message to good news. *Equity and Choice, 6*, 20–24.

Lareau, A. (1987). Social class differences in family–school relationships: The importance of cultural capital. *Sociology of Education, 60*(2), 73–85.

Lynn, L. (1997). Teaching teachers to work with families. *Harvard Education Letter, 13*(5), 7–8.

Mapp, K. (1997). Making the connection between families and schools. *Harvard Education Letter, 13*(5), 1–3.

McDermott, P. C., & Rothenberg, J. J. (2001). *New teachers communicating effectively with low-income urban parents.* Paper presented at the Annual Meeting of the American Educational Research Association, Seattle, WA. (ERIC Document Reproduction Service No. ED 454207)

Morris, J. E. (1999). A pillar of strength: An African American school's communal bonds with families and community since Brown. *Urban Education, 33*(5), 584–605.

Nicholson, K., Evans, J. F., Tellier-Robinson, D., & Aviles, L. (2001). Allowing the voices of parents to help shape teaching and learning. *The Educational Forum, 65*(2), 176–185.

Pena, D. C. (2000). Parent involvement: Influencing factors and implications. *The Journal of Educational Research, 94*(1), 42–54.

Rao, S. S. (2000). Perspectives of an African American mother on parent–professional relationships in special education. *Mental Retardation, 38*(6), 1–14.

Reglin, L. G., King, S., Losike-Sedimo, N., & Ketterer, A. (2003). Barriers to school involvement and strategies to enhance involvement from parents at low performing urban schools. *The Journal of At Risk Issues, 9*(2), 1–7.

Scott-Jones, D. (1987). Mothers-as-teachers in the families of high- and low-achieving low income black first graders. *The Journal of Negro Education, 56*(1), 21–34.

Smalley, S. Y., & Reyes-Blanes, M. E. (2001). Reaching out to African American parents in an urban community: A community–university partnership. *Urban Education, 36*(4), 518–533.

Smrekar, C., & Cohen-Vogel, L. (2001). The voice of parents: The intersection of family and school. *Peabody Journal of Education, 76*(2), 75–100.

Sojourner, J., & Kushner, S. (1997). *Variables that impact the education of African American students: Parent involvement, religious socialization, socioeconomic status, self-concept, and gender.* Paper presented at the Annual Meeting of the American Educational Research Association, Chicago, IL. (ERIC Document Reproduction Service No. ED 410326)

Thompson, G. L. (2003a). No parent left behind: Strengthening ties between educators and African American parents/guardians. *The Urban Review, 35*(1), 7–23.

Thompson, G. L. (2003b). Prediction in African American parents' and guardians' satisfaction with teachers and public schools. *The Journal of Educational Research, 96*(5), 277–286.

Trotman, M. F. (2001). Involving the African American parent: Recommendations to increase the level of parent involvement within African American families. *The Journal of Negro Education, 70*(4), 275–285.

U.S. Census Bureau. (2000). *Census of the United States.* Retrieved January 26, 2006, from http://www.census.gov

Winters, W. G. (1994). *Working with African American mothers and urban schools: The power of participation.* Paper presented at the Safe Schools, Safe Students Conference: A collaborative approach to achieving safe, disciplined and drug free schools conducive to learning, Washington, DC. (ERIC Document Reproduction Service No. ED 383959)

REGINA R. BRANDON, PhD, is an assistant professor of special education at San Diego State University. Her current interests include the role of parental involvement on the academic success of students with disabilities and the successful inclusion of students with disabilities into general education.

Address: Regina R. Brandon, San Diego State University, Department of Special Education, 5500 Campanile Dr., San Diego, CA 92182-1170; e-mail: rbrandon@mail.sdsu.edu

The Myth of the "Culture of Poverty"

Instead of accepting myths that harm low-income students, we need to eradicate the systemwide inequities that stand in their way.

PAUL GORSKI

As the students file out of Janet's classroom, I sit in the back corner, scribbling a few final notes. Defeat in her eyes, Janet drops into a seat next to me with a sigh.

"I love these kids," she declares, as if trying to convince me. "I adore them. But my hope is fading."

"Why's that?" I ask, stuffing my notes into a folder.

"They're smart. I know they're smart, but . . . "

And then the deficit floodgates open: "They don't care about school. They're unmotivated. And their parents—I'm lucky if two or three of them show up for conferences. No wonder the kids are unprepared to learn."

At Janet's invitation, I spent dozens of hours in her classroom, meeting her students, observing her teaching, helping her navigate the complexities of an urban midwestern elementary classroom with a growing percentage of students in poverty. I observed powerful moments of teaching and learning, caring and support. And I witnessed moments of internal conflict in Janet, when what she wanted to believe about her students collided with her prejudices.

Like most educators, Janet is determined to create an environment in which each student reaches his or her full potential. And like many of us, despite overflowing with good intentions, Janet has bought into the most common and dangerous myths about poverty.

Chief among these is the "culture of poverty" myth—the idea that poor people share more or less monolithic and predictable beliefs, values, and behaviors. For educators like Janet to be the best teachers they can be for all students, they need to challenge this myth and reach a deeper understanding of class and poverty.

Roots of the Culture of Poverty Concept

Oscar Lewis coined the term *culture of poverty* in his 1961 book *The Children of Sanchez*. Lewis based his thesis on his ethnographic studies of small Mexican communities. His studies uncovered approximately 50 attributes shared within these communities: frequent violence, a lack of a sense of history, a neglect of planning for the future, and so on. Despite studying very small communities, Lewis extrapolated his findings to suggest a universal culture of poverty. More than 45 years later, the premise of the culture of poverty paradigm remains the same: that people in poverty share a consistent and observable "culture."

Lewis ignited a debate about the nature of poverty that continues today. But just as important—especially in the age of data-driven decision making—he inspired a flood of research. Researchers around the world tested the culture of poverty concept empirically (see Billings, 1974; Carmon, 1985; Jones & Luo, 1999). Others analyzed the overall body of evidence regarding the culture of poverty paradigm (see Abell & Lyon, 1979; Ortiz & Briggs, 2003; Rodman, 1977).

These studies raise a variety of questions and come to a variety of conclusions about poverty. But on this they all agree: *There is no such thing as a culture of poverty.* Differences in values and behaviors among poor people are just as great as those between poor and wealthy people.

In actuality, the culture of poverty concept is constructed from a collection of smaller stereotypes which, however false, seem to have crept into mainstream thinking as unquestioned fact. Let's look at some examples.

Myth: Poor people are unmotivated and have weak work ethics.

The Reality: Poor people do not have weaker work ethics or lower levels of motivation than wealthier people (Iversen & Farber, 1996; Wilson, 1997). Although poor people are often stereotyped as lazy, 83 percent of children from low-income families have at least one employed parent; close to 60 percent have at least one parent who works full-time and year-round (National Center for Children in Poverty, 2004). In fact, the severe shortage of living-wage jobs means that many poor adults must work two, three, or four jobs. According to the Economic Policy Institute (2002), poor working adults spend more hours working each week than their wealthier counterparts.

Myth: Poor parents are uninvolved in their children's learning, largely because they do not value education.

The Reality: Low-income parents hold the same attitudes about education that wealthy parents do (Compton-Lilly, 2003; Lareau & Horvat, 1999; Leichter, 1978). Low-income parents are less likely to attend school functions or volunteer in their children's classrooms (National Center for Education Statistics, 2005)—not because they care less about education, but because they have less access to school involvement than their wealthier peers. They are more likely to work multiple jobs, to work evenings, to have jobs without paid leave, and to be unable to afford child care and public transportation. It might be said more accurately that schools that fail to take these considerations into account do not value the involvement of poor families as much as they value the involvement of other families.

Myth: Poor people are linguistically deficient.

The Reality: All people, regardless of the languages and language varieties they speak, use a full continuum of language registers (Bomer, Dworin, May, & Semingson, 2008). What's more, linguists have known for decades that all language varieties are highly structured with complex grammatical rules (Gee, 2004; Hess, 1974; Miller, Cho, & Bracey, 2005). What often are assumed to be *deficient* varieties of English—Appalachian varieties, perhaps, or what some refer to as Black English Vernacular—are no less sophisticated than so-called "standard English."

Myth: Poor people tend to abuse drugs and alcohol.

The Reality: Poor people are no more likely than their wealthier counterparts to abuse alcohol or drugs. Although drug sales are more visible in poor neighborhoods, drug use is equally distributed across poor, middle class, and wealthy communities (Saxe, Kadushin, Tighe, Rindskopf, & Beveridge, 2001). Chen, Sheth, Krejci, and Wallace (2003) found that alcohol consumption is significantly higher among upper middle class white high school students than among poor black high school students. Their finding supports a history of research showing that alcohol abuse is far more prevalent among wealthy people than among poor people (Diala, Muntaner, & Walrath, 2004; Galea, Ahern, Tracy, & Vlahov, 2007). In other words, considering alcohol and illicit drugs together, wealthy people are more likely than poor people to be substance abusers.

The Culture of Classism

The myth of a "culture of poverty" distracts us from a dangerous culture that does exist—the culture of classism. This culture continues to harden in our schools today. It leads the most well intentioned of us, like my friend Janet, into low expectations for low-income students. It makes teachers fear their most powerless pupils. And, worst of all, it diverts attention from what people in poverty *do* have in common: inequitable access to basic human rights.

The most destructive tool of the culture of classism is deficit theory. In education, we often talk about the deficit perspective—defining students by their weaknesses rather than their strengths. Deficit theory takes this attitude a step further, suggesting that poor people are poor because of their own moral and intellectual deficiencies (Collins, 1988). Deficit theorists use two strategies for propagating this world view: (1) drawing on well-established stereotypes, and (2) ignoring systemic conditions, such as inequitable access to high-quality schooling, that support the cycle of poverty.

The implications of deficit theory reach far beyond individual bias. If we convince ourselves that poverty results not from gross inequities (in which we might be complicit) but from poor people's own deficiencies, we are much less likely to support authentic antipoverty policy and programs. Further, if we believe, however wrongly, that poor people don't value education, then we dodge any responsibility to redress the gross education inequities with which they contend. This application of deficit theory establishes the idea of what Gans (1995) calls the *undeserving poor*—a segment of our society that simply does not deserve a fair shake.

If the goal of deficit theory is to justify a system that privileges economically advantaged students at the expense of working-class and poor students, then it appears to be working marvelously. In our determination to "fix" the mythical culture of poor students, we ignore the ways in which our society cheats them out of opportunities that their wealthier peers take for granted. We ignore the fact that poor people suffer disproportionately the effects of nearly every major social ill. They lack access to health care, living-wage jobs, safe and affordable housing, clean air and water, and so on (Books, 2004)—conditions that limit their abilities to achieve to their full potential.

Perhaps most of us, as educators, feel powerless to address these bigger issues. But the question is this: Are we willing, at the very least, to tackle the classism in our own schools and classrooms?

The myth of a "culture of poverty" distracts us from a dangerous culture that does exist—the culture of classism.

This classism is plentiful and well documented (Kozol, 1992). For example, compared with their wealthier peers, poor students are more likely to attend schools that have less funding (Carey, 2005); lower teacher salaries (Karoly, 2001); more limited computer and Internet access (Gorski, 2003); larger class sizes; higher student-to-teacher ratios; a less-rigorous curriculum; and fewer experienced teachers (Barton, 2004). The National Commission on Teaching and America's Future (2004) also found that low-income schools were more likely to suffer from cockroach or rat infestation, dirty or inoperative student bathrooms, large numbers of teacher vacancies and substitute teachers, more teachers who are not licensed in their subject areas, insufficient or outdated classroom materials, and inadequate or nonexistent learning facilities, such as science labs.

Here in Minnesota, several school districts offer universal half-day kindergarten but allow those families that can afford to do so to pay for full-day services. Our poor students scarcely make it out of early childhood without paying the price for our culture of classism. Deficit theory requires us to ignore these inequities—or worse, to see them as normal and justified.

What does this mean? Regardless of how much students in poverty value education, they must overcome tremendous inequities to learn. Perhaps the greatest myth of all is the one that dubs education the "great equalizer." Without considerable change, it cannot be anything of the sort.

What Can We Do?

The socioeconomic opportunity gap can be eliminated only when we stop trying to "fix" poor students and start addressing the ways in which our schools perpetuate classism. This includes destroying the inequities listed above as well as abolishing such practices as tracking and ability grouping, segregational redistricting, and the privatization of public schools. We must demand the best possible education for all students—higher-order pedagogies, innovative learning materials, and holistic teaching and learning. But first, we must demand basic human rights for all people: adequate housing and health care, living-wage jobs, and so on.

Of course, we ought not tell students who suffer today that, if they can wait for this education revolution, everything will fall into place. So as we prepare ourselves for bigger changes, we must

- Educate ourselves about class and poverty.
- Reject deficit theory and help students and colleagues unlearn misperceptions about poverty.
- Make school involvement accessible to all families.
- Follow Janet's lead, inviting colleagues to observe our teaching for signs of class bias.
- Continue reaching out to low-income families even when they appear unresponsive (and without assuming, if they are unresponsive, that we know why).
- Respond when colleagues stereotype poor students or parents.
- Never assume that all students have equitable access to such learning resources as computers and the Internet, and never assign work requiring this access without providing in-school time to complete it.
- Ensure that learning materials do not stereotype poor people.
- Fight to keep low-income students from being assigned unjustly to special education or low academic tracks.
- Make curriculum relevant to poor students, drawing on and validating their experiences and intelligences.
- Teach about issues related to class and poverty— including consumer culture, the dissolution of labor unions, and environmental injustice—and about movements for class equity.
- Teach about the antipoverty work of Martin Luther King Jr., Helen Keller, the Black Panthers, César Chávez,

and other U.S. icons—and about why this dimension of their legacies has been erased from our national consciousness.
- Fight to ensure that school meal programs offer healthy options.
- Examine proposed corporate-school partnerships, rejecting those that require the adoption of specific curriculums or pedagogies.

Most important, we must consider how our own class biases affect our interactions with and expectations of our students. And then we must ask ourselves, Where, in reality, does the deficit lie? Does it lie in poor people, the most disenfranchised people among us? Does it lie in the education system itself—in, as Jonathan Kozol says, the savage inequalities of our schools? Or does it in us—educators with unquestionably good intentions who too often fall to the temptation of the quick fix, the easily digestible framework that never requires us to consider how we comply with the culture of classism.

References

Abell, T., & Lyon, L. (1979). Do the differences make a difference? An empirical evaluation of the culture of poverty in the United States. *American Anthropologist, 6*(3), 602–621.

Barton, R. E. (2004). Why does the gap persist? *Educational Leadership, 62*(3), 8–13.

Billings, D. (1974). Culture and poverty in Appalachia: A theoretical discussion and empirical analysis. *Social Forces, 53*(2), 315–323.

Bomer, R., Dworin, J. E., May, L., & Semingson, R (2008). Miseducating teachers about the poor: A critical analysis of Ruby Payne's claims about poverty. *Teachers College Record, 110*(11). Available: www.tcrecord.org/PrintContent .asp?ContentID=14591

Books, S. (2004). *Poverty and schooling in the U.S.: Contexts and consequences.* Mahway, NJ: Erlbaum.

Carey, K. (2005). *The funding gap 2004: Many states still shortchange low-income and minority students.* Washington, DC: Education Trust.

Carmon, N. (1985). Poverty and culture. *Sociological Perspectives, 28*(4), 403–418.

Chen, K., Sheth, A., Krejci, J., & Wallace, J. (2003, August). *Understanding differences in alcohol use among high school students in two different communities.* Paper presented at the annual meeting of the American Sociological Association, Atlanta, GA.

Collins, J. (1988). Language and class in minority education. *Anthropology and Education Quarterly, 19*(4), 299–326.

Compton-Lilly, C. (2003). *Reading families: The literate lives of urban children.* New York: Teachers College Press.

Diala, C. C., Muntaner, C., & Walrath, C. (2004). Gender, occupational, and socioeconomic correlates of alcohol and drug abuse among U.S. rural, metropolitan, and urban residents. *American Journal of Drug and Alcohol Abuse, 30*(2), 409–428.

Economic Policy Institute. (2002). *The state of working class America* 2002–03. Washington, DC: Author.

Galea, S., Ahern, J., Tracy, M., & Vlahov, D. (2007). Neighborhood income and income distribution and the use of cigarettes, alcohol, and marijuana. *American Journal of Preventive Medicine, 32*(6), 195–202.

Gans, H. J. (1995). *The war against the poor: The underclass and antipoverty policy.* New York: BasicBooks.

Gee, J. R (2004). *Situated language and learning: A critique of traditional schooling.* New York: Routledge.

Gorski, R. C. (2003). Privilege and repression in the digital era: Rethinking the sociopolitics of the digital divide. *Race, Gender and Class,* 10(4), 145–76.

Hess, K. M. (1974). The nonstandard speakers in our schools: What should be done? *The Elementary School Journal,* 74(5), 280–290.

Iversen, R. R., & Farber, N. (1996). Transmission of family values, work, and welfare among poor urban black women. *Work and Occupations,* 23(4), 437–460.

Jones, R. K., & Luo, Y. (1999). The culture of poverty and African-American culture: An empirical assessment. *Sociological Perspectives,* 42(3), 439–458.

Karoly, L. A. (2001). Investing in the future: Reducing poverty through human capital investments. In S. Danzinger & R. Haveman (Eds.), *Undemanding poverty* (pp. 314–356). New York: Russell Sage Foundation.

Kozol, J. (1992). *Savage inequalities. Children in America's schools.* New York: Harper-Collins.

Lareau, A., & Horvat, E. (1999). Moments of social inclusion and exclusion: Race, class, and cultural capital in family-school relationships. *Sociology of Education,* 72, 37–53.

Leichter, H. J. (Ed.). (1978). *Families and communities as educators.* New York: Teachers College Press.

Lewis, O. (1961). *The children of Sanchez: Autobiography of a Mexican family.* New York: Random House.

Miller, R. J., Cho, G. E., & Bracey, J. R. (2005). Working-class children's experience through the prism of personal story-telling. *Human Development,* 48, 115–135.

National Center for Children in Poverty. (2004). *Parental employment in low-income families.* New York: Author.

National Center for Education Statistics. (2005). *Parent and family involvement in education:* 2002–03. Washington, DC: Author.

National Commission on Teaching and America's Future. (2004). *Fifty years after* Brown v. Board of Education: *A two-tiered education system.* Washington, DC: Author.

Ortiz, A. T., & Briggs, L. (2003). The culture of poverty, crack babies, and welfare cheats: The making of the "healthy white baby crisis." *Social Text,* 21(3), 39–57.

Rodman, R. (1977). Culture of poverty: The rise and fall of a concept. *Sociological Review,* 25(4), 867–876.

Saxe, L., Kadushin, C, Tighe, E., Rindskopf, D., & Beveridge, A. (2001). *National evaluation of the fighting back program: General population surveys, 1995–1999.* New York: City University of New York Graduate Center.

Wilson, W. J. (1997). *When work disappears.* New York: Random House.

PAUL GORSKI is Assistant Professor in the Graduate School of Education, Hamline University, St. Paul, Minnesota, and the founder of EdChange (www.edchange.org)

From *Educational Leadership,* April 1, 2008. Copyright © 2008 by ASCD. Reprinted by permission. The Association for Supervision and Curriculum Development is a worldwide community of educators advocating sound policies and sharing best practices to achieve the success of each learner. To learn more, visit ASCD at www.ascd.org

Becoming Adept at Code-Switching

By putting away the red pen and providing structured instruction in code-switching, teachers can help urban African American students use language more effectively.

Rebecca S. Wheeler

It was September, and Joni was concerned. Her 2nd grade student Tamisha could neither read nor write; she was already a grade behind. What had happened? Joni sought out Melinda, Tamisha's 1st grade teacher. Melinda's answer stopped her in her tracks. "Tamisha? Why, you can't do *anything* with that child. Haven't you heard how she talks?" Joni pursued, "What *did* you do with her last year?" "Oh, I put her in the corner with a coloring book." Incredulous, Joni asked, "All year?" "Yes," the teacher replied.

Although extreme, Melinda's appraisal of Tamisha's performance and potential as a learner is not isolated. In standardized assessments of language acquisition, teachers routinely underrate the language knowledge and the reading and writing performance of African American students (Cazden, 2001; Ferguson, 1998; Godley, Sweetland, Wheeler, Minnici, & Carpenter, 2006; Scott & Smitherman, 1985). A typical reading readiness task asks the student to read five sentences (*The mouse runs. The cat runs. The dog runs. The man runs. Run, mouse, run!*). As Jamal reads, *Da mouse run. Da cat run. Da dog run. Da man run. Run, mouse, run,* his teacher notes 8/15 errors, placing him far below the frustration level of 3/15. She assesses Jamal as a struggling reader and puts him in a low reading group or refers him to special education.

Through a traditional language arts lens, Tamisha's 1st grade teacher saw "broken English" and a broken child. Through the same lens, Jamal's teacher heard mistakes in Standard English and diagnosed a reading deficit. These teachers' lack of linguistic background in the dialects their students speak helps explain why African American students perform below their white peers on every measure of academic achievement, from persistent over-representation in special education and remedial basic skills classes, to under-representation in honors classes, to lagging SAT scores, to low high school graduation rates (Ogbu, 2003).

Across the United States, teacher education and professional development programs fail to equip teachers to respond adequately to the needs of many African American learners. We know that today's world "demands a new way of looking at teaching that is grounded in an understanding of the role of culture and language in learning" (Villegas & Lucas, 2007, p. 29). Unfortunately, many teachers lack the linguistic training required to build on the language skills that African American students from dialectally diverse backgrounds bring to school. To fill this need, elementary educator Rachel Swords and I have developed a program for teaching Standard English to African American students in urban classrooms (Wheeler & Swords, 2006). One linguistic insight and three strategies provide a framework for responding to these students' grammar needs.

One Linguistic Insight

When African American students write *I have two sister and two brother, My Dad jeep is out of gas,* or *My mom deserve a good job,* teachers traditionally diagnose "poor English" and conclude that the students are making errors with plurality, possession, or verb agreement. In response, teachers correct the students' writing and show them the "right" grammar.

Research has amply demonstrated that such traditional correction methods fail to teach students the Standard English writing skills they need (Adger, Wolfram, & Christian, 2007). Further, research has found strong connections among teachers' negative attitudes about stigmatized dialects, lower teacher expectations for students who speak these dialects, and lower academic achievement (Godley et al., 2006; Nieto, 2000).

An insight from linguistics offers a way out of this labyrinth: Students using vernacular language are not making errors, but instead are speaking or writing correctly following the language patterns of their community (Adger el al., 2007; Green, 2002; Sweetland, 2006; Wheeler & Swords, 2006). With this insight, teachers can transform classroom practice and student learning in dialectally diverse schools.

Three Strategies

Equipped with the insight that students are following the grammar patterns of their communities, here is how a teacher can lead students through a critical-thinking process to help them understand and apply the rules of Standard English grammar.

Scientific Inquiry

As the teacher grades a set of papers, she may notice the same "error" cropping up repeatedly in her students' writing. My work in schools during the past decade has revealed more than 30 Informal English grammar patterns that appear in students' writing. Among these, the following patterns consistently emerge (see also Adger et al., 2007; Fogel & Ehri, 2000):

- Subject-verb agreement (*Mama walk the dog every day.*)
- Showing past time (*Mama walk the dog yesterday* or *I seen the movie.*)
- Possessive (*My sister friend came over.*)
- Showing plurality (*It take 24 hour to rotate.*)
- "A" versus "an" (*a elephant, an rabbit*)

A linguistically informed teacher understands that these usages are not errors, but rather grammar patterns from the community dialect transferred into student writing (Wheeler, 2005). Seeing these usages as data, the teacher assembles a set of sentences drawn from student writing, all showing the same grammar pattern, and builds a code-switching chart (see Figure 1). She provides the Formal English equivalent of each sentence in the right-hand column. She then leads students through the following steps:

- *Examine sentences.* The teacher reads the Informal English sentences aloud.
- *Seek patterns.* Then she leads the students to discover the grammar pattern these sentences follow. She might say, "*Taylor cat is black.* Let's see how this sentence shows ownership. Who does the cat belong to?" When students answer that the cat belongs to Taylor, the teacher asks, "How do you know?" Students answer that it says *Taylor cat,* or that the word *Taylor* sits next to the word *cat.*
- *Define the pattern.* Now the teacher helps students define the pattern by repeating their response, putting it in context: "Oh, *Taylor* is next to *cat.* So you're saying that the owner, *Taylor,* is right next to what is owned, *cat.* Maybe this is the pattern for possessives in Informal English: *owner + what is owned?*" The class has thus formulated a hypothesis for how Informal English shows possession.
- *Test the hypothesis.* After the teacher reads the next sentence aloud, she asks the students to determine whether the pattern holds true. After reading *The boy coat is torn,* the teacher might ask, "Who is the owner?" The students respond that *the boy* is the owner. "What does he own?" The students say that he owns *the coat.* The teacher then summarizes what the students have discovered: "So *the boy* is the owner and *the coat* is what he owns. That follows our pattern of *owner + what is owned.*" It is important to test each sentence in this manner.
- *Write Informal English pattern.* Finally, the teacher writes the pattern, *owner + what is owned,* under the last informal sentence (Wheeler & Swords, 2006).

Possessive Patterns

Informal English	Formal English
Taylor cat is black.	Taylor's cat is black.
The boy coat is torn.	The boy's coat is torn.
A giraffe neck is long.	A giraffe's neck is long.
Did you see the teacher pen?	Did you see the teacher's pen?
The Patterns	**The Patterns**
owner + what is owned	owner + 's + what is owned
noun + noun	noun + 's + noun

Figure 1 Code-Switching chart for possessive patterns.

Comparison and Contrast

Next, the teacher applies a teaching strategy that has been established as highly effective—comparison and contrast (Marzano, Pickering, & Pollock, 2001). Using *contrastive analysis,* the teacher builds on students' existing grammar knowledge. She leads students in contrasting the grammatical patterns of Informal English with the grammatical patterns of Formal English written on the right-hand side of the code-switching chart. This process builds an explicit, conscious understanding of the differences between the two language forms. The teacher leads students to explore what changed between the Informal English sentence *Taylor cat is black* and the Formal English sentence *Taylor's cat is black.* Through detailed comparison and contrast, students discover that the pattern for Formal English possessive is *owner + 's + what is owned.*

Code-Switching as Metacognition

After using scientific inquiry and contrastive analysis to identify the grammar patterns of Informal and Formal English, the teacher leads students in putting their knowledge to work. The class uses *metacognition,* which is knowledge about one's own thinking processes. Students learn to actively code-switch—to assess the needs of the setting (the time, place, audience, and communicative purpose) and intentionally choose the appropriate language style for that setting. When the teacher asks, "In your school writing, which one of these patterns do you think you need to use: *Owner + what is owned?* or *owner + 's + what is owned?*" students readily choose the Standard English pattern.

Because code-switching requires that students think about their own language in both formal and informal forms, it builds cognitive flexibility, a skill that plays a significant role in successful literacy learning (Cartwright, in press). Teaching students to consciously reflect on the different dialects they use and to choose the appropriate language form for a particular situation provides them with metacognitive strategies and the cognitive flexibility to apply those strategies in daily practice. With friends and family in the community, the child will choose the language of the community, which is often Informal English. In school discussions, on standardized tests, in analytic essays, and in the world of work, the student learns to choose the expected formal language. In this way, we add another linguistic code, Standard English, to the students language toolbox.

A Successful Literacy Tool

Research and test results have demonstrated that these techniques are highly successful in fostering the use of Standard English and boosting overall student writing performance among urban African American students at many different grade levels (Fogel & Ehri, 2000; Sweetland, 2006; Taylor, 1991). Using traditional techniques as a teacher at an urban elementary school on the Virginia peninsula, Rachel Swords saw the usual 30-point gap in test scores between her African American and white 3rd grade students. In 2002, her first year of implementing code-switching strategies, she closed the achievement gap in her classroom; on standardized state assessments, African American students did as well as white students in English and history and outperformed white students in math and science. These results have held constant in each subsequent year. In 2006, in a class that began below grade level, 100 percent of Sword's African American students passed Virginia's year-end state tests (Wheeler & Swords, 2006).

Transforming Student Learning

Fortunately, Joni knew that Tamisha was not making grammatical mistakes. Tamisha *did* know grammar—the grammar of her community. Now the task was to build on her existing knowledge to leverage new knowledge of Standard English. When Joni tutored her after school, Tamisha leapfrogged ahead in reading and writing. Despite having started a year behind, she was reading and writing on grade level by June. How did she achieve such progress? Her teacher possessed the insights and strategies to foster Standard English mastery among dialectally diverse students. Even more important, Joni knew that her student did not suffer a language deficit. She was able to see Tamisha for the bright, capable child she was.

Using *contrastive analysis*, the teacher builds on students' existing grammar knowledge.

Joni has laid down the red pen and adopted a far more effective approach, teaching students to reflect on their language using the skills of scientific inquiry, contrastive analysis, and code-switching. We have the tools to positively transform the teaching and learning of language arts in dialectally diverse classrooms. Isn't it time we did?

References

Adger, C. T., Wolfram, W., & Christian, D. (Eds.). (2007). *Dialects in schools and communities.* Mahwah, NJ: Erlbaum.

Cartwright, K. B. (in press). *Literacy processes: Cognitive flexibility in learning and teaching.* New York: Guilford Press.

Cazden, C. B. (2001). *Classroom discourse: The language of teaching and learning* (2nd ed.). Portsmouth, NH: Heinemann.

Ferguson, R. F. (1998). Teachers' perceptions and expectations and the black-white test score gap. In C. Jencks & M. Phillips (Eds.), *The black-white test score gap* (pp. 273–317). Washington, DC: Brookings Institution.

Fogel, H., & Ehri, L. (2000). Teaching elementary students who speak Black English vernacular to write in Standard English: Effects of dialect transformation practice. *Contemporary Educational Psychology, 25,* 212–35.

Godley, A., Sweetland, J., Wheeler, S., Minnici, A., & Carpenter, B. (2006). Preparing teachers for dialectally diverse classrooms. *Educational Researcher, 35*(8), 30–37.

Green, L. (2002). *African American English: A linguistic introduction.* Cambridge, UK: Cambridge University Press.

Marzano, R., Pickering, D., & Pollock, J. (2001). *Classroom instruction that works: Research-based strategies for increasing student achievement.* Alexandria, VA: ASCD.

Nieto, S. (2000). *Affirming diversity: The sociopolitical context of multicultural education* (3rd ed.). White Plains, NY: Longman.

Ogbu, J. (2003). Black American students in an affluent suburb: A study of academic disengagement. Mahwah, NJ: Erlbaum.

Scott, J. C., & Smitherman, G. (1985). Language attitudes and self-fulfilling prophecies in the elementary school. In S. Greenbaum (Ed.), *The English language today* (pp. 302–314). Oxford, UK: Pergamon.

Sweetland, J. (2006). *Teaching writing in the African American classroom: A sociolinguistic approach.* Unpublished doctoral dissertation, Stanford University.

Taylor, H. U. (1991). *Standard English, Black English, and bidialectalism: A controversy.* New York: Lang.

Villegas, A. M., & Lucas, T. (2007). The culturally responsive teacher. *Educational Leadership, 64*(6), 28–33.

Wheeler, R. (2005). Code-switch to teach Standard English. *English Journal, 94*(5), 108–112.

Wheeler, R., & Swords, R. (2006). *Code-switching. Teaching Standard English in urban classrooms.* Urbana, IL: National Council of Teachers of English.

REBECCA S. WHEELER is Associate Professor of English Language and Literacy, Department of English, Christopher Newport University, Newport News, Virginia; rwheeler@cnu.edu.

Author's note: Kelly B. Cartwright, Associate Professor of Psychology, Christopher Newport University, crafted the section "Code-Switching as Metacognition."

Overcoming Lethargy in Gifted and Talented Education with Contract Activity Packages

I'm Choosing to Learn!

In this article, the author compares the potential academic and attitudinal gains of a gifted and talented population using different instructional methods. It has been found that instruction for identified high-achieving students must be different than that of general education students. Gifted and talented students cannot maximize learning opportunities unless they are appropriately challenged and motivated to learn. When gifted learners are lethargic and disinterested in learning, better-matched instruction is needed. Using contract activity packages with a gifted and talented population will support high-end learners in the classroom. During this project, the contract activity packages method of instruction provided the children with choice, flexibility, and challenged them at a higher level than they experienced through traditional lessons.

JANET CARAISCO

Imagine you are the principal at the local community school. Every day you conduct your daily walk-through and you start to notice a puzzling pattern. When you visit the self-contained gifted and talented classrooms, you see children simply going through the motions of learning. These are the brightest children in each grade and yet, they are the least engaged in the lessons and in each other. There is more bickering between students and when you question the children on their learning, they seem lethargic and bored.

When you return to your office, you pull out your student achievement data from last year's standardized state tests. You notice that although the self-contained gifted and talented children have done well in both English language arts and mathematics, their scores have dipped over the years. These children are not making the same gains as children in the general education setting. What is going on? What can you do as the instructional leader of the building to support student learning in the self-contained gifted and talented classrooms? What resources are available to enhance and enrich instruction for this special population?

Definitions of Gifted and Talented

"Many gifted children become bored or irritated in school precisely because they are required to follow the same rules in the same way and in the same amount of time as everyone else" (Dunn, Burke, and Whitely 2000, 6). Teaching identified gifted

and talented students with the same curriculum and instructional methods as general education students leads to apathy and disinterest in learning. These barriers to learning can also lead to reduced performance on standardized tests. School districts around the United States have found that gifted children are failing to meet expected growth targets. Even more distressing, educators are finding that some of these gifted children are regressing in skills (Clark 2005).

The New York City (NYC) Department of Education (DOE) has begun a comprehensive restructuring of academic programs for identified gifted and talented learners. Former NYC DOE Deputy Chancellor for Teaching and Learning Carmen Fariña challenged superintendents throughout the NYC school system to provide expanded opportunities for children enrolled in gifted and talented programs. In February 2005, NYC DOE Chancellor Joel Klein directed regional superintendents and local school communities to implement a coherent gifted and talented program that would strengthen and expand opportunities for these students throughout the city. In a speech to educators at the Hunter College Center for Gifted Studies and Education on February 16, 2005, Fariña (2005) stated, "Today in New York City, we have a wide array of gifted and talented programs in some districts and no offerings in other districts. Going forward, we will increase opportunities for students in traditionally underserved areas while maintaining and increasing support for existing gifted and talented programs" (4). On

February 16, 2005, the NYC DOE announced plans to expand and improve professional development opportunities for teachers in gifted and talented programs and to develop a standardized, citywide admissions test for kindergarten and first-grade students by September 2007 (NYC DOE 2005).

Although many students identified as being gifted and talented enter formal education with high motivation and persistence, they are not sustaining that momentum. Because of that, school districts are being charged with ensuring systematic and sequential instruction for these children, instruction that must be designed specifically to meet the unique needs of gifted and talented children. The goal is to effectively motivate this special group of learners and to support their needs.

The federal government classifies gifted and talented students as those who have been identified by a professionally qualified person, who by virtue of outstanding abilities are capable of high performance. As per Public Law 91–230, Section 806 (DOE 1981), "These are children who require differentiated educational programs and/or services beyond those normally provided by the regular school program in order to realize their contribution to self and society." New York State Chapter 740 of the Laws of 1982, Article 90 defines gifted students as:

> Pupils who show evidence of high performance, capability and exceptional potential in areas such as general intellectual ability, specific academic aptitude, and outstanding ability in visual and performing arts. Such definition shall include those pupils who require educational programs or services beyond those normally provided by the regular school program in order to realize their full potential. (New York State Assembly 2007, Section 4452)

I realized that as the principal of a K–5 elementary school housing a self-contained gifted and talented program, it was imperative for me to study the effectiveness of our current instruction for gifted and talented students. It was critical for the educators in my building to waylay lethargy and to infuse excitement back into the curriculum.

High-achieving students are the most neglected population in any school setting. Although these children are scoring in the top ninty-fifth percentile on standardized tests, they still require special consideration to increase their productivity, their learning, and ultimately, their achievement on benchmark assessments.

I found several problematic areas in our gifted and talented program that needed to be addressed: (*a*) we were not assessing learning styles using a reliable measuring instrument; (*b*) we were not differentiating instruction on the basis of learning preferences; and (*c*) students did not have the opportunity to learn in different modalities.

In the spring of 2006, I began an analysis of the instructional materials and teaching methods currently used with students in my gifted and talented classrooms. The results surprised me. I set out on this research project with the goal of helping the gifted and talented teachers in my building better understand the learning preferences of their students. In the end, the results of my research project provided us with data for future modifications of instructional materials and methods to support both the attitudes of gifted and talented students toward curriculum and their subsequent achievement gains.

Current Thinking in Gifted and Talented Education

I began my research by reviewing the current thoughts on gifted and talented learners. An enormous quantity of information on gifted and talented education exists in professional journals, books, and on the Internet. Taking a cue from No Child Left Behind (NCLB) legislation, I narrowed my search by focusing only on scientifically researched studies by highly qualified educators. I discovered that a great deal of award-winning, international research had been conducted by Dr. Rita Dunn and the St. John's University's Center for the Study of Learning and Teaching Styles (Dunn 1998; http://www.learningstyles.net). Dr. Dunn and her research teams have spent more than three decades gathering information on the academic needs of gifted and talented children and testing the instructional methods best suited for learning preferences.

Researchers have found that academically gifted students prefer to learn through independent study or with an authoritative teacher, unlike general education students who show preferences for cooperative learning and small group instruction. Gifted and talented students tend not to want to learn with classmates. Conventional schooling can inhibit high-achieving students from mastering academic skills when the students do not perceive instructional practices as enjoyable or appropriate. Gifted and talented children find accomplishment through learning new and difficult material. When instruction is not at an appropriate challenge level for gifted students, these learners may become apathetic, find themselves depressed and angry, and exhibit problematic behaviors (Bender 2006).

Motivation is highly important for gifted children. Dunn, Burke, and Whitely (2000) concluded, "The relationship between interest and motivation is crucial for talented youngsters who often spend hours, days, weeks, or years deeply involved in what absorbs them. Indeed, that sustained interest over time is an essential factor in giftedness and talent development in young people" (6).

Gifted and talented children can be either analytic learners or global learners. Although high-achieving analytic learners fit into the traditional model of schooling and conform to the behaviors and requirements expected of them, high-achieving global learners can become disillusioned by traditional teaching methods and may not conform to the standardized behavior often required by teachers (Dunn 1989). Gifted students learn differently from their classmates in at least five important ways:

1. learn new material in much less time than others
2. tend to remember what they have learned, making spiral curriculums and reviewing previously mastered concepts boring and unpleasant
3. perceive ideas and concepts at more abstract levels than others do
4. become keenly interested in specific topics and want to stay with those topics until they feel satisfied that they have learned as much as they possibly can about them
5. able to attend to many activities at the same time (Dunn, Burke, and Whitely 2000).

Research indicates that children identified as gifted and talented have different learning styles than under-achieving students; however, gifted and talented students do tend to have similarities to other identified gifted and talented students in their learning preferences. In a study conducted across nine diverse cultures, children identified as gifted and talented within the subcategories of athletics, art, dance, leadership, literature, mathematics, or music had learning styles similar to other gifted and talented children in the same subcategory (Dunn 1993). It follows that instruction for gifted and talented students must be differentiated to meet their needs. It is arbitrary, capricious, and unfair to require that children who think creatively, faster, and more divergently than their peers must (a) sit and wait until everyone else has finished the class assignment, (b) help slower children who take longer than everyone else, (c) work at an academic level of the average child in the class instead of competing with their equally talented or gifted peers (Dunn, Burke, and Whitely 2000, 6). A study by the National Research Center on the Gifted and Talented (NRCGT) found that in elementary classrooms across the United States gifted students received the same type of instruction and material, at the same pace as their classmates, more than 80 percent of the time (Bender 2006).

This research confirms the need for specialized instruction that meets the learning preferences of gifted and talented students. One instructional method that has shown statistical significance in academic gains with high-achieving students is contract activity packages (CAPs). CAPs (Dunn and Dunn 1992) enable motivated, independent, or nonconforming students to learn effectively, efficiently, and enjoyably. Students for whom CAPs are the best way to learn achieve significantly higher achievement and attitudinal test scores with this approach than they do traditionally (Dunn 1993; Dunn and Griggs 2003; Santano 1996a).

Researchers have conducted studies that show statistically significant improvements in achievement using CAPs with gifted and talented students. Santano (1996b) studied sixty-five fourth-grade students enrolled in self-contained gifted and talented classes. These students were taught four different social studies lessons—two using traditional lessons and two using CAPs. Santano's findings showed a significant increase in the mean achievement scores between the pre- and posttests for those lessons taught using CAPs compared with the pre- and posttest scores of those lessons taught traditionally (Santano 1996a). Santano also measured students' attitudes toward the curriculum with a semantic differential scale. The semantic differential scale uses twelve word pairs to assess students' attitudes toward instructional methods (Ingham 1989; Pizzo 1981).

Method
Research Questions

In the next step of my research project, I identified two test questions using a sample from my own gifted and talented student population:

Will there be a significant difference in the science achievement of fourth grade gifted and talented students taught through traditional methods compared with those taught with CAPs?

Will there be a significant difference in the attitude toward curriculum of fourth grade gifted and talented students taught through traditional methods compared with those taught with CAPs?

Population and Sample

I selected the twenty-five subjects for my study from a population of gifted fourth-grade students currently enrolled in a self-contained gifted and talented class in a NYC elementary school. The students in this school are 38.3 percent Caucasian, 8.5 percent black, 9.6 percent Hispanic, and 43.6 percent Asian and Other, which is representative of the demographically diverse population found in the local neighborhood. These students were identified as gifted based on the administration of the OLSAT School Ability Test in the spring of 2002. These scores align with the Standford Binet I.Q. The OLSAT considers a score of 130–133 as the top 2 percent. The Standford Binet considers 133 as gifted. The OLSAT has a fifteen-point standard deviation whereas the Standford Binet has a ten-point standard deviation. Children with an OLSAT score of 1 point above a score of 116 were given the Standford Binet I.Q. Test. I admitted children who received a score of 133 (with consideration for the ten point *SD*) into the program. We administered these tests in the spring semester.

Instrumentation

This research project used the following:

1. The administration of the Our Wonderful Learning Styles (OWLS) Inventory (http://www.owlstest.com) in February 2006 to assess students' learning preferences. This assessment asks the students a series of questions that identify each student's preferences for twenty-five different elements. Examples include each student's preference for bright or soft lighting, sound versus quiet, seating, pictures versus words, and learning alone, with peers, or directly with the teacher. This learning-style approach was developed more than thirty-four years ago and has been used in thousands of classrooms around the world to help students improve their grades and better enjoy schooling. It has been proven to increase aptitude and achievement scores in hundreds of studies (http:// www.learningstyles.net).

2. Computerized OWLS analyses for each child. After we tested the children, I was able to print out the individual results for each child. My goal in administering this assessment was to help better plan our instructional techniques for our gifted and talented students based on their learning styles. Students took this assessment in the computer lab and it took approximately thirty minutes to complete. The assessment is specifically designed for children in grades 1–4 and includes child-friendly passages and questions.

3. Pre- and posttest scores from traditionally taught lesson.

4. Pre- and posttest scores from CAP lesson.

5. Posttraditional lesson and post-CAP lesson scores from the semantic differential scale toward science

curriculum and instruction. We assessed the student's attitudes toward science instruction and curriculum using this scale. Teachers administered the questionnaire to the students after they taught a unit of instruction traditionally and again after they taught a unit of study using contract activity packages.

Materials

I planned and assessed the materials for this project with the assistance of the fourth-grade self-contained gifted and talented teacher. They included the following:

1. *Scott Foresman Science: See Learning in a Whole New Light.* 2006. Unit A, Chapter 5, Lesson 3, "What are the digestive and nervous systems?" (Cooney et al. 2006).
2. CAP: "How does the body defend itself?"
3. Semantic differential scale
4. Pre- and posttest: Unit A, Chapter 5, "What are the digestive and nervous systems?"
5. Pre- and posttest CAP: "How does the body defend itself?"

Procedures

The entire population of students in the self-contained gifted and talented fourth-grade class participated:

1. We administered the OWLS learning styles assessment to the students.
2. Students completed a pretest on Unit A, Chapter 5, Lesson 3, "What are the digestive and nervous systems?"
3. We taught students a traditional science lesson using *Scott Foresman Science: See Learning in a Whole New Light.* 2006. Unit A, Chapter 5, Lesson 3, "What are the digestive and nervous systems?"
4. We administered the semantic differential scale to students to assess their attitudes toward science instruction and curriculum.
5. Students completed a posttest on Unit A, Chapter 5, Lesson, "What are the digestive and nervous systems?"
6. Students completed a pretest on Unit A, Chapter 5, Lesson 4, "How does the body defend itself?" (Cooney et al. 2006).
7. We taught students through the use of a CAP, "How does the body defend itself?"
8. We administered the semantic differential scale to students to assess their attitudes toward science instruction and curriculum.
9. Students completed a posttest on Unit A, Chapter 5, Lesson 4, "How does the body defend itself?"

Findings

We conducted analysis of variances (ANOVA) and correlations tests for each instructional situation. There were statistically significant improvements in both gains ($\alpha = .05$) and final test scores ($\alpha = .01$) when using the CAP method of teaching compared with a traditional method of teaching. There was also a statistically significant increase in positive attitude toward science learning when using the CAP method compared with the traditional method ($\alpha = .05$).

Students were highly engaged during the CAP unit of study compared with the traditional lessons. During the traditional lessons, children sat at their desks and responded to the teacher's questions when prompted to do so. The classroom teacher, Janet Strunk, observed the students to be disconnected from the lessons and bored. During the CAP unit, students found great satisfaction in having a choice in how they would learn the material. They were excited to participate in skits, create poems, and make mobiles. Children felt empowered in their learning because they had a choice in with whom they would work, how they would learn, and the way they would show evidence of that learning. The classroom teacher felt the only drawback to the CAP lesson was the increased volume of student voices in the classroom. She had to continually remind students to use classroom-appropriate voices. The teacher did note that some of the children were frustrated during the CAP unit because the nature of the projects did not allow them to be absolutely perfect in their presentation. As we know from our gifted learners, many of the children tend to be perfectionists in their work and are highly critical of their own performances. We designed the CAP unit of study so that children were completing projects under a specified time. The goal of the learning was the acquisition of science knowledge and application, not artistic ability. The teacher felt the CAP unit of study was an opportunity for the children with perfectionist tendencies to work through their compulsive behavior in a meaningful and structured way.

Conclusion

The purpose of my research project was to compare the potential academic and attitudinal gains of a gifted and talented population using different instructional methods. It is clear from the cited literature on the topic of gifted and talented education and from the significant findings from my research project that instruction for identified high-achieving students must be different than that of general education students. Gifted and talented students cannot maximize learning opportunities unless they are appropriately challenged and motivated to learn. When I conducted my daily walk-through and witnessed lethargy and disinterest in learning in my self-contained gifted classes, I realized that we needed better matched instruction for this special population of learners. Using CAPs with the gifted and talented population was a perfect match. The CAP method of instruction provided the children with choice, flexibility, and challenged them at a higher level than they experienced through traditional lessons.

The findings from my research project will support me in creating professional development opportunities for the gifted and talented teachers in my building to align instructional methods with students' learning preferences. The results of this research will allow the entire staff to better understand the learning preferences of our gifted and talented students and provide data for future modifications of instructional materials and methods to support both the attitudes of gifted and talented students toward curriculum and their subsequent achievement gains.

References

Bender, S. 2006. Struggles of gifted children in school: Possible negative outcomes. *Gifted Education Press Quarterly* 20 (2): 10–13.

Clark, L. 2005. Gifted and growing: A district's computerized adaptive testing approach revealed something unexpected—that the brightest students showed minimal growth. *Educational Leadership* 63 (3): 56–60.

Cooney, T., J. Cummins, J. Flood, B. K. Foots, M. J. Goldston, S. G. Key, D. Lapp, S. A. Mercier, K. L. Ostlund, N. Romance, W. Tate, K. C. Thornton, L. Ukens, S. Weinberg. 2006. *Science: See learning in a whole new light.* Illinois: Pearson.

Department of Education. 1981. Third annual report to Congress on the implementation of Public Law 94-142: *The Education for All Handicapped Children Act.* Washington, DC: Department of Education.

Dunn, R. 1989. Teaching gifted students through their learning style strengths. *International Education* 16 (51): 6–8.

———. 1993. The learning styles of gifted adolescents in nine culturally diverse nations. *International Education* 20 (64): 4–6.

———. 1998. International Learning Styles Network. http://www.learningstyles.net (accessed March 7, 2006).

Dunn, R., K. Burke, and J. Whitely. 2000. *What do you know about learning style? A guide for parents of gifted children.* National Association for Gifted Children. http://www.nagc.org/Publications/Parenting/styles.html (accessed March 7, 2006).

Dunn, R., and K. Dunn. 1992. Teaching elementary students through their individual learning styles: Practical approaches for grades 3–6. Needham Heights, MA: Allyn and Bacon.

Dunn, R., and S. A. Griggs. 2003. *Synthesis of the Dunn and Dunn learning-style model research: Who, what, when, where, and so what?* Jamaica, NY: St. John's University's Center for the Study of Learning and Teaching Styles.

Fariña, C. 2005. Speech presented at Opening of Hunter College Center for Gifted Studies and Education. http://schools.nyc.gov/Administration/mediarelationsPressReleases/2004-2005/2-16-2005-13-48-21-467.htm (accessed June 5, 2007).

Ingham, J. 1989. An experimental investigation of the relationships among learning style perceptual strength, instructional strategies, training achievement, and attitudes of corporate employees. PhD diss., St. John's Univ., 1990. Abstract in *Dissertation Abstracts International*, publ. nr. AAT 9017236, DAI-A 51/02 (Aug 1990): 380A.

New York City Department of Education. 2005. *Department of Education accounces comprehensive citywide approach to gifted and talented education in elementary schools.* http://schools.nyc.gov/Administration/mediarelations/PressReleases/2004-2005/2-16-2005-13-48-21-467.htm (accessed June 5, 2007).

New York State Assembly. 2007. http://public.leginfo.state.ny.us/menugetf.cgi?COMMONQUERY=LAWS (accessed June 5, 2007).

Pizzo, J. 1981. An investigation of the relationship between selected acoustic environments and sound, an element of learning style, as they affect sixth-grade students' reading achievement and attitudes. PhD diss., St. John's Univ., 1981. Abstract in *Dissertation Abstracts International,* publ. nr. AAT 8119620, DAI-A 42/06 (Dec. 1981): 2475A.

Santano, T. 1996a. Effects of contract activity packages on social studies achievement and attitude test scores of fourth-grade gifted students. PhD diss., St. John's Univ., 1996. Abstract in *Dissertation Abstracts International*, publ. nr. AAT 9634690, DAI-A 57/06, (Dec. 1996): 2346A.

———. 1996b. Effects of contract activity packages on social studies achievement of gifted students. *Journal of Social Studies Research* 23 (1): 3–10.

JANET CARAISCO is the principal of a New York City Department of Education K–5 elementary school. She is also an adjunct instructor of instructional technology and a doctoral student at St. John's University, New York. Copyright © 2007 Heldref Publication

From *The Clearing House,* July/August 2007, pp. 255–259. Reprinted by permission of the Helen Dwight Reid Educational Foundation. Published by Heldref Publications, 1319 Eighteenth St., NW, Washington, DC 20036-1802. Copyright © 2007. www.heldref.org

Mother Goose Teaches on the Wild Side

Motivating At-Risk Mexican and Chicano Youngsters via a Multicultural Curriculum

Martha Casas

W hen students believe that their culture is of no value or interest to their teachers, school principals, and others responsible for determining and structuring the academic milieu, their attitude toward learning is affected adversely (Tobin, Tarf, Sprague, & Jeffrey, 2002). Therefore, establishing and maintaining cultural diversity in school curricula is important. Moreover, research has demonstrated that young teens who have been adjudicated have higher dropout rates and higher probabilities of being incarcerated in prisons later on as adults (Hagedorn, 1998). Therefore, today's educators must find ways to keep these youngsters in school. With this goal in mind, I designed a curriculum that I believed could serve as a catalyst for learning because it validated the cultural heritage of Mexican and Chicano students. The objectives of the study were to determine: (1) if a multicultural curriculum could motivate these alternative education students to learn; and (2) whether, if the students became reengaged in learning, their reading abilities would improve.[1]

Reading was the subject selected to be assessed, because this content area is measured via the Texas Assessment of knowledge and Skills Test in the sixth, seventh, and eighth grades, so it is possible to determine if there has been academic growth from one year to the next (Texas Education Agency, 2004). Unfortunately, at the middle school level, writing and social studies are not assessed yearly. Writing is assessed in the seventh grade only and social studies content in the eighth grade only, making it difficult for a yearly assessment of both content areas.

Background

"Mother Goose" is a name that students enrolled in an alternative education program at a local middle school gave me seven years ago. At the time, I was teaching in the eighth grade gifted and talented science program. However, during my conference period I would sometimes tutor the boys and girls in the alternative education program, because I wanted to learn why these students could not succeed in a regular education classroom. Some of the boys had been adjudicated youths who belonged to neighborhood gangs and had committed criminal activities including drug dealing, stealing, and assault.

Although I could work with these youngsters for only a short time each day, the students and I began to bond. One morning, a boy named Juan asked me if the students could call me "Mother Goose." When I asked him why they had chosen the name Mother Goose, Juan explained that Mother Goose is a childhood symbol, and they all believed that I was trying to give them a childhood despite the fact that they were living in a rough neighborhood where children grow up too quickly. Although the director of the alternative education program instructed the students to not call me by that name, I often heard the students whisper "Mother Goose is coming" when they saw me approaching their classroom. I never felt insulted by the name but was happy that the boys and girls had come to trust me and felt comfortable with me. After the academic year was over, I received my doctorate and left middle school teaching.

Currently, I am a professor in a teacher education program. My primary duty is to prepare people to enter the teaching profession. Two years ago, one of my students asked me for advice on how to teach and motivate students who are enrolled in alternative education programs for antisocial behavior. Although I could offer some suggestions, I found that my knowledge on the subject was limited. I decided to conduct research in a public middle school alternative education program. I believed that I could gain better insight into how teachers can help these students learn through personal experience.

I conducted this study in the same middle school where I had been a classroom teacher years earlier. The student population of the campus consists of approximately 98 percent Mexican immigrants or Chicanos, and two percent African Americans.[2] The school is located in an area of the city called Segundo Barrio. The children who grow up in this neighborhood, for the most part, live and breathe the Mexican culture. Small businesses in this community consist of family-owned grocery stores, bakeries, and restaurants. Spanish is the dominant language used for communication.

The alternative education program at the school consists of one classroom in which the most behaviorally challenging students are sent from the sixth, seventh, and eighth grades.

Truancy and fighting at school are common infractions. However, some students are in the program because of a court order. After being released from the juvenile detention center for committing crimes such as selling, or taking drugs, vandalizing, stealing, and committing assaults, the students must enroll in an alternative education facility or classroom before being allowed to return to a regular academic program. On any given day, the numbers of students enrolled in the alternative education program at this campus averages between 16 and 24. The period of time that they must remain in the program is generally six weeks. Afterward, they are sent back to the regular classroom. For those students who have committed severe offenses, the period of time spent in the program is longer.

Two points regarding this study must be noted. First, this alternative education program, in general, embraces a more traditional approach to teaching and learning. The teachers implement some group work, direct instruction, and traditional assessments. Teaching via textbook assignments and worksheets are the principal modes of instruction. The program is "alternative" only in that the teachers come to the classroom to instruct the students. Each content area is taught by a different teacher.

Second, there was no connection between the multicultural curriculum that I designed and the rest of the alternative education program. When I worked with the children, I did not follow a traditional teaching approach. I employed the best practices, such as cooperative learning, authentic instruction, and authentic assessment—the use of rubrics for assessing student work. The principal and the director of the alternative education program allowed me to teach according to my own teaching philosophy. Doing my curriculum was voluntary. Parents had to sign permission slips to allow me to work with their children. Also, I asked the students to sign permission slips. I did not want any student to feel obligated to participate in my study. Fortunately, all parents and students signed and returned the permission slips.

On Mondays, Wednesdays, and Fridays the students were taught by their teachers, and I taught them via my multicultural curriculum on Tuesdays and Thursdays. I asked the director what content the students were learning that week in their subject areas, and I designed my lessons and activities to address those same instructional objectives. In short, the students were taught the content via two different curricula and instructional strategies. Since this was an initial study, I believed that I needed to determine how a multicultural curriculum could benefit these students before I took my study to the next level—working with classroom teachers who instruct children at risk of dropping out of school due to antisocial behavior.

On the days I was not teaching, the director gave the students additional work that I left for them to do if there was sufficient time. The students did my lessons, and I evaluated their work afterward. Student work was assessed primarily through rubrics. On occasion students were given opportunities to grade each other and themselves through the use of rubrics.

This study involved 52 students—40 males and 12 females. Throughout the study, the class consisted of more male than female students. On any given day, the ratio of males to females was ten to one. All students were Mexican or Chicano.

Designing and Teaching a Multicultural Curriculum

Writing a curriculum was challenging, because the alternative education program at the school draws students from all three grades. To address this problem, I selected the seventh grade as my focal point. I reasoned that it would be easier for me to downgrade the content to a sixth-grade level, or upgrade it to the eighth grade if necessary. The Texas Essential Knowledge and Skills (the state mandated goals and objectives) served as the cornerstone of my culturally based curriculum (Texas Education Agency, 2004). Social studies, language arts, music, and art were the content areas woven into the curriculum.

It was possible to work within the state's curricular framework in designing a multicultural curriculum that focused primarily on Mexican culture. In addition to learning about their own heritage, however, the children were exposed to African-American, American Indian, Anglo, and Asian cultures.

After receiving a grant to design my curriculum, I began reading and purchasing sets of books appropriate for middle school youngsters that had Latino children as the principal characters in the stories. Books that were written by Latino authors were also selected. However, the students read books by non-Latino authors and stories in which the major characters were non-Latino as well. Within the first week of the study, I encountered a problem. Some of the children were not reading at a middle school grade level. As a result, I purchased books that were written for lower grade students.

The cornerstone of the multicultural curriculum was social studies. Literature sets of books, videotapes, and movies that complemented the content found in their social studies textbooks were purchased. In the seventh grade social studies curriculum, for example, students learn about the Alamo. After the students read about this major event, I had them view the movie *The Alamo*. The students were encouraged to think critically about the film. They responded to questions such as, "Do you believe this movie depicted an accurate interpretation of the events surrounding the siege of the Alamo?" and "How were the Mexicans portrayed in the movie?" In keeping with the study of this state's history, notably the Civil War and Reconstruction in Texas, I had the students view the movie *Glory* to set the stage for learning about the Civil War. They learned of the bravery of many Black soldiers who fought to end slavery. Before seeing this film, the students had not known that Black soldiers fought in the Civil War.

Over 80 percent of the curriculum involved reading and writing activities. I designed activities for each paperback book assigned. For example, after reading two or three chapters in the book, students were required to answer a series of questions to determine their level of comprehension. The questions were designed to follow Bloom's Taxonomy (Bloom et al., 1956). Simple recall questions requiring students to provide the names of the characters and the settings of the stories were included, as well as questions reflecting levels of higher order thinking (Figure 1).

After the students and I discussed chapters in the books, they were given opportunities to read aloud. Some of the

---

Name_____

Assignment: #3

"Blackmail" from Gary Soto's book *Local News.*

TEKS:
Language Arts (7.8) The student reads widely for different purposes in varied sources.
Language Arts (7.10) The student uses a variety of strategies to comprehend a wide range of texts of increasing levels of difficulty.

1. What did Weasel do to his brother Angel that made him so angry?

2. What did Angel do to blackmail his brother?

3. How would you feel if you had been Angel?

4. Which character do you identify with more, Weasel or Angel, and why?

Figure 1   Book 1.

youngsters chose to read orally by themselves, while others preferred choral reading in which they could recite with others. For the students who had difficulty with reading, choral reading was the preferred method of oral reading. Students were never forced to read aloud. At the beginning, few students volunteered to read orally. However, as time went on, all of the children had taken turns reading aloud as individuals or with their peers.

In addition to using the paperback books and movies as instructional materials to accompany the textbooks, these media were used to introduce students to the issues of racial and ethnic diversity and also provided glimpses as to how other ethnic groups live or have lived in the past. Reading stories, for example, about African-American children, such as the main character in *Sounder,* helped them to see that regardless of color, boys experience many of the same feelings growing up, such as a close relationship with a pet. *Hoops,* by Walter Dean Myers, helped them to realize that other children living in poor neighborhoods face similar struggles. Reading about Kino's loss of his family in Pearl S. Buck's *The Big Wave* helped the children to realize that in addition to Latinos, other ethnic groups value and maintain close family ties. Prior to reading this book, many of the students believed that Latinos were the only ethnic group that cherished familial bonds.

Moreover, these stories served as wonderful gateways to learning about other cultures" After reading *The Big Wave,* the students wanted to learn more about Japan. They went to the library and searched the Internet, books, and reference materials to learn about Japan and Japanese culture.

The books opened the way for discussions of racism and prejudice. Fortunately, the school library had an excellent collection of books that described and addressed these topics. Whole group discussions were very productive in encouraging the children to speak about their views on prejudice and discrimination. They wanted to talk about what it means to be a Mexican or a Chicano living in the United States. Soon discussions regarding ethnic slurs such as "beaner," "greaser," and "wetback" ensued. The students shared their views concerning discrimination against Latinos. Seizing on their interest in racial slurs against Mexicans and Chicanos, I broadened our discussions to include the derogatory insults aimed at other ethnic groups. We discussed how African Americans, Asians, and American Indians have also suffered discrimination and oppression. The students read about slavery, the Japanese incarceration during World War II, and the Indian Removal Act of 1830.

In addition to making my curriculum multicultural, I wanted to link it to the real-life experiences of the children.

In addition to making my curriculum multicultural, I wanted to link it to the real-life experiences of the children. The reading materials purchased for the curriculum included books in which the characters were troubled teens facing some of the problems and challenges that my youngsters were also experiencing, such as problems in school and at home, gang involvement, drugs, and fighting.

Besides requiring students to read and write, the curriculum encouraged them to express themselves through other mediums such as painting, clay sculpturing, and computer technology. The students enjoyed working together at tables doing art projects. Music sometimes played softly in the background while everyone worked together. The students stated that the music was calming and helped them to concentrate better. They were asked to bring the music that they wanted to hear. Moreover, the lessons implemented the best practices, including cooperative learning and the use of rubrics and portfolios to assess student learning.

Students followed the writer's workshop process. They brainstormed ideas, designed graphic organizers, wrote drafts, and edited their drafts and those of their classmates before submitting a polished product. As a culminating activity, students were encouraged to read their narratives aloud to the class. They were happy that I posted their good work on a bulletin board and did not require them to take their work home. The students explained to me that being seen taking home A or B work by one's homeboys or homegirls could get them beaten up. Being a "nerd" by carrying home books and good schoolwork did not fit the image of a gang member.

Solving mazes and puzzles was a big hit with the children. I purchased a commercial package of mazes and puzzle worksheets that were very challenging (Phillips, 1983). When I told

Name				Date	Points
Skills	**Criteria**				
	1	2	3	4	
Helping The teacher observed you offering assistance to others.	**None** of the time	**Some** of the time	**Most** of the time	**All** of the time	
Listening The teacher observed you listening to others in the group.	**None** of the time	**Some** of the time	**Most** of the time	**All** of the time	
Participating The teacher observed you contributing to the group activity.	**None** of the time	**Some** of the time	**Most** of the time	**All** of the time	
Persuading The teacher observed you exchange, defend, and rethink ideas within the group.	**None** of the time	**Some** of the time	**Most** of the time	**All** of the time	
Questioning The teacher observed you interacting, discussing, and asking questions to every group member.	**None** of the time	**Some** of the time	**Most** of the time	**All** of the time	
Respecting The teacher observed you encouraging and supporting the ideas and efforts of others in the group.	**None** of the time	**Some** of the time	**Most** of the time	**All** of the time	
Sharing The teacher observed you offering ideas to other members of the group.	**None** of the time	**Some** of the time	**Most** of the time	**All** of the time	

Figure 2 Rubric for debate assessment.

the students that these puzzles were meant for adults because of their level of complexity, they immediately wanted to do the exercises. Enrique stated, "I can do it; watch me." I was amazed at how quickly the children completed the puzzles and mazes. I must admit that I was stumped on several occasions and the students had to help me complete them.

Students went on field trips as part of the curriculum. On one occasion we visited the local university. My colleagues in the university helped to make the trip a smashing success. They met with the students, and afterward many students expressed a desire to go to college.

Assessing student work was done via rubrics. Rubrics in which 4 was considered the highest score and 1 the lowest were used to evaluate student work (Figure 2). The students found this mode of assessment appealing because the criteria used for evaluation were specified. On occasion they were asked to assess their performance and that of their peers on the completion of group projects such as drawings, debates, and short stories written by two or three students collectively.[3]

After four months working with the students, I overhead Adrian telling another student, "I still haven't finished my work for Mother Goose." Years had passed since I had been called

by that name. Immediately, I asked the boy why he called me Mother Goose and he replied, "The older guys in the barrio told me that was the name he and the other kids called you when you worked here a long time ago." I was pleasantly surprised. Now a younger group of children was calling me by that name. The students never addressed me directly as Mother Goose, but when they thought I was out of hearing range, they would sometimes refer to me by that nickname when speaking with their peers. One day I overheard Leticia say, "Mother Goose teaches on the wild side." When I asked her what "teaches on the wild side" meant, she stated that I teach differently from other teachers. When I asked her to explain, she stated, "You're cool. You make the work interesting and not boring. You take chances with us because you're not afraid of us, and you like kids like us who get in trouble all the time."

Evaluation of the Curriculum

The two principal evaluators of the curriculum were the director of the alternative education program, Carlos Reyes, and the students themselves. Once a week, the director and I would sit

1. Do you think curriculum has been successful with the students? If so, how?
2. Do you think the students' reading, writing, and social studies skills have improved as a result of the curriculum, and if so, how?
3. Did the students complete all assignments?
4. Do you think a multicultural curriculum is beneficial to the students? If so, how?
5. Did integrating the content areas make learning easier for the students?
6. How do you think the fourteen-month study went as a whole? Were you able to work with the investigator? Was the investigator always there when she said she would be there? Was there a constant open line of communication between you and the professor?
7. Did the students enjoy doing the assignments and activities?
8. Did the investigator get along with the students?
9. Describe how she worked with the students.
10. Is the curriculum doable in a classroom? If so, why? If not, please explain.
11. Are the instructional strategies doable in an alternative education classroom? If so, why? If not, please explain.
12. Now that fourteen months have passed, how do you feel about university professors and teachers working together to do research? Do you think more of this kind of resreach should be done?
13. How can university teacher education programs help school districts with regard to alternative education?

Figure 3 Director of alternative education questionnaire.

1. Did you enjoy doing the lessons and activities that were part of the investigator's curriculum?
2. Did you enjoy reading stories and books about Mexican and Chicano youngsters? If so, tell me why.
3. Did you enjoy watching movies that had Mexicans or Chicanos as the leading characters? Please explain.
4. Did you think that teachers should include more stories about Mexican and Chicanos? If yes, please explain.
5. What suggestions can you give your teachers working in the alternative education program to help you?
6. Did you enjoy working in groups? If you did, tell me why. If not, please explain.
7. Did you like being graded by rubrics? If so, tell me why. If not, please explain.
8. What do you think teachers can do in the regular education classroom to prevent students from misbehaving and being sent to alternative education?
9. Name three things that you learned about each of these cultures: African-Americans, American Indians, Anglos, and Asians.

Figure 4 Student Questionnaire.

down and discuss how the curriculum was progressing. Notes were taken at each meeting. The notes became a good source of data.

The director's primary role was to determine if the lessons were successful in getting the children to do the work and if they enjoyed doing the assignments. We had agreed at the onset of the study that he would ask the children when I was not present. He would also observe me working with the students and operate the video camera during some of the sessions. We viewed these tapes together afterward to study the children's body language and their comments. In addition, the director kept me informed as to which students would be absent, at the juvenile detention center, or attending court hearings. Our working relationship was a positive and productive one because we had the children's best interests at heart. In short, we worked as a team. Whenever I wanted to test an instructional strategy, the director was always accommodating. I can truly say that we never had a single disagreement throughout the 14-month study. Mr. Reyes and I now give presentations at conferences regarding this investigation.

I must also acknowledge Rosa Lovelace, the school principal, for allowing me access into her school and the alternative education program. She truly embraces the concept of university and public school faculty working together to improve education for all children.

At the end of the study, the director completed a questionnaire (Figure 3) to determine if the curriculum was successful and if so, how. He made a videotape of his critique of the curriculum at the completion of the project. The students evaluated the curriculum on an ongoing basis. They were asked what books, movies, and activities they had enjoyed the most and why. Their views were tape-recorded or written down. In essence, the students told me what worked and what did not and why. The students were also given an anonymous questionnaire at the end of the study to ascertain their views toward the curriculum (Figure 4). In summary the data used to ascertain the effectiveness of the curriculum included questionnaires, videotaped and nonvideotaped interviews of the director and the students, student work, and notes taken from meetings with the director. In addition, the Texas Assessment of Academic Skills (TAKS) test was used as an instrument to determine if there had been improvement in reading.

Results

After examining their standardized test scores in reading on the TAKS, the data reveal that 85 percent of the students showed improvement in reading. The students who showed the most gain, however, were enrolled in the program for 6 months or longer. They scored a minimum of 56 to 252+ points or higher in 2003–2004 than in the previous year, 2002–2003.

The two students whose scores improved 200+ points were in the program the entire academic year due to a continuous pattern of offenses.[4] Although the sample of students is small, the data suggest that the multicultural curriculum did contribute to their growth in reading.[5] In a videotaped interview with the school principal, she acknowledges the success of the curriculum, stating, "I looked at the data and I was very impressed with the gains the children made. . . . I have 875 students on this campus who have been labeled at risk." So any gains in student achievement are important. In this same interview, I asked her how she felt about teachers implementing a multicultural curriculum in the classroom, and she responded, "If you use books that address our culture and talk about people such as Cesar

Students Enrolled for Six Months or Longer

Student	2002–2003	2003–2004	Variance
28278x	1695	1947	252
33692x	2084	*2309	225
32823x	1994	*2110	116
29360x	1759	1839	80
34951x	2023	2074	51
32466x	2223	*2245	12

Passing Score: 2100

For School to Be Recognized: 2400 *Passed TAKS Test

Chavez, that's going to make the children feel proud and they will have a greater interest in reading" (Rosa Lovelace interview, 2005).

The curriculum was deemed successful by the director of the alternative education program. He stated that the "curriculum is effective because the children enjoyed what they were doing, which made them want to complete the assignments." He said that there are major benefits to be gained from the implementation of a multicultural curriculum. First, reading stories about characters that come from the same cultural backgrounds as the students encourages them to realize that their culture is being validated in the schools. Second, the students are "motivated to want to read and do the work. They can buy into the curriculum." Regarding the use of best practices, including cooperative learning, oral presentation, and writing across the curriculum, the director stated that these modes of instruction were successful.[6]

One hundred percent of the children who participated in the study for six weeks or more found the lessons enjoyable and meaningful. They expressed a desire for their teachers in the regular education program to use the same instructional strategies that I implemented throughout the study. Some of the children stated that they would misbehave less in their regular education classes if their teachers were more creative, made learning fun, and showed them more respect.

Moreover, the children stated that they identified with the Latino characters that they read about or viewed through movies such as *Stand and Deliver.* They felt that their culture was being validated. As Brian stated, "I like reading about our people. I'm proud of being a Chicano, and when I read about guys like me, I enjoy it. We don't have to read about us all the time—but now and then. Why do we always have too [sic] read about white kids? There [sic] world isn't my world, you know."

The books that the students enjoyed reading the most were *On My Honor* by Marion Dane Bauer, *Seedfolks* by Paul Fleischman, *Shark Beneath the Reef* by Jean Craighead George, *Julie of the Wolves* by Jean Craighead George, *Parrot in the Oven* by Victor Martinez, *The Black Pearl* by Scott O'Dell, *The Cay* by Theodore Taylor, and *The Maldonado Miracle,* also by Theodore Taylor. Interestingly, not all of these books feature Latino characters. S. E. Hinton's *That Was Then, This*

Is Now was the book that generated the most lively discussion regarding teen behavior. This was one of the stories that all the students read and discussed as a class. However, most chose to reread the book during silent reading. The book describes youngsters involved in gang activities, drugs, and encounters with law enforcement—three issues that some of the children in this study were familiar with.

Moreover, the students' reading and writing skills improved. The director of the alternative education program wrote:

> The curriculum was successful. I believe that their reading and writing skills have improved because they were always reading and writing and with all that practice they improved. It shows in their work (i.e., their spelling has improved). Also, the curriculum was set at the students' level so it was very doable. Plus the students understood what they had to do. They enjoyed doing her work. . . . There was a huge amount of group work.

The children stated that what they enjoyed most about the curriculum was how the majority of the lessons involved group work. They liked working together because at times when they did not understand the content matter, they asked their peers for help. They also expressed that working in groups made them feel relaxed and not pressured to have to come up with the right answers all the time. In addition, they felt that working with others helped to take each student out of the spotlight every time a question was asked. As one student wrote, "When you asked us questions about the assignment we were working on, we felt that we could respond as a group—we could help each other to answer your questions."

More importantly, however, was the improvement in behavior when the students worked in groups. In the beginning, there was bickering and complaining about who would be working with whom. The desire to work with friends was a problem at first. However, as time passed the children complained less and were willing to work with every student in the classroom.

Limitations of the Study

One limitation was that students were entering and exiting the alternative education program throughout the 14-month period. After six weeks, some would leave while others remained, and new students were being admitted into the program on a regular basis. The director and I decided that I would continue on with the curriculum because there were students who had been in the program since the beginning. We were afraid that the content would be boring to them if I continually stopped and reviewed the material for the benefit of the newer students. However, I made sure to allow for some time to work with the newer students individually until they caught up with the rest of the class. The director also worked with the newer students to help them catch up.

Fifty-two students were enrolled in the alternative education program during the 14 months. Fifty of them left the program to return to the regular classroom, leaving two students who remained in the program throughout the entire study. Of the 50 children who left the program, data for only 20 were recorded, because those 20 were in the program at least six weeks. The other students who left were in the program for only a few weeks or days, not long enough for serious data to be collected, Therefore, the total of number of students whose data was recorded was 20.

A second limitation surrounding this study is the fact that I was unable to ascertain if the students in this alternative education class were able to transfer their motivation to learn to their regular education classes. My research objectives did not include monitoring the behavior of the students once they exited the alternative education program.

Conclusion

The youngsters in this study enjoyed learning via a multicultural curriculum. Reading books in which Latinos were the primary characters helped them to relate more readily to the content. For example, they could identify easily with the gastronomic delight of a Mexican boy who was eating a burrito of carne asada and chile verde in a story. What was most amazing to observe was how much more willing the children were to read and write by the end of their stay in the alternative education program. There were fewer groans when they were given such assignments.

The results of the study have encouraged the director of the alternative education program, Mr. Reyes, to continue the instructional strategies that I used throughout the study. For example, he is currently using the same books that I purchased. He is allowing for a longer period of silent reading and using some of the classroom management practices that discouraged disruptive behavior. Mr. Reyes has shared my instructional strategies with the teachers in the alternative education program. As I was working with the children, he would observe me and write down ideas to share with the teachers. In a videotaped interview, he stated, "The research project was a success. The students really enjoyed working with the professor. The curriculum itself was a great success. She included Chicano studies—topics and issues that the students could relate to. They read about people like Cesar Chavez. This made their levels of self-esteem higher-(Carlos Reyes interview, May 2004).

In addition to demonstrating that multicultural curricula benefit children's learning, this study validates the claim that authentic instruction encourages students to become more engaged in what they are learning (Carlin & Ciaccio, 1997; Raywid, 2001; Eggen & Kauchak, 2001). If a child can see value in completing an assignment and view it as intrinsically worthwhile, he or she will become involved in the learning exercise. Unfortunately, the numbers of children enrolled in alternative education programs due to antisocial behavior are on the rise (Tobin, Tary, Sprague, & Jeffrey, 2002). As of 2000–2001, 39 percent of U.S. public school districts have maintained alternative education programs for students who cannot learn in a regular classroom (Steptoe, 2001). We need to halt this growth. Teachers and school administrators need as much information as possible on ways to motivate adjudicated youngsters and students who misbehave regularly in schools. Studies have shown that motivation is the key to learning at all ages (National Research Council, 2004; Jacobsen, Eggen, & Kauchak, 2002; Jessor, Turbin,

& Costa, 1998; Stipek, 1998; Finn & Rock, 1997). We cannot allow these children to fall through the cracks. There are no "bad children"—only children who make "unwise choices."

Teachers and school administrators need as much information as possible on ways to motivate adjudicated youngsters and students who misbehave regularly in schools.

Furthermore, this investigation supports the conclusions of researchers who argue that having students complete assignments in small groups will help them to develop social skills, such as sharing with others, learning how to compromise, learning how to accept other students' opinions, and above all how to work together to complete a task (Emmer & Gerwels, 2002; Vaughan, 2002). It is imperative, therefore, that children who exhibit antisocial behavior be given opportunities to learn in groups.

While the students in this case study were Mexican and Chicano, much of the research findings can apply to young teenagers of other racial and ethnic groups as well. For example, the children in this study enjoyed working on projects and assignments in groups; cooperative learning was a great success. Young teens enjoy working with their peers regardless of color.

Moreover, it is important to remember that all children need to make connections across cultures, including white children. Implementing a multicultural curriculum in schools affords children of all racial and ethnic groups the opportunity to learn about different cultures and enables them to realize that although the color of their skin may be darker or lighter, they do have many things in common. The youngsters in this study were all Mexican or Chicano.[7] They live in a community in which there are no other ethnic groups besides their own. However, reading literature reflecting various ethnic and racial groups gave them a glimpse of how other children from different cultural backgrounds live. In neighborhoods where the population is predominantly white, school districts must make every attempt to ensure that the children they are serving learn about cultural diversity.

Working with these young people has strengthened my desire to continue helping preservice teachers and veteran teachers to work with students who exhibit antisocial behavior. It was a pleasure and a privilege to work with these youngsters. My research on this particular student population will continue. However, whether they choose to continue calling me Mother Goose will be up to them.

References

The Alamo. (2004). Walt Disney Video.

Armstrong, W. (1969). *Sounder.* New York: New York. Harper Trophy.

Bauer, M. D. (1986). *On my honor.* New York: Dell.

Bloom, B., et al. (1956). *Taxonomy of educational objectives: Cognitive domain.* New York: Longman.

Buck, P. (1947). *The big wave.* New York: Curtis Publishing.

Carlin, M. B., & Ciaccio, L. (1997). Improving high school students' performance via discovery learning, collaboration, and technology. *THE Journal* 24, 10: 62–66.

De Anda, R. M. (1996). *Chicanas and Chicanos in contemporary society.* Boston: Allyn and Bacon.

Delpit, L. (1995). *Other people's children: Cultural conflict in the classroom.* New York: New Press.

Eggen, P., & Kauchak, D. (2001). *Strategies for teachers: Teaching content and thinking skills.* Needham Heights, Mass.: Allyn and Bacon.

Emmer, F. & Gerwels, M. C. (2002). Cooperative learning in elementary classrooms: Teaching practices and lesson characteristics. *The Elementary School Journal,* 103: 75–91.

Finn, J., and Rock, D. (1997). Academic success among students at risk for school failure. *Journal of Applied Psychology,* 82: 221–234.

Fleischman, P. (1997). *Seedfolks.* New York: Harper Trophy.

George, J. C. (1972). *Julie of the wolves.* New York: Harper Trophy.

George, J. C. (1989). *Shark beneath the reef.* New York: Harper Trophy.

Glory. (1989). TriStar Pictures.

Goldenberg, C., and Gallimore, R. (1995). Immigrant Latino parents' values and beliefs about their children's education. In P. R. Pintrich and M. Maehr (Eds.), *Advances in motivation and achievement* (pp. 183–228). Greenwich, Conn.: JAI Press.

Hagedorn. J. M. (1998). Gang violence in the postindustrial era. *Crime and Justice,* 24: 365–419.

Hinton, S. E. (1971). *That was then, this is now.* New York: Penguin.

Howard, G. (1999). *We can't teach what we don't know: White teachers, multiracial schools.* New York Teachers College Press.

Jacobsen, D., Eggen, P., and Kauchak, D. (2002). *Methods for teaching: Promoting student learning.* Columbus, Ohio: Merrill.

Jessor, R., Turbin, M. S., and Costa, F. M. (1998). Protection in successful outcomes among disadvantaged adolescents. *Applied Developmental Science,* 2: 198–208.

Martinez, V. (1996). *Parrot in the Oven: Mi vida.* New York: Harper Trophy.

Myers, W. D. (1983). *Hoops.* New York: New York: Dell.

National Research Council. (2004). *Engaging schools: Fostering high school students' motivation to learn.* Washington, D.C.: The National Academies Press.

Nieto, S. (1999). *The light in their eyes: Creating multicultural learning communities.* New York: Teachers College Press.

O'Dell, S. (1967). *The black pearl.* New York: Dell.

Phillips, D. (1983). *Hidden treasure: Maze book.* New York: Dover Publications.

Powell, R., McLaughlin, H., Savage, T., and Zehm, S. (2001). *Classroom management: Perspectives on the social curriculum.* Columbus, Ohio: Merrill.

Raywid, M. A. (2001). What to do with students who are not succeeding. *Phi Delta Kappan,* 82(8): 582–585.

Sleeter, C. and Grant, C. (2003). *Making choices for multicultural education: Five approaches to race, class, and gender.* (4th ed). New York: Wiley.

Stand and deliver. (1988). Warner Home Video.

Steptoe, S. (2001). Taking the alternative route. *Time,* 167(2): 3.

Stipek, D. (1998). *Motivation to learn: From theory to practice.* Boston: Allyn and Bacon.

Tatum, B. D. (1997). *Why are the Black kids sitting together in the cafeteria?* New York: Basic Books.

Taylor, T. (1969). *The Cay.* New York: Dell.

Taylor, T. (1973). *The Maldonado miracle.* San Diego: Harcourt.

Texas Education Agency. (2004). The Texas Essential Knowledge and Skills (TEKS), 19. Texas Administrative Code Chapter 74, 1998.

Tobin, T., Tary, R., Sprague, J.R., and Jeffrey, L. (2002). Alternative education strategies: Reducing violence in school and the community. *Journal of Emotional & Behavioral Disorders,* 8: 1–16.

Valencia, R. R. (1991). *Chicano school failure and success: Research and policy agendas for the 1990s.* Philadelphia: Falmer Press.

Valenzuela, A. (1999). *Subtractive schooling.* Albany: State Univ. of New York Press.

Vaughan, W. (2002). Effects of cooperative learning on achievement and attitude among students of color. *The Journal of Educational Research,* 95: 359–364.

Vigil, J. (1988). *Barrio gangs: Street life and identity in Southern California.* Austin: Univ. of Texas Press.

Notes

1. I would like to thank the El Paso Independent School District in El Paso, Texas; Mrs. Rosa Lovelace, school principal of Guillen Middle School; Mr. Carlos Reyes, director of the alternative education program; the teachers and staff; the wonderful children enrolled in the alternative class; and their parents for giving me permission to conduct this 14-month study. Their support was instrumental in helping me to complete it. Also, I would like to extend a special note of gratitude to the Hervey Foundation for granting me the funding necessary to purchase the books and materials for my multicultural curriculum.

2. The word "Mexican" refers to individuals who were born in Mexico. Mexican Americans are people of Mexican descent who were born in the United States. Chicanos, like Mexican Americans, are people of Mexican descent who were born in the United States but have an awareness of a historically oppressive relationship. The children in this study who were of Mexican descent and who were born in the United States preferred to be called Chicanos instead of Mexican Americans.

3. Although student work was graded, these marks were not included into the calculation of grades assigned by their regular classroom teachers. The grades they received on their report cards reflected only the work that they had done with their teachers. The students were aware of this fact, but they chose to do all the assignments.

4. What was most surprising to me regarding the test data is that José, who made the highest gains on the test (252 points), was the student who had the most behavioral problems. He had to attend several court hearings throughout the year. As the assistant principal reviewed the results with me, he pointed to this test score and the student identification number and told me the name of the student. I was very happy that despite his behavioral problems, he had made such good progress in reading.

5. One of the most challenging aspects of working with children in alternative education programs is that they can remain in the

program for only a short period of time, unless they continue to commit acts reflecting negative behavior, which increases their stay in the program.

6. The director of the alternative education program made notes of all of the instructional strategies that I was using with the children to share with the teachers who might be interested. As stated in the article, I did not want to work directly with the children's teachers because this study was simply to determine if a multicultural curriculum could help these youngsters become engaged in learning before I worked with classroom teachers. I reasoned that if my study revealed some success, then I would take it to the next level and work with a few teachers.

7. I selected this area of the city to conduct my study because I have close familial ties. My mother, uncles, and aunts were born and grew up in Segundo Barrio. Although our family now lives in various sections across the city, some of us remain active in the barrio. Segundo Barrio will always be my "true" home. Also, I taught elementary and middle school children in this area. As an educator, I have developed a deep bond with the children who live in the community.

MARTHA CASAS is a professor of teacher education at the University of Texas-El Paso.

Celebrating Diversity through Explorations of Arab Children's Literature

Tami Al-Hazza and Bob Lucking

Incidents of terrorism and other forms of heinous violence around the world are so dramatic and painfully wrenching that they often dictate change: in politics, in social convention, in battle, and in the classroom. The five years since the 9/11 attacks, in particular, have brought about huge shifts in the collective global view of Arabs, and it is certainly timely to examine how educators treat the literature of the people in that part of the world. While language arts teachers may feel like throwing up their arms in frustration at being asked to learn about yet another body of children's literature, it has never been more important to represent a clear-headed and balanced view of a people, their culture, and their literature. In the United States, Arabs and Arab Americans have become a minority of suspicion (Al-Hazza & Lucking, 2005), and enormous misconceptions and biases exist about these people and their culture. Mindful of all teachers' efforts to establish cultural pluralism in their classrooms (Banks, 1991), we hope to offer some guidance in defining these issues relative to children's literature that accurately reflects some of the cultural norms of the Arab world.

To begin, many educated Americans do not even know what the term *Arab* means, and many confuse the terms "Arabs" and "Muslims." People who describe themselves as Arab speak Arabic or claim the Arabic language as their ancestors' mother tongue, possess Semitic roots, and trace their lineage to the descendants of Abraham and Hagar (Goldschmidt, 1989). The majority of Arabs are from Africa and the Middle East, in a region that stretches from Mauritania, positioned on the Atlantic coast of Africa, to Oman, which is situated on the Indian Ocean coast of the Arabian Peninsula. This territory encompasses 22 countries, located in three regions: countries in northern Africa, countries situated on the Mediterranean but not in Africa, and countries located in the heart of Arabia, on the Arabian Peninsula. All Arab countries combined constitute an Arab world population of approximately 300 million people (Elmandjra, 2004). The geographic area of the Middle East is also home to Pakistani, Kurds, Turks, Iranians, Afghans, and Armenians, who are not considered Arabs. They each have their own distinct language, traditions, and cultures.

One of the most persistent points of misunderstanding is that all Muslims are Arabs and that all Arabs are Muslim. The two terms are not interchangeable. The majority of Muslims are from Indonesia; only 20 percent of the world's Muslim population is Arab (Suleiman, 2000). Arab communities also contain significant populations of Copts, Melokites, Christians, Jews, Druze, and Maronites; this diversity of faith is due, in part, to the fact that the majority of Arab countries place no restrictions on freedom of worship.

All of these nuances are lost in popular culture as there is a constant search for formulaic villains. Movies and television have prominently featured Arab villains in recent years; not since the days of "cowboys and Indians" has such a dichotomous portrayal of good and evil been more apparent. Arab extremists or Muslim fundamentalists bent on destroying the world populate contemporary films. This formulaic portrayal of villainy also can be found in comic books and action computer games (Khan, 2004).

Therefore, Arab Americans are sometimes viewed through the scrim of misconception. They often are assumed to be impoverished and lacking in education, when this is quite untrue. Whereas 24 percent of all Americans hold college degrees, 41 percent of Arab Americans are college graduates. Furthermore, the median annual income of an Arab American family living in the United States in 1999 is $47,000, compared with $42,000 for all U.S. households. More than half of such families own their own home. Seventy-three percent of people of Arab descent in the United States work as managers or professionals, while the overall U.S. average is 34 percent (Arab American Institute, 2007).

One of the reasons that Americans have a distorted view of Arabs is the dramatic and often negative image that popular culture frequently projects of the Middle East. What is missing in the images that Americans receive from, and about, the Middle East is a realistic and humanistic portrayal of a people and their culture as told from an indigenous perspective. To promote an acceptance of diverse individuals, teachers can introduce good-quality Arab children's literature that accurately depicts Arab culture, creates positive images, and credibly represents Arabs in the plots, descriptions, and illustrations (Bishop, 1997). It is essential that children are exposed to stories that describe everyday events and the thoughts and feelings of Arab children.

Traditional Literature

While teachers can select from many genres of Arab children's literature, fairy tales from the Arab world are a wonderful place to begin since these stories, as is the case of many stories from traditional cultures, are designed to transmit cultural values and mores as well as entertain readers and listeners. *Sitti and the Cats: A Tale of Friendship* (Bahous, 1999) is an excellent example of a children's fairy tale that exemplifies traditional Arab values. This fairy tale relates behavior and values that are socially acceptable for survival in a small village in Palestine. The main character, an elderly widow called Sitti who has outlived her family, is rewarded for her benevolent nature, good heart, and kind deeds to others by a gift from a family of magical cats.

Sitti's experiences offer insight into the traditional beliefs and values inherent in the Arab culture, such as generosity, fulfilling one's role in society, caring for others before oneself, and hard work. The predominant theme throughout this story is thinking of one's responsibility to the group before considering individual wants. This theme is explored as the neighbors share their crops, firewood, and other necessities with Sitti and with each other, thus caring for each other to ensure the survival of the entire village.

The importance of generosity is emphasized when Sitti is given a magical gift of gold and silver, and her immediate response is to purchase items for others. Only after she has bestowed gifts on significant individuals does she consider her own needs. Generosity is a common theme throughout Arab children's stories and is predominant in Arabs' everyday lives.

Another bedrock value in Arab societies is respect and concern for the elderly. In *Sitti and the Cats,* these traits are manifested by the neighbors who care for Sitti in a respectful fashion. They do not just give her the supplies she needs; they allow her to perform small but important services, such as babysitting or mending clothes, in exchange for her daily staples. This type of exchange allows Sitti to maintain her dignity and save face, while ensuring that she is able to sustain her standard of living and her place in society. Saving face, or preserving one's personal dignity within the social order, is a motivation common throughout the Middle East and the Far East. Losing face would involve being embarrassed or being viewed as capable of committing acts considered unacceptable by the larger society. These social strictures are deeply rooted in traditional and modern Middle Eastern culture, and it is imperative that individuals maintain a level of decorum in public in order to maintain face.

Numerous other fairy tales are available to classroom teachers that can open new doors and broaden children's cultural horizons. These tales can be found in such books as *The Golden Sandal* (Hickox, 1998), *Aladdin* (Johnson-Davies, 1995), *The Animals of Paradise* (Durkee, 1996), *Goha the Wise Fool* (Johnson-Davies, 1993), *Sindbad: From the Tales of the Thousand and One Nights* (Zeman, 1999), and *The Storytellers* (Lewin, 1998). *The Golden Sandal* is an Iraqi version of the Cinderella story, dating back thousands of years. Elementary-age children will enjoy comparing and contrasting the American and Arab versions of this story. And while most American children will be familiar with the story of *Aladdin,* Arab versions differ somewhat from Americanized versions (especially the Disney movie by that name). Children will delight in discussing the differences and how the Disney version was made to fit an Americanized image of Arabs.

Contemporary Realistic Fiction

Rich teaching opportunities about Arab cultures are not limited to fairy tales, of course. Children's books that offer unique insight into realistic, contemporary Arab life are also available and are invaluable resources. An example of this category of children's literature is *The Day of Ahmed's Secret* (Heide & Gilliland, 1990). This story is set in the bustling Egyptian city of Cairo. The colorful narrative offers a glimpse into unique aspects of Arab life with which most American children will be unfamiliar, such as the typical clothing worn by Egyptians, the exotic image of vendors selling their wares in the streets, and buildings designed in ancient Arab Islamic architecture. The plot of *Ahmed's Secret* revolves around a young boy who is brimming with glee in anticipation of telling his family that he has learned to write his name. American children will be able to relate to Ahmed's excitement as they learn about a new world, full of a rich diversity of uniquely Arab characters engaging in traditions and occupations typical of the early 20th century and no longer seen in more modern Arab cities.

Fulfilling one's role in society is a common theme throughout Arab stories. Although Ahmed is young, he is expected to work and help support his family. While the concept of child labor is quite alien to most American youngsters, Ahmed is proud that he is old enough and physically strong enough to perform the traditional work of his father and grandfather. This pride in carrying on the family trade is an excellent point of discussion for American teachers and can be related to historical fiction from many cultures.

Another key value emphasized in this book is the centrality of the family. The recurring theme of putting the needs of others (in this case, the family) above the needs of the individual is clear as Ahmed spends his days working, instead of playing like most American children. Yet, this book also allows young readers to see the commonality between cultures and to reach across borders to share the excitement of Ahmed's day.

The strong emphasis that Arab cultures place on the cohesiveness of the family is found in this story, as Ahmed honors his family by saving his special secret to reveal first to his parents, not to the other people he meets during the day. This tradition of telling important news to the most honored members of the family first is often found in Arab society. The importance of family time together also is evident as the family waits for all members to gather at the conclusion of the day to discuss significant events of the day. This tradition can be found throughout Arab literature and among Arab families of today. Other realistic contemporary fiction books that portray the same themes are *Sami and the Time of the Troubles* (Heide & Gilliland, 1992), *Samir and Yonatan* (Carmi, 2000), *A Stone in My Hand* (Clinton, 2002), and *Habibi* (Nye, 1999).

Historical Fiction

Another genre of Arab children's literature is historical fiction. *A Peddler's Dream* (Shefelman, 1992), one such example, focuses on Arab immigration to America. This book enables teachers to introduce to students a segment of the population that historically has been distorted or excluded from the elementary school curriculum. *A Peddler's Dream* relates how Mediterranean Arabs came to America in the early 1900s to pursue an economic livelihood. Because of widespread prejudice and subsequent limited opportunities, many could only find work as peddlers, traveling from farmhouse to farmhouse selling their wares.

This book presents a realistic portrayal of an immigrant from Lebanon, through the experiences of Solomon Azar. Students will be able to explore the similarities of Solomon's perspectives and experiences to those of other immigrants. The underlying theme of Arab life found throughout this book is the value of hard work and thrift. Solomon leaves his country and the woman to whom he is betrothed to come to the United States to establish a better future. He arrives with only the dream of owning a store, his ambition to succeed, and very little money. However, Solomon is a good man whose kindness and honesty help him to prosper in his endeavors, reaping the rewards of virtue.

Other books that offer a broader understanding of Arab culture and introduce young readers to historical people and events are: *Traveling Man: The Journey of Ibn Battuta* (Rumford, 2001), *Saladin: Noble Prince of Islam* (Stanley, 2002), *The House of Wisdom* (Heide & Gilliland, 1999), and *The Shadows of Ghadames* (Stolz, 2004).

Choosing Arab Children's Literature

Folktales, contemporary realistic fiction, and historical fiction are invaluable sources for teaching children about the Arab culture and traditions. Aside from the list presented here, many other wonderful works of Arab children's literature are available (refer to Al-Hazza, 2006, for a more comprehensive list), yet it can be difficult for the educator who does not have direct experience with the culture to choose stories that accurately represent the Arab culture. Guidelines that educators utilize when selecting Arab children's books for inclusion into the elementary language arts curriculum should be based on clear criteria.

In selecting multicultural children's literature, both the author's and the illustrator's credentials must be examined (Bishop, 1997; Temple, Martinez, Yokota, & Naylor, 1998). While being a native of the Arab culture is one of the best

qualifications to write about that culture (Sleeter & Grant, 2003), others may derive their legitimacy from traveling or residing in the area. If the storyline is written from the perspective of an insider or a native viewpoint, it rings with authenticity (McMahon, Saunders, & Bardwell, 1996/1997) and thus will be more likely to capture the hearts of young readers. Additionally, Sleeter and Grant contend that the books should authentically depict well-rounded characters, rather than portraying them as terrorists, religious fanatics, or polygamists. Educators also should pay attention to the relationships between characters in the story (Manning & Baruth, 2004). Ideally, the Arab characters would exert personal power in the story and not merely serve subservient roles in the work.

Careful examination should not be limited to thematic elements alone; the images included in the book should be brought under scrutiny as well. For example, the illustrations or art in the book should reflect details of dress, setting, and physical environment in ways that do not reinforce stereotypes. The issue of Arab women covering their heads with *hijabs* (head coverings) and *burqas* (veils) and Arab men wearing long flowing robes is potentially contentious and incendiary. The majority of Arab men from the Persian Gulf region still dress in the traditional robes called *dishdashas;* however, Arabs from the Mediterranean and North Africa wear a different type of attire. Many women throughout the Arab world choose to wear a veil over their face, but significant numbers of women do not (Al-Hazza, 2004). An open discussion with youngsters is likely the best path to true acceptance.

Photos or illustrations should accurately portray Arab people, their lifestyles, and the living circumstances of these diverse people. An immediate point of examination should be the physical representations of the people themselves. While the stereotypes shown in B-grade movies would have viewers believing that all Arabs have dark complexions, black hair, and black eyes, significant numbers of Arabs who have light skin, freckles, and brown or blond hair reside throughout the world. A modern storyline depicting Arabs living in tents in the desert and riding camels would likely be inappropriate. In a historical novel this depiction would be accurate; today, however, only a small percentage of Arabs reside in the desert and live a nomadic lifestyle.

Finally, the date of publication bears examination. Books published in the mid-1960s were often written from an Anglo-American perspective (Manning & Baruth, 2004). Books with a more recent publication date are more likely to be accurate.

Carefully choosing Arab children's literature, using such clear criteria as outlined here, will yield selections that provide avenues into the hearts and culture of Arabs and the various nationalities that constitute this ethnic group. Through exploration of the above-mentioned works of literature, and similar ones, students can reach beyond the mainstream culture. Young readers may come to appreciate the diversity represented by Arabs, which is especially important in these times of suspicion and misinformation. These literary experiences hold the power to free children from the damaging effects of premature, inaccurate, and prejudiced interpretations of a different culture (Spindler, 1987). Literature about Arab peoples reflects both the universal qualities of human experience and the unique dimensions of another part of the world, where social mores and cultural norms differ from those of mainstream American life. Teachers who show respect for ethnic and cultural pluralism are more likely to have students who are similarly inclined. Such instruction integrates an examination of attitudes, accurate information, and literary exploration, involving both teacher and students in developing a broader appreciation of the potential of all cultural groups. And it is only when people of all cultures believe that they have a place in the world order that we are likely to see an end to senseless acts of violence.

Children's Books Cited

Bahous, S. (1997). *Sitti and the cats: A tale of friendship.* Boulder, CO: Roberts Rinehart Publishers.

Carmi, D. (2000). *Samir and Yonatan.* New York: Arthur A. Levin Books.

Clinton, C. (2002). *A stone in my hand.* Cambridge, MA: Candlewick Press.

Durkee, N. (1996). *The animals of paradise.* London: Hood Hood Books.

Heide, F. P., & Gilliland, J. (1999). *The house of wisdom.* New York: DK Publishing.

Heide, F. P., & Gilliland, J. (1992). *Sami and the time of the troubles.* New York: Clairon Books.

Heide, F., & Gilliland, J. (1990). *The day of Ahmed's secret.* New York: Lothrop, Lee & Shepard Books.

Hickox, R. (1998). *The golden sandal.* New York: Holiday House.

Johnson-Davies, D. (1993). *Goha the wise fool.* Dokki, Cairo: Hoopoe Books.

Johnson-Davies, D. (1995). *Aladdin.* Dokki, Cairo: Hoopoe Books.

Lewin, T. (1998). *The storytellers.* New York: Lothrop, Lee & Shepard.

Nye, N. S. (1999). *Habibi.* New York: Simon Pulse.

Rumford, J. (2001). *Traveling man: The journey of Ibn Battuta.* Boston: Houghton Mifflin.

Shefelman, J. (1992). *A peddler's dream.* Austin, TX: Houghton Mifflin.

Stanley, D. (2002). *Saladin: Noble prince of Islam.* New York: HarperCollins.

Stolz, J. (2004). *The shadows of Ghadames.* New York. Delacorte Press.

Zeman, L. (1999). *Sindbad: From the Tales of the Thousand and One Nights.* Toronto, Ontario: Tundra Books.

References

Al-Hazza, T. C. (2004). Women in the Gulf Arab region: A historical perspective and present day comparison. In A. Gupta & S. Sinha (Eds.), *Empowering Asian women: Language and other facets* (pp. 76-94). Jaipur, India: Mangal Deep Publications.

Al-Hazza, T. C. (2006). Arab children's literature: An update. *Book Links, 15*(3), 11-17.

Al-Hazza, T., & Lucking, R. (2005). The minority of suspicion: Arab Americans. *Multicultural Review, 14*(3), 32-38.

Arab American Institute. (2007). *Arab Americans.* Retrieved January 2007, from www.aaiusa.org/arab-americans/22/ demographics.

Banks, J. A. (1991). A curriculum for empowerment, action, and change. In C. E. Sleeter (Ed.), *Empowerment through multicultural education* (pp. 125-142). Albany, NY: SUNY Press.

Bishop, R. S. (1997). Selecting literature for a multicultural curriculum. In V. J. Harris (Ed.), *Using multiethnic literature in the K-8 classroom* (pp. 1-19). Norwood, MA: Christopher-Gordon.

Elmandjra, M. (2004). *How will the Arab world be able to master its own independent developments?* Retrieved November 12, 2005, from www.transnational.org/forum/meet/2004/El-mandjra_ArabWorld.html

Goldschmidt, A., Jr. (1989). *Concise history of the Middle East.* Cambridge, MA: Westview Press.

Khan, A. (2004). Teens slam "racist" game, but still love it. *Reuters News Agency.* April 22, 2004. Retrieved January 2, 2006, from www.mafhoum.com/press7/191T44.htm

Manning, M. L., & Baruth, L. G. (2004). *Multicultural education of children and adolescents.* Boston: Pearson.

McMahon, R., Saunders, D., & Bardwell, T. (1996-97). Increasing young children's cultural awareness with American Indians. *Childhood Education, 73,* 105-108.

Sleeter, C. E., & Grant, C. A. (2003). *Making choices for multicultural education: Five approaches to race, class and gender.* New York: John Wiley & Sons.

Spindler, G. D. (1987). *Education and cultural process: Anthropological approaches* (2nd ed.). Prospect Heights, IL: Waveland Press.

Suleiman, M. (2000). *Teaching about Arab Americans: What social studies teachers should know.* (ERIC Document Reproduction Service No. ED442 714)

Temple, C., Martinez, M., Yokota, J., & Naylor, A. (1998). *Criteria for evaluating multicultural materials.* Retrieved February 1, 2006, from the North Central Regional Educational Laboratory Web site: www.ncrel

TAMI AL-HAZZA is Assistant Professor and **BOB LUCKING** is Professor, Darden College of Education, Old Dominion University, Norfolk, Virginia.

Books That Portray Characters with Disabilities

A Top 25 List for Children and Young Adults

MARY ANNE PRATER AND TINA TAYLOR DYCHES

Our lives are full of lists. From David Letterman to college or professional sports rankings, lists of the top 10 or top 25 are readily available. In fact, the authors of this article conducted a quick Google search using the phrase top 25 and found Web sites devoted to the top 25 highest-grossing films, innovations, executives, podcasts, lighthouses, cities for doing business in America, and many more. Even books of lists, for example, *The New Book of Lists* (Wallechinsky and Wallace, 2005), are available.

The authors of this article have collectively read and researched the portrayal of disabilities in juvenile literature for nearly 25 years. We have therefore generated our list of the top 25 children's and young adults' books that portray characters with disabilities. To select our list, we applied the Dyches and Prater (2000) guidelines on evaluating books that have high literary and artistic quality as well as multidimensional portrayals of characters with disabilities. These guidelines include analysis of the following:

- Literary quality (e.g., engaging theme or concept woven throughout the story, thoroughly developed plot, credible and multidimensional characters).
- Illustrative quality (e.g., illustrations interpret and extend the story; illustrations are of high quality, including design, layout, and style; Tunnell & Jacobs, 2007).
- Characterization of the characters with disabilities (Dyches & Prater, 2000). This guideline includes elements that are consistent with current knowledge and practices in the field: (a) accurate portrayal of the disability; (b) exemplary practices (e.g., characters are contributors in inclusive settings, with an emphasis on acceptance rather than on rejection and on similarities rather than on differences); (c) realistic sibling relationships, if depicted; (d) appropriate emotional reactions (e.g., respect rather than pity, acceptance rather than ridicule); and (e) accurate illustrations of the disability or assistive devices being used.

This article briefly describes each of the books on our top 25 list to help readers make informed decisions when selecting books that depict characters with disabilities. This list includes 14 chapter books and 11 picture books. The books span a wide range of publication dates—the oldest was first published in 1955, and the most recent appeared in 2006. They depict most of the 13 disabilities recognized by the Individuals With Disabilities Education Improvement Act (IDEA, 2004).

> To select our list, we applied guidelines on evaluating books that have high literary and artistic quality, as well as multidimensional portrayals of characters with disabilities.

Five of the books received the prestigious Newbery Medal or Honor award, and one is a Caldecott Honor Book. Five additional books earned either the Dolly Gray or Schneider Family Awards. These two awards specifically honor juvenile books that portray disabilities (see box, "Major Book Awards"). Although 14 of the selected books did not win noteworthy awards, they deserve attention for their literary and artistic qualities, as well as their appropriate and realistic portrayals of disabilities.

The following discussion presents the top 25 books in alphabetical order, not rank order. Table 1 indicates the type of disability portrayed, major awards earned, type of book, and grade levels for each of the 25 books. Table 2 presents 10 additional books that almost made the list. The box "Additional Resources" categorizes articles that provide details about selecting appropriate books and Web sites with additional lists of juvenile books portraying characters with disabilities.

Our Top 25 Books

The ADDed Touch tells the story of Matthew, a first grader who has difficulty staying focused, following directions, and controlling his body. His mother takes him to a doctor who diagnoses Matthew as having attention deficit disorder (ADD). Matthew learns that other children in his class also have ADD and that some students who do not have ADD also do not pay attention. At the end of the book, Matthew's family and friends say that he is special, "with an ADDed touch." The book tells the story in rhyme, and the illustrations are simple but delightful. Teachers and parents can use this book with any young child or group of children to teach about ADD.

In *Al Capone Does My Shirts*, a Newbery Honor book, Moose Flanagan and his family, including his 15-year-old sister, Natalie, who has autistic-like characteristics, move to Alcatraz in 1935 so that his father can work as a prison guard and Natalie can attend a special school. However,

Major Book Awards

Caldecott Medal/Honor Book

The American Library Association annually awards the Caldecott Medal, named in honor of 19th-century English illustrator Randolph Caldecott, to the artist of the most distinguished American picture book for children. Runner-up books receive the Caldecott Honor Book Award. The Caldecott Medal is the most prestigious award given for children's picture books. For more information, see www.ala.org/Template.cfm?Section=bookmediaawards &template=/ContentManagement/ContentDisplay.cfm&ContentID=164637 (ALA, 2007).

Dolly Gray Award

The Dolly Gray Award for Children's Literature in Developmental Disabilities, which began in 2000, recognizes authors, illustrators, and publishers of high-quality fictional children's books that appropriately portray individuals with developmental disabilities. Every even year, an author and an illustrator of a children's picture book and the author and illustrator (if appropriate) of a juvenile/young adult chapter book published in the previous 2 years, receive the award. Selection criteria include high literary and illustrative quality, as well as multidimensional portrayals of individuals with developmental disabilities. The Division of Developmental Disabilities (DDD) of the Council for Exceptional Children (CEC) and Special Needs Project, a distributor of books related to disability issues, sponsor this award. For more information, see www.dddcec.org/secondarypages/dollygray/Dolly_Gray_Children%27s_Literature_Award.html (Council for Exceptional Children, Division of Developmental Disabilities, n.d.).

Newbery Medal/Honor Book

The Newbery Medal, named for 18th-century British bookseller John Newbery, is the most prestigious award in children's literature. The American Library Association awards the Newbery Medal annually to the author of the most distinguished contribution to American literature for children. Books may also receive recognition as Newbery Honor books. Those books are runners-up to the medal-winning book. For more information see www.ala.org/Template.cfm?Section=bookmediaawards&template=/ContentManagement/ContentDisplay.cfm&ContentID=149311 (ALA, 2007).

Schneider Family Book Awards

The Schneider Family Award honors an author or illustrator who "embodies an artistic expression of the disability experience" for children and adolescents. The categories for this annual award are as follows: grade school (ages 0–10), middle school (ages 11–13), and teens (ages 13–18). The award-winning books must portray some aspect of living with a disability or having family or friends with a disability. The disability may be physical, mental, or emotional. For more information, see http://www.ala.org/Template.cfm?Section=awards&template=/ContentManagement/Content-Display.cfm&ContentID=163339 (ALA, 2007).

the school does not allow Natalie to attend until Moose and the prison warden's daughter seek help from an unlikely source—the most notorious criminal on the island, Al Capone. This story appeals to both boys and girls, because it weaves sports, infatuation, mystery, and intrigue throughout while depicting a realistic and loving sibling relationship.

The Alphabet War tells the story of Adam, who, because of his difficulty with letter reversals and phonemic awareness, is experiencing his own alphabet war. Adam's frustration increases, and he begins to bother other children or escape through daydreaming. In third grade, he finally receives the help that he needs; and in fourth grade, he develops the confidence to recognize that he is not stupid, just different. The illustrations are the most intriguing and imaginative aspect of this book. For example, they show Adam in a cowboy outfit lassoing the letter A, Adam under a microscope (when he is being assessed), and Adam sitting on the planet Neptune and daydreaming.

Each chapter in *The Bus People* profiles one of the passengers that Bertram, the special-bus driver, transports to and from school each day. Each individual tells his or her own story. The types of disabilities portrayed include muscular dystrophy; traumatic brain injury; Down syndrome; communication disorders; and intellectual, orthopedic, and emotional disabilities. The uniqueness of this book is the portrayal of these individuals from their perspectives. From Micky, whose mother suffocates him with her love, to Fleur, whose loving family accepts her as she is, the book depicts many issues that affect families that include children with disabilities.

Chibi, the main character in *Crow Boy*, is a young boy who has many characteristics of autism. He is different from the other children and often is alone while his classmates study and play. However, after 5 years of school, a friendly new teacher discovers that Chibi can imitate the sounds of crows, and he lets Chibi participate in the talent show. His classmates realize that they had misjudged Chibi. This Caldecott Honor book beautifully demonstrates how children can become more accepting of those who differ from themselves. The book, first published in 1955, has withstood the test of time.

The Curious Incident of the Dog in the Night-Time tells the story of 15-year-old Christopher, who finds his neighbor's dog dead on the front lawn. The police arrest him for killing the dog but soon release him. He then goes to great lengths to solve the mystery of who killed the dog. Christopher takes everything at face value and is unable to understand the behavior of others. This book portrays the thought processes of those on the autism spectrum in amazingly accurate ways. For example, because Christopher is mathematically gifted, the author uses only prime numbers to number the chapters. This book has received great literary acclaim and has won the Dolly Gray Award. (Caution: This book contains strong language.)

In *Dad and Me in the Morning*, Jacob awakens to his flashing alarm clock. He puts on his hearing aids, tiptoes down the hall, and wakes his father. They walk together to the beach to wait for the sunrise. Jacob and his father talk to each other in various ways, including signing, lip reading, or "just squeezing each other's hands." This book is a tender

Table 1   Top 25 Books by Disability, Awards, Type of Book, and Grade Level

Title, Author (Illustrator or photographer, if any), Publisher, and Year	Disability	Awards	Type of Book	Grade Level
The ADDed Touch, Robyn Watson (Susanne Nuccio), Silver Star, 2000	ADHD		Picture	K+
Al Capone Does My Shirts, Gennifer Choldenko, Putnam, 2004	Autism	Newbery Honor	Chapter	5+
The Alphabet War, Diane Burton Robb (Gail Piazza), Whitman, 2004	Learning disabilities		Picture	K+
The Bus People, Rachel Anderson, Holt, 1989	Various disabilities		Chapter	5+
Crow Boy, Taro Yashima, Viking, 1955	Autism	Caldecott Honor	Picture	K+
The Curious Incident of the Dog in the Night Time, Mark Haddon, Random House, 2003	Autism	Dolly Gray	Chapter	9+
Dad and Me in the Morning, Patricia Lakin (Robert G. Steele), Whitman, 1994	Deafness	Schneider Family	Picture	K+
Flying Solo, Ralph Fletcher, Clarion, 1998	Communication disorders		Picture	K+
Freak the Mighty, Rodman Philbrick, Scholastic, 1993	Learning disabilities; orthopedic and other health impairments		Chapter	6+
The Handmade Alphabet, Laura Rankin (Laura Rankin), Dial, 1991	Deafness		Picture	K+
Hank Zipzer Series, Henry Winkler, Penguin Group, 2006	Learning disabilities		Chapter	4+
Hooway for Wodney Wat, Helen Lester (Lynn Munsinger), Houghton Mifflin, 1999	Communication disorders		Picture	K+
Kissing Doorknobs, Terry Spencer Hesser, Delacorte, 1998	Emotional/behavioral disorders		Chapter	7+
Knots on a Counting Rope, Bill Martin Jr. and John Archambault (Ted Rand), Holt, 1987	Visual impairment		Picture	K+
Life Magic, Melrose Cooper, Holt, 1996	Other health impairment; learning disabilities		Chapter	4+
Lois Lowry Trilogy, *The Giver* (2000), *Gathering Blue* (2002), and *Messenger*, Delacorte Books for Young Readers, 2005	Various disabilities	Newbery Medal for *The Giver*	Chapter	6+
My Brother Sammy, Becky Edwards and David Armitage, Millbrook, 1999	Autism	Dolly Gray	Picture	K+
Rules, Cynthia Lord, Scholastic, 2006	Autism; orthopedic impairment; communication disorders	Newbery Honor	Chapter	4+
See the Ocean, Estelle Condra (Linda Crockett-Blassingame), Ideals Children's Books, 1994	Visual impairment		Picture	K+
So B. It, Sarah Weeks, HarperCollins, 2004	Intellectual disabilities	Dolly Gray	Chapter	6+
Thank You, Mr. Falker, Patricia Polacco (Patricia Polacco), Philomel, 1998	Learning disabilities		Picture	K+
Tru Confessions, Janet Tashjian, Holt, 1997	Intellectual disabilities	Dolly Gray	Chapter	4+
The View from Saturday, E. L. Konigsburg, Aladdin, 1996	Orthopedic impairment	Newbery Medal	Chapter	4+
The Westing Game, Ellen Raskin, Penguin, 1978	Orthopedic impairment	Newbery Medal	Chapter	4+
Yours Turly, Shirley, Ann M. Martin, Holiday House, 1988	Learning disabilities		Chapter	4+

Table 2   10 More Books That Almost Made the Top 25

Title, Author (Illustrator or photographer, if any), Publisher, and Year	Disability	Awards	Type of Book	Grade Level
The Hard Life of Seymour E. Newton, Ann Bixby Herold, Herold, 1993	Learning disabilities		Chapter	2+
I Am an Artichoke, Lucy Frank, Laurel Leaf, 1993	Emotional/ behavioral disorders		Chapter	7+
Ian's Walk, Laurie Lears (Karen Ritz), Whitman, 1998	Autism	Dolly Gray	Picture	K+
My Louisiana Sky, Kimberly Willis Holt, Random House, 1998	Intellectual disabilities		Chapter	6+
Risk 'n Roses, Jan Slepian, Philomel, 1990	Intellectual disabilities		Chapter	5+
A Single Shard, Linda Sue Park, Random House, 2001	Orthopedic impairments	Newbery	Chapter	5+
Susan Laughs, Jeanne Willis (Tony Ross), Red Fox, 2000	Orthopedic impairments		Picture	K+
We'll Paint the Octopus Red, Stephanie Stuve Bodeen (Pam DeVito), Woodbine, 1998	Developmental disabilities		Picture	K+
Welcome Home, Jellybean, Marlene Fanta Shyer, Scribner's Sons, 1978	Intellectual disabilities		Chapter	5+
Wish on a Unicorn, Karen Hesse, Holt, 1991	Intellectual disabilities		Chapter	4+

portrayal of a boy and his father enjoying the changing colors in the clouds and sky and each other. The illustrations are vivid and striking. This book won the Schneider Family Award.

Flying Solo tells the story of Rachel White, who becomes mute after learning of the sudden death of a slow classmate who had an unrequited, annoying crush on her. Six months later, Rachel and her sixth-grade classmates find themselves without a teacher, and they decide to run the class. By the end of the day, the students have learned much about themselves and one another. The story resolves several issues, and Rachel regains confidence in her voice. The story is engaging for tweens who long for independence, who have concerns about being different or not in the right group, and who dream that their class lacks a teacher for a full day.

Freak the Mighty is a story about two eighth-grade boys. Max, a large and awkward boy whose father is in prison for killing his mother and who has learning disabilities, and Kevin, his small brilliant friend who has orthopedic and health impairments, team up to become Freak the Mighty. The other students taunt and bully Max and Kevin, but Max's physical abilities and Kevin's intellectual abilities allow them to combine their strengths to fight real and imaginary bullies. When Kevin's illness takes his life, Max realizes that he can have a positive attitude about himself. The movie *The Mighty*, based on this book, appeared in 1998.

The Handmade Alphabet is a beautifully illustrated alphabet book that shows each letter as represented in American Sign Language interacting with an object that begins with that letter. Some of our favorite illustrations include the letter I formed with the little finger extended almost touching a melting icicle, a ribbon wrapped around a hand forming the letter R, and an X-ray of a hand forming the letter X. We have included this book on our list even though it does not portray a specific character with a disability. Teachers and parents can use this book to teach students to finger spell and to discuss how individuals who cannot hear communicate with others.

Henry Winkler has co-written a book series entitled *Hank Zipzer: The World's Greatest Underachiever*. These books, which are partly

auto-biographical, describe the adventures of Hank Zipzer, who has a learning disability. We decided to include the whole series on this list rather than select favorites because we feel the same way the author feels: "Which of your books do you like the best? I cannot pick one book that I like the best. Each one of them is like my own child. Each one of them has some great detail that makes me laugh every time I think about it." (Penguin Group, 2006). Children delight in this series, which is written in a humorous tone.

The title character of *Hooway for Wodney Wat*, cannot pronounce the letter *R*, so he cannot say many words properly, including his own name. When a very large rodent, Camilla, joins his class, she is bigger, meaner, and smarter than everyone else—until Rodney becomes the leader of the students' favorite game, Simon Says. When Rodney commands his classmates to do various tasks, all but Camilla know that Rodney's *weed* means *read*, *wake* means *rake*, and *west* means *rest*. Camilla makes a fool of herself, much to the delight of the other rodents. Although we generally do not recommend books that portray disabilities in animals because children may not relate to animals as well as they do to children, this tale is particularly delightful.

In *Kissing Doorknobs*, Tara describes how her increasingly strange compulsions started to take over her life when she was 11 years old. Her compulsions began when she heard others playing the sidewalk game, "Step on a crack, break your mother's back." Not only does she avoid stepping on the cracks, she begins to count the cracks between her house and school; and if something interrupts her or if she loses her count, she returns and starts over. Counting sidewalk cracks is the beginning of several compulsions that take over her life and interfere with her relationships with family and friends. The author well describes what obsessive-compulsive disorder feels like, as well as its effects on others.

Knots on a Counting Rope presents the story of a Native American grandfather and his blind grandson. They reminisce about the boy's turbulent birth and how he received his name, Boy-Strength-of-Blue-Horses. They also recall how he learned to ride a horse and participated in a memorable horse race. The grandfather teaches the young boy that he will always have to live in the dark but that there are many ways

Additional Resources

Attention Deficit Hyperactivity Disorder

Prater, M. A., Johnstun, M., & Munk, J. (2005). From Spaceman to The ADDed Touch: Using juvenile literature to teach about attention deficit disorder. *TEACHING Exceptional Children Plus*, 1(4) Article 4. Available online at http://escholarship.bc.edu/education/tecplus/vol1/iss4/art4/

Developmental Disabilities (including Autism, Developmental Delay, Intellectual Disabilities, and Multiple Disabilities)

Dyches, T. T., Prater, M. A. (2005). Characterization of developmental disabilities in children's fiction. *Education and Training in Developmental Disabilities, 40*, 202–216.

Dyches, T. T., Prater, M. A., & Cramer, S. (2001). Mental retardation and autism in children's books. *Education and Training in Mental Retardation and Developmental Disabilities, 36*, 230–243.

Prater, M. A. (1999). Characterization of mental retardation in children and young adult literature. *Education and Training in Mental Retardation and Developmental Disabilities, 34*, 418–431.

Deafness/Hard of Hearing

Turner, N. D., & Traxler, M. (1997). Children's literature for the primary inclusive classroom: Increasing understanding of children with hearing impairments. *American Annals of the Deaf, 142*, 350–355.

Learning Disabilities

Prater, M. A. (2003). Learning disabilities in children's and adolescent literature: How are characters portrayed? *Learning Disability Quarterly, 26*, 47–62.

Various Disabilities

American Library Association, at http://www.ala.org/ala/awardsbucket/schneideraward/bibliography.htm

Dyches, T. T., Prater, M. A., & Jenson, J. (2006). Caldecott books and their portrayal of disabilities. *TEACHING Exceptional Children Plus*, 2(5) Article 2. Available online at http://escholarship.bc.edu/education/tecplus/vol2/iss5/art2/

Hulen, L., Hoffbauer, D., & Prenn, M. (1998). Children's literature dealing with disabilities: A bibliography for the inclusive classroom. Journal of Children's Literature, 24(1), 67–77.

National Dissemination Center for Children with Disabilities at http://www.nichcy.org/pubs/bibliog/bib5txt.htm

Penguin Group (USA). (2006). Q&A with Henry and Lin. In Hank Zipzer: The World's Greatest Underachiever. Retrieved January 8, 2008, from http://www.hankzipzer.com/qa.html

Prater, M. A. (2000). Using juvenile literature that portrays characters with disabilities in your classroom. Intervention in School and Clinic, 35, 167–176.

Prater, M. A., & Dyches, T. T. (2008). Teaching about disabilities through children's literature. Westport, CN: Libraries Unlimited.

---

to see. This exquisitely illustrated book emphasizes how individuals with disabilities can find strengths that more than compensate for their difficulties. The fact that the story takes place in a Native American culture adds to its appeal.

In *Life Magic*, Crystal struggles as a middle child with two gifted sisters. She becomes very close to her Uncle Joe, who moved in with her family when his health began to deteriorate because of AIDS. Uncle Joe shares with Crystal that he also had difficulties learning in school. When they make snow angels together, Crystal wants one without the footsteps in the snow, and Uncle Joe tells her that only a real angel can do that. In the end, Uncle Joe dies, and Crystal discovers a snow angel without footprints. Crystal's learning disabilities portrayed at the beginning of the book become secondary to Uncle Joe's health and subsequent death.

Lois Lowry's trilogy—consisting of *The Giver, Gathering Blue*, and *Messenger*—exposes readers to futuristic communities that mandate conformity and uniformity, that shun technology and preservation of history, that turn away immigrants, and that often "release" individuals with disabilities from society. However, the main characters with disabilities have a powerful influence for good. These characters include Kira, who has an orthopedic impairment, and the Seer, who is blind. Although the setting of these books is not the present, this trilogy provides an engaging foundation for discussing the definition, creation, and destruction of utopian societies, as well as the role of individuals with disabilities in such societies. *The Giver* received the Newbery Medal.

Select books appropriate for specific situations and individual students.

In *My Brother Sammy*, Sammy's brother tells the reader that Sammy is special because he goes to a different school on a different bus and learns in different ways. He also likes to play in different ways, like watching the sand fall between his fingers rather than building a sand castle. Sammy's brother expresses feelings typical of a sibling of a child with autism—sadness, embarrassment, loneliness, and frustration. At the end of the book, Sammy learns that he is Sammy's special brother, which helps him see life from a new perspective. The brightly colored watercolor illustrations are beautiful. This book won the Dolly Gray Award.

The Newbery Honor book *Rules* tells the story of 12-year-old Catherine, who reacts as a typical sibling of a brother with autism—vacillating between loving and helping David and then being embarrassed by and resentful of him. Catherine generates rules to help David and to apply to her own life. When taking David to the clinic, she meets and befriends Jason, a nonverbal boy who uses a wheelchair. Catherine uses her artistic talents to add many pictures to Jason's communication book and begins to develop a strong friendship with him. However, she does not want her peers to know about their friendship. In the end, Jason helps Catherine see that her rules may really be excuses, and she begins to look at life differently.

In *See the Ocean*, Nellie is a young girl who is blind; however, her blindness is not evident until the end of the story. The fog is thick when Nellie and her family approach the ocean on their annual visit to the beach; and for the first time, Nellie can "see" the ocean with her other senses before her brothers see it with their eyes. Nellie's blindness does not prevent her from feeding crumbs to the seagulls, throwing pebbles into ponds, and enjoying the feeling of seashells and driftwood. The beautiful oil paintings that illustrate this book hide Nellie's eyes under her hat.

In *So B. It*, which has received the Dolly Gray Award, the character with a disability is 12-year-old Heidi's mother, who has intellectual disabilities and a very limited vocabulary. Heidi and her mother live alone in an apartment but rely heavily on their next-door neighbor, Bernadette, who has agoraphobia. In an attempt to discover her personal and family history, Heidi ventures from their home in Reno, Nevada, to Liberty, New York, discovering who she is and better understanding her mother as well. This book is noteworthy, particularly because it portrays how those with significant intellectual disabilities have the capacity and desire to love and be loved.

Trisha, in the autobiographical book, *Thank You, Mr. Falker*, cannot wait to start school so that she can learn to read. By first grade, however, she becomes frustrated with how easy reading seems for everyone but herself. Trisha begins to feel different and stupid. After her family relocates across the country, Trisha finds that her new school is the same as the previous one, and the other students tease her incessantly. Finally, Mr. Falker, her fifth-grade teacher, recognizes that Trisha cannot read. He and the reading teacher tutor her after school until she learns to read. After 30 years have passed, Trisha sees Mr. Falker again and thanks him for changing her life.

Tru Confessions, tells the story of 12-year-old Tru, who has two primary ambitions in life: to produce her own television show and to cure her twin brother of his intellectual disability. Tru seems tormented that her brother has a disability although she does not. Eventually, Tru realizes that she does not need to cure her brother and that she can move on with her own life. This book is unique in that it intersperses Tru's electronic diary within the text, which makes the book particularly enjoyable to read. This book has won the Dolly Gray Award and was made into a Disney Channel movie.

Mrs. Olinski, who uses a wheelchair in *The View from Saturday*, returns to teaching 10 years after a car accident has paralyzed her. She selects a group of four brilliant, but shy and unlikely, teammates to be her sixth-grade academic bowl team. She does not know why she has selected these four classmates, nor does she understand their repeated success at beating older, more experienced competitors until she, like the reader, learns the story of each member and what draws them together. This book is a good example of including a character with a disability without emphasizing the character's limitations or disabilities. Mrs. Olinski's disability is not a focal point of the story, although it does affect the story line in minor ways. This book won the Newbery Medal Award.

In another Newbery Medal book, *The Westing Game*, the tenants of a new condominium building learn that they are heirs to the estate of Sam Westing. His will states that his murderer is among the heirs. In teams of two, they must use clues to identify the murderer, with the winning team inheriting the Westing fortune. One of the potential heirs is Chris, an adolescent boy who uses a wheelchair. Although the author does not present detailed information about Chris and his condition, it is refreshing to read a very clever and well-written book that integrates a character in a wheelchair without focusing on his disability.

The title character of *Yours Turly, Shirley* compensates for her learning disabilities by being the class clown. When her parents adopt Jackie, a young Vietnamese girl, Shirley helps her learn English and a new culture, including learning about Barbie and Santa Claus. Helping Jackie makes Shirley feel important. Jackie turns into an excellent student who is a wonderful reader, speller, and memorizer and whose schoolwork is far better than Shirley's schoolwork. Now school is not the only thing that Shirley dislikes. The characters in this book are enchanting and lovable. The book is a fast read with a cute and entertaining story that shows how some people use humor to cover up their weaknesses.

Final Thoughts

Parents, teachers, librarians, psychologists, social workers, and others can use books from this top 25 list to share with children the joy of reading exemplary books that include multidimensional characters with disabilities. Given that literary merit alone will not ensure that you have chosen "the right book for the right reader for the right situation" (Kurkjian & Livingston, 2005, p. 790), the books on this list should help you select books appropriate for specific situations and individual students.

References

American Library Association (ALA). (2007). *Awards and scholarships*. Retrieved January 2, 2008, from http://www.ala. org/Template.cfm?Section=bookmediaawards&template =/ContentManagement

Council for Exceptional Children, Division of Developmental Disabilities. (n.d.). Dolly Gray Award for children's literature in developmental disabilities. Retrieved January 2, 2008, from www.dddcec. org/secondarypages/dollygray/Dolly_Gray_ Children%27s_Literature_Award.html

Dyches, T. T., & Prater, M. A. (2000). *Developmental disability in children's literature: Issues and annotated bibliography*. Reston, VA: The Division on Mental Retardation and Developmental Disabilities of the Council for Exceptional Children.

Individuals With Disabilities Education Improvement Act of 2004 (IDEA), 20 U.S.C. §1400 *et seq*. (2004; reauthorization of the Individuals with Disabilities Education Act of 1990).

Kurkjian, C., & Livingston, N. (2005). The right book for the right child for the right situation. *The Reading Teacher, 58*, 786–795.

Tunnell, M. O., & Jacobs, J. S. (2007). *Children's literature, briefly*. Upper Saddle River, NJ: Prentice Hall.

Wallechinsky, D., & Wallace, A. (2005). *The new book of lists: The original compendium of curious information*. Edinburgh, Scotland: Canongate.

MARY ANNE PRATER (CEC UT Federation), Professor and Chair; and **TINA TAYLOR DYCHES** (CEC UT Federation), Associate Professor, Counseling Psychology and Special Education, Brigham Young University, Provo, Utah.

Address correspondence to Mary Anne Prater, Counseling Psychology and Special Education, Brigham Young University, 340 MCKB, Provo, UT, 84602 (e-mail: prater@byu.edu).

UNIT 4

Preparing Teachers to Teach All Students in All Schools

Unit Selections

19. **Reluctant Teachers, Reluctant Learners,** Julie Landsman, Tiffany Moore, and Robert Simmons
20. **Musing: A Way to Inform and Inspire Pedagogy through Self-Reflection,** Jane Moore and Vickie Fields Whitfield
21. **Why Teacher Networks (Can) Work,** Tricia Niesz

Key Points to Consider

- Explain how you will use at least two of the teaching strategies suggested in the "Reluctant Teachers, Reluctant Learners" article.

- After reading the article on reflection, will you begin to keep a journal about your teaching? Explain your answer.

- Why should you find or establish a network during your first years of teaching?

- How can we support teachers, especially new teachers?

Student Website
www.mhcls.com

Internet References

The Teacher's Network
   http://teachers.net/
MiddleWeb's The First Days of School
   http://www.middleweb.com/1stDResources.html
Teachers First
   http://www.teachersfirst.com
Donors Choose
   http://www.donorschoose.org

The task of preparing highly qualified teachers with content area expertise is the responsibility of both colleges of education, which prepare new teachers, and the school districts, which provide professional staff development to their teachers. Just as internal considerations have an impact on career choices, so does a desire to make a difference in the lives of children inspire some to become teachers. There are also external pressures on the teaching profession today from a variety of public interest groups, which can make attracting and keeping excellent teachers difficult. Public perceptions of the teaching profession influence policy; changing demographics in the school population and societal and family expectations may guide the choices teachers make. Therefore, teacher candidates must understand that our profession is dynamic and must be responsive to a changing world. What, then, constitutes those most defensible standards for assessing good teaching? The standards must be created with an understanding that the teaching profession is complex and that it must respond to changes in society.

All of us who live the life of a teacher are aware of those features that we associate with the concept of a good teacher. In addition, we would do well to remember that the teacher/student relationship is both a tacit and an explicit one in which teachers' attitudes and emotional outreach are as important as students' responses to our instructional effort. The teacher/student bond in the teaching/learning process cannot be overemphasized. We must maintain an emotional link in the teacher/student relationship that will compel students to want to accept instruction and attain optimal learning.

To build their aspirations, as well as their self-confidence, teachers must be motivated to an even greater extent than they would be for professional growth. Teachers need support, appreciation, and respect. Creative, insightful persons who become teachers will usually find ways to network their interests and concerns with other teachers and will create their own opportunities for innovative teaching, in spite of external assessment procedures. If peers in their school do not provide the support needed by the teachers, they look for support and opportunities for sharing elsewhere. The websites provided above will give you a place to find a network suitable for your personal needs. Or do a Google search for teacher blogs and read a few; by doing this you will be able to see how important it is to build a community of support for teachers. For many of the bloggers, their blogs are the journals they keep for self-reflection and problem solving. Teachers describe in detail their experiences in classrooms, ask

© Photodisc Collection/Getty Images

for help regarding difficult issues, share their lesson plans, and sometimes develop support groups that meet off-line.

In this unit, we enter a dialogue about how to be an inspired teacher who uses networkfs, mentors, and self-reflection to improve pedagogy. New teachers, whether just out of college or second career educators, often state that teaching is the hardest job they ever had and certainly harder than their internship teaching with a mentor teacher. How do teachers keep their motivation for teaching and working with students who do not seem motivated? These are questions answered by Landsman, Moore, and Simmons. First, they discuss why teacher may be reluctant with reluctant learners. Next, they suggest building relationships with other teachers and with their own students. Finally, their suggestions are supported with examples that will help readers understand how to use these in any classroom across grades and content areas. In support of the previous authors' suggestion to join networks, Tricia Niesz explains why *communities of practice* form networks where teachers engage in learning from shared experiences and describes the four components of teacher networks with examples and personal stories. As noted above, some teachers find self-reflection their path to improving their teaching skills and thinking through problems. Some teachers, like Francesca, are lucky enough to find a mentor, perhaps another grade level teacher, a college professor, or their partner.

Reluctant Teachers, Reluctant Learners

The key to helping seemingly unmotivated students may be in the teacher's hands.

JULIE LANDSMAN, TIFFANY MOORE, AND ROBERT SIMMONS

How would students teach someone who doesn't want to learn? Here's what a few 9th graders we talked with at South High School in Minneapolis, Minnesota, had to say:

- "I don't believe that there are kids who 'don't want to learn.' I do believe though, that some kids have trouble learning or don't understand what the teacher is saying or teaching."
- "I think what motivates kids to learn is different for each individual student."
- "Well, first of all, I'd address the problem in a good way and find out the reason they don't want to learn."

By focusing on what we *can* do, we can reach many learners who appear to have given up.

As teachers, there are many things we can't control: district budgets, state legislatures' attitudes toward education and financing, No Child Left Behind and how it's interpreted, and inequality of wealth and educational privilege. But these 9th graders mentioned some things teachers can control. By focusing on what we *can* do, we can reach many learners who appear to have given up.

But first we need to reframe the problem.

Who Is Really Reluctant?

The discussion about reluctant learners seems to imply that students alone must become more involved in the schooling process. To reframe the conversation about the reluctant learner, we must also consider the "reluctant teacher."

Reluctant teachers often avoid students who do not look, act, or talk like them. They may categorize such students as being at risk, having behavior problems, or being unteachable. Ladson-Billings (2006) indicates that teachers who define students in such terms create a classroom environment that is no longer a place of learning and high expectations, but rather a place rooted in control and management. Such conditions will not help the reluctant learner become successful.

Just as all reluctant learners have the potential to become star students and contributors to our human family, all is not lost with the reluctant teacher. To succeed, the reluctant teacher must adopt attitudes and practices that reach every learner, particularly those who seem turned off to school.

Motivation in the Face of Difficulty

Those who become teachers want to make a difference in the world. They love and care about children. They also want a fulfilling job. Unfortunately, the reality of teaching today often does not match these expectations. Large class sizes, standardized testing, mandated curriculum, behavior issues, and school bureaucracy can make teaching more stressful than fulfilling. New teachers often comment that teaching is much more difficult than their training prepared them for Second-career teachers say that teaching is the hardest job they have ever had. One study found that around one-quarter of new hires leave teaching within five years. In schools that serve low-income urban areas, the retention rate dips to 50 percent within the first five years (Hare, Heap, & Raack, 2001).

How can teachers stay motivated when so many factors make teaching so difficult?

How can teachers stay motivated when so many factors make teaching so difficult? First, educators can create a network of peers to rely on when times are tough. They can eat lunch with supportive colleagues, take time out of a prep hour to chat with others, or go out and have fun with colleagues after work.

Second, teachers need to grab on to those small and all-too-rare expressions of gratitude they receive from students, parents, and administrators. All of us have experienced such welcome expressions as classroom teachers. Tiffany, for example, tucked away this note, left on her desk after she taught a unit on global warming to her social studies students at South High School in Minneapolis, Minnesota:

> Thank you for teaching me about how I can have an impact on my world. After you taught me about global warming, I went home and turned off all the lights we weren't using and rode my bike to the store rather than have my brother drive me in his car.

Tiffany had no idea the student had taken their class discussions to heart. That note reminded her of her influence on not only this one student, but also the entire planet.

Cultural Competence

For many learners, the school door represents a barrier that disconnects the classroom from their real life. The reluctant learner may feel isolated and turned off from school, be it because of family problems, cultural differences, language, dialect, or economic difficulties. His or her teachers often are more well off, speak differently, dress differently, and have a different color skin. Students who have had little prior exposure to the language and culture of schools can feel lost. Such students may resist the school environment and become apathetic, angry, restless, or disruptive, depending on their temperaments.

One avenue toward making the life of the classroom more accessible for students is for teachers to daily recognize the students' world outside the classroom. For example, posting a poem, quote, joke, song, or picture of a famous person from the students' culture demonstrates an awareness of and respect for students' backgrounds.

Becoming culturally competent means experiencing a culture that is not your own—and suspending judgment of that culture. Specifically, it may mean going to community meetings and shopping where students' families shop. It certainly means learning about the different basic facts, concepts, holidays, and economics of the cultures in your school.

Relationships with Students

Positive, caring relationships are vital for all students, especially those who seem hesitant. Students want teachers to understand that they have problems outside the classroom. They appreciate teachers who are willing to listen and guide them. Unfortunately, just as students can be disengaged from learning, many teachers can be disengaged from their students. This is not to say that they don't care about the students, but the students may not *feel* that caring (Kuykendall, 2004).

So how can teachers show students that they do care? They can begin by establishing a positive atmosphere on the first day of school. Some teachers may ask students to write pieces about themselves and share them with the class. Teachers can also have students guess the teacher's age or try to figure out where the teacher is from. This leads to lots of laughter and discussion about first impressions and stereotypes.

Teachers can maintain these positive relationships throughout the year by greeting students at the door and asking them how they are doing. These conversations only take a few minutes, and they ensure that, even in large classes, each student has been acknowledged in some way. This builds the trust that is vitally important for reaching reluctant students.

Many teachers, worrying about the curriculum they have to cover, don't want to lose instructional days by laying the groundwork for building community. Yet these relationships can actually make it easier to cover the curriculum efficiently because students feel invested in the classroom. The time required to develop relationships with students may be substantial. However, without this time, the reluctant learner may never become engaged in learning.

Connection to Families

Over the years, we have seen numerous teachers attempting to build relationships with students. Although many efforts have been sincere and well intentioned, too often they are disconnected from the students' families.

Robert discovered the value of connecting with families when, at the end of a long day, the father of one of his 8th grade science students at Elmdale Conservatory for the Visual and Performing Arts in Detroit, Michigan, stopped by to invite him to their home for dinner. Never one to turn down a home-cooked meal, Robert packed his things and headed to their home. This was not the first time that he had broken bread with a family, but it was the first time that he had dinner with *this* family. This student was in his 5th period class and was working with him on a science fair project, yet they had never connected beyond the usual good morning and afternoon.

During dinner, the parents commented on the number of times that Robert had called home to share positive information about their son. Their son was never a demonstrative student, so he appeared to Robert to be a reluctant learner. The parents believed that Roberts commitment to sharing good news fostered a sense of pride in their son. The student's participation in the science fair project was a by-product of Robert's proactive approach in contacting the parents.

Connection to Communities

Service learning projects give students an opportunity to connect what they learn in school with the communities in which they live. Several years ago, Robert and his 8th grade science students started a service learning project by discussing their Detroit community. The schools neighborhood had many vacant lots, burned-out homes, and trash on the streets and sidewalks.

The students and Robert developed a list of 10 problems they wanted to address. One student, Jamal, was adamant about placing mattresses on the list. A shy student who did not often participate, Jamal was alive with energy about this topic. Robert was unclear about why mattresses needed to be on the list, but service learning is about community needs, and this was Jamal's community.

In his service learning project, Jamal began a journey from reluctant learner to outspoken advocate for community awareness to award-winning science student. To support the science requirement for the project, Jamal cut out a piece of a mattress lying in a vacant lot and contacted a local company to help him analyze the contents. The bacteria and other particles contained in that small piece would turn anyone's stomach.

This project helped Jamal become much more engaged in class, and his grades began to improve. Projects in which students connect school with their communities can engage the most reluctant of learners.

Student Input

D. W., a South High 9th grader, offers this suggestion for teaching students who don't seem interested in learning:

I would simply ask them what their favorite things are and use these things as examples to teach these students.

Reluctant learners need to feel that they are heard, that *their* stories, *their* voices, *their* questions, and *their* contributions matter. The best teachers make student voices the center of the class. Sometimes they build whole themes and activities around student interests and concerns. One teacher, for example, created a science, history, music, and literary curriculum centered on hairstyles and the history of fashion (Delpit & Dowdy, 2002).

Reluctant learners need to feel that they are heard, that *their* stories, *their* voices, their questions, and *their* contributions matter.

Although No Child Left Behind may make such an imaginative approach difficult, teachers can modify subject and class assignments by incorporating such engaging activities as surveys, free-writing exercises, and storytelling. Small-group work, time before and after class to talk with teachers, or even organized after-school study sessions can also make reluctant learners feel connected.

The most important way to nurture students and keep them in school is to create opportunities for them to determine for themselves what will go on in the classroom. Contracts that give students choices, discussions or projects related to issues that pique students' interest, and classroom strategy meetings with students who seem to be drifting send a message to the young man who is sleeping in the back row or the young woman who has been skipping school: "Your voice, your thoughts, your concerns are important here."

Classroom Management

Nothing alienates students more than threatening them, and nothing creates more reluctant learners than force. Unfortunately, too many teachers begin their career without a tool kit full of strategies for managing student learning. Therefore, they end up disciplining students with force and threats.

A strong, well-planned lesson that has enough work to fill a class period from bell to bell can go a long way toward keeping students involved. The minute students walk into the classroom, there should be an activity to engage them: a warm-up journal topic; a crazy question about science (Do fish sleep?); or a puzzle to solve. Writing the learning objective and agenda for the class on the board each day—with specific directions—helps students transition from one activity to the next. Students also remain focused when they have a concrete outcome due at the end of the class period. If they have "until tomorrow" to finish an assignment, students will put off doing the work.

Another proactive strategy is to have a set of classroom guidelines and procedures that students (and parents) have agreed on. Once students know the rules and consequences and see that they will be enforced, they are less likely to argue. Creating a procedure and a place in the classroom for turning in work and for obtaining and storing supplies can add to the order of a classroom. Students who come from chaotic or disorganized homes or who feel intimidated by school generally welcome this predictability.

Even the teacher with the best relationship with students, the most organized classroom, and the best-planned lesson will face days when students do not want to participate. To keep students on task on such days, teachers must maintain an altitude of "with-it-ness," stopping to survey the class every couple of minutes. Students notice how "with-it" a teacher is and act accordingly.

When students are disruptive, the teacher can often simply "stop and stare" or move closer to the student who is misbehaving, giving no verbal attention to the problem. If this doesn't work, then the teacher should simply say the student's name and "please stop." If the student doesn't stop, the teacher may, if it's feasible, ask the student to move into the hall for a talk. Some teachers are brilliant at student hall talks. They speak quietly, get the student to tell what is happening, and then discuss what can be done. The calmer the teacher remains, the more students will respect the rules. This is especially true for students who need to feel they are being heard.

Self-Reflection

No matter how experienced, the best teachers are willing to change. Reflective teachers admit mistakes and create open conversations with students and colleagues in order to improve. They ask themselves whether their students are learning, and when they don't like the answer, they immediately change how they are teaching.

Some educators reflect and learn by writing down their thoughts and observations daily. Some attend workshops on areas where they need support. Others find a mentor to bounce ideas off of. Some learn from their students by giving surveys, asking students to write in a journal, or having an open class discussion about topics of teacher concern. Whatever their approach to learning, they remain open to new ideas and always seek new ways to ensure that all students are learning.

What We Can Do

Zoe, a South High 9th grader, says that teachers should "try to inspire [students]. Try to work with them, not against them. Try to make the class interesting."

Individual teachers can't control tax structures or national trends. We can't fix broken homes. We can't revamp our economic system to make things more equitable. However, we can do what Zoe suggests: We can inspire students with our own fire, motivation, research, and ideas. We can give students confidence in their ability and their future. And we can create classrooms that are so vibrant, so full of life and laughter, with such high expectations and such a clear connection to the world, that even the most reluctant learner will be tempted to join in.

The reluctant learner creates a thin veneer of resistance to cover his or her yearning. This veneer is penetrable by teachers who take the time—who themselves are not reluctant to teach and learn from all students.

References

Delpit, L., & Dowdy, J. K. (2002). *The skin that we speak.* New York: New Press.

Hare, D., Heap, J., & Raack, L. (2001). Teacher recruitment and retention strategies in the Midwest: Where are they and do they work? *NCREL Policy Issues, 8,* 1-8. Available: www.ncrel.org/policy/pubs/pdfs/pivol8.pdf

Kuykendall, C. (2004). *From rage to hope: Strategies for reclaiming black and Hispanic students* (2nd ed.). Bloomington, IN: National Educational Service.

Ladson-Billings, G. (2006). Yes, but how do we do it? Practicing culturally relevant pedagogy. In J. Landsman & C. Lewis (Eds.), *White teachers/Diverse classrooms: A guide to building inclusive schools, promoting higher expectations and eliminating racism* (pp. 29–42). Sterling, VA: Stylus.

JULIE LANDSMAN is a retired teacher; author of *A White Teacher Talks About Race* (Scarecrow, 2001); and coeditor of *White Teachers/ Diverse Classrooms* (Stylus Press, 2006); jlandsman@goldengate.net. **TIFFANY MOORE** is a teacher mentor for Minneapolis Public Schools in Minnesota; tiffany.moore@mpls.k12.mn.us. **ROBERT SIMMONS** is Assistant Professor of Teacher Education at Eastern Michigan University, Ypsilanti; rsimmon6@emich.edu.

Musing: A Way to Inform and Inspire Pedagogy through Self-Reflection

JANE MOORE AND VICKIE FIELDS WHITFIELD

Teaching is a complex profession that involves grappling with a variety of management styles; federal, state, and local mandates; local policies and agendas; and informed curriculum practices that affect pedagogy. Teachers work in increasingly diverse schools, and they must be reflective practitioners to deal with the many social and educational issues that converge in such places. A reflective practitioner is better able to grow and defend teaching practices.

This is the time of year when teachers in many parts of the world begin to pack up their classrooms and prepare for a brief respite over the summer—only to begin anew in a few short months. It is the perfect time to create an atmosphere for and in support of reflection and learning so that, as teachers, we can unite to become professionals committed to perpetual growth—both personally and for those we teach.

Dewey (1933) introduced the idea of reflective thought to teachers. His basic assumption was that learning improves according to the degree of effort that comes out of the reflective process. Reflection is thinking over time by linking recent experiences to earlier ones in order to promote a more complex and interrelated mental schema. The thinking involves looking for commonalities, differences, and interrelations beyond superficial elements (Shermis, 1999).

To muse is a phrase that comes to mind when thinking about reflective thought. When looking up the word *muse* in a dictionary, it is defined as a verb, noun, and a proper noun. As a verb it means to ponder, to become absorbed in thought, or to meditate. As a noun, the word is described as the spirit or power of deep thought—the source of genius or inspiration. The proper noun definition leads to Greek mythology and the nine sister goddesses who presided over song and poetry and the arts and sciences.

In order to awaken self-reflection on our teaching practices, the following questions have been designed to assist teachers in reflecting on the skills and habits they have developed. By raising self-awareness of personal strengths and weaknesses, teachers can find and exploit the strengths of

their students. Intrinsic, rather than extrinsic, motivation to reflect may produce better results. The nature of the stimulus to reflect will affect the quality of the reflection. Surbeck, Han, and Moyer (1991) identified three levels of reflection:

1. Reacting—commenting on feelings toward the learning experience, such as reacting with a personal concern(s) about an experience
2. Elaborating—comparing reactions with other events, such as referring to a general principle, theory, or a philosophical position
3. Contemplating—focusing on constructive personal insights or on problems or difficulties, such as education issues, training methods, future goals, attitudes, ethical matters, or moral concerns

The nature of the stimulus or directive initially provided, as well as the feedback received after initial reflection, will determine the extent to which one reaches the contemplative level of reflection. Dewey (1933) added that when teachers speculate, reason, and contemplate using open-mindedness, wholeheartedness, and responsibility, they will act with foresight and planning rather than base their actions on tradition, authority, or impulse.

In our November 2007 column, we focused on how each coach and mentor could reflect on his or her performance to enhance teacher productivity. In this column, we would like to invite the teacher to engage in the reflective process, thereby promoting a community of reflective thinking. The following list is not exhaustive but is designed to stimulate reflection on the pedagogy practiced, thus raising self-awareness and the ability to articulate these practices. The questions also may be used to reflect on skills developed and to assist in guiding personal development planning.

If we are truthful to ourselves during the reflective process, the results can become our muses—our source of inspiration and renewal. Honest self-examination helps us identify what motivates and inspires us. Forms of inspiration are vital to our happiness and important to sustain us in our work. The process can aid us in developing an acute awareness of what we teach, how we teach, and why we teach. Ultimately, that which inspires and directs our teaching may lead to student success.

The process is simple. Honestly mull over, ruminate, and spend time musing over any number of the questions offered in the following list. Self-reflection is for personal growth. If you are comfortable with your self-reflection, however, you might take it a step further and have a reflective conversation with a revered colleague, coach, mentor, or significant other.

Personal Growth

- What do you do with the feedback on your performance evaluations or annual evaluations?
- Have you created a specific development plan? How were your needs identified?
- When you have been made aware of, or have discovered for yourself, a problem in your work performance, what was your course of action? What did you learn?
- What makes learning difficult or easy for you?
- What are you concerned about? What do you look forward to?

Curriculum Decisions

- How diligent are you in the use of relevant, available data?
- What information do you take into account before coming to a conclusion?
- What do you reflect on at the end of the working day? Do you spend more time on what went well and why, or do you analyze any problems that may have occurred?
- Think about your favorite lesson. What made it work well? Can you apply this to other lessons?
- How are support services and interventions being implemented?

Flexibility

- Think about a time when priorities changed quickly. What did you do? What was the outcome?
- How do you handle interruptions?
- Are you facing new content or grade-level changes next year? What will you do to prepare?
- Are you amenable to criticism, advice, or suggestions?
- How flexible are you in meeting the differentiated needs of learners?

Professional Development

- What have you done to further your own professional development outside of your formal studies?
- How do you keep record of your achievements?
- What activities do you participate in to develop your skills?
- Do you readily seek opportunities to develop your skills and competencies?
- How often do you update a learning log or résumé?

Technology

- How do you think technological knowledge can support the planning, designing, or implementation of learning?
- How do you embrace the use of technology in your teaching?
- In what areas do you need more technological knowledge?
- How do you demonstrate your knowledge of technological advances and the impact of these on working practices and organizational strategies?
- Where do you find support to assist growth in this area?

Planning

- How do you typically plan your day to manage your time effectively?
- Describe how you are able to contribute to district or school goals. What are the goals or mission?
- Consider a time when you had to adopt a new approach or style to accomplish a task. How did you plan and manage the transition?
- How do you differentiate and prioritize short- and long-term needs?
- How does your classroom management augment your teaching?

Other Musings

- What inspires or drives you?
- What issue stands out as a focus for next year?

A Note to the Coach

Vygotsky (1934/1978) defined the Zone of Proximal Development as the distance between the actual developmental level and the level of potential development under adult guidance or collaboration with more capable peers. The role of the coach is enhanced when teachers can be led to reflection and then to form questions that assist in asking for resources, training, or mentoring. The actual development level and the potential level of the teacher's skills, strategies, and understandings remain constants. Training will no longer need to be reliant on group, grant, or management foci but rather to differentiate each teacher's growth and opportunity.

In Greek mythology, the muses were daughters of Zeus and Mnemosyne, the goddess of memory. For over 2,500 years and throughout Western civilization, artists of every sort have attributed most of their inspirations, creativity, and talent to the muses. Teaching is both art and science, so muse to become inspired, creative, and talented so that each child you touch may become successful.

References

Dewey, J. (1933). *How we think: A restatement of the relation of reflective thinking to the educative process.* Boston: D.C. Heath.

Shermis, S.S. (1999). Reflective thought, critical thinking. *ERIC Digest,* D143.

Surbeck, E., Han, E.P., & Moyer, J. (1991). Assessing reflective responses in journals. *Educational Leadership, 48*(6), 25–27.

Vygotsky, L.S. (1978). *Mind in society: The development of higher psychological processes* (M. Cole, V. John-Steiner, S. Scribner, & E. Souberman, Eds. & Trans.). Cambridge, MA: Harvard University Press. (Original work published 1934)

JANE MOORE is a literacy coach for the Dallas Independent School District, Texas, USA; e-mail drjanemoore@gmail.com. VICKIE FIELDS WHITFIELD works for istation.com in curriculum development; e-mail vickiewhitfield7@gmail.com.

Why Teacher Networks (Can) Work

Communities of practice, in which learning and teaching are interwoven in social networks, may someday lead to a movement to put thoughtful professional expertise back into schooling.

TRICIA NIESZ

During my first month of graduate school, I read that Japanese teachers' school days included time to discuss their practice and plan lessons with their colleagues. Many years have gone by since I came across that information, but sometimes I still think about it.

The reason that image of teacher collaboration made such an impression on me, I think, is because I had recently left elementary school teaching after only a few months as a long-term substitute teacher. An important factor in my decision had been that I felt so isolated from other teachers who might have goals similar to mine. The experience of isolation was especially profound because I had just graduated from a small, alternative teacher preparation program called "Learning Community" that was based on social theories of learning. The program practiced what it preached. We preservice teachers were engaged in learning in the social context of a community; we studied and discussed practice together, co-taught, supported one another, formed friendships, and developed ongoing collaborations and conversations with colleagues with similar interests. Less than one year after graduating from the Learning Community program, I was in my first teaching job—alone and starved for the kinds of connections I had had and the ideas and support that they had provided.

It was only in hindsight, once I began to study teacher networks as a researcher, that I recognized why I was so struck by that article about teaching in Japan. Researching school change in an urban middle school in Philadelphia, I met Jennifer and Ellen, two teachers who were exceptionally well connected to networks of educators drawn together around common interests. These interests included multicultural education, community service learning, teacher research, teaching writing for English-language learners, and more. I was struck by the way Jennifer and Ellen were revitalized by meeting outside the school day with other educators who shared their passions. They were excited by the new ideas that they brought to the school from their networks, and they could trace their own changing practice in terms of those ideas. As was the case for the Japanese teachers

and for me in Learning Community, for Jennifer and Ellen, learning and teaching were interwoven in social networks.

Since the completion of my research project, I have read the growing literature on teacher professional development networks and have learned that Jennifer and Ellen are not alone. In recent years, teacher networks—defined here as groups of teachers organized for purposes related to teacher learning, inquiry, support, or school improvement—have been embraced by researchers and practitioners alike for their approach to teacher professional development.[1] In contrast to such traditional professional development approaches as workshops or inservice days, networks often reflect a social or constructivist orientation to teacher learning. Many are based on the premises that contexts for teacher learning should endure over time, build on teachers' knowledge and experiences, provide opportunities for critical dialogue and inquiry, and foster the public sharing of practice and understandings. Turning to learning communities outside of their schools, teachers can find everything that schools, too often, are not.

Networks are poised to be a powerful source of teacher learning and school improvement.

Networks as Communities of Practice

Researchers and advocates of teacher networks have suggested that one of the reasons that there is so much excitement about this approach to teacher professional development is that networks are examples of *communities of practice*,[2] a concept developed by Jean Lave and Etienne Wenger.[3] In my view, the power of this idea is in the conceptualization of learning-as-social-participation, which begins with the assumption that "engagement in social practice is the fundamental process by which we learn and so become who we are."[4]

Wenger's model of communities of practice incorporates four "deeply interconnected and mutually defining" components of this social theory of learning:

- Community: learning as belonging;
- Identity: learning as becoming;
- Practice: learning as doing; and
- Meaning: learning as experience.[5]

In interesting ways, this framework captures much of what is noted in the literature on teacher networks—a literature heavy on concepts like identity, community, and participation. Teacher networks are explicitly or implicitly contrasted with traditional approaches to teacher professional development, such as workshops or inservice days, which are faulted for failing to recognize that the kind of learning that inspires change in practice takes time and social support. In addition, teachers often view conventional professional development offerings as a waste of time because they are disconnected from everyday practice and the pressing questions that arise therein. Indeed, professional development is often pursued without any attempt to understand—or sometimes even respect—existing practice and its underlying assumptions. In short, traditional professional development in schools has often been undertaken without attention to communities, identities, practice, and meanings.

Networks take a different tack. In many networks, it is not that tools, skills, discrete knowledge, and technical fixes are eschewed, but rather that they are considered within social contexts where a great deal of attention is given to communities, identities, practice, and meanings. What you do, who you are in engagement with others, and whom you want to become are central to the professional development approach of many networks.

Readers will note that I am idealizing networks in this article. In practice, most networks have strengths and weaknesses, and few represent the ideal I write about here. My argument is that networks are *poised to be* a powerful source of teacher learning and school improvement—especially if they are designed and actualized in ways that respect the assumptions underlying communities of practice.

Community:
Learning as Belonging

Ann Lieberman and Milbrey McLaughlin write that "networks that engage and sustain teachers' interest and commitment blend, rather than differentiate between, personal and professional, social and work-related activities."[6] By making the context for professional development one of interpersonal connection and interaction, networks foster the commitment of time, energy, and perhaps something of ourselves.

Last year I was a member of a learning community of university professors. For months our community was functioning very much like a formal seminar, and the formality seemed to be hindering our work together. We have since talked about

the fact that many of us were unsure about the expectations for our collaborative work. Many of us had questions that were not asked or concerns that were not expressed.

One day we all met early, before the official meeting time, to discuss a presentation that we were to give as a group. As I walked up to the group, I saw that one member was sharing pictures of her son. Soon, many of us were sharing pictures of our children and stories of our personal lives. Then we got to work. Something changed in our work together that day. We were both more relaxed and more invested. We were more vulnerable and more trusting. We were more honest. All of these characteristics—trust, honesty, vulnerability, comfort, investment—lead to better learning, more meaningful learning, and an openness to hear and change. Connecting to one another made us connect more to our work together. With much of the formality gone, the distance that characterized our early work together began to disappear. We claimed a new ownership over our joint enterprise.

Recently, I attended one of the last class meetings of an extended professional development experience for science teachers that functioned for some as a network. Although I had heard from some of the participants that they valued the network-like aspects of the series of meetings—talking about current practice and new learning with peers, posing questions and hearing stories of the impact of new ideas—I was still surprised when a couple of the teachers pulled out cameras and began to take photos of their instructors and new friends. This told me that the experience was more than just a class. It reminded me of my Learning Community experience in college, which was more than just a teacher preparation program. We made sweatshirts representing our community. We kept in touch through a newsletter for 10 years following our graduation, sharing news of major life events, both exciting and tragic, as well as reporting on where our work as educators was taking us.

In both of these cases, to different extents, learning experiences were intertwined with interpersonal experiences and relationships. Critics might respond, "Sure, experiences like these are 'nice' and 'pleasant,' but do they matter for our learning?" I would argue that they do, because the social connections we make with others whom we learn to trust and respect invest us in the process of change. Moreover, these experiences have the potential to do much more than develop our technical professional expertise; they can contribute to or even transform our identities as educators.

Identity: Learning as Becoming

In addition to the effect that belonging to a group has on identity, networks often have explicit philosophies, missions, values, assumptions, and orientations that help shape participants' identities. When teachers voluntarily join a network, they often do so based on their personal and professional interests. Teachers choose networks that engage them and are responsive to their passions and questions and to how they see themselves as professionals. Then, through being associated with the network and pursuing a joint vision, teachers gain new experiences, language, and resources.

Jennifer, for example, joined networks that focused on the range of educational issues that mattered to her: English-language learners and literacy, social justice and multicultural education, and more. She joined these networks because of who she was as a teacher and a person. Yet who she was as a teacher and a person was further refined through her participation. As she interacted with and learned from peers with similar interests and ultimately advanced into leadership roles that allowed her to share her practice with others, her identity was transformed and strengthened.

Ellen's experience was different, in that she was introduced to a community service learning network almost by accident, through an opportunity suggested by her principal. The idea aligned with who she was as a teacher, and she attended a conference. She became quite taken with the approach, and within a year of that conference, she was an expert in community service learning.

Teachers' associations with other like-minded professionals outside the school can be powerful, especially for those who feel isolated within their school. Networks often include old-timers whom newcomers can emulate. While Jennifer, having moved into leadership roles, was an old-timer in a few of her networks, she had less experience than some of the more senior teachers in her teacher research group. When she talked about that group, I could hear how much she respected them. In addition to learning from these colleagues and their experiences, simply being associated with teachers she respected so much contributed to her view of herself.

The mission of a network, which links colleagues with similar interests in a community of practice, is important, but there is another dimension of identity that networks offer teachers: professionalism. Networks offer learning opportunities in a context of dignity and respect that teachers do not always experience. Being treated as a professional, with one's experiences and perspectives valued, contributes to teachers' efficacy, agency, commitment, and engagement in the work of the network and the work of teaching; being treated as a professional may also help teachers construct an identity that is more rewarding and a better fit with how they see themselves.

In the school where Jennifer and Ellen worked, teachers were constantly responding to new mandates from the district and school administration that informed them what curriculum and reform programs were going to be implemented or eliminated, what new school policies would change their daily work lives, and even how much time they had to spend preparing their students for a slate of standardized tests. For very experienced teachers like Ellen, and for very well-respected teacher leaders like Jennifer, being given so little control over aspects of their work lives was frustrating. However, when they worked on projects in the context of educational networks, they were no longer receivers of information, but contributors to ongoing conversations about teaching practice. Their experience mattered, and their professional views were respected.

The literature is clear on the fact that, historically, teachers' work has been de-professionalized and de-skilled. Within the field of education, there is often a chasm between those acknowledged as the producers of knowledge and those who have traditionally been viewed as the receivers.[7] Networks bridge this chasm by taking teachers' knowledge and practice as the starting point for learning and having teachers themselves lead the work of professional development. As Ann Lieberman and Diane Wood write, in this model, teachers become "active and interactive, developers rather than developed, passionate instead of passive."[8] Being treated as professionals has a powerful impact on teachers' identities.

Jennifer and Ellen both brought new ideas, assumptions, and language to their school from their teacher networks.

Practice: Learning as Doing

While talk of teaching practice has generally been difficult to find in schools, it is central to the work of networks. Even though the school where Jennifer and Ellen worked was going through a number of changes and reforms during the time of my research there, teachers had few places to talk about their practice with respect to the changes, and so most of the new school-sponsored ideas and programs remained peripheral to their work. Many teachers at the school felt alienated from the changes, if not completely unaware of what they meant for their practice. In contrast, Jennifer in particular was active in teacher networks that were structured around teachers' sharing their practice and making it public.

Some networks take professional development beyond talk about practice and into the realm of "learning as doing" by incorporating inquiry into the experience. Jennifer was involved in a number of networks, but there was one that was far and away the most important to her. It was a teacher research group. In it, she worked with colleagues who shared her passion for multicultural education. Engaging in research in their own classrooms and then coming together to share their findings enabled the group members to learn from one another's inquiry. Jennifer looked forward to sharing her developing ideas with her fellow teacher researchers and found that their perspectives pushed her to broaden her understandings of multicultural education. Moreover, teacher inquiry became an important aspect of her daily practice.

Many teachers indicate that sharing practice or engaging in inquiry with others makes for a powerful experience. Analysts suggest that networks "reward participants with a renewed sense of purpose and efficacy"[9] and provide "nourishment"[10] and "intellectual and emotional stimulation."[11] I certainly saw this with Jennifer and Ellen. When frustrations mounted at the school site, they could weather them because they were so engaged with and excited by what they were doing in their networks.

Not all networks are created equal; not all embrace an inquiry approach to teacher learning. But the structure of a social network offers the potential for teachers to intellectually engage with what brought them into the profession or to find new passions through work in a community of practice. It is difficult for traditional professional development to do that.

Meaning: Learning as Experience

The fourth component of Wenger's social theory of learning is *meaning;* he argues that learning is the negotiation of meaning through participation. Participation in communities is the context in which we learn to assign meaning to our lives over time. Schools can be seen as the primary community of practice to which teachers belong, because of days, months, and years of accumulated experience. However, I would argue that much of the power for changing practice comes from negotiating meanings across two competing communities: schools and teacher professional development networks. The substance of the learning and the trajectory of the development of professional identities differ in these two communities. However, practice is shaped by negotiating meaning across both of them.

For example, Jennifer and Ellen both brought new ideas, assumptions, and language to their school from their teacher networks. They used their broadened experience to contest what they viewed as the limitations of school policy and practice. Jennifer, for example, challenged her colleagues' shallow interpretation of multicultural education—a "multicultural fair" approach—and advocated for the infusion of a more fundamental multiculturalism throughout the curriculum. Ellen advocated for ways to actively engage the school's students through local neighborhood/community participation and tried to pull colleagues into her students' service-learning projects.

Thus their networks inspired them enough to take action in their schools but also provided *legitimacy* for their ideas and advocacy. Their networks linked them not only to other educators but also to sites of knowledge production in the field. When teachers come together in network spaces to discuss and think about educational practice generally and their own practice specifically, they also become connected to the research, theory, and scholarship supporting the mission of the network. At this intersection, educators are poised to produce new cultural practices, new orientations to their work. Ann Lieberman and Maureen Grolnick write.

> Education networks bridge two cultures. On the one hand they are connected to a system that organizes the delivery of education to school-age children through an elaborate system of codes, regulations, standards, and assessments. On the other hand, they support the professional development of teachers and administrators who work within that system, who need to be free to step outside of it in order to consider ways to improve the very schools and system within which they work.[12]

This is the sort of negotiation of meaning that makes networks promising spaces for professional development. Educators involved with networks don't just step outside of their bureaucratic systems, they also step into a world of ideas and practice-focused discourse. Networks, even those that privilege teachers' knowledge and interests, aren't neutral about where they want their participants to end up. The goal is always sound improvement informed by big ideas.

Thus networks occupy an interesting place in the educational landscape. First, they are explicitly designed for learning and change. Second, the structure of networks, unlike that of schools and other workplaces, is flexible rather than bureaucratic, so networks aren't often faced with contradictory goals that compete with teacher learning. Third, because participation is voluntary, teachers' own goals align with those of the network. Teacher networks offer a good foil for the schools, where bureaucracy, politics, and myriad other factors often compete with teacher learning and thoughtful school improvement.

Networks in Today's Schools

Despite all that we know about education and learning, schools today are increasingly overpowered by technical, test-driven approaches. What professional educators believe is important for learning has been pushed to the margins by political pressures on schools. It was not surprising to me that Jennifer and Ellen were critics and resisters of teach-to-the-test pressures and used the resources of their networks to justify their stances. Both teachers had big dreams for their students and saw powerful learning experiences related to critical thinking and problem solving as a way to realize them. Their participation in networks let them know that they weren't alone in their big dreams and big ideas and provided support and strategies for teaching against the grain.

Although thus far there has been only limited research on how teachers' participation in networks specifically changes actual classroom practice,[13] networks have been on the rise as an approach to teacher professional development for some time. It will be interesting to see whether the current political climate for public schooling reverses this trend, as teachers are confronted with ever more prescribed curricula and pedagogy, or whether more teachers flock to networks as a survival strategy. If a movement can be mounted to put thoughtful professional expertise back into schooling, it might well emerge from networks.

Notes

1. Networks have become so popular that they have been used as strategies to implement and support particular school or district reforms, but these are of less interest to me. Distinguishing between policy-implementation networks and professional development networks is important because the power of professional development networks lies in their voluntary nature; teachers turn to them because they address particular professional or personal interests.

2. Ann Lieberman and Diane R. Wood, *Inside the National Writing Project: Connecting Network Learning and Classroom Teaching* (New York: Teachers College Press, 2003); and Joseph P. McDonald and Emily J. Klein, "Networking for Effective Learning: Toward a Theory of Effective Design," *Teachers College Record,* vol. 105, 2003, pp. 1606–21.

3. Jean Lave and Etienne Wenger, *Situated Learning: Legitimate Peripheral Participation* (Cambridge: Cambridge University Press, 1991); and Etienne Wenger, *Communities of Practice: Learning, Meaning, and Identity* (Cambridge: Cambridge University Press, 1998).

4. Wenger, p. 1.

5. Ibid., p. 5.

6. Ann Lieberman and Milbrey W. McLaughlin, "Networks for Educational Change: Powerful and Problematic," *Phi Delta Kappan,* May 1992, p. 674.

7. Marilyn Cochran-Smith and Susan Lytle, *Inside/Outside: Teacher Research and Knowledge* (New York: Teachers College Press, 1992).

8. Ann Lieberman and Diane Wood, "When Teachers Write: Of Networks and Learning," in Ann Lieberman and Lynn Miller, eds., *Teachers Caught in the Action: Professional Development That Matters* (New York: Teachers College Press, 2001), p. 184.

9. Lieberman and McLaughlin, p. 674.

10. Ann Lieberman and Maureen Grolnick, "Networks and Reform in American Education," *Teachers College Record,* vol. 1, 1996, p. 41.

11. Lieberman and McLaughlin, p. 674.

12. Lieberman and Grolnick, pp. 36–37.

13. McDonald and Klein, op. cit.

TRICIA NIESZ is an assistant professor of research methodology and cultural foundations of education at Kent State University, Kent, Ohio.

UNIT 5

Cornerstones to Learning: Reading and Math

Unit Selections

22. **Response to Intervention (RTI): What Teachers of Reading Need to Know,** Eric M. Mesmer and Heidi Anne E. Mesmer
23. **You Should Read This Book!,** Jennifer Hartley
24. **Getting Children In2Books: Engagement in Authentic Reading, Writing, and Thinking,** William H. Teale et al.
25. **Using Literature Circles with English Language Learners at the Middle Level,** Pamela J. Farris, Pamela A. Nelson, and Susan L'Ailler
26. **Losing the Fear of Sharing Control: Starting a Reading Workshop,** Lesley Roessing
27. **Nine Ways to Catch Kids Up,** Marilyn Burns
28. **The Classroom That Math Built: Encouraging Young Mathematicians to Pose Problems,** Ann H. Wallace, Deborah Abbott, and Renee McAlhaney Blary

Key Points to Consider

- What are the issues surrounding literacy expressed in these articles?

- Why should teachers be concerned that students read for pleasure?

- Literature circles may help student who are English Language Learners, but who else might be helped with this method? Provide rationales for your choices.

- Which of the nine ways to catch kids up will you use? Explain why.

- Why do you think helping students pose their own problems would be successful? What learning theories support this teaching method?

Student Website

www.mhcls.com

Internet References

Literature Circles Resource Center
   http://www.litcircles.org
Teacher Scholastic: Meet the Expert
   http://teacher.scholastic.com/professional/readexpert/laurarobb.htm
The Literacy Web
   http://www.literacy.uconn.edu/index.htm
The National Council of Teachers of English (NCTE)
   http://www.ncte.org/collections/secell
Read, Write, Think
   http://www.readwritethink.org/
National Council of Teachers of Mathematics
   http://www.nctm.org

In this unit of the Annual Edition we focus on core skills that are taught in all public schools, reading and math. We have selected this topic because these skills are fundamental skills acquired from printed materials, which are a primary source of knowledge. Additionally, being able to read and calculate are fundamental rights of all citizens in a democratic society. Many of us who read for both learning and pleasure cannot imagine a life without reading. Just as reading is an essential skill for learning and living a successful life, so are math skills. Imagine not being able to balance your checking account, keep a budget, or understand and check the deductions on your paycheck. Good math skills are even more important when you try to read the fine print on car and home mortgage loans or credit card bills. These issues are a reality for persons who lack basic math skills. In school, students may have the intellectual ability to attend college, but cannot pass those higher level math classes required in college prep programs. Thus we are adding several articles about math to this section on cornerstones to learning.

As we begin this exploration, we must acknowledge that reading and math include accessing words in different ways. For the child who is visually impaired, this may mean reading Braille materials, listening to audio recordings, or using a screen reader to access information on a computer and the Internet. Students who have learning disabilities and dyslexia may use the same audio and digital resources as the visually impaired. In fact, some students may wish to use these methods even when they are able to read print, because they like to doodle while listening because it helps them keep their focus. Students with visual impairments or learning disabilities may need to use an abacus or calculator to complete math problems. Students who are English Language Learners may wish to continue reading and working math word problems in their native language while they are learning English. Still, other students prefer to read graphic novels for pleasure. No matter what reason compels students to use resources other than the traditional print materials, we should remember that they *are reading* and calculating even when it does not match our notion of those tasks. Promoting lifelong reading habits and math usage may mean that, as teachers, we need to be flexible and revise our thinking. The articles in this unit will offer new ways of considering how we teach students.

One indicator that students are struggling with academic tasks is a reading level below that of same-age peers. These students may be recommended for special education screening because they are not progressing as well as their peers. However, there are many problems with the discrepancy model used by many school districts to identify students who are eligible for special education. First appearing in special education law, Response to Intervention (RTI) was developed to help school personnel shift the emphasis from identifying and labeling students to providing support to students who struggle with academic tasks. We have included an article regarding RTI in this section because much of the initial work is completed by reading teachers. Mesmer and Mesmer provide definitions, information about the legislation, and numerous of examples of teachers using RTI. Readers who are beginning their teaching careers will find this article helpful in sorting through the requirements of this relatively new method for determining student needs.

As readers and teachers, we understand that fluency is a key to reading well and with pleasure. But even if they are fluent, some

© amana images inc./Alamy

readers resist silent reading activities in school. Hartley shares the story of her repeated efforts to engage urban students in sustained silent reading. Her realization that she needed to give up control and that her students needed to make their own choices on what to read was a breakthrough moment. In yet another urban setting, Teale and others worked to get students into books. Their efforts yielded results when students engaged themselves in authentic reading, writing, and thinking. These two articles illustrate that students read when given choices and authentic learning tasks.

When we work with middle schoolers who are English Language Learners in multicultural classrooms, we may face a different set of issues, for example, a cultural clash between students who belong to groups that have been enemies historically. Farris, Nelson, and L'Allier suggest that literature circles can be useful as teachers can combine literary skills and strategies in a supportive atmosphere of non-threatening peers. In multicultural literature circles, students can learn skills that extend across their lives, such as making decisions and compromises collaboratively.

Another problem that many middle and high school language arts teachers face is when a student can read, but cannot comprehend complex text material. Can we expect upper level teachers to teach reading as well as their core-content knowledge? Roessing faced just such a problem in her eighth-grade language arts class. She provides insight into her journey to become a content area teacher who taught reading, but not in the way you might expect. Her article gives sufficient detail for others to follow what she has done.

The articles on teaching math offer readers two methods for helping students who lack deep understanding of the underlying concepts and help teachers engage students more authentically with math problems. Burns offers a nine-step process for remediating basic skills and teaching for understanding. Her explanations and examples will help readers use her methods. Wallace, Abbott, and Blary explain ways to use student's imaginations and the classroom environment to create math problems that had real meaning to the students with authentic tasks. They describe in detail a five-day progress that engages students in problem-posing investigation of their classroom and school.

This collection of articles is presented to stimulate your thinking about ways to help your students (or prospective students) become lifelong readers and competent users of math.

Response to Intervention (RTI): What Teachers of Reading Need to Know

Clear definitions, details of relevant legislation, and examples of RTI in action help explain this approach to identifying and supporting learners who may be struggling.

ERIC M. MESMER AND HEIDI ANNE E. MESMER

In the most recent "What's hot, what's not for 2008?" *Reading Today* survey, 75% of prominent literacy researchers believed that Response to Intervention (RTI) was "very hot" and the same percentage believed that it should be "hot" (Cassidy & Cassidy, 2008). RTI is a new approach to identifying students with specific learning disabilities and represents a major change in special education law, the Individuals With Disabilities Act (IDEA). This change shifts the emphasis of the identification process toward providing support and intervention to struggling students early and is similarly reflected in the Reading First provisions of No Child Left Behind, which calls for proven methods of instruction to reduce the incidence of reading difficulties. RTI will alter the work of reading teachers because more than 80% of students identified for special education struggle with literacy (Lyon, 1995), and the law names "reading teachers" as qualified participants in the RTI process because of the International Reading Association's (IRA, 2007) lobbying efforts. However, RTI has only recently attracted the attention of the reading community (Bell, 2007), despite having roots in approaches such as prereferral intervention (Flugum & Reschly, 1994; Fuchs, Fuchs, & Bahr, 1990), curriculum-based measurement (Shinn, 1989), and Reading Recovery (Clay, 1987; Lyons & Beaver, 1995).

RTI in Theory
Background and Rationale
RTI was developed because of the many problems with the discrepancy model for identifying students with learning disabilities (e.g., Francis et al., 2005; O'Malley, Francis, Foorman, Fletcher, & Swank, 2002; Stanovich, 2005; Vellutino, Scanlon, & Lyon, 2000; Walmsley & Allington, 2007). In 1977, a learning disability was defined as "a severe discrepancy between achievement and intellectual ability" (U.S. Department of Education, 1977, p. G1082). In practice, this involves schools administering IQ

tests and achievement tests and then examining scores for discrepancies between intellect and achievement to identify a learning disability (see Table 1). The discrepancy model has drawn four major criticisms. First, it requires that a learning problem becomes considerably acute in terms of an IQ/achievement discrepancy before a learner can receive additional support, a problem called "waiting to fail" (Vaughn & Fuchs, 2003, p. 139). Second, establishing a discrepancy is not necessary to improve outcomes for struggling readers, as students both with and without a discrepancy are qualitatively the same in their literacy instructional needs (Fuchs, Mock, Morgan, & Young, 2003; Vellutino et al., 2000). Third, the IQ/ achievement discrepancy has shifted focus away from understanding the impact of other possible factors, such as opportunities to learn (Walmsley & Allington, 2007). These factors need to be considered prior to determining that a learning disability exists. Fourth, under the discrepancy model, many districts and states have seen skyrocketing percentages of students identified as learning disabled, particularly minorities (IRA, 2007; Walmsley & Allington, 2007).

The Law
In 2004, IDEA, Public Law 108-446, introduced RTI language (U.S. Department of Education, 2006). In Table 2, the section entitled "Specific learning disabilities" (§ 300.307) asserts that states cannot be required to use the discrepancy model for identifying learning disabilities but may "permit the use of a process based on the child's response to scientific, research-based intervention." This is RTI, a process measuring whether a learner's academic performance improves when provided with well-defined, scientifically based interventions. In an RTI model, the "tests" of whether students possess learning disabilities are not standardized measures but students' measured responses to interventions. Within RTI, student potential (IQ) is replaced by a goal that allows for the evaluation of a performance relative to a defined academic standard (e.g., performance of other students

Table 1 Definitions of RTI Terms

Term	Definition
Discrepancy model	The standard for identifying students with learning disabilities based on the 1977 federal regulations. This process required that a significant difference be documented between a student's ability (IQ) and achievement in order for a learning disability to be identified. RTI models respond to the many problems identified with the discrepancy model.
Intervention	Targeted instruction provided in addition to the regular classroom program that addresses a student's documented instructional needs.
	Instruction that intends to prevent students who are struggling from falling farther behind their peers and intends to improve their future educational trajectory.
Level data	Information that reflects how students are performing in comparison to peers at a specific point in time.
	Slope data Information that reflects how a student is learning across time in comparison to his or her previous learning. These data capture rate of learning and can also be called growth rates. Slopes that are steeper show more growth over a smaller period of time than slopes that are flatter. Slope data are obtained by repeatedly measuring student performance in a particular area. They are displayed using a line graph.
Student progress monitoring	An assessment technique required by RTI regulations. Teachers administer quick assessments (1–5 minutes) frequently (weekly) to gauge the improvement of a student. The assessments provide information about the student's rate of learning and the effectiveness of a particular intervention (National Center on Student Progress Monitoring, 2007).
Literacy screening	The process of assessing the most basic and predictive literacy skills for all students in a school. The goal of screenings is to select learners whose reading achievement is significantly below standards. Literacy screenings are intended to identify students who require additional help so that further slippage and literacy failure can be prevented.

in the class or grade level). Students responding quickly and significantly to interventions are less likely to possess a disability than students responding more slowly or not at all. However, data showing a student's response to an intervention serves as only one source of information for determining whether a learning disability is present. Learning disabilities cannot be diagnosed when appropriate instruction, socioeconomic status, culture, sensory issues, emotional issues, or English as a second language may be of concern.

In the section entitled "Determining the existence of a specific learning disability" (§ 300.309), the law states that a learning disability may be present when a student's performance is not adequate to meet grade-level standards when provided with appropriate instruction and research-based interventions. The term *appropriate* refers to instruction in the classroom that matches a student's skill level. The descriptors *scientific* or *research-based* indicate that interventions should be based on practices that have produced verifiable results through research studies.

RTI Processes

The processes undergirding RTI have been used for evaluating the success of schoolwide supports, individualized interventions, and special education (O'Connor, Fulmer, Harty, & Bell, 2005; Powell-Smith & Ball, 2002; Taylor-Greene et al., 1997). However, in this article we focus on RTI as an initial referral and identification process for students suspected of having learning disabilities.

Step 1

Universal literacy practices are established. Prevention begins with universal literacy screenings to identify students who could be at risk (see Table 3). Any state receiving Reading First monies has identified a literacy screening in grades K–3. All students are screened on basic literacy skills approximately three times per year. Typically, student performance is compared with minimal benchmark scores and students not meeting benchmarks receive help.

Step 2

Scientifically valid interventions are implemented. When students do not meet benchmarks, they need additional instruction. Within most RTI models, interventions are first delivered to a small group and are intended to assist students in developing skills that will allow them to improve their reading skills.

Step 3

Progress of students receiving intervention instruction is monitored. RTI requires that progress-monitoring data are continuously collected as students receive interventions. Progress-monitoring assessments should address the skills that are being targeted for intervention and should indicate if the intervention is changing the student's reading. Also, the assessments should be administered repeatedly (weekly or biweekly) without introducing test-wise bias, which occurs when the results of an assessment reflect the testtaker's acquired knowledge about a test rather than true performance. In addition, the assessments

Table 2 Additional Procedures for Identifying Children with Specific Learning Disabilities

IDEA terminology	IDEA definition
§ 300.307 Specific learning disabilities.	A State must adopt, consistent with 34 CFR 300.309, criteria for determining whether a child has a specific learning disability as defined in 34 CFR 300.8(c)(10). In addition, the criteria adopted by the State: • Must not require the use of a severe discrepancy between intellectual ability and achievement for determining whether a child has a specific learning disability, as defined in 34 CFR 300.8(c)(10); • Must permit the use of a process based on the child's response to scientific, research-based intervention; and • May permit the use of other alternative research-based procedures for determining whether a child has a specific learning disability, as defined in 34 CFR 300.8(c)(10). A public agency must use the State criteria adopted pursuant to 34 CFR 300.307(a) in determining whether a child has a specific learning disability. [34 CFR 300.307] [20 U.S.C. 1221e-3; 1401(30); 1414(b)(6)]

§ 300.309 Determining the existence of a specific learning disability.	The group described in 34 CFR 300.306 may determine that a child has a specific learning disability, as defined in 34 CFR 300.8(c)(10), if:
	
	• The child does not achieve adequately for the child's age or to meet State-approved grade-level standards in one or more of the following areas, when provided with learning experiences and instruction appropriate for the child's age or State-approved grade–level standards:
	
	    • Oral expression.
	    • Listening comprehension.
	    • Written expression.
	    • Basic reading skills.
	    • Reading fluency skills.
	    • Reading comprehension.
	    • Mathematics calculation.
	    • Mathematics problem solving.
	
	• The child does not make sufficient progress to meet age or State-approved grade-level standards in one or more of the areas identified in 34 CFR 300.309(a)(1) when using a process based on the child's response to scientific, research-based intervention; or the child exhibits a pattern of strengths and weaknesses in performance, achievement, or both, relative to age, State-approved grade-level standards, or intellectual development, that is determined by the group to be relevant to the identification of a specific learning disability, using appropriate assessments, consistent with 34 CFR 300.304 and 300.305; and the group determines that its findings under 34 CFR 300.309(a)(1) and (2) are not primarily the result of:
	
	    • A visual, hearing, or motor disability;
	    • Mental retardation;
	    • Emotional disturbance;
	    • Cultural factors;
	    • Environmental or economic disadvantage; or
	    • Limited English proficiency.
	
	To ensure that underachievement in a child suspected of having a specific learning disability is not due to lack of appropriate instruction in reading or math, the group must consider, as part of the evaluation described in 34 CFR 300.304 through 300.306:
	
	• Data that demonstrate that prior to, or as a part of, the referral process, the child was provided appropriate instruction in regular education settings, delivered by qualified personnel; and
	• Data-based documentation of repeated assessments of achievement at reasonable intervals, reflecting formal assessment of student progress during instruction, which was provided to the child's parents.

Note. From U.S. Department of Education. (2006). *Assistance to states for the education of children with disabilities and preschool grants for children with disabilites* (Federal register 34 CFR Parts 300 and 301). Washington, DC: Author.

Table 3 Examples of Literacy Screening Assessments

Screener	Authors
Dynamic Indicators of Basic Early Literacy Skills (DIBELS)	Good & Kaminski, 2002
Phonological Awareness Literacy Screening (PALS)	Invernizzi, Juel, Swank, & Meier, 2005
Texas Primary Reading Inventory (TPRI)	Texas Education Agency & University of Texas System, 2006
Illinois Snapshots of Early Literacy (ISEL)	Illinois State Board of Education, 2008

should be sufficiently sensitive to small changes in the student's reading performance (i.e., those that might occur within a few days) because it students are showing growth on the more sensitive, microlevel progress-monitoring measures, they will also be showing growth in the more comprehensive measures (Deno, Mirkin, & Chiang, 1982; Fuchs & Deno, 1981; Riedel, 2007). Finally, progress-monitoring measures must be reliable, valid, and brief (National Center on Student Progress Monitoring, 2007). For a list of tools for progress monitoring, see the National Center on Student Progress Monitoring website at www.studentprogress.org/chart/chart.asp.

Step 4

Individualize interventions for students who continue to struggle. Students who continue to struggle despite receiving initial intervention instruction will require more intense, targeted interventions. These interventions may require additional assessments to clarify the nature of the difficulty. The data generated from these additional assessments should be used collaboratively by teachers, reading specialists, school psychologists, and parents to develop more intensive intervention strategies. Upon implementation, the student's progress continues to be monitored.

Step 5

A decision-making process to determine eligibility for special education services occurs when necessary. In the last step, a team of school-based professionals and the student's parents review all data to determine whether the student is eligible for special education services. Special services may be indicated when the student has not responded to interventions that have been well implemented for a sufficient period of time. If the team suspects that the student's lack of response may be explained by some other factor (i.e., not explained by a learning disability), then it should request additional assessment of the student's social, behavioral, emotional, intellectual, and adaptive functioning.

RTI in Real Life: Making a Difference for Mark

To illustrate RTI processes, we use a vignette (with pseudonyms) based on our experiences in schools. This vignette shows how a team including Donisha, a reading teacher, Julie, a special educator, Carol, a second-grade teacher, and Sandra, a school psychologist, worked collaboratively (and sometimes painstakingly) within an RTI model to assist a student named Mark.

Step 1: Universal Literacy Practices Are Established

In September, Mark was administered the Phonological Awareness and Literacy Screening (PALS; Invernizzi, Juel, Swank, & Meier, 2005), an assessment that begins with two screening measures, the first-grade word list, given in the fall of grade 2, and a spelling assessment. From these measures, an entry benchmark score is formed. If the benchmark score does not meet the grade-level minimum, then additional diagnostics are administered (preprimer and primer lists, letter naming, letter sounds, concept of word, blending, and sound-to-letter). Students also read passages through which accuracy, reading rate, phrasing (a 3-point subjective scale), and comprehension scores are collected.

In the fall, Mark received a benchmark score of 22 (7/20 on the first-grade word list) and 15/20 on the spelling assessment. An expected benchmark score of 35, based on 15 words on the first-grade list, and 20 spelling feature points is expected for the beginning of second grade. Mark read instructionally at the primer level (1.1) with moderate phrasing and expression and answered five-sixths of the questions correctly. He read the 120 words in the primer story in 4 minutes and 20 seconds, a rate of about 28 words correct per minute (WCPM) and 20 words below the 50th percentile for second graders in the fall (Parker, Hasbrouck, & Tindal, 1992). When diagnostic assessments were administered, data showed that Mark had mastered alphabetic skills, such as phonemic awareness and letters. Carol described her initial analysis: "Mark seemed to have the basic building blocks for reading but needed more practice at his level." Initially, Mark received small-group classroom instruction, including reading daily in on-level materials and working with Carol on comprehension and decoding. In September, October, and November, Carol took running records on the books that Mark and the other students had been reading. Although the accuracy and book levels of other students were steadily increasing, Mark's accuracy was averaging 90% in less difficult books. Carol explained, "I felt like Mark needed more help, and we needed to act because I was concerned that he would continue to fall behind."

Step 2: Scientifically Valid Interventions Are Implemented

RTI requires that instructional interventions be scientifically valid, public, implemented with integrity, and systematically evaluated. Julie, who had recently attended the district's RTI workshop, explained that "The who, what, when, where, and how of interventions must be clear." The content of the intervention should be designated, the teacher responsible for implementing it identified, and the assessments determined. Often different team members plan, implement, or assess the intervention based on availability and expertise. For this reason, educators must collaborate and share information.

The team discussed Mark's needs and designed an intervention. Based upon its review of the data, the team determined that accurate, fluent reading in connected text seemed to be the problem. Mark could easily understand books above his reading level, but his progress was being impeded by word recognition. The group decided that an intervention increasing the amount of reading practice for Mark would build up his reading level. The designed intervention comprised the following components: modeling of fluent reading, repeated readings, error correction, comprehension questions, and self-monitoring. They decided that Donisha would implement the intervention with three other students in the classroom in 20-minute sessions, three times per week. In addition, Carol continued to work with Mark in the classroom during small-group instruction. Specifically, she had Mark read from the same materials used by Donisha to further increase practice opportunities, and she set a daily goal for Mark on comprehension questions. Mark checked his answers each day and provided the results to his teacher at the end of the reading block.

Step 3: Progress of Students Receiving Intervention Instruction Is Monitored

As the intervention was implemented, Sandra tracked Mark's accuracy and fluency in reading passages at the primer and second-grade levels, because the goal was to understand Mark's progress toward grade-level norms. She used a PDA device loaded with passages at different levels. As Mark read these passages weekly, Sandra kept track of his accuracy (percentage of words correct) and reading rate (WCPM). Figure 1 shows Mark's accuracy and Figure 2 shows his reading rate before and after implementing the intervention for six weeks. Mark demonstrated some gains in accuracy and fluency, but his progress was not increasing at a rate that would allow him to meet established second-grade goals.

As we have described RTI to this point, it sounds smooth and trouble free. But it was anything but that for the professionals involved. Donisha's first reaction to RTI was strong:

> At first, I felt like this group was shrinking reading down to something very simplistic. I had to advocate for comprehension questions to be included in the intervention. Even though Mark's comprehension was fine, we did not want him to believe that comprehension didn't matter. We also clarified that interventions are *additive* and by nature narrower because their power lies in solving specific problems. The comprehensive reading program is broad and multifaceted, and it keeps going on while a child is receiving an intervention. So Carol wasn't going to stop guided reading or doing the rest of her program.

We liken the intervention and the reading program to a balanced diet. The intervention is like an extra serving of milk, but it doesn't replace meat, fruits, or vegetables.

Donisha was also concerned that the intervention would be scripted. Scripts ate directions to teachers that are read verbatim during instruction. Interventions are specific and systematic, but nothing in the law requires them to be scripted.

Carol also had concerns. "I was not used to people asking me specific questions about exactly what I was doing, and how often, and what my results were. At first, it felt invasive and suspicious." Given the frequency with which blame is placed on classroom teachers, Carol's reaction was understandable. However, the team members pointed out that the instruction was working well for almost all of the other students and acknowledged the time limitations and demands placed on Carol as a classroom teacher. Although she had felt it in the past, Carol did not feel as though fingers were being pointed at her. Sandra had faced equal frustration before:

> I come in because a teacher has a concern and when I start asking questions, I get tight responses and defensiveness. It's like asking questions is stepping on toes. I can't help others further understand the problem or contribute to a useful intervention if we can't talk nitty-gritty. Once I had a teacher tell me, "You're not a teacher. You won't be able to help." While I am not a teacher, I can contribute to the development of interventions, and I have particular skill in measuring effects.

In addition to reviewing Mark's progress during the six weeks of intervention instruction, Mark's midyear PALS scores were evaluated by the team. He was independent at the primer (1.1) level and barely instructional at the first-grade level with 14 errors and a reading rate of 42 WCPM. Despite his increase in instructional level and fluency, the team remained concerned about the lack of reduction in the number of errors that Mark was making. The team decided that these errors would ultimately become detrimental to Mark's fluency and comprehension, particularly as text increased in difficulty. The team determined that individualized intervention was warranted.

Step 4: Individualize Interventions for Students Who Continue to Struggle

Because they had no measure of decoding, the team decided to assess Mark using the Word Attack Test from the Woodcock Reading Mastery Test. Results from this assessment revealed that Mark was having difficulty decoding words with more than one syllable or those that contained difficult vowel patterns. This resulted in reduced accuracy and fluency. The team enhanced the intervention by adding practice with problem words. Mark practiced incorrectly read words, received instruction in how to analyze word parts, extended analytic skills to similar words, and practiced through word sorts. Following word sorts, Mark read each word within a sentence. Donisha implemented this individualized intervention for 10 minutes each day following the reading practice intervention (discussed earlier in the article).

Mark's reading accuracy and fluency continued to be monitored weekly by Sandra. The team determined that the intervention would be implemented for a minimum of 6 weeks, as this time frame would correspond with the end of the school year. However, the team recognized that interventions in early

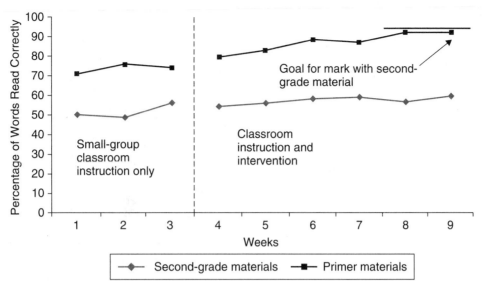

Figure 1 Mark's accuracy during intervention instruction.

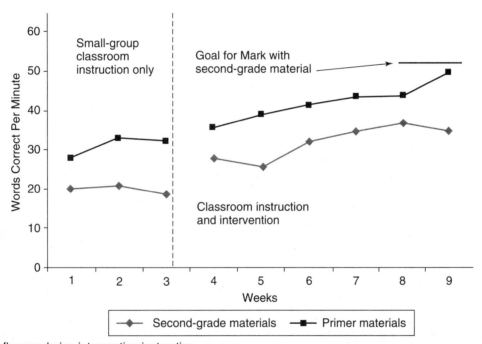

Figure 2 Mark's fluency during intervention instruction.

literacy often need to run longer, between 10 and 20 weeks, depending on factors such as the needs of the student and the intensity of the intervention (University of Texas Center for Reading and Language Arts, 2003; Wanzek & Vaughn, 2008). Moreover, Mark's progress was measured each week so that the intervention could be modified if he failed to make adequate gains. His response to the individualized reading intervention is provided in Figures 3 and 4. Figure 3 shows that Mark quickly responded to the word attack intervention. Data were collected once per week on the percentage of words read correctly from second-grade passages. Mark's response to the intervention contrasted dramatically with his performance reading unknown

words prior to the intervention. By the sixth week, Mark correctly read 100% of words presented when prior to intervention he was only reading 55% to 60% accurately. Figure 4 shows that Mark improved in reading fluency as well. Prior to word attack intervention, the effects of the fluency intervention had leveled off. With the addition of the word attack intervention, Mark's fluency steadily improved until he met the second-grade goal. By the end of May, Mark met the PALS summed score benchmark. His end-of-the-year PALS (58 summer score) showed him meeting the benchmark, reading instructionally at second-grade level with comprehension, and reading at a rate of about 60 WCPM.

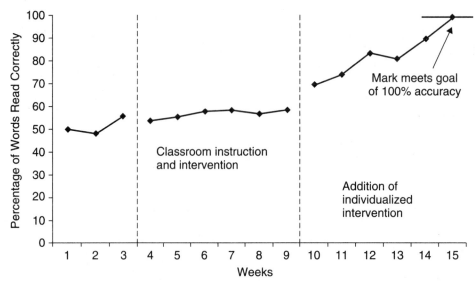

Figure 3 Mark's accuracy during individualized intervention.

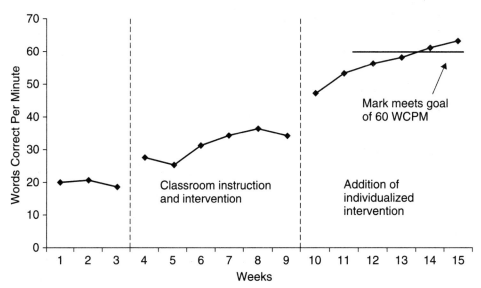

Figure 4 Mark's fluency during individualized intervention.

Step 5: Decision-Making Process to Determine Eligibility for Special Education Services

Despite falling below the second-grade benchmark in September, Mark demonstrated growth on accuracy, fluency, and decoding as a result of the efforts of school personnel. The team reviewed Mark's intervention data and determined that special education services were not necessary. However, Julie voiced concerns about Mark and the continued need for support:

> I could see that Mark had made great progress, but I knew that summer could potentially influence his starting point in the rail and that his progress was the result of substantive instruction *in addition* to the regular classroom. So I insisted that a meeting be scheduled for him in the fall to be proactive about his needs.

Mark's progress was significant relative to where his skills were at the beginning of the year. If the interventions had not met Mark's needs, the team would have been charged with determining whether the lack of response was indicative of a learning disability.

Why RTI?

As illustrated, RTI is a process that incorporates both assessment and intervention so that immediate benefits come to the student. Assessment data are used to inform interventions and determine the effectiveness of them. As a result of the intervention-focused nature of RTI, eligibility services shift toward a supportive rather than sorting function. A testing model that identifies and sorts students into programs or services is predicated upon the effectiveness of those services. Unfortunately, the effectiveness of special education, particularly placement of students in separate classrooms, has been variable at best (Bentum & Aaron, 2003; Kavale, 1990), even as an increasing percentage of students have been identified as learning disabled over the past 30 years (Gresham, 2002). Within the RTI model, instruction can at last be addressed.

Queries, Concerns, and Future Research

We have worked with state departments of education, school districts, schools, and teachers long enough to have questions about RTI. The first issue is that definitions of scientific research privilege experimental and quasi-experimental research (Eisenhart & Towne, 2003; Pressley, 2003). Experiments occur when subjects are randomly assigned to different conditions and the results measured, and they are the best way to know if a practice is causing a certain learning outcome. However, they depend on delivering an instructional treatment in a standardized way, often with study personnel. When teachers do participate in experiments, they often receive intensive support that may not be available when the strategy is widely implemented. The artifices of experiments can limit the degree to which the instructional treatment can be implemented in the real world (Pressley, 2003).

Second, if scientifically based interventions are to be implemented, then research findings must get to schools. We are concerned that the label *scientifically based* will be misused and will proliferate as publishers and companies slap it on everything they market to schools. The final issue is that diverse ways to screen in literacy are still emerging (Gersten & Dimino, 2006). Researchers note that phonologically based competencies, such as phoneme awareness, letter/sound knowledge, and decoding, contribute to part of what makes a student a successful reader (Gersten & Dimino, 2006; Paris, 2005; Scarborough, 2005). Readers must also have a deep knowledge of word meanings and be able to comprehend text. We know oral reading fluency is a good predictor of grade 1 comprehension (Riedel, 2007) but powerful, direct screenings in the areas of vocabulary and comprehension have yet to be developed for elementary learners. Nonetheless, intervening in these areas is important despite the fact that few screening tools exist.

Despite the challenges with RTI, we have seen this approach increase the quantity and quality of instruction for struggling readers. RTI is an initial attempt to provide an alternative to the dominant and damaging discrepancy model in which so much time is spent admiring the student's reading problem. By this we mean people discuss the problem, collect data on it, and write about it, months before they *do* anything about it. IDEA 2004 provides school districts with a choice to opt out of the discrepancy model.

References

Bell, M. (2007). *Reading teachers play key role in successful response to intervention approaches.* Retrieved May 31, 2007, from www.reading.org/downloads/resources/IDEA_RTI_teachers_role.pdf

Bentum, K.E., & Aaron, P.G. (2003). Does reading instruction in learning disability resource rooms really work?: A longitudinal study. *Reading Psychology, 24*(3–4), 361–382. doi:10.1080/02702710390227387

Cassidy, J., & Cassidy, D. (2008). What's hot, what's not for 2008? *Reading Today, 25*(4), *1*, 10–11.

Clay, M.M. (1987). Learning to be learning disabled. *New Zealand Journal of Educational Studies, 22*(2), 155–173.

Deno, S.L., Mirkin, P.K., & Chiang, B. (1982). Identifying valid measures of reading. *Exceptional Children, 49*(1), 36–45.

Eisenhart, M., & Towne, L. (2003). Contestation and change in national policy on "scientifically based" education research. *Educational Researcher, 32*(7), 31–38. doi:10.3102/0013189X032007031

Flugum, K., & Reschly, D. (1994). Prereferral interventions: Quality indices and outcomes. *Journal of School Psychology, 32*(1), 1–14. doi:10.1016/0022-4405(94)90025-6

Francis, D.J., Fletcher, J.M., Stuebing, K.K., Lyon, G.R., Shaywitz, B.A., & Shaywitz, S.E. (2005). Psychometric approaches to the identification of LD: IQ and achievement scores are not sufficient. *Journal of Learning Disabilities, 38*(2), 98–108. doi:10.1177/00222194050380020101

Fuchs, D., Fuchs, L., & Bahr, M. (1990). Mainstream assistance teams: A scientific basis for the art of consultation. *Exceptional Children, 57*(2) 128–139.

Fuchs, D., Mock, D., Morgan, P.L., & Young, C.L. (2003). Responsiveness-to-intervention: Definitions, evidence, and implications for the learning disabilities construct. *Learning Disabilities: Research & Practice, 18*(3), 157–171. doi:10.1111/1540-5826.00072

Fuchs, L.S., & Deno, S.L. (1981). *The relationship between curriculum-based mastery measures and standardized achievement tests in reading* (Research Report No. 57). Minneapolis: University of Minnesota Institute for Research on Learning Disabilities. (ERIC Document Reproduction Service No. ED212662)

Gersten, R., & Dimino, J.A. (2006). RTI (Response to Intervention): Rethinking special education for students with reading difficulties (again). *Reading Research Quarterly, 41*(1), 99–108. doi:10.1598/RRQ.41.1.5

Good, R., & Kaminski, R. (2002). *DIBELS oral reading fluency passages for first through third grades* (Technical Report 10). Eugene: University of Oregon.

Gresham, F. (2002). Responsiveness to intervention: An alternative approach to the identification of learning disabilities. In R. Bradley, L. Danielson, & D. Hallahan (Eds.), *Identification of learning disabilities: Research to practice* (pp. 467–519). Mahwah, NJ: Erlbaum.

Illinois State Board of Education. (2008). *Illinois Snapshots of Early Literacy.* Retrieved June 5, 2007, from www.isbe.state.il.us/curriculum/reading/html/isel.htm

International Reading Association. (2007). *Implications for reading teachers in Response to Intervention (RTI).* Retrieved May 31, 2007, from www.reading.org/downloads/resources/rti0707_implications.pdf

Invernizzi, M., Juel, C., Swank, L., & Meier, J. (2005). *Phonological awareness literacy screening.* Virginia: The Rector and The Board of Visitors of the University of Virginia.

Kavale, K. (1990). Effectiveness of special education. In T.B. Gutkin & C.R. Reynolds (Eds.), *Handbook of school psychology* (2nd ed., pp. 868–898). New York: Wiley.

Lyon, G.R. (1995). Research initiatives in learning disabilities: Contributions from scientists supported by the National Institute of Child Health and Human Development. *Journal of Child Neurology, 10*(Suppl. 1), S120–S126.

Lyons, C., & Beaver, J. (1995). Reducing retention and learning disability placement through reading recovery: An educationally sound cost-effective choice. In R. Allington & S. Walmsley (Eds.), *No quick fix: Rethinking literacy programs in America's elementary schools* (pp. 116–136). New York: Teachers College Press.

National Center on Student Progress Monitoring. (2007). Common questions for progress monitoring. Retrieved May 20, 2007, from www.studentprogress.org/progresmon.asp#2

O'Connor, R.E., Fulmer, D., Harty, K.R., & Bell, K.M. (2005). Layers of reading intervention in kindergarten through third grade: Changes in teaching and student outcomes. *Journal of Learning Disabilities, 38*(5), 440–455. doi:10.1177/00222194050380050701

O'Malley, K., Francis, D.J., Foorman, B.R., Fletcher, J.M., & Swank, P.R. (2002). Growth in precursor and reading-related skills: Do low-achieving and IQ-discrepant readers develop differently? *Learning Disabilities Research & Practice, 17*(1), 19–34. doi:10.1111/1540-5826.00029

Paris, S.G. (2005). Reinterpreting the development of reading skills. *Reading Research Quarterly, 40*(2), 184–202. doi:10.1598/RRQ.40.2.3

Parker, R., Hasbrouck, J., & Tindal, G, (1992). Greater validity for oral reading fluency: Can miscues help? *The Journal of Special Education, 25*(4), 492–503.

Powell-Smith, K., & Ball, P. (2002). Best practices in reintegration and special education exit decisions. In A. Thomas & J. Grimes (Eds.), *Best practices in school psychology-IV* (pp. 541–557). Bethesda, MD: National Association of School Psychologists.

Pressley, M. (2003). A few things reading educators should know about instructional experiments. *The Reading Teacher, 57*(1), 64–71.

Riedel, B. (2007). The relation between DIBELS, reading comprehension, and vocabulary in urban first grade students. *Reading Research Quarterly, 42*(4), 546–567. doi:10.1598/RRQ.42.4.5

Scarborough, H. (2005). Developmental relationships between language and reading: Reconciling a beautiful hypothesis with some ugly facts. In H.W. Catts & A.G. Kamhi (Eds.), *The connections between language and reading disabilities* (pp. 3–24). Mahwah, NJ: Erlbaum.

Shinn, M, (1989). *Curriculum-based measurement: Assessing special children.* New York: Guilford.

Stanovich, K. (2005). The future of a mistake: Will discrepancy measurement continue to make the learning disabilities field a pseudoscience? *Learning Disability Quarterly, 28*(2), 103–106. doi:10.2307/1593604

Taylor-Greene, S., Brown, D., Nelson, L., Longton, J., Cohen, J., Swartz, J., et al. (1997). School-wide behavioral support: Starting the year off right. *Journal of Behavioral Education, 7*(1), 99–112. doi:10.1023/A:1022849722465

Texas Education Agency & University of Texas System. (2006). *Texas Primary Reading Inventory.* Retrieved from www.tpri.org/products/

University of Texas Center for Reading and Language Arts. (2003). *Three-tier reading model: Reducing reading difficulties for kindergarten through third grade students.* Austin, TX: Author.

U.S. Department of Education. (1977). *1977 code of federal regulations.* Washington, DC: Author.

U.S. Department of Education. (2006). *Assistance to states for the education of children with disabilities and preschools grants for children with disabilities, final rule.* Retrieved May 17, 2007, from eric.ed.gov/ERICDocs/data/ericdocs2sql/content_storage_01/0000019b/8011b/e9/95.pdf

Vaughn, S., & Fuchs, L.S. (2003). Redefining learning disabilities as inadequate response to instruction: The promise and potential problems. *Learning Disabilities Research & Practice, 18*(3), 137–146. doi:10.1111/1540-5826.00070

Vellutino, F.R., Scanlon, D.M., & Lyon, G.R. (2000). Differentiating between difficult-to-remediate and readily remediated poor readers: More evidence against the IQ-discrepancy definition of reading disability. *Journal of Learning Disabilities, 33*(3), 223–238. doi:10.1177/002221940003300302

Walmsley, S., & Allington, R. (2007). *No quick fix, the RTI edition: Rethinking literacy programs in America's elementary schools.* Newark, DE: International Reading Association.

Wanzek, J., & Vaughn, S. (2008). Response to varying amounts of time in reading intervention for students with low response to intervention. *Journal of Learning Disabilities, 41*(2), 126–142. doi:10.1177/0022219407313426

ERIC M. MESMER teaches at Radford University, Radford, Virginia, USA; e-mail emesmer@radford.edu. **HEIDE ANNE E. MESMER** teaches at Virginia Polytechnic Institute and State University, Blacksburg, USA; e-mail hamesmer@vt.edu.

From *The Reading Teacher*, December 2008/January 2009, pp. 280–290. Copyright © 2009 by International Reading Association. Reprinted by permission.

You Should Read This Book!

Sustained silent reading was the breakthrough for these urban learners—but only because their teacher tried and tried again.

JENNIFER HARTLEY

One Monday, my 5th grade students were, as usual, visiting the classroom library, returning and checking out books. One of my boys pulled a bookmark out from about 10 pages into his book. When I asked why he was returning his book, he said, "Because I'm finished." When I questioned him about the story, he could only give details about the very beginning. He checked out another book and went on his way. Although my kids always had a book available to read after they finished their class work, I began to notice the pattern: Many students turned books in whether they were finished with them or not. Perhaps my students were not reading as much as I had thought.

I teach in an urban elementary school; 98 percent of my students are economically disadvantaged. My 5th grade class that year consisted of 20 black students, 11 boys and 9 girls. Their reading abilities ranged from a low 1st grade level to a middle school level. To begin gathering information about their reading habits, I surveyed students' parents about their children's reading behaviors at home. Most of my students were not reading outside of school, and many parents indicated that they wished their child could and would read more. Although we had shared and guided reading daily, my students were only reading assigned materials at assigned times. True, I gave them choices, but their choices came from a list of *my* choices. The truth was, my students were not getting enough time to sit and really read what *they* wanted to read.

After discovering Pilgreen's (2000) research about making independent reading a success, I committed to changing my book selections, my classroom's appearance, and my instruction. Sustained silent reading is a time when everyone, including the teacher, reads silently for a given length of time (Butler & Turbill, 1987). To get essential information from my students about what they enjoyed and did not enjoy about reading, I gave each student a short reading survey. The results revealed that most of my students were not motivated to read—especially the boys, many of whom claimed they did not like to read at all.

Ready, Set—Chaos!

Clearly, I had to begin updating my classroom library. I started by ordering *Sports Illustrated Kids* and *National Geographic for Kids*. Right away I noticed that the boys, and many of the girls, gravitated toward the magazine section. My next step was to get the students involved in choosing books for our classroom library. During our book fair, when boys got to pick two books apiece to add to our collection, they came up with graphic novels featuring Batman and Spiderman, as well as the Goosebumps graphic novel series. They also selected multiple nonfiction books, of which we had few to start with, centered on science, sports heroes, and world records. Girls also picked for the library, choosing mostly fiction that highlighted female characters and books based on TV shows.

My next step was to change the class library's appearance. I needed a shelf that screamed, "Choose me!" On our new display shelf, books face forward with their covers visible; the shelf reads "Excellent 5th Grade Reads." At Wal-Mart, I found cushions, chairs, mats, and beanbags for reading comfort.

My final step was to incorporate silent reading into our daily classroom routine. I knew my students would initially be reluctant, but I was hoping the added books and comfy seating arrangement would make the transition easier for them.

The first day of our new sustained silent reading trial, students decorated their own folders and picked out books they wanted to read. They could sit anywhere they wanted. I was hoping that finding a comfortable reading position would help motivate them to read.

What I got was chaos! Students ran around the room fighting over the cushions or a place to read on the carpet. Some chose reading materials that were too difficult for them, and some chose books they could finish in two minutes. Needless to say, we did not get a lot of reading done that day. I was disheartened and frustrated. How was I going to get students to love reading?

Setting up Supports

Instead of scrapping the whole idea, I hit the computer to do a little research on the best way to implement sustained silent reading in my classroom. Steve Gardiner (2005) discussed how he models for his classes what good adult readers do. I began working with my students on how to choose appropriate reading materials at their ability levels by evaluating books through the "five-finger test." Students determine whether a book is too hard for them by skimming a page and raising a finger every time they come to a word they do not understand. If they raise all five fingers, the book is too difficult to read without help. We talked about different physical places where a reader might feel comfortable reading. Students described situations that might distract them when they read, giving them a way to determine whether their reading location was appropriate for focusing on reading.

We discussed different ways students could monitor and support their own reading using strategies like predicting, asking questions, rereading for meaning, and making connections. Students decided to use reading logs to track what they were reading, how much they were reading, and when they finished a book. Because they wanted to share what they read with other students, I downloaded from the Internet (at www.abcteach. com/free/f/form_bookrecommendation.pdf) a form we could use titled "You Should Read This Book!" The form gives readers the opportunity to share their favorite parts of each text and articulate why they would recommend favored books to their peers.

I also modeled ways students could set personal reading goals. Goals included such achievements as completing one to three pages every five minutes (for my lowest-achieving readers); choosing harder and longer books; or focusing on a particular comprehension strategy, such as summarizing or questioning. Students let me know how many books they wanted to read each week and month. We discussed their reading levels and book choices and made goals together depending on the types of books each student decided to read.

We had two rules for sustained silent reading, adapted from Kelley and Clausen-Grace (2006):

- Students must have self-selected reading materials in their desks before the reading period begins. If a student forgets to bring something to read, the teacher gives the reader a book, selecting something he or she might like.
- No one moves around during the reading period.

Success!

The second time we tried silent reading, students came in after lunch, pulled out their reading folders, and began to read at their desks. After a couple of minutes, I announced that students should choose a reading spot somewhere around the room. Each reader could pick his or her own place, but if the reader was distracted—or distracting—in that spot, I would suggest a better location. Some pulled out beanbags, some settled under their desks on mats and pillows, and one tucked up underneath the computer tables. Contrary to the second s in *sustained silent reading*, my classroom was not completely quiet. You could hear whisper-reading and hushed talking throughout the room and the occasional burst of laughter when someone read something funny.

The class worked up from reading 5 minutes to 25 minutes each day. It wasn't long before students were begging me to let them share what they were reading with their peers. The reading by itself was not satisfying enough, and they wanted to go beyond filling out the "You Should Read This Book!" form.

So we instituted partner sharing. After each reading stretch, students returned to their desks and turned to a partner to share what they were reading. This practice actually helped with accountability; unfocused readers now had a motivating reason to delve into their books. Occasionally, students asked to share with the whole class. These presentations gave students ideas for books they wanted to read and initiated some excellent book discussions.

Eventually, we combined the partner and whole-group sharing through a strategy called "Rap" (Kelley & Clausen-Grace, 2006). After one partner shared what he or she had experienced in a book, the other partner would turn around and pass on what he or she had heard to the rest of the class. This technique helped my students become better listeners and improved their retelling skills, which standardized tests in our district evaluate. One unexpected outcome of this method of operating was that my classroom blossomed into a learning community

Worth All the Work

After nine weeks of this daily reading, students again filled out the reading survey they took at the beginning. The results were astounding: Surveys showed a major increase in students' motivation to read. Students read more at home, embraced more variety in their reading selections, and were more likely to finish their books. Many students reported that they enjoyed the peer sharing and the quiet atmosphere, which they didn't have at home. Throughout the year, I assessed students using the ThinkLink test, Rigby Running Records, and the DIBELS assessment. Students' scores on all assessments improved as we continued to do sustained silent reading. All but one of my students were eager to continue the program, and my readers made comments like, "Sustained silent reading gives you more time to communicate with books. You get the feeling you want to read all the way through the book, and you get to know the characters."

Although introducing silent reading into my classroom took a lot of hard work and multiple adjustments, it was a success that will contribute to these students' future learning. They grew to love reading, and they used books to expand their knowledge both at school and at home. Now, whenever we miss a day of silent reading, my students beg me to let them read.

References

Butler, A., & Turbill, J. (1987). *Towards a reading-writing classroom.* Portsmouth, NH: Heinemann.

Gardiner, S. (2005). A skill for life. *Educational Leadership, 63*(2), 67–70.

Kelley, M., & Clausen-Grace, N. (2006). R5: The sustained silent reading makeover that transformed readers. *The Reading Teacher, 60*(2), 148–156.

Pilgreen, J. (2000). *The SSR handbook: How to organize and manage a sustained silent reading program.* Portsmouth, NH: Heinemann.

JENNIFER HARTLEY teaches 5th grade at Hardy Elementary School in Chattanooga, Tennessee; jhartley@comcast.net.

Getting Children In2Books

Engagement in Authentic Reading, Writing, and Thinking

Getting children excited about—"in2"—reading and writing is the first step in developing high-level literacy. An innovative program based on this premise is producing excellent results with urban elementary students who had struggled with language arts. The authors suggest this program shows that there are better approaches than focusing merely on phonemic awareness, phonics, and word recognition.

WILLIAM H. TEALE ET AL.

Literacy reigns in U.S. elementary schools. Because of recent federal and state policies, more instructional emphasis than ever before has been placed on reading and writing. Such a development should bode well for raising the reading comprehension, vocabulary knowledge, and critical-thinking skills of children in the U.S., which, according to the National Assessment of Educational Progress (NAEP), have been basically static for the past 30 years. Moreover, according to such international assessments as the Programme for International Student Assessment (PISA), these are areas in which U.S. children lag behind children in a number of other developed nations.[1] However, there are signs that the current emphasis may be doing the very thing recent federal legislation was designed to avoid: leaving U.S. students, especially children from our poorest neighborhoods, even further behind in what really counts when it comes to literacy—comprehension and critical thinking.

If children are to excel in reading, writing, and critical thinking, they need to learn how to read different types of texts deeply and critically and how to write different types of texts in ways that clearly and powerfully communicate ideas.

How could this possibly happen? Because K-3 reading instruction in many schools has focused so heavily on phonemic awareness, phonics, and word recognition that comprehension, vocabulary, and writing have been given short shrift. Because so much emphasis has been placed on K-3 reading that literacy instruction at higher grade levels has not been given the attention that it requires. Because the results on standardized reading tests have served as the sole criterion of literacy progress and consequently elementary school literacy programs have become mechanized and test-driven rather than content- and meaning-driven. Because instruction focused on reading skills has ended up reducing the teaching of science and social studies in the elementary schools to a minimum and in some cases has even crowded these subjects out of the school day altogether.[2] Ironically, developments such as these have occurred largely in response to state and federal mandates intended to *raise* the quality and level of literacy instruction.

We applaud the idea of giving literacy the primary emphasis in the instructional day in U.S. elementary schools. But we also have observed that, unless fundamental principles of good literacy curriculum and instruction are kept firmly at the forefront of daily teaching in all subjects, the new emphasis may have little effect at best and at worst may negatively affect student literacy. If children are to excel in reading, writing, and critical thinking, they need to learn how to read different types of texts deeply and critically and how to write different types of texts in ways that clearly and powerfully communicate ideas. If the children who are not faring well in literacy learning in our schools are to succeed, they need teaching that both accelerates their learning and goes beyond what are commonly regarded as the "basics" of literacy. Instruction must promote children's engagement with text while also developing their skill at understanding and creating texts for a variety of purposes and across a range of subjects.

For the past few years we have worked in urban public elementary schools to implement literacy instruction that emphasizes higher-level reading, writing, and thinking while also maintaining instructional focus on the skills of decoding, word recognition, and fluency. Our aim has been to help students learn what they really need to learn in order to become engaged and accomplished readers and writers—literate beings capable of interpreting text; developing connections between themselves and texts; critically analyzing, evaluating, and synthesizing; critiquing the usefulness of information in a text; writing on a variety of topics and for many different audiences; revising and editing ideas and forms of expression; and carrying out other higher-level processing that is involved in reading and writing.[3]

Engaging Children in Authentic Reading, Writing, and Thinking

Our efforts have involved implementing an initiative called In2Books. During the past five years, we have worked with more than 6,000 urban children and their teachers in grades 2 through 5 in Washington, D.C., and Chicago. Over 80% of the children attended Title I schools, and most of them were struggling readers and writers. In2Books is a program that was developed to motivate children to engage in authentic literacy activities across the curriculum while also teaching them higher-level thinking, composing, and comprehension skills. It centers on a pen-pal exchange, with adult volunteers and students writing to one another about a common set of children's books they have read. The program is designed to create a context in which students are motivated to read books and to comprehend them deeply because they will write about the books to an adult who engages them in dialogue about what they have both read. In the students' classrooms, teachers use a range of instructional activities—from discussion and questioning to process writing and vocabulary and fluency activities—in order to develop children's literacy skills and content-area knowledge and so enable them to write good letters to their pen pals and apply their reading and writing strategies effectively in a variety of contexts.

During a school year, In2Books students receive five grade-level books in different genres: fiction, folklore, biography, and informational nonfiction (social studies and science). For each genre cycle, students can choose one of three books of varying difficulty. The books are then the students' to keep. All the books align with the content standards at each grade level and are selected by a committee of nationally recognized experts in children's literature. They are chosen to be age appropriate, compelling, and diverse, and they demonstrate successful problem solving, resilience, and the importance of interpersonal and family relationships. In addition to these core books, there is a set of related books the teacher reads aloud in conjunction with each genre.

Students are matched with adult pen pals, recruited from various businesses, nonprofit organizations, and government agencies in the area. The adults are coached through Pen Pal Place®, a rich website environment that helps them learn how to write effective letters about the books in language the children will understand and to pose thought-provoking questions. Pen pals submit their letters electronically, and the letters are screened, printed out, and then delivered to the children in an envelope.

In class, on an appointed delivery day, each student receives the "hard copy" of his or her pen pal's letter. This is always a time of great excitement for the children. They read and reread their letters, and then, over a number of days, they complete the culminating activity for each cycle—writing letters about the books in response to those from their pen pals.

During each cycle, the children not only study the genre and especially the core book, but they also branch out to other print and electronic texts on similar topics or with similar text features. The varied activities that surround the genre study create a context for deeper understanding and higher-level discussions and writing.

For support in establishing and maintaining this rich learning environment in their classrooms, teachers participate in one of three distinct yearlong professional development sequences (determined by the number of years the teacher has implemented In2Books). Each sequence has different content, but all of the sequences focus on core principles: 1) improving literacy through strategic reading of books, 2) writing to a real pen pal in response to literature, and 3) using informal data (i.e., the letters the students write) as the basis for teachers' instructional decisions. The professional development sessions are highly participatory and designed to support teachers in using the core books, the related read-aloud books, and a range of other instructional and assessment activities that are detailed in cycle-related curriculum guides.

Effects of In2Books

What has happened to students' literacy as a result of implementing In2Books? We do not yet have a full answer, but one large-scale study conducted to date provides important indications. During the 2003-04 school year, an evaluation was conducted in the District of Columbia Public Schools (DCPS) to help determine how participation in In2Books related to student literacy achievement patterns. The analysis compared the SAT-9 reading test scores of over 2,000 DCPS students in grades 2 through 4 who were in In2Books classrooms with the scores of approximately 8,500 students in comparison classrooms who had not participated in In2Books. As two of the authors have reported elsewhere, at all three grade levels, students in the classrooms of veteran In2Books teachers (teachers who had used the program for more than one year) scored statistically significantly higher in reading than the control students.[4] Performance comparisons also showed that students in first-year In2Books classrooms scored significantly higher in grades 3 and 4 than students in non-In2Books classrooms, while scores were statistically equivalent across groups for grade-2 students.

Overall, these results indicated that students who experienced In2Books as part of their instructional program were significantly more likely to have higher levels of achievement in reading than students not in the program. Furthermore, it is worth noting that In2Books students managed to score significantly higher on this high-stakes, standardized reading test than non-In2Books students while having a curriculum that deliberately avoided didactic test-preparation exercises in favor of authentic, challenging literacy instruction. This outcome strongly suggests that a focus on authentic instruction can work as well in traditionally low-achieving schools as in any other type of school.

What Is at Work in Such an Approach?

The test results, a review of two years of questionnaire responses from classroom teachers, periodic observations of In2Books classrooms, and the assessment of hundreds of letters written by the children and their pen pals have led us to conclude that devoting classroom time to emphasizing higher-level reading, writing, and thinking skills in conjunction with core instruction on the technical basics of reading and writing can develop elementary school children's decoding and word-recognition skills at least as well as a core program that concentrates mainly on the technical basics. The bonus for children in In2Books classrooms is that they have many more opportunities to read and write for authentic purposes across content areas. What exactly makes such an experience possible? We identified four interrelated factors that seemed to matter.

- *An active and supportive learning community.* Children, teachers, and pen pals worked together to create a classroom community that emphasized learning from one another and the benefits of a cooperative approach. The attitude promoted in In2Books classrooms is one of participation: each person's contributions are expected, respected, and built on by a group engaged in inquiry together. In order to support teachers in establishing such an environment in their classrooms, the professional development sequences stressed the notion of the classroom and the pen pals as a learning community. In addition, the concept was an important feature of the training of pen pals through Pen Pal Place®. The aim from the beginning was to establish a community of children, teachers, and other adults who read, talk, and write together in ways that enhance their understanding of the world they share. Such a focus helped all participants feel that they were contributing and valuable members of the overall community.

The role of pen pals in the program proved to be a very powerful one because it demonstrated that the learning community did not stop at the walls of the classroom or the school. We often hear about the importance of community involvement, but what distinguished this case of involvement was that the community, in essence, became personalized for each child in the form of the one-on-one relationship with a pen pal. This relationship with someone who responded in an individualized and caring way sparked a genuine desire among the children to communicate.

- *Engagement in authentic, purposeful, and challenging work that promotes critical thinking.* Closely related

to the role that the learning community played was the idea of having an actual person to write to. This made children's work in literacy authentic and purposeful and encouraged them to talk in substantive ways about themselves, the books they read, and their everyday worlds.

Writing a good letter about a book was a challenging task for the children, most of whom had struggled in language arts. However, because the work was personally meaningful, they were motivated to do their best in writing their letters. This highly motivating context for literacy instruction increased student engagement. And greater engagement meant that children were more likely, for example, to read their books more than once so that they could respond to the questions about the overall theme or specific details that pen pals posed in their letters. Questions from pen pals and teachers encouraged children to evaluate what they had read, to connect to it, and to respond thoughtfully through discussion and writing. To accomplish this, children had to listen carefully and participate in classroom discussions that helped them think critically about their reading. In speaking, listening, reading, and writing, then, children were asked to link ideas, to analyze, and to express their thinking in personally relevant ways.

Teacher reports and our classroom observations show that children approached the task of writing with more enthusiasm than usual. For children who typically struggle in language arts, this was both unusual and encouraging. Focusing on authentic, purposeful reading and writing activities helped create extended, cumulative conversations that kept children involved and learning, despite the fact that the cognitive demands on them increased over time. Ultimately, because of their participation in the higher-level reading, writing, and thinking involved in these cumulative conversations, many children were able to make unexpected progress.

Among the keys to achieving such high levels of student engagement and learning were the instructional routines employed to support children's development. Over the course of the program, children engaged many times in a variety of social practices related to literacy: read and reread a book, discuss it, write a letter about it. But each time the same social practice was somewhat different: different books, different content, different questions, different expectations for their performance, and so on. Thus, while there were routines, they were not routinized to the point that they became merely exercises practiced over and over. In addition, the program's integrated assessment that focused on the letters the students wrote helped teachers target children's developing needs and adjust teaching routines to meet those needs.[5]

- *Contextualized literacy skills work.* Unlike many programs and approaches advocated since NCLB began to affect practices in underachieving schools, In2Books maintained a higher-level focus and gave authentic purpose to the learning of literacy skills. For example, surface features such as sentence structure, grammar, spelling, and punctuation were taught in the context of purposeful reading and writing tasks. Even when immediate attention was focused on the smaller parts of the task or on skills, the overall context was one of communicating in written language for personal, meaningful purposes.

- *Teacher empowerment through professional growth.* Over the course of their implementation of In2Books, teachers changed their beliefs, attitudes, and practices as a result of participating in a professional learning community. They became empowered to make learning more meaningful to their students and to act as reflective practitioners who were skilled in assessing student work in order to make better instructional decisions. They came to understand how they themselves could learn in this context and embraced the value of ongoing professional development that helped them work in productive and effective ways in their classrooms. A key factor was increasing teachers' professional communication—getting teachers to talk more with one another about teaching, both within and across school buildings. They recognized the importance of decision making in daily instruction and connected to what others were doing in this respect. They increasingly centered their practices on making literacy learning and instruction meaningful to students, and they trusted that they and their students deserved more than a stripped-down focus on the technical basics of reading and writing.

We should always keep in mind that deep and thoughtful reading, effective and purposeful writing, and critical thinking are every bit as basic to high-quality literacy instruction in U.S. elementary schools as phonemic awareness, phonics, and word recognition. We have discussed In2Books not as *the* way to conduct literacy instruction but as a program whose principles are worth considering. It stands as one successful example of how literacy instruction in the classroom lives of urban children can focus on rich, intellectual reading and writing experiences that are meaningful and engaging. In2Books blended the community with classroom literacy and subject-matter study to make learning "authentic" and to motivate students to hone their critical thinking, reading, and writing skills.

We read a great deal about what our children will need for life in the 21st century. But we believe that among the most important skills they can possess is to be critically, not merely functionally, literate. And our experience with In2Books argues strongly that reading and writing instruction that engages children for authentic purposes can help achieve this end.

References

1. *First Results from PISA 2003: Executive Summary* (Paris: Organisation for Economic Co-operation and Development, 2004).
2. Sam Dillon, "Schools Cut Back Subjects to Push Reading and Math," *New York Times*, 26 March 2006, p. 1.
3. The NAEP reading and writing frameworks are available at www.nagb.org/pubs/r_framework_05/761507-ReadingFramework.pdf and http://nces.ed.gov/nationsreportcard/writing/whatmeasure.
4. William H. Teale and Linda Gambrell, "Raising Urban Students' Literacy Achievement by Engaging in Authentic, Challenging Work," *Reading Teacher*, in press.
5. Kathryn Glasswell and William H. Teale, "Authentic Assessment of Authentic Student Work in Urban Classrooms," in Jeanne R. Paratore and Rachel L. McCormack, eds., *Classroom Literacy Assessment: Making Sense of What Students Know and Do* (New York: Guilford, forthcoming).

WILLIAM H. TEALE is a professor of education at the University of Illinois, Chicago. **NINA ZOLT** is advisor to and founder of In2Books, Washington, D.C. **JUNKO YOKOTA** is a professor of education and director of the Center for Teaching Through Children's Books at National-Louis University, Skokie, Ill. **KATHRYN GLASSWELL** is an assistant professor of education at the University of Illinois, Chicago. **LINDA GAMBRELL** is a professor of education at Clemson University, Clemson, S.C., and president-elect of the International Reading Association. ©2007, Nina Zolt.

Using Literature Circles with English Language Learners at the Middle Level

PAMELA J. FARRIS, PAMELA A. NELSON, AND SUSAN L'ALLIER

This We Believe Characteristics

- An inviting, supportive, and safe environment
- Students and teachers engaged in active learning
- Curriculum that is relevant, challenging, integrative, and exploratory
- Multiple learning and teaching approaches that respond to their diversity

Students gather in small groups of three and four to discuss their literature selections as the teacher floats around the room, stopping from time to time to listen to the conversation and other times serving to facilitate the discussion leader's efforts. Sticky notes are prevalent as students jot down ideas, quotes, and questions, pasting them on their clipboards to take back to their desks. Now starting day three of their literature circle assignment, they have been reading two chapters a day and completing their assigned role jobs as part of combined language arts and social studies class requirements.

Yusaf is teamed with his buddies José, Saddat, and Zeke. Wandering off task is easy for this group, as they are also players on the middle school's soccer team and often share stories and jokes. Being grouped together has not always been easy. Two weeks ago, Yusaf flew into a rage upon discovering José's father's name was Israel Lopez. Yusaf could not conceive that his best friend's father could bear a name that he had been taught to hate growing up in his Palestinian family. Conversely, José could not understand why Yusaf was spewing hateful remarks about his father when he had not even met him. Cultural clashes often occur in diverse classroom settings. Fortunately, in this instance a calm, understanding teacher interceded and arranged for Yusaf to spend some time with Jose and his dad during the last period of the school day. It did not hurt that as a young man, Mr. Lopez had been a soccer player with fairly nimble feet, so sports yielded a common ground for conversation. The hurt, shock, and dismay spread over a few days time eventually evaporated.

Nearby, four girls huddle together, hastily scribbling notes for later reference. Kimmie is relatively new to the United States and has no idea about its history—only that it is a place for "oppoortoity" (opportunity) according to her Chinese parents.

Angelina is trying hard to fit in, crossing borders to meet the demands of her Hispanic background and family and those of the American culture. Ramona, too, tries to balance her native culture (Romanian) with her new American one. Unlike Kimmie, Ramona, and Angelina, Maria balks at trying to learn American ways. She refuses to stand for the morning pledge to the flag. At lunch she seeks out the food kiosk with tacos, even though she complains they do not taste like those prepared by her mother and "abulela" (grandmother). Ever so patiently the teacher has nudged Maria to try to view things openly, yet she knows Maria yearns to return to Mexico and live with her grandparents.

Balancing literacy instruction with cultural attributes makes for an interesting teaching assignment for teachers of English Language Learners (ELLs). Scenes like the above happen in schools throughout the country as students try to straddle cultural borders at school. Literature circles can help students better understand each other's culture when appropriate multicultural books and historical novels are selected.

Since 1991, the enrollment of Limited English Proficient (LEP) students in United States schools has increased by 105%, while the total school enrollment has increased only 12%. Of the total LEP enrollment, 67% are in the elementary grades (National Clearing House for English Language Acquisition, 2002), soon to be entering middle school. During the past two decades, immigrants have been largely from Latin American, Arabic, and Asian countries, with increasing numbers of children from Russia and the Ukraine. Not since the late 1880s and 1920s have we seen such changes in the composition of our classrooms.

Literature Circles

The focus of literature circles is to combine literacy skills and strategies in a supportive social atmosphere of a non-threatening peer group (Daniels, 2002). Learning to engage in meaningful discussions, make compromising stances, and work cooperatively are all essential elemental skills students should develop as part of the literature circle experience. Students engage in reading aloud, independent and shared reading, as well as oral discussion and writing based on one selection of literature. Students are encouraged to make connections: text-to-self, text-to-text, and text-to-world. Higher level thinking evolves, as students challenge their peers and themselves with questions about the text, its plot, theme, and characterization.

Raphael and Hiebert (1996) pointed out that literature discussions where students can state their opinions and insights about the book in a community of readers who are interested in discovering, permit the students to develop greater understanding and compassion for others, as they examine differences and commonalities viewed from the perspectives of their peers. Minority students generally gain confidence in speaking before groups and stating their opinions as a result of engaging in conversations about books they are reading (Raphael & Members of the Book Club, 1999). Shy or reluctant students, or those who lack proficiency in English can develop literacy skills through learning the various roles offered in literature circles as they share, discuss, and interpret the various pieces of literature (Martinez, 2000).

The very nature of literature circles provides opportunities for ELL students to practice and refine their language and literacy skills as they analyze, reflect upon, and negotiate the views and ideas of their peers and those presented by the authors they are reading (Martinez-Roldan & Lopez-Robertson, 1999/2000; Samway & Whang, 1996).

Modifying Roles of Literature Circle Members

Typically, three to eight students read the same piece of historical fiction for a combined language arts/social studies integrated assignment, with four being the ideal group size for working with ELLs. The literature circle roles are those outlined for social studies instruction by Farris (2004, pp. 270–271) as follows:

Discussion Leader: Monitors other group members and gives assistance with tasks when needed. Leads the discussion when the group meets together. This requires that the teacher select the ELL student who is dependable and willing to take on a leadership role for the initial literature circle group meetings. Extremely reserved or shy students often feel unduly pressured in this role until they have some experience under their belts.

Historian: Traces the major historical events of the chapter. Often ELLs are lacking in knowledge of their own culture's history as well as that of the United States or world history. The teacher can assist by giving a time line of historical events of the period (e.g., the Revolutionary War or Civil War) or by providing a resource book on the period such as Stephen Ambrose's (2000) *The Good Fight*, a picture book overview of World War II.

Geographer/Cartographer: Draws a map related to the setting of the book and depicts journeys of the main character. Students with an artistic bent or who like geography are well suited for this task in the initial go round.

Word Warrior: Keeps a list of unusual or unfamiliar words from the book and writes down the sentences in which they were used and their definitions. ELLs can easily get bogged down with this task. It is best to limit the number of words to no more than five or six per chapter; otherwise, the student may not be able to complete the reading of the book and the accompanying task in a reasonable time period.

Phrase Keeper: Jots down interesting phrases from each chapter, noting the page number for each. This task can be a superb means of generating discussion in the group.

Character Analyst: Compares and contrasts the main characters of the book; yet another task that opens the discussion door for students, hence, the selection of literature with strong, appealing characters is critical.

Introducing Literature Circles

All students need teacher modeling if literature circles are to work effectively. This is especially true for ELL students, as they need more structure to complete tasks efficiently. Too few directions and too little modeling by the classroom teacher often leave ELL students bewildered. Handing them a sheet of paper and telling them to follow the directions on it simply does not suffice. The teacher needs to carefully demonstrate what needs to take place. This modeling should not be rushed.

The most efficient means of modeling literature circles is for the teacher to find a one- or two-page article, possibly from *Time for Kids, Cobblestone,* or *National Geographic.* Each student is given a copy of the selection to follow along. The teacher then reads aloud a portion of the piece while demonstrating the literature circle role to be accomplished. For instance, the first few paragraphs may demonstrate comparing and contrasting characters. The next section of the text may have new vocabulary words. It is best to have introduced two roles each day to lessen student confusion.

After all the roles have been shared during the week with students given another short text selection for guided practice in performing the roles, the teacher demonstrates how to be a good discussion leader. This includes how to get organized, preparing good questions in advance, and having a checklist to make certain all tasks are accomplished successfully.

Initiating Literature Circles

A quality picture book offers an exceptional opportunity to present all roles in a relatively short period of time to ensure that the students understand not only their respective roles but the need to communicate with other members of their group. *The Pot That Juan Built* (2002) by Nancy Andrews-Goebel provides a superb text, not too long but with sufficient content that piques student interest that the teacher can share as a read aloud with the entire class. In the prose of a cumulative tale, Andrews-Goebel tells the story of Juan Quezada's discovery of how potters in his native Mexican village of Mata Ortiz centuries ago created their unique pottery. Juan's determination to bring back the traditional style helped to provide the natives of Mata Ortiz with a stable economy, as museums, galleries, and patrons of the arts throughout the world seek out the beautiful pottery made in this tiny Mexican village.

After reading the prose on a page, the teacher then reads aloud the accompanying explanatory notes, thus providing both narrative and informational text for the students to consider in their literature circles. New vocabulary is listed on the overhead along with the sentence in which it is used and page number and with the students serving as word reporters copying the information down and creating a definition of the word. Upon completion of the entire book, the teacher presents three questions that the discussion leaders use to stimulate debate and share information.

1. Why did Juan take such an interest in how pottery was made hundreds of years ago?
2. What are the critical steps in making the pottery?
3. Juan is famous for his work throughout the world. He could live anywhere he desires, yet he stays in the small Mexican village of Mata Ortiz. What kind of person is Juan? Why does he not leave and enjoy the riches that accompany a famous artist like famous athletes or musicians do?

The literature circle groups are given 10 minutes to discuss these questions. The class reconvenes to examine the different responses shared by each group. The next day, the students engage in their respective tasks. Each group has access to a copy of the book for reference. The groups then do a follow-up activity—making pottery in art, sharing Mexican artwork or murals, developing a readers' theatre and presenting it, and so on.

The teacher is now ready to present read alouds of the various book choices. Read alouds have been found to foster engagement and learning in social studies at the middle school level (Albright, 2002). The teacher should read the first chapter of the historical fiction novel and select the portion he wishes to read aloud before sharing it with the students. Using different voices for the various characters, setting the tone of the book, using appropriate intonation, and speaking loudly, yet not reading too rapidly are also important tips. Stopping and encouraging students to respond to the reading and share what they are thinking by querying, "What do you think about this?" will spark some discussion, and most likely, interest in the books you are promoting for literature circles (Albright & Ariail, 2005).

Suggested Literature

Since diverse populations are together in the classroom, sometimes books from different cultures lend themselves to sharing. In particular, it is efficient to combine a picture book from one culture with that of another culture. Students can read the picture book and discuss it as both an icebreaker to initiate their literature circle group as well as to discuss commonalities and differences among cultures. One possibility is pottery as a common cultural element. *The Pot that Juan Built* by Nancy Andrews-Goebel with pictures by David Diaz is a combination prose/biography of Juan Quezada, the premier potter in Mexico. On the left-hand page is the prose.

This is the pot that Juan built.

These are the flames so sizzling hot

That flickered and flared and fired the pot.

The beautiful pot that Juan built.

Asian

Cha, Disa, Chiie Thao Cha, & Nhia Thao Cha. (1996). *Dia's story cloth: The Hmong people's journey of freedom*. New York: Lee & Low. (Picture book Hmong)

Cheng, Andrea. (2000). *Grandfather counts*. New York: Lee & Low. (Picture book-Chinese)

Fleming, Candace. (2005). *Lowji discovers America*. New York: Atheneum. (Picture book-East Indian)

Lord, Bette. (1984). *In the year of the boar and Jackie Robinson*. New York: HarperRow. (Novel-Chinese)

Park, Linda. (2001). *A single shard*. New York: Dell Yearling. (Novel-Korean)

Park, Linda. (2005). *Project mulberry*. New York: Clarion. (Novel-Korean)

Hispanic

Andrews-Goebel, Nancy. (2002). *The pot that Juan built* (David Diaz, Illus.). New York: Lee & Low. (Picture book-Hispanic)

Bernier-Grand, Carmen. (2004). *Cesar*. New York: Marshall Cavendish. (Picture book-Hispanic)

Garza, Carmen. (1996). *In my family/En mi familia*. San Francisco: Children's Book Press. (Picture book-Hispanic)

Garza, Carmen. (2005). *Family Pictures/Cuadros de familia*. San Francisco: Children's Book Press. (Picture book-Hispanic)

Jimenez, Francisco. (1997). *The circuit: Stories from the life of a migrant child*. Boston: Houghton Mifflin. (Autobiography-Hispanic)

Perez, L. King. (2002). *First day in grapes*. New York: Lee & Low. (Picture book-Hispanic)

Ryan, Pam. (2001). *Esperanza rising*. New York: Scholastic. (Novel-Hispanic)

Ryan, Pam. (2004). *Becoming Naomi Leon*. New York: Scholastic. (Novel-Hispanic)

Other cultures

Ellis, Deborah. (2000). *Breadwinner*. Toronto, Canada: Groundwood Books. (Novel-Afghanistan)

Heide, Florence Parry, and Judith Heide Gilliland. (1992). *Sami and the time of the troubles*. New York: Clarion. (Picture book-Lebanese)

Naidoo, Beverly. (Ed.). (2004). *Making it home: Real-life stories from children forced to flee*. New York: Puffin. (Short autobiographical vines-Afghanistan, Bosnia, Burundi, Congo, Iraq, Liberia, and Sudan)

Nye, Naomi Shibab. (1997). *Habibi*. New York: Aladdin. (Novel-Israeli/Palestinian)

Figure 1 Children's and young adult literature.

The right-hand side offers the historical background of Juan Quezada's life—how he uses ancient methods and natural materials in making pottery in Mata Ortiz, Mexico. *The Pot that Juan Built* couples nicely with *A Single Shard* by Linda Park (2001), the Newbery Award winning story about a 12-year-old orphan boy who becomes an apprentice to a master potter who makes fine celadon ware. The boy travels on a dangerous journey to the king's court to show the potter's work.

Figure 1 presents a list of suggested literature circle books including picture books for read alouds by the teacher or group as well as novels. In selecting books, keep in mind gender issues

Alphabet Book—The students create an alphabet book based on the characters, key events, historical information, geographical locations, and so on from the book.

Accordion Book—Each student in the group creates one scene that they believe is significant in the sequence of the storyline.

Character Bookmark—Each student creates a bookmark representing an important character from the book.

Jackdaw—Using a shoe box, collect artifacts and label them as they relate to the story.

Newspaper—Create a newspaper with events of the period and some of the major events of the book.

PowerPoint Presentation—Since most middle school students take a computer technology course, the students can download illustrations or pictures from the period and write an historical overview that is read to accompany the pictures.

Reader's Theatre—Students take significant passages and transform them into a reader's theatre.

Reenacting Major Scenes from the Book—Students may select one to three scenes and dress up in simple costumes and reenact in a short drama.

Timeline—Each student takes a section of the book and creates a timeline for that portion of the story. The entire timeline gives the major events of the story along with the historical backdrop of the period.

Figure 2 Extension projects.

as male students who are reluctant readers may balk completely if the book choices have female protagonists and vice versa with female students.

Extension Activities

At the conclusion of the literature circle, having the students engage in an extension project helps students to continue their discussions about the book and gain more meaning. With historical fiction, students can search out information in the library or via the Internet and gain additional understanding from a historical viewpoint. Often, the other social sciences (economics, sociology, geography) are enhanced for the student through such inquiry. Figure 2 displays a list of some possible extension projects for historical novels.

The sharing of these extension activities should celebrate the groups' work. Effort and the final products should be duly noted, as students share and rejoice in their group's completion of the roles and their extension project. This is also a learning time for the peer groups who view only the extension activities. Groups can be limited to 10 minutes for their presentations.

Conclusion

Teachers who elect to incorporate literature circles as part of their literacy and social studies instruction of ELLs find that the time to structure the assignment, model the roles, and have the students engage in the actual literature circles is beneficial in literacy growth and acquisition of social studies knowledge by their students. Careful selection of literature as well as formation of the groups are critical aspects for successful implementation of literature circles with ELLs.

References

Albright, L. K. (2002). Bringing the Ice Maiden to life: Engaging adolescents in learning through picture book read-alouds in content areas. *Journal of Adolescent & Adult Literacy, 44,* 418–428.

Albright, L. K., & Ariail, M. (2005). Tapping the potential of teacher read-alouds in middle schools. *Journal of Adolescent & Adult Literacy, 48,* 582–591.

Daniels, H. (2002). *Literature circles: Voice and choice in the student-centered classroom.* York, ME: Stenhouse.

Farris, P. J. (2004). Communicating in social studies. In P. J. Farris (Ed.), *Elementary and middle school social studies: An interdisciplinary and multicultural approach,* 4th ed. (pp. 238–288). Boston: McGraw-Hill.

Martinez, C. M. (2000). Bilingual students' responses to multicultural children's literature on discrimination. *The Dragon Lode, 18*(2), 17–23.

Martinez-Roldan, C. M., & Lopez-Robertson, J. M. (1999/2000). Initiating literature circles in a first grade bilingual classroom. *The Reading Teacher, 53,* 270–281.

National Clearinghouse for English Language Acquisition (NCELA). (2002). Office of English Language Acquisition, Language Enhancement, and Academic Achievement for Limited English Proficient Students. Washington, DC: Author. Retrieved May 19, 2005, from http://www.ncela.gwu.edu/expert/faq/081eps.htm

Raphael, T. E., & Hiebert, E. (1996). *Creating an integrated approach to literacy instruction.* Fort Worth, TX: Harcourt.

Raphael, T. E., & Members of the Book Club. (1999). What counts as teacher research: An essay. *Language Arts, 78,* 333–342.

Samway, K., & Whang, G. (1996). *Literature study circles in a multicultural classroom.* York, ME: Stenhouse.

Pamela J. Farris is a distinguished teaching professor of literacy education at Northern Illinois University, DeKalb. E-mail: pamelafarris@comcast.net **Pamela A. Nelson** is an assistant professor of literacy education at Northern Illinois University, DeKalb. E-mail: panelson@niu.edu **Susan L'Allier** is an assistant professor of literacy education at Northern Illinois University, DeKalb. E-mail: alallier@niu.edu

From *Middle School Journal,* March 2007, pp. 38–42. Copyright © 2007 by National Middle School Association. Reprinted by permission.

Losing the Fear of Sharing Control
Starting a Reading Workshop

LESLEY ROESSING

This We Believe **Characteristics**

- An inviting, supportive, and safe environment
- High expectations for all members of the learning community
- Students and teachers engaged in active learning
- Curriculum that is relevant, challenging, integrative, and exploratory
- Multiple teaching and learning approaches that respond to their diversity
- Assessment and evaluation programs that promote quality learning

W e stood in the empty classroom. Lisa looked up at me. "I couldn't understand what I read last night," she said.

I looked at her, speechless. The class was reading a novel, and I wondered why Lisa had been failing the daily quizzes. These were genuine "right-there" questions, designed only to see if the students had read their nightly assignments.

Of course, you do. You're a good student. I bit back my thoughts.

"I did the reading both nights; really, I did. I just don't understand what I read."

I looked down at this little, trusting face. Goodness! This child expected me to teach her reading. Even worse, she *needed* me to be a reading teacher, not the literature teacher I considered myself, with degrees in English and comparative literatures, courses in literature, literary theory, speech and writing, and one lone course in Reading Across the Curriculum in my Secondary Education Masters program. I was here to teach eighth graders how to *appreciate* literature, not how to *read* it! I sighed; Lisa and her problem were not going to go away.

Then it dawned on me. I might not be trained as a reading teacher, but I was a *reader.* I thought about what *I* do as a reader. I connect the reading to my life, to other works, to what is going on in the world; I question; I visualize what I am reading; I read between the lines and predict what is going to happen. Sometimes I even reread or grab a dictionary for clarity.

Lisa and I sat down, and I made a plan for her. The next day we met again. For two days I asked her to try various strategies.

The third day Lisa came to class. "I understood what I read last night, and I remember it!" That class period she passed the quiz and contributed to the group discussion.

Too close for comfort, I thought. I realized that Lisa was motivated enough to tell me that she could not comprehend the text. How many more were just coasting along on class discussions? There was no way to avoid it; I needed to become a reading teacher. That summer I enrolled in the Pennsylvania Writing & Literature Project's Literature Institute. There, I read the masters, Atwell to Zimmerman, and planned for next year.

The Control Issue

Reflecting on my teaching style, I realized that the way I taught gave me control of the classroom and control of my students. Control was safe; I knew what I was doing, but were the students learning? Obviously, not all of them. I resolved that I would read and apply the insights recorded by others—that I would work out a feasible plan that addressed teaching the state standards and fit into a middle school curriculum. After reading and reading, I vowed to change my classroom into a true reading-writing workshop so that my students could improve their reading skills and learn to love reading and literature as much as they loved writing. As I had previously done with writing (Roessing, 2004), I would trade total *control* for some student *choice.*

I began my journey to release this total control of my classes' reading, to share responsibilities with my students. But, I needed a plan. I teach two eighth grade heterogeneous language arts classes in a 6–8 middle school. For the past 15 years, my literature curriculum had been comprised of a mixture of short stories, poetry, folk tales, a play, and two or three novels. I interspersed magazine and news articles and essays, typically as background for the novel units or as examples for expository writing. In my language arts classes, all the students read the same literary works at the same time and for the same amount of time, all of which I controlled. The only choice the students had was their independent reading 25 minutes per night, and I did give them a (limited) choice of responses.

Did my students like reading? Not especially, although a few did mention that they particularly liked one chapter in *Rifles for Watie*. Was I in control of what we did and what we thought in my classroom? You bet! And everything moved along smoothly. I assumed that everyone was reading, and that, if I force-fed enough culture and showed them how to find the answers, one day they would all love to read as much as I do and would read as well as I do.

Then came Lisa. And there was Richard, who admitted he never even opened the book; he just listened in class and scored the highest grade on the test "since the teacher did such a thorough job of explaining the book and answering her own questions." There was Alan, who did not even pretend to read, who said he would rather go to summer school where they did not have to read so much. And there were the students who insisted that they loved to read but stopped so that they would not have to read my books.

The depth of my problem suddenly struck me when I read a quote from one of Wilhelm's students. Randy defined *school* as "a bunch of crap that doesn't mean anything . . . you just do a bunch of crap for someone else [the teacher] so you can get through the year" (Wilhelm, 1997, p. 12). That sentence really got to me. It affected me, not just because it was true, but because I had ambivalent feelings about it. First of all, I could see many of *my* students saying the same thing, and, second, I really thought that my "crap" was important. I worried that my students needed my crap—that they could not become educated without it. And that is when I knew I needed to change.

First of all, where did I get this idea that I needed to control all aspects of my classroom, especially reading, afraid that students would not learn what they needed, that the product would not remain sacred? Through writing workshops, I had somewhat successfully turned over responsibility of writing to the students. But reading was a different matter. Thinking about my classes with this new insight, I felt the same as Atwell (1998), who said that after her "writing revolution" she realized, "Writing was something that students did, and literature was something I did to students" (p. 21). I was determined to empower my readers and move toward a reader-centered classroom. I decided that I would learn to share control of reading: *what* (choice of literature read), *how* (movement from a variety of shared readings to book club readings to individual reading experiences), *where* (a realistic combination of reading workshop and at-home reading time), and, most importantly, *why* (validation of reader response). I began to agree with Wilhelm (1997) when he wrote, "Creating this new environment [would be] a new and difficult direction to move in as a teacher" (p. 11).

My Plan

The first step was admitting that my teaching methods had become ineffective. Students needed to read better, and they needed to be able to read well to enjoy reading. Therefore, if my goal was to have students love reading as much as I do, they needed to read as I do. However, as pointed out by Purves, Rogers, and Soter (1995), "We found an assumption that reflects our (teachers of secondary English) own experiences rather than

that of the contemporary adolescent student: 'I' love literature, and 'I' managed to 'get hooked on it,' and somehow, so will they; 'I' will help them get there. The teacher is still the director" (p. 21). No one directs *my* reading; no one tells me what to read, although I appreciate recommendations, and I find that I expand my tastes when I am introduced to diverse types of literature—especially when the introduction serves a purpose. I love to talk about my reading with people who are reading the same book and also with those who are not reading that same book (or article or poem). And I appreciate time to read. My students needed the same—recommendations not requirements, peers with whom to discuss their readings, and time to read.

I recognized that, in my role as teacher, I could not break my control abruptly—not for my benefit, but for my students, I needed to prepare them for the transfer of power. I had to give them the tools they would need to assume control of their own reading and learning. An analogy came to mind. When I stopped smoking, I went "cold turkey," which successfully broke my habit but was not effective for my weight; I should have planned for a substitution for the cigarettes (other than food). In the same way, I could not just say, "Go forth and read. See you in June." Giles (1993) (cited in Spiegel 1996) wrote, "Teacher trust of students does not mean teacher abandonment of students" (p. 335). I needed to train my readers with demonstrations and strategy lessons. Purvis, Rogers, and Soter (1995) explained Rosenblatt's *Literature as Explorations,* writing, "Exploration doesn't mean being lost in the woods. It means finding out about new territory for the explorer. The students are the explorers, but they need guides who help them" (p. 77). I needed to become a guide, and my lessons would become their maps, assessments their compasses.

I decided that the most effective journey toward independence would be to begin with shared readings—short stories, poetry, and informational articles first, then a novel. Rief (1992), a strong proponent of reading workshop, advocated differentiated reading experiences, "We read fine literature in many different ways: kids choose their own books, we read different books to each other, and sometimes we read the same books together. I think we need to get at reading from all those angles" (p. 101).

Starting the Path Toward Independence—Shared Readings

In September my classes began reading short stories so that I could teach reading strategies using writings that we could read during class time and discuss *together*. I introduced each new concept with an approximately 25-minute lesson that included an example, guided practice, and independent practice and repeated the same strategy over the next week or so with 10-minute follow-up lessons. Most of these initial concepts focused on reading strategies, such as questioning, visualization, inferring, and connecting, and others focused on literary elements and classroom procedures (collectively referred to as "focus lessons"). We read these stories in varied ways: I read aloud, modeling strategies; students read aloud, using Reader's Theater techniques; and students read silently. The method depended on the story and the students' reading proficiencies. I know that student reading improves most by reading, but I felt it was important to model reading and strategies. Reading aloud is primary, especially in training readers.

Each class began with a focus lesson. Next, we would read the story, and we would discuss the story, focusing on the strategy or literary element being taught or practiced, scaffolding on past lessons. Many times, when I read aloud, we would practice a strategy, questioning or inferring *as* we read. When students were more practiced in the strategy, they would read silently, using sticky notes to mark strategies used.

After introducing a variety of reading strategies and skills through shared stories and, later, factual magazine and news articles, my classes segued into a shared novel. One aspect of control I retained was in choosing shared readings that I really like, that I am passionate about. As Rief (1992) pointed out in *Seeking Diversity,* "If I am not passionate about the book and what it says, I will not pass on that love of learning from reading" (p. 105). On the other hand, I chose stories and books that we read together based on the interests of adolescents and relevance of the texts to my students and their lives. "Selection . . . is a significant factor in engaging many adolescents (and any reader) in what they read" (Purves, Rogers, & Soter, 1995, p. 24). There were three reasons for my choice of novel: I had enough class sets (practicality); it was a story that most, if not all, would find interesting and that a heterogeneous class could read with some assistance; and the novel lent itself to practicing such reading strategies as questioning, inference, and visualization. I knew it was important to choose a novel that everyone could and would read and that would generate discussion and even debate.

Continuing the Path— Book Clubs

After these shared readings, the students were ready for the next step: Book Clubs (also known as literature circles (see Daniels, 2002; Latendresse, 2004)). For this experience I looked for books for which I could round up five or six copies of enough novels of different genres and topics, and diverse reading levels to give choice to every group—class novels from years past, novels of which I had duplicates and the library had a copy or two, novels from the summer reading list donated by students.

The students looked through the offered selection of novels and chose their books and, thereby, formed their book clubs. Lessons associated with this experience focused on choosing appropriate books by reading level and interest, working cooperatively in a group, and other club management issues. We had practiced literature circles a few times for our discussions of the shared novel so the class was familiar with meeting in this way.

I explained that in book clubs the members would first meet and decide how they were going to read the book. They would meet every other day to discuss their reading and would be given time for in-class reading. I gave them an approximate finish date, and the club was to decide how many pages to read for each meeting. It was left up to the discretion of the members to make such decisions as to whether to read more or less over weekends; take other activities in consideration; start slowly and, as they became familiar with the plot, move more quickly; to co-operatively prepare their schedule. It was also within their jurisdiction to plan the in-class

reading time. They could choose to read aloud to each other or read silently or work on response journals during that stage.

Instead of assigning roles to each student, I deviated from Daniels' (2002) original model by requiring each student to bring to each club meeting a discussion point, a quote or passage to share aloud, an analysis of a new vocabulary word, and one question, prediction, or connection made with the text. That way, absenteeism did not leave a gap in the discussion, a problem I had discovered in past years of literature circles. I found that most of the students kept up with the readings and that the few who did not still benefited from the discussions, were "caught up" by the meetings, and wanted to read for the next session so that they could participate (and not incur the disdain of the peers who took this deficit personally since it now affected them). At times, members of groups met with other groups to compare characters, settings, plots, or writing styles.

> **Each student was required to bring to each club meeting a discussion point, a quote or passage to share aloud, an analysis of a new vocabulary word, and one question, or connection made with the text.**

After students finished reading and discussing the book, each book club prepared a presentation of their choice to share the book with the rest of the class. We had quite a variety—brown bag projects, readers' theater, skits, interactive class activities, and a Jerry Springer talk show. These gave my other students ideas of other books to read during the next stage: individual reading.

The End of the Path: Individual Reading

Now my classes were ready for individual reading—what some might refer to as "reading workshop," although I felt that we had been workshopping all year. Atwell (1998) defined workshop as "student-centered in the sense that individuals' rigorous pursuit of their ideas is the primary content of the course" (p. 71). By this point I had introduced and they had practiced all the reading strategies and were familiar with literary elements as well as a variety of writers' crafts. They had read literature chosen by me and self-chosen literature; students had read aloud and read silently; they had discussed writings in large groups and in small groups; they had reflected together and individually. They had also practiced a variety of reading responses. The classes had been trained toward independence. Also, beginning with shared readings and progressing to book clubs and now to individual reading, each class had built a reading *community*. In this way, by the time students were reading self-chosen texts, they did not feel they were reading alone; they were reading separately but not in isolation—individually, not independently.

As the first step in preparation for the individual readings, I thought about my classroom library. I realized that, since many of the books had belonged to my own children, variety was missing; for example, there were few horror or sports books. I needed to think of the interests and reading levels of all of my students and offer a variety of reading levels, lengths, and genres. I ordered from book clubs, hit the second-hand bookstores, and, during the year, asked my students for donations of books. Well into reading workshop, students would send me to the bookstore on weekends with a list.

By the time students were reading their own texts, they did not feel they were reading alone; they were reading separately, but not in isolation—individually, not independently.

A valuable activity was having the students rearrange the classroom library. For years my library of approximately 400 books was organized by author. The books sat there, year after year. After teaching genre, I distributed books to my classes and asked students to read the covers, look through the books, talk to others, and decide on genre classifications for their books. Productive discussion among students flourished. There were discussions about genre but also discussions about authors and books read. Short book talks spontaneously took place. We then re-shelved the books by genre, labeling each shelf: Horror, Mystery, Fantasy, Sci-Fi, Historic Fiction, Biography & Memoir, Folktales, Multicultural Lit, Adolescent Life, Romance, Sports, Classics, Drama, Poetry, Short Stories, Nonfiction. Almost immediately, books started flying off the shelves. The students felt more secure; a boy who wanted a sports book did not fear ending up with a romance and did not mind trying a new author since he knew that the book would be somehow related to sports. Mystery readers tried Agatha Christie and Sherlock Holmes, authors above their usual pleasure reading level. And, if students were looking for particular authors or books, they usually knew under which genre to find them.

Next, the students needed to be prepared for individual choices. Lessons on choosing books for a variety of interests and purposes, on authors, and on varying genres for varying purposes, as well as examples of book talks given by our librarian, students, and me helped my students to "cross the bridge" to independence. Natalie said, "Over this year . . . I also read books suggested by other students, which I have never really done before."

Individual Reading Workshop Begins

I had explained the process of reading individually as opposed to book club reading. I explained the concept, and the students knew that they could choose what to read and where in the classroom to read; they could get comfortable and would be reading for at least a half hour per workshop class, which was a little more time than they usually had in book clubs. Finally, I held my breath, and we began. I presented my focus lesson (nothing new there) and told the students that they could now go to places in the classroom where they could comfortably read. I

looked on in amazement as Heather took out her fleece blanket and headed to lean against the back wall, Tommy pulled out a Spiderman pillow and sat *under* a table, and a few students sat on the carpeted floor in various parts of the classroom; many stayed seated at desks but moved, turning their desks sideways and even backwards.

They are making a mockery of this, I thought pessimistically. What have I done? I'll never get control back.

Then they got out their books and read—each of them, all of them! I got my file folder with overlapping individual 3″ × 5″ cards taped inside and a pen and started making the rounds of conferences, asking them about their choices, whistling inside but looking like all this was expected. I felt like Sally Fields at the Oscars saying, "You like me! You really like me!" But, in this case, referring to reading workshop.

And, in each reading workshop they read. And in each reading workshop until the end of the year, I was amazed and thrilled. I would like to give an example of the students who did not read and the brilliant plans I used to get them to read, but the simple truth is that, this year, everyone read in class every time. Surely, not all students always remembered to bring their books, but they were trained to go to our bookshelves and get a book of short stories or poetry, or even a magazine, for the period. When students finished their books, they went to the bookshelves for another—with some conferring with me or other students—or to our school library. By March or April, readers usually knew what book they wanted next.

I often tell the story of when my two classes got off the same schedule. My second class of the day walked in with their books, and I said, "It can't be your reading day; the last class said it was their reading workshop. I must have forgotten to change the workshop signs on the hall bulletin board last night." They started laughing. One student said, "Period 3 told us they lied to you. It was their writing day, but they wanted to read." Lying to read? I didn't know whether to be angry or proud.

Scheduling Workshops

During the earlier time of shared readings (short stories and our novel), I had also taught writing with shared writings. Our school is on a modified block schedule: Language arts classes are 85-minute periods, all year. Therefore, usually this writing was accomplished during the half period before or after reading or on days after a reading was finished. As the classes moved to book clubs, I began alternating reading and writing workshop days, posting a sign outside my door to remind students. Typically, I began class with a non-workshop lesson such as language study or standardized test-taking skills. I started workshop time with a 15-minute lesson (including the reading aloud of a picture book, poem, excerpt, or continuing story, the focus lesson itself, and guided practice of the skill or strategy presented or reviewed in the lesson). After individual reading time of 30 to 35 minutes, we ended with a 10-minute share, discussion, and, at times, a book talk. Thirty minutes, in my estimation, was the perfect length for reading and writing some responses. As the students read, I circulated, conferring with about one-third of the class for about 15 minutes; the remainder of the time I read. Experts differ, but

I think it is important for students to see me, as a model, read and react to my reading—laughing, crying, gasping. I also talked about my books during share time and gave book talks. I read a range of adolescent books, "adult" books, and books which my students lent me. Students also borrowed the books I was reading. There were some books that I was still in line for at the end of the year. I was part of the community, and it felt good. I got to know my students as readers and could, therefore, recommend books. They got to know me as a reader and also recommended books.

To improve reading, reading should occur daily. For homework during workshop, students read for 25 minutes each night, five nights a week, and wrote journal entries, sharing their at-home reading experiences.

Student Response

Through my personal professional development, I became familiar with Rosenblatt's reader-response theory. As Wilhelm (1997) explained it, "reading is a 'transaction' in which the reader and the text converse together in a particular situation to make meaning." (p. 19) In other words, readers construct meaning from their transactions with the text. Teaching that focuses on finding the correct answers or interpretations or teacher meaning is efferent or informational reading, and to teach students to experience, enjoy, and own literature, or, as she would say, read aesthetically, I must not even try to control the reader's response. Gone were my lists of questions, the lists of topics that must be covered. I let readers engage with the text on their own playing fields. How can literature be life changing and lead to self-discovery, as it has for me, if I am inserting my life and values between the literature and the self?

As I thought back, I wondered why I was afraid that my students would miss the "right answer," the correct interpretation of the text. I remember telling a friend that my problem with literature circles was that, even though the students were talking about the reading and were on task, I was afraid that they might not catch *everything*. She told me to think of my book clubs; did we cover everything when we discussed the book? Exactly who is the arbiter of "everything" (And why did I think it was me)? Where did the reader fit in?

I found, in my search, that I was not alone. In *The Literature Workshop*, Blau (2003) pointed out,

> As a profession, we have for the past twenty or twenty-five years tended to teach composition in ways that are process-oriented, learning-centered (or learner-centered) and collaborative while we have continued . . . to teach literature in a way that has been product-oriented . . . [and] text-centered. (p. 3)

Because of this, students feel that they have to search for not *a* but *the* meaning in a text. They surmise that only teachers have the meaning; unfortunately, many teachers also feel this way. But I am learning that there are many meanings and that "literary meaning is largely an individual engagement, that it results from the creative effort of a reader working from a text." (Probst, 1994, p. 41). Probst further explains,

> We must try, first of all, to *respect the natural influence of literary texts upon readers* [emphasis in the original].

He continues, "Our first task, if we accept that position, is to make sure that the literature has the chance to work its effect on the readers, to make sure we don't get in the way, substituting other matters for that vital influence. . . . Implicit within this vision of literary experience is a *respect for the uniqueness of the individual reader and the integrity of the individual reading.* We have tended in the past—influenced strongly by the professional tendency to insist upon the rightness of certain readings, upon conformity to established interpretations—to seek consensus in the classroom. (pp. 37–38)

Probst also suggested that teachers guide the design of instruction to incorporate certain principles, such as "invite response to the text," "give students time to shape and take confidence in their responses," and "let the talk build and grow as naturally as possible, encouraging an organic flow for the discussion," among others (p. 42).

> **Students feel that they have to search for, not a, but *the* meaning in a text. They surmise that only teachers have the meaning; unfortunately, many teachers also feel this way.**

However, here again I gradually loosened control of the students. They needed to be guided to make valid responses. Rosenblatt (1978) defined "valid" response as "an interpretation [which] is not contradicted by any element of the text, and . . . nothing is projected for which there is no verbal basis" (p. 115). Even though readers are free to make unique and personal responses, they need to base their interpretations on their understanding of the actual text. I taught students a variety of journaling techniques throughout the year so that they were responding in diverse ways. By the end of the year, most students had identified their favorite type of response or modified their journaling to fit their particular reading.

Student Assessment and Evaluation

The purpose of assessment is to judge students' learning and, practical ly, the quantity and quality of work accomplished. Assessment also makes students accountable and provides feedback to both the students and their parents. I attempted to design a system that (a) would balance an evaluation of both student effort and achievement, (b) was based on observation (by me) and performance (by the student), and (c) would not penalize any student risk-taking in either choosing lengthy books or trying and abandoning books that were not right for them. Readers were required to keep a reading log with the date, literary work, and pages read, along with a response journal that I checked weekly. I expected daily entries in the log, and the journal was to contain responses or reflections from all reading. One student said, "[The requirement] forced me to read each night."

Assessment was based on quantity and quality of the journal responses and by a demonstration of quantity, quality, and genre variety in reading evidenced by log entries and a genre record card that listed 19 genres plus a personal choice category. This card was divided into genres and, when students finished books, they would place a star sticker in the appropriate box. I was not really looking for quantity of stars (I knew from the log that the lengths of the books varied), but for stars in a variety of boxes. On the other side of the card, students listed each literary work read, genre, dates began and finished (or abandoned), appraisal of the reading level for them, and if they wrote a book review or gave a book talk, one being required each quarter. In celebration of finishing a book, students were also encouraged to write the titles of their books and their names on laminated posters of library books hung on the back wall of the classroom. By June 1, the readers had filled in all 300 books listed on the posters and were clamoring for me to buy another set of posters, ignoring the fact that the school year was ending.

Students were also assessed by their preparation for and participation in workshops, both by the actual time spent reading and the discussions following, neither of which turned out to be a problem. The marking-period grade also reflected writings (based on the shared readings) or projects (book club) created in response to readings and book talks or written book reviews (based on individual reading), all of which were collected into a binder for other readers to peruse for book suggestions and some of which were submitted to magazines. The evaluation process ended with students' self-evaluation of themselves as readers. These diverse criteria for the assessment of my students' learning also served to assist me in evaluating the success of my workshop program.

Self-Assessment of Reading Workshop: Did It Work?

The reading workshop incorporates what Hansen called the "four key elements" of learning environments: time, ownership, response, and community, which Keene noted as being timeless, relevant to the creation of meaningful environments, and critical to the passionate engagement of learning (Keene & Zimmermann, 1997, p. 7).

During this first year, I observed that students read more, read better, and read willingly. When asked to comment on how their reading changed this year and on reading workshop in general, my students observed these same details about themselves. However, I found it interesting that different students focused their comments on different components of the workshop:

> Chris wrote, "My reading has changed a lot since the beginning of the year. In the beginning of the year I absolutely hated to read. By the end of the year I started to like reading. I started reading books that I usually would not have read before like *Murder on the Orient Express*. Usually I wouldn't read such a long book. I think this was the first book I read that had more than 200 pages. I was proud of myself." [Chris read 14 novels in nine genres]

John wrote: that "I thought reading workshop was a good idea for the school to use. It made me a better reader, and it was cool how we were able to move around the class and find a comfortable place to read." [John read 10 books in seven genres and sat in four different places]

Lauren wrote: "My reading has changed a lot this year. Reading workshop made me want to read more, and it taught me strategies that I used during reading. I used to read close to nothing but now I like it a lot." She continued, "Reading workshop was my favorite thing this year in language arts. I liked it so much because I really enjoy reading now and it really got me into reading more than I ever have before. I enjoyed the lessons in the beginning most of the time too." [Lauren read 17 novels in six genres]

But I think that Emily made one of the most important points:

> "I like reading workshop because everyone can read at their own pace and not worry about [it]."

My students chose how they read and how they responded. And what about me? I read right along with them, sharing my revelations—guiding and guided.

References

Atwell, N. (1998). *In the middle*. Portsmouth, NH: Heinemann.

Blau, S. (2003). *The literature workshop*. Portsmouth, NH: Heinemann.

Daniels, H. (2002). Literature circles: Voice and choice in the student-centered classroom. Portland, ME: Stenhouse Publishers.

Keene, E. O., & Zimmermann, S. (1997). *Mosaic of thought*. Portsmouth, NH: Heinemann.

Latendresse, C. (2004). Literature circles: Meeting reading standards, making personal connections, and appreciating other interpretations. *Middle School Journal, 35*(3), 13–20.

Probst, R. E. (1994). Reader-response theory and the English curriculum. *English Journal, 83*(3), 37–44.

Purves, A. C., Rogers, T., & Soter, A. O. (1995). *How porcupines make love III: Readers, texts, cultures in the response-based literature classroom*. White Plains, NY: Longman.

Rief, L. (1992). *Seeking diversity*. Portsmouth, NH: Heinemann.

Roessing, L. (2004). Toppling the idol. *English Journal, 94*(1), 41–46.

Rosenblatt, L. (1978). *The reader, the text, the poem: The transactional theory of the literary work*. Carbondale, IL: Southern Illinois University Press.

Spiegel, D. L. (1996). The role of trust in reader-response groups. *Language Arts, 73*, 332–339.

Wilhelm, J. D. (1997). *You gotta BE the book*. New York: Teachers College Press.

LESLEY ROESSING, a teacher-consultant for the PA Writing and Literature Project, is an eighth grade language arts teacher at Ridley Middle School, Ridley Park, Pennsylvania. E-mail: lroessing@comcast.net or Lesley_roessing@ridleysd.k12.pa.us

From *Middle School Journal*, January 2007, pp. 44–51. Copyright © 2007 by National Middle School Association. Reprinted by permission.

Nine Ways to Catch Kids Up

How do we help floundering students who lack basic math concepts?

MARILYN BURNS

P aul, a 4th grader, was struggling to learn multiplication. Paul's teacher was concerned that he typically worked very slowly in math and "didn't get much done." I agreed to see whether I could figure out the nature of Paul's difficulty. Here's how our conversation began:

Marilyn: Can you tell me something you know about multiplication?

Paul: [*Thinks, then responds*] 6 × 8 is 48.

Marilyn: Do you know how much 6 × 9 is?

Paul: I don't know that one. I didn't learn it yet.

Marilyn: Can you figure it out some way?

Paul: [*Sits silently for a moment and then shakes his head.*]

Marilyn: How did you learn 6 × 8?

Paul: [*Brightens and grins*] It's easy—goin' fishing, got no bait, 6 × 8 is 48.

As I talked with Paul, I found out that multiplication was a mystery to him. Because of his weak foundation of understanding, he was falling behind his classmates, who were multiplying problems like 683 × 4. Before he could begin to tackle such problems, Paul needed to understand the concept of multiplication and how it connects to addition.

Paul wasn't the only student in this class who was floundering. Through talking with teachers and drawing on my own teaching experience, I've realized that in every class a handful of students are at serious risk of failure in mathematics and aren't being adequately served by the instruction offered. What should we do for such students?

Grappling with Interventions

My exchange with Paul reminded me of three issues that are essential to teaching mathematics:

- It's important to help students make connections among mathematical ideas so they do not see these ideas as disconnected facts. (Paul saw each multiplication fact as a separate piece of information to memorize.)

- It's important to build students' new understandings on the foundation of their prior learning. (Paul did not make use of what he knew about addition to figure products.)

- It's important to remember that students' correct answers, without accompanying explanations of how they reason, are not sufficient for judging mathematical understanding. (Paul's initial correct answer about the product of 6 × 8 masked his lack of deeper understanding.)

For many years, my professional focus has been on finding ways to more effectively teach arithmetic, the cornerstone of elementary mathematics. Along with teaching students basic numerical concepts and skills, instruction in number and operations prepares them for algebra. I've developed lessons that help students make sense of number and operations with attention to three important elements—computation, number sense, and problem solving. My intent has been to avoid the "yours is not to question why, just invert and multiply" approach and to create lessons that are accessible to all students and that teach skills in the context of deeper understanding. Of course, even well-planned lessons will require differentiated instruction, and much of the differentiation needed can happen within regular classroom instruction.

But students like Paul present a greater challenge. Many are already at least a year behind and lack the foundation of mathematical understanding on which to build new learning. They may have multiple misconceptions that hamper progress. They have experienced failure and lack confidence.

Such students not only demand more time and attention, but they also need supplemental instruction that differs from the regular program and is designed specifically for their success, I've recently shifted my professional focus to thinking about the kind of instruction we need to serve students like Paul. My colleagues and I have developed lessons that provide effective interventions for teaching number and operations to those far behind. We've grappled with how to provide instruction that is engaging, offers scaffolded instruction in bite-sized learning experiences, is paced for students' success, provides the practice students need to cement fragile understanding and skills, and bolsters students' mathematical foundations along with their confidence.

In developing intervention instruction, I have reaffirmed my longtime commitment to helping students learn facts and skills— the basics of arithmetic. But I've also reaffirmed that "the basics" of number and operations for all students, including those who struggle, must address all three aspects of numerical proficiency—computation, number sense, and problem solving. Only when the basics include understanding as well as skill proficiency will all students learn what they need for their continued success.

Essential Strategies

I have found the following nine strategies to be essential to successful intervention instruction for struggling math learners. Most of these strategies will need to be applied in a supplementary setting, but teachers can use some of them in large-group instruction.

1. Determine and Scaffold the Essential Mathematics Content

Determining the essential mathematics content is like peeling an onion—we must identify those concepts and skills we want students to learn and discard what is extraneous. Only then can teachers scaffold this content, organizing it into manageable chunks and sequencing these chunks for learning.

For Paul to multiply 683×4, for example, he needs a collection of certain skills. He must know the basic multiplication facts. He needs an understanding of place value that allows him to think about 683 as $600 + 80 + 3$. He needs to be able to apply the distributive property to figure and then combine partial products. For this particular problem, he needs to be able to multiply 4 by 3 (one of the basic facts); 4 by 80 (or 8×10, a multiple of 10); 4 and by 600 (or 6×100, a multiple of a power of 10). To master multidigit multiplication, Paul must be able to combine these skills with ease. Thus, lesson planning must ensure that each skill is explicitly taught and practiced.

2. Pace Lessons Carefully

We've all seen the look in students' eyes when they get lost in math class. When it appears, ideally teachers should stop, deal with the confusion, and move on only when all students are ready. Yet curriculum demands keep teachers pressing forward, even when some students lag behind. Students who struggle typically need more time to grapple with new ideas and practice new skills in order to internalize them. Many of these students need to unlearn before they relearn.

3. Build in a Routine of Support

Students are quick to reveal when a lesson hasn't been scaffolded sufficiently or paced slowly enough: As soon as you give an assignment, hands shoot up for help. Avoid this scenario by building in a routine of support to reinforce concepts and skills before students are expected to complete independent work. I have found a four-stage process helpful for supporting students.

Students are quick to reveal when a lesson hasn't been scaffolded sufficiently or paced slowly enough: As soon as you give an assignment, hands shoot up for help.

My "Aha!" Moment

My "aha" moment came long after I had finished a masters in mathematics, taught mathematics in secondary school and college, and completed a doctorate in mathematics education. Although I enjoyed the rigor of learning and applying rules, mathematics was more like a puzzle than an elegant body of knowledge.

Many years of work on a mathematics program for elementary schools led to that moment. I realized that mathematics was more than rules—even the beginnings of mathematics were interesting. Working with elementary students and teachers, I saw that students could make sense of basic mathematical concepts and procedures, and teachers could help them do so. The teachers also posed problems to move students forward, gently let them struggle, and valued their approaches. What a contrast to how I had taught and learned mathematics!

With vivid memories of a number-theory course in which I memorized the proofs to 40 theorems for the final exam, I cautiously began teaching a number-theory course for prospective middle school teachers. My aha moment with these students was a semester long. We investigated number-theory ideas, I made sense of what I had memorized, and my students learned along with me. My teaching was changed forever.

—Mary M. Lindquist, Professor of Mathematics Education, Columbus College, Georgia. Winner of the National Council of Teachers of Mathematics Lifetime Achievement Award.

In the first stage, the teacher models what students are expected to learn and records the appropriate mathematical representation on the board. For example, to simultaneously give students practice multiplying and experience applying the associative and commutative properties, we present them with problems that involve multiplying three one-digit factors. An appropriate first problem is $2 \times 3 \times 4$. The teacher thinks aloud to demonstrate three ways of working this problem. He or she might say,

I could start by multiplying 2×3 to get 6, and then multiply 6×4 to get 24. Or I could first multiply 2×4, and then multiply 8×3, which gives 24 again. Or I could do 3×4, and then 12×2. All three ways produce the same product of 24.

As the teacher describes these operations, he or she could write on the board:

$$2 \times 3 \times 4 \qquad 2 \times 3 \times 4 \qquad 2 \times 3 \times 4$$
$$6 \times 4 = 24 \qquad 8 \times 3 = 24 \qquad 2 \times 12 = 24$$

It's important to point out that solving a problem in more than one way is a good strategy for checking your answer.

In the second stage, the teacher models again with a similar problem—such as $2 \times 4 \times 5$—but this time elicits responses from students. For example, the teacher might ask, "Which two factors might you multiply first? What is the product of those two factors? What should we multiply next? What is another way to start?" Asking such questions allows the teacher to reinforce correct mathematical vocabulary. As students respond, the teacher again records different ways to solve the problem on the board.

During the third stage, the teacher presents a similar problem—for example, $2 \times 3 \times 5$. After taking a moment to think on their own, students work in pairs to solve the problem in three different ways, recording their work. As students report back to the class, the teacher writes on the board and discusses their problem-solving choices with the group.

In the fourth stage, students work independently, referring to the work recorded on the board if needed. This routine both sets an expectation for student involvement and gives learners the direction and support they need to be successful.

4. Foster Student Interaction

We know something best once we've taught it. Teaching entails communicating ideas coherently, which requires the one teaching to formulate, reflect on, and clarify those ideas—all processes that support learning. Giving students opportunities to voice their ideas and explain them to others helps extend and cement their learning.

Thus, to strengthen the math understandings of students who lag behind, make student interaction an integral part of instruction. You might implement the *think-pair-share* strategy, also called it *turn and talk*. Students are first asked to collect their thoughts on their own, and then talk with a partner; finally, students share their ideas with the whole group. Maximizing students' opportunities to express their math knowledge verbally is particularly valuable for students who are developing English language skills.

5. Make Connections Explicit

Students who need intervention instruction typically fail to look for relationships or make connections among mathematical ideas on their own. They need help building new learning on what they already know. For example, Paul needed explicit instruction to understand how thinking about 6×8 could give him access to the solution for 6×9. He needed to connect the meaning of multiplication to what he already knew about addition (that 6×8 can be thought of as combining 6 groups of 8). He needed time and practice to cement this understanding for all multiplication problems. He would benefit from investigating six groups of other numbers—6×2, 6×3, and so on—and looking at the numerical pattern of these products. Teachers need to provide many experiences like these, carefully sequenced and paced, to prepare students like Paul to grasp ideas like how 6×9 connects to 6×8.

6. Encourage Mental Calculations

Calculating mentally builds students' ability to reason and fosters their number sense. Once students have a foundational understanding of multiplication, it's key for them to learn the basic multiplication facts—but their experience with multiplying mentally should expand beyond these basics. For example, students should investigate patterns that help them mentally multiply any number by a power of 10. I am concerned when I see a student multiply 18×10, for example, by reaching for a pencil and writing:

$$\begin{array}{r} 18 \\ \times\ 10 \\ \hline 00 \\ 18 \\ \hline 180 \end{array}$$

Revisiting students' prior work with multiplying three factors can help develop their skills with multiplying mentally. Helping students judge which way is most efficient to multiply three factors, depending on the numbers at hand, deepens their understanding. For example, to multiply $2 \times 9 \times 5$, students have the following options:

$2 \times 9 \times 5$	$2 \times 9 \times 5$	$2 \times 9 \times 5$
$18 \times 8 = 90$	$10 \times 9 = 90$	$2 \times 45 = 90$

Guiding students to cheek for factors that produce a product of 10 helps build the tools they need to reason mathematically.

When students calculate mentally, they can estimate before they solve problems so that they can judge whether the answer they arrive at makes sense. For example, to estimate the product of 683×4, students could figure out the answer to 700×4. You can help students multiply 700×4 mentally by building on their prior experience changing three-factor problems to two-factor problems: Now they can change a two-factor problem—700×4—into a three-factor problem that includes a power of 10—$7 \times 100 \times 4$. Encourage students to multiply by the power of 10 last for easiest computing.

7. Help Students Use Written Calculations to Track Thinking

Students should be able to multiply 700×4 in their heads, but they'll need pencil and paper to multiply 683×4. As students learn and practice procedures for calculating, their calculating with paper and pencil should be clearly rooted in an understanding of math concepts. Help students see paper and pencil as a tool for keeping track of how they think. For example, to multiply 14×6 in their heads, students can first multiply 10×6 to get 60, then 4×6 to get 24, and then combine the two partial products, 60 and 24. To keep track of the partial products, they might write:

$$\begin{array}{r} 14 \times 6 \\ 10 \times 6 = 60 \\ 4 \times 6 = 24 \\ 60 + 24 = 84 \end{array}$$

They can also reason and calculate this way for problems that involve multiplying by three-digit numbers, like 683×4.

Player 1 chooses two numbers from those listed (in the game shown here, 6 and 11) and circles the product of those two numbers on the board with his or her color of marker.

Player 2 changes just one of the numbers to another from the list (for example, changing 6 to 9, so the factors are now 9 and 11) and circles the product with a second color.

Player 1 might now change the 11 to another 9 and circle 81 on the board. Play continues until one player has completed a continuous pathway from one side to the other by circling boxes that share a common side or corner. To support intervention students, have pairs play against pairs.

72	36	49	88	54
84	77	96	132	56
63	81	48	108	121
(66)	99	144	64	42

6　　7　　8　　9　　11　　12

Figure 1　Pathways multiplication game.

8. Provide Practice

Struggling math students typically need a great deal of practice. It's essential that practice be directly connected to students' immediate learning experiences. Choose practice problems that support the elements of your scaffolded instruction, always promoting understanding as well as skills. I recommend giving assignments through the four-stage support routine, allowing for a gradual release to independent work.

Games can be another effective way to stimulate student practice. For example, a game like *Pathways* (see Figure 1 for a sample game board and instructions) gives students practice with multiplication. Students hone multiplication skills by marking boxes on the board that share a common side and that each contain a product of two designated factors.

9. Build In Vocabulary Instruction

The meanings of words in math—for example, *even, odd, product,* and *factor*—often differ from their use in common language. Many students needing math intervention have weak mathematical vocabularies. It's key that students develop a firm understanding of mathematical concepts before learning new vocabulary, so that they can anchor terminology in their understanding. We should explicitly teach vocabulary in the context of a learning activity and then use it consistently. A math vocabulary chart can help keep both teacher and students focused on the importance of accurately using math terms.

When Should We Offer Intervention?

There is no one answer to when teachers should provide intervention instruction on a topic a particular student is struggling with. Three different timing scenarios suggest themselves, each with pluses and caveats.

While the Class Is Studying the Topic

Extra help for struggling learners must be more than additional practice on the topic the class is working on. We must also provide comprehensive instruction geared to repairing the student's shaky foundation of understanding.

- *The plus:* Intervening at this time may give students the support they need to keep up with the class.
- *The caveat:* Students may have a serious lack of background that requires reaching back to mathematical concepts taught in previous years. The focus should be on the underlying math, not on class assignments. For example, while others are learning multidigit multiplication, floundering students may need experiences to help them learn basic underlying concepts, such as that 5×9 can be interpreted as five groups of nine.

Many students needing math intervention have weak mathematical vocabularies.

Extra help for struggling learners must be more than additional practice.

Before the Class Studies the Topic

Suppose the class is studying multiplication but will begin a unit on fractions within a month, first by cutting out individual fraction kits. It would be extremely effective for at-risk students to have the fraction kit experience before the others, and then to experience it again with the class.

- *The plus:* We prepare students so they can learn *with* their classmates.
- *The caveat:* With this approach, struggling students are studying two different and unrelated mathematics topics at the same time.

After the Class Has Studied the Topic

This approach offers learners a repeat experience, such as during summer school, with a math area that initially challenged them.

- *The plus:* Students get a fresh start in a new situation.
- *The caveat:* Waiting until after the rest of the class has studied a topic to intervene can compound a student's confusion and failure during regular class instruction.

How My Teaching Has Changed

Developing intervention lessons for at-risk students has not only been an all-consuming professional focus for me in recent years, but has also reinforced my belief that instruction—for all students and especially for at-risk students—must emphasize understanding, sense making, and skills.

Thinking about how to serve students like Paul has contributed to changing my instructional practice. I am now much more intentional about creating and teaching lessons that help intervention students catch up and keep up, particularly scaffolding the mathematical content to introduce concepts and skills through a routine of support. Such careful scaffolding may not be necessary for students who learn mathematics easily, who know to look for connections, and who have mathematical intuition. But it is crucial for students at risk of failure who can't repair their math foundations on their own.

Marilyn Burns is Founder of Math Solutions Professional Development, Sausalito, California; 800-868-9092; mburns@mathsolutions.com.

The Classroom That Math Built
Encouraging Young Mathematicians to Pose Problems

Ann H. Wallace, Deborah Abbott, and Reneé McAlhaney Blary

The idea of problem posing is not now, but it has received increased attention in light of new approaches to mathematics education. The National Council of Teachers of Mathematics (NCTM 1991, 2000) has called on teachers to set up problem-solving experiences that encourage children to devise and solve their own problems.

Mathematical problem posing builds on young children's natural curiosity. It promotes children's "engagement in authentic mathematical activity"; enables children to "encounter many problems, methods, and solutions rather than only one of each"; and fosters creativity (Silver & Cai 2005, 129). For example, children may see an illustration of pentagons in a book or worksheet. The implied question is, "What is 2 + 3?" However, the picture can be used as a vehicle for additional problem posing. Various children may ask the following questions:

- If these are all tables, how many guests could sit at each table? How many guests could you seat at all the tables?
- If there are two adults at each table, how many places are left for children?
- If 16 seats are filled, how many seats are empty?
- Why is there a gap? How many shapes would fill the gap?

Some teachers find it difficult to let children pose and explore their own problems. They may assign textbook problems that often are of little interest to the class and that generally have one solution reached only after following a particular procedure (Baxter 2005). Traditionally it was the teacher's role to lead students down that specific path to the solution.

But real things are not so neatly packaged in the natural world, where there are no set procedures or pat answers. Early educators must move away from posing math problems with one way to reach a solution to offering math experiences with things and situations that are meaningful to children. As children explore their environment, they ask and pose questions. Effective teachers recognize and provide opportunities and experiences to build math skills and concepts within that environment. One way to do this is by guiding classroom discussions about children's problem-solving experiences.

Teacher input into the problem-posing process is critical. Their questions frame the concept or idea available for exploration, analysis, and consideration (Whitin 2006). In the previous example, a child referred to the pentagons as tables. The teacher then pursued this idea and encouraged children to pose problems as if that were the case. This gave a context to children who may have been struggling with their own problems to pose. In classroom environments that encourage and support exploration, problem solving becomes important to children. They can think about, analyze, and solve problems that matter to them.

This article describes how one teacher encouraged children to pose their own math problems during a five-day investigation in their classroom. Included are examples of teacher questions and children's posed problems and solutions.

Deborah's Class

Second-grade teacher Deborah Abbott, one of the authors of this article, consistently strives to create a classroom environment in which she and the children share and support the construction of mathematical thinking. Her goal is to promote critical thinking across all disciplines. To enhance hands-on, authentic learning activities, she stocked the classroom with multiple and varied math resources, including manipulatives such as two- and three-dimensional geometric shapes, linking cubes, counters, number tiles, and pattern blocks; tools such as measuring tapes, rulers, calculators, graph paper, and writing supplies; and books focusing on authentic use and real-world math experiences specific to a topic or project—for example, for a study of the community, *Numbers on the Street* (Math All Around series), by Jennifer Rozines Roy and Gregory Roy, and *Shapes around Town,* by Nathan Olson.

Open-ended class discussions and encouragement are integral parts of the learning process. Children have opportunities to recognize, verbalize, explore, and evaluate in an environment that fosters the problem-solving process and where teacher and students alike ask and answer questions.

Open-ended class discussions and encouragement are integral parts of the learning process.

Deborah wanted to incorporate problem posing into her teaching. Its open-ended process fit her philosophy of providing opportunities for children to investigate multiple approaches to solving problems. She had never thought about setting up an initial problem to spawn new questions and was curious as to whether her second-graders could create their own extensions from a problem situation. She planned a five-day investigation based on inquiry and process skills.

Deborah knew she could not just begin with, "Here is a problem. What question do you want to pose?" and expect the children to respond. Any initial problem situation had to interest and make sense to the children or they would not become engaged. Deborah speculated that "if my students had to determine how many hamburgers were eaten in one day at school, they would love it!"

After deciding to focus and build on something the children saw every day—their classroom—she asked herself, What do the students notice about this classroom? If they had to create their own, could they? What would their classroom look like? She wondered if the children could

- realize or recognize the size of classroom items (tables, bookcases, rug, and so on),
- identify the arrangement of objects,
- comprehend amounts (like the number of books or blocks), and
- understand the mathematics involved in finding out these things.

To get students thinking about everyday numbers—where we see them and how we use them—Deborah asked the children questions like the following:

- Our school is filled with math. Where do you see numbers here?
- At home, in the car or store, where do you see numbers?
- How do we use these numbers every day?
- How do you use the numbers you see in our school?

A lively discussion began. The children mentioned the cost of lunch, cooking cups, calendar days, and telling time. This was just a brainstorming and preliminary session, So the class did not keep a record of the everyday numbers.

Day 1: Building Interest

To help students make connections between mathematics and their world, Deborah introduced *The House That Math Built*, from Time-Life Books, as a context for the problem-posing investigation. The book highlights the importance of early math skills through original stories, poems, riddles, games, and hands-on activities. It encourages children to see math as a natural part of their everyday environment. The book takes readers on a tour of a wacky mansion filled with math challenges. Every room has a theme, like the Shape Room and the Measuring Room. Using the book's suggestions for extending the focus of each page, Deborah prepared additional questions to ask as she read. For example, in the Pattern Bathroom, she asked the children:

- What color is the missing wallpaper flower?
- What is the pattern on the shower curtain?
- Can you extend the pattern?

Then Deborah posed the question, "What if the next room we walked into was a classroom? I wonder what it would look like." She asked the children to close their eyes and use their mind's eye to see what the classroom would look like. She asked questions that helped create visual images:

- What would you put in your classroom?
- How many would you need?
- Where would things go?
- Do you need exact numbers of things?
- Does it matter?

What if the next room we walked into was a classroom? I wonder what it would look like.

Children shared their ideas. "I see a lot of desks," one said. "Kids!" said another. "Books!" "Book bags," and more. Deborah then wondered about drawing the imaginary classroom. "Hmm," she said, "How would we begin such a drawing? Would we have to plan first? What things do you think we should include?"

Deborah asked the children to draw diagrams of the classrooms they visualized. She walked around, observing and commenting on the children's work. She reminded everyone to think about what items would be needed in the room. She often asked probing questions:

- Do you think that's enough?
- Will the teacher need different materials than the students?
- Does the teacher need more or fewer of certain items?
- Do you think it will all fit?
- How can you find out?
- What things does your classroom have to have?
- Do you think you're finished?
- Are you satisfied?

Her many questions were designed to assess whether every child could understand and interpret the problem.

Day 2: Introducing a Problem

The children gathered to share and discuss the classroom diagrams they had drawn the previous day. Together they generated a master list of items they decided were needed for a classroom, noting things they had not included and considering other suggestions. The thorough list included tables, chairs, calendar, computers, bulletin boards, books, posters, tissue boxes, and many more items.

The thorough list included tables, chairs, calendar, computers, bulletin boards, books, posters, tissue boxes, and many more items.

"Now," said Deborah, "if you were going to design your own classroom—let's call it 'The Classroom That Math Built'—are these the items you would need?" She had to figure out how to transition from the generated list to further exploration, encouraging the children to ask questions they could answer. Knowing that this would be a challenge, she had planned in advance how to get the children thinking about quantity. She prodded,

- Is the size or the amount of the items important?
- Does length matter?
- Would it matter how many desks we had? Could they be too big or too small?
- How big is the carpet? Why do we care how big it is?
- How can we answer these questions?

Referring back to the list of items, she asked, "Can we turn some of the things on our list into problems or questions?" One child responded, "I'd like to know how long the shelves are." "How do we figure that out?" Deborah asked. Several children replied in unison, "Measure!"

Deborah followed up: "What tool would we use to measure the shelf?" She asked one child to choose the best measuring tool for determining the length of the shelf. The boy picked up both the yardstick and the measuring tape, pondered a moment, and then decided on the tape. Deborah inquired, "Why did you choose the measuring tape over the yardstick?" He responded, "There's more and it's easier. I just have to roll out the tape one time, and I don't have to start and stop, like with the yardstick."

The class created a list of available measurement tools—rulers, yardsticks and meter sticks, measuring tape, calculators. They also mentioned scales but decided it was a measuring tool they probably would not need.

The children then selected at least one item from the list and worked with partners to generate a question to ask about the item(s). Deborah provided a few constraints:

- The room must be the same size as their real classroom.
- There would be no extra windows or doors.
- The classroom would have one teacher and 20 students.

By the end of math class, the children had discussed a variety of items and the tools with which to measure them. They were ready to begin solving their problems.

A Five-Step Problem-Solving Process

1. **Understand the problem.**
   What is your question? Do you know what you need to do? Do you know what you're looking for? Do you count or measure? Do you need to record things? Do you need to make notes? Can you explain this to your partner?

2. **Devise a plan.**
   Do you need to draw a picture? What tools do you need? Share your thinking with your partner. Do you agree?

3. **Carry out the plan.**
   Do you need a record of your investigation? How will you keep a record?

4. **Answer the question.**
   Do you have an answer to the question you posed? Is there anything else you would like to know?

5. **Does your answer make sense?**
   Check your work. Are 200 desks correct? Is the carpet way too big? Why is it important to check our work?

Adapted from George Polya, *How to Solve It: A New Aspect of Mathematical Method,* 2nd ed. (Princeton, NJ: Princeton University Press, [1957] 2004).

Day 3: Let the Problem Solving Begin

Deborah reviewed an adaptation of a classic problem-solving process (polyà [1957] 2004) that the children had previously used (see "A Five-Step Problem-Solving Process"). While going over each step, she asked questions to help the children focus on the questions they had posed.

With their chosen tools, the children measured and talked about solving their problems for the remainder of the math period. They tallied, counted, and calculated numbers all over the classroom, measuring the perimeter of rugs and the length, width, and height of the bulletin board, bookcases, tables, and other things.

Deborah was pleased with their serious approach to problem solving. She saw that the problems were important to the children and that they were taking an active approach to solving them. As she observed the work, she asked questions to examine and extend the children's thinking and to help them connect mathematical ideas. To show respect for their ideas, however conventional or unconventional, she listened to various approaches and possible solutions. Children worked with their partners and only turned to Deborah for help or direction when necessary.

For the question, "How many desks and chairs do we need for the 20 students in the class?" Deborah guided problem-solving partners by asking additional questions, such as "Do you need exactly 20? What would happen if we got a new student? Would the student have to sit on the floor? What size desks do you think we need?"

With another team investigating how many bookcases the classroom would need, Deborah facilitated their thinking by asking, "What size should they be? How many shelves are needed? Do the shelves have to be the same size? Will your journals fit on one of the shelves?"

The children became so involved that they wanted to continue beyond math time.

Day 4: Sharing

Each pair or group of students shared with the class the problem they had solved, their method(s) for solving it, and the answer(s) they had found. Deborah occasionally asked questions to foster sense making and promote reasoning. She structured the flow of discussion so that everyone in the class could understand the explanations. For example, she asked,

- Would anyone have answered that question in a different way?
- How could you improve your methods?
- How could you check your results?
- Would checking be important?
- If you didn't have the tools you had, what would have happened?
- What other tools would have been helpful?

The class concluded that recording their work to communicate their findings was very important. Deborah wondered, "Could you measure things again if you were asked? Why was recording important?" Although the children had used pencils, paper, and calculators, they said they thought that computers could be used for bigger projects.

Day 5: Reflecting

On the final day of problem posing, Deborah and her clinical intern interviewed each pair of children. She asked them to describe their thinking process for the question(s) they had answered. When she asked David and Cody what materials they had used to determine the perimeter of the rug, David replied, "Well, we used four yardsticks and we used a 12-inch ruler. We had to put the rulers together to get the exact length." Cody added, "First it was 120—it said so on the calculator—and then David said that's the wrong answer, and then I said it's 133." When asked how they had reached their answer, David explained, "We had to use the rulers plus the markers to mark our areas. I counted how many marks we made. I came to the conclusion by adding up this number sentence: $4 \times 30 + 13 = 133$."

Alexis and Diamond had measured the perimeter of their desks put together. Alexis reported, "We took the ruler and then we put it on the desk and we measured how much around." Diamond clarified, "We wrote on a piece of paper so that we can remember what we got. We counted a little bit. Like we used the pencils, so that it could help us, as we get to a point we can put a mark down." When asked, "Were there things you didn't find out that you wanted to?" Alexis responded, "We can measure other things that I want to know, like the whole classroom, like big stuff—bigger than this desk or bigger than the board."

Bethany, working by herself, had asked the unconventional and ambitious question, "What do we need for everyone to eat breakfast?" For a class of 17, she had determined that 17 cereal bowls, 17 cartons of milk, 17 spoons, 17 napkins, and 17 cereal bars would be needed. She added $17 + 17 = 34, 34 + 17 = 51, 51 + 17 = 68, 68 + 17 = 85$. She had concluded that the class would need 85 items for breakfast. When Deborah asked Bethany why she had used 17 when there were 20 students in the class, Bethany responded that three children did not eat breakfast. When asked if she could use the same method to solve a different problem, she said, "I guess—pencils or batteries or clipboards."

Bethany wasn't done. She said she wanted to figure out how many school supplies would be needed for 85 people. (She chose the number 85 from the number of breakfast items she had previously found.)

Lessons Learned

This five-day experiment reinforced the importance of a classroom environment that promotes mathematical thinking. Such a classroom is led by a teacher who is flexible and eager to listen to what children have to say, and who accepts their ideas.

Deborah says the experience served the needs of a wide variety of mathematical learners. It opened math gateways for children with differing intellectual needs and desires. In expressing their math ideas, some children drew, some wrote, Some tallied, Some recorded, some created graphs, and so on.

There was David, the self-proclaimed class mathematician, and his partner Cory, who was still struggling with one-to-one correspondence. The vast difference in their mathematical skills did not deter them from exploring and solving their problem.

Deborah understood the importance of capturing the children's interest before posing the problem she wanted them to explore. She began with the engaging story of the wacky mansion and followed with a series of questions. Only after she had piqued the children's interest did she introduce the focus for the lesson, the classroom. As a result, the children relied less on her direction and more on themselves to come up with problems to be solved. She further found Polyà's ([1977] 2004) problem-solving process helpful in guiding students in what to do with the questions they posed.

Although the children did not extend their problems by posing additional questions, Deborah believes her classroom culture invites this kind of expansion. She suspects the children had little or no prior experience in posing problems, and she thinks the initial challenge, imaginary classrooms, may have been too narrow. There might have been further explorations if she had transitioned from focusing on the classroom to exploring other places of interest to the children (like their bedrooms or the zoo or mapping the neighborhood).

In the future, Deborah plans to incorporate problem posing throughout the year, perhaps by enlisting older children to help the second-graders with math exploration. The older children may bring different ideas about what problems to pose or questions to ask. She will continue to cultivate the classroom environment by creating positive mathematical experiences for her students.

Conclusion

This experience demonstrates the value of allowing children to take responsibility for their own learning and emphasizes the crucial role the teacher plays in this process. Effective early childhood educators teach children how to think. The goal of problem posing is for children to figure out how to ask a question from or about a given situation.

The children in Deborah's class had to figure out what to do when they were not being told what to do. They relied less on the teacher's questions and answers and become comfortable not following a predetermined process. They talked through problems to figure out other problems. They speculated, pursued alternatives, and determined whether their approaches were valid. They discarded ideas that did not work and focused on those that did. As Deborah says, "These are the essential skills they will need for their future success in the world."

References

Baxter, J. 2005. Some reflections on problem posing: A conversation with Marion Walter. *Teaching Children Mathematics* 12 (3): 122–28.

NCTM (National Council of Teachers of Mathematics). 1991. *Professional standards for teaching mathematics.* Reston, VA: Author.

NCTM. 2000. Standards for grades Pre-K–2. In *Principles and standards for school mathematics,* 29–140. Reston, VA: Author.

Polyá, G. [1957] 2004. *How to solve it: A new aspect of mathematical method.* 2nd ed. Princeton, NJ: Princeton University Press.

Silver, E.A., & J. Cai. 2005. Assessing students' mathematical problem posing. *Teaching Children Mathematics* 12 (3): 129–35.

Whitin, D. 2006. Problem posing in the elementary classroom. *Teaching Children Mathematics,* 13 (1): 14–18.

ANN H. WALLACE, PhD, is an assistant professor of mathematics education at the College of Charleston in South Carolina. Ann is interested in children's problem posing as a companion to problem solving. Together, she says, they allow children to generate more diverse thinking and reinforce basic mathematics concepts. E-mail: wallacea@cofc.edu. **DEBORAH ABBOTT,** MEd, teaches second grade in Charleston. Deborah is interested in mathematics curriculum implementation that focuses on providing and faciltating authentic learning opportunities in the classroom. E-mail: Deborah_abbott@charleston.k12.sc.us. **RENEÉ MCALHANEY BLARY,** BS, teaches fourth grade science and social studies in Yemassee, South Carolina, During this project, Renee was Deborah's intern for clinical practice at the College of Charleston. E-mail: rblary@hamptonl.org.

UNIT 6

Rethinking Behavior Management: Getting the Behavior You Want and Need to Teach Effectively

Unit Selections

29. **Tackling a Problematic Behavior Management Issue: Teachers' Intervention in Childhood Bullying Problems,** Laura M. Crothers and Jered B. Kolbert
30. **The Under-Appreciated Role of Humiliation in the Middle School,** Nancy Frey and Douglas Fisher
31. **The Power of Our Words,** Paula Denton
32. **Marketing Civility,** Michael Stiles and Ben Tyson
33. **Classwide Interventions: Effective Instruction Makes a Difference,** Maureen A. Conroy et al.
34. **Developing Effective Behavior Intervention Plans: Suggestions for School Personnel,** Kim Killu

Key Points to Consider

- Have you even been a victim of bullying? What effect did it have?

- Stiles and Tyson suggest improving communication will increase civility in classrooms. What is your response to their suggestions? Provide a rationale for your answer.

- Frey and Fisher make three recommendations for reducing humiliation in the middle school. Explain how you will use at least two of those recommendations in either your field experiences or future teaching.

- What was your first reaction when you read the Denton article? How will this affect your own use of words with students?

- How might general education teachers use Behavior Intervention Plans for non-disabled students?

Student Website

www.mhcls.com

Internet References

The OSEP Technical Assistance Center of Positive Behavior Interventions & Supports (PBIS)
http://www.pbis.org/school/what_is_swpbs.aspx
Bully OnLine
http://www.bullyonline.org/
Teaching Tolerance
http://www.tolerance.org

National Education Association: Classroom Management
http://www.nea.org/tools/ClassroomManagement.html
Teacher Vision
http://www.teachervision.fen.com/
Center for Safe and Responsible Internet Use
http://www.cskcst.com

When teachers (and prospective teachers) discuss what concerns them about their roles (and prospective roles) in the classroom, the issue of discipline (how to manage student behavior) will usually rank near or at the top of their lists. Teachers need a clear understanding of what kinds of learning environments are most appropriate for the subject matter and ages of the students. Any person who wants to teach must also want his or her students to learn well, to acquire basic values of respect for others, and to become more effective citizens.

All teachers have concerns regarding the quality of life in classroom settings. Teachers and students want to feel safe and accepted when they are in school. There exists today a reliable, effective knowledge base on classroom management and how to prevent unwanted behaviors in schools. This knowledge base has been developed from hundreds of studies of teacher/student interaction and student/student interaction that have been conducted in schools in North America and Europe. We speak of classroom management because there are many factors that go into building effective teacher/student and student/student relationships. If teachers think about managing their classroom rather than controlling or ruling over the classroom, there is a shift in thinking that makes a difference. Managers are collaborative, cooperative, and sensitive to those they manage. Teachers who control are more commanding than cooperative, more punishing than managing, and tend to use fear as the dominant emotion in their classrooms. Furthermore, the term *discipline* is too narrow and refers primarily to teachers' negative responses to unwanted behavior. We can better understand methods of managing student behavior when we look at the totality of what goes on in classrooms, with teachers' responses to student behavior as a part of that totality.

Teachers' core ethical principles come into play when deciding what constitutes defensible and desirable standards of student conduct. Teachers need to realize that before they can control behavior, they must identify what student behaviors are desired in their classrooms. They need to reflect, as well, on the emotional tone and ethical principles implied by their own behaviors. To optimize their chances of achieving the classroom atmosphere that they wish, teachers must strive for emotional balance within themselves; they must learn to be accurate observers; and they must develop just, fair strategies of intervention to aid students in learning self-control and good behavior. A teacher should be a good model of courtesy, respect, tact, and discretion. Children learn by observing how other persons behave and not just by being told how they are to behave. There is no substitute for positive, assertive teacher interaction with students in class.

Teachers bear moral and ethical responsibilities for being witnesses to and examples of responsible social behavior in the classroom. We now have a body of research that attests to widespread prejudicial discipline measures being used with African American and Hispanic students. Teachers must examine their practices for such prejudice. Do we see threats in the actions and behaviors of black and Hispanic boys and youth? Those of us who teach or have taught in urban settings may have noted that African American and Hispanic males are more often the ones in the hallways with teachers scowling and shaking their fingers. What message does this send to all students, including the ones sitting compliantly in their seats? We must be careful about the silent messages we send that clearly betray our innermost fears.

Furthermore, teachers are responsible for the emotional climate that is set in a classroom. Whether students feel secure and safe and whether they want to learn depend to an enormous extent on the teacher's psychological frame of mind. Teachers must be able to manage

© OJO Images/Getty Images

their own selves first in order to effectively manage the development of a humane and caring classroom environment. This is why we address the issues of bullying again in this edition. Crother and Kolbert offer eight strategies to address bullying as a management issue. We also offer two articles about dealing with bullying problems that often begin in middle school, but the humiliation can carry through high school and into adulthood as noted in two articles (Frey and Fisher; Stiles and Tyson). Responsible and responsive adults can make a difference. Denton reminds us that respect and caring are attitudes that a teacher must communicate to receive them in return. Open lines of communication between teachers and students enhance the possibility for congenial, fair dialogical resolution of problems as they occur. Several articles in this unit address the bullying issue.

In the course of a teaching career, any one teacher may have one or more children whose behavior requires more than the usual classroom management strategies. Conroy and co-authors suggest six classroom tools that work based on effective instructional practices. However, some students may have deeper needs, including emotional or behavioral disabilities, or a conduct disorder. These students may require a Behavior Intervention Plan (BIP), especially if they have an Individual Education Plan (IEP). These plans help guide teachers, families, and students in their treatment and management of serious unwanted behaviors and should be viewed as a positive. These plans should be designed to help students change their behavior rather than being punitive in nature. For example, teachers may have students who have ADHD, and a behavior plan that outlines positive self-monitoring methods for helping the student to be more attentive and less active. Since general education teachers should be part of the team that writes these plans, we have included an article about BIPs by Killu.

Helping young people learn the skills of self-control and motivation to become productive, contributing, and knowledgeable adult participants in society is one of the most important tasks that good teachers undertake. These are teachable and learnable skills; they do not relate to heredity or social conditions. They can be learned by any human being who wants to learn them and who is cognitively able to learn them. All that is required is the willingness of teachers to learn these skills themselves and to teach them to their students. In this unit we have included an article on teaching self-regulation in early childhood settings, but some of these methods can generalize to higher grade levels.

Tackling a Problematic Behavior Management Issue

Teachers' Intervention in Childhood Bullying Problems

In coping with and addressing a common child behavioral problem, classroom teachers may benefit from viewing bullying as a behavior management issue in the educational setting. The authors offer eight suggestions that specifically address childhood bullying problems in the classroom. Teachers can add these to their toolkit of behavior management strategies.

LAURA M. CROTHERS AND JERED B. KOLBERT

Child disciplinary problems can be stressful for a classroom teacher. Teachers find accommodating behavioral difficulties more challenging and less feasible than making instructional modifications for academic problems (Ritter, 1989). In fact, researchers have suggested the existence of a relationship between disruptive student behavior patterns (e.g., disrespect, poor social skills) and teacher burnout (Hastings & Bham, 2003).

When asked about managing problematic student behavior, teachers often respond in one of two ways: It is not much of a concern, because their classroom management strategies are typically effective in resolving student behavioral concerns, or they feel overwhelmed and impotent to address behavioral difficulties that threaten to disrupt the learning process and subsequent academic achievement of students (Discipline Problems Take a Toll, 2004). Those in the latter group often explain that they were not adequately trained to manage students with behavior problems or they believe that teachers who are effective classroom managers are inherently talented in rectifying disciplinary issues demonstrated by children at school.

The use of such external attributions or excuses can compromise a teacher's ability to successfully take responsibility for student behavior and learning in the classroom. Early intervention is critically important in preventing and reducing children's behavior problems (Dodge, 1993). Interestingly, the primary difference between successful and unsuccessful behavior managers is not the manner in which they handle discipline problems but rather the number of discipline problems they encounter. Effective classroom managers create a structured environment and manage behavioral antecedents to diminish the likelihood of behavior problems ever occurring (Duke, 1982; Elliott, Witt, Kratochwill, & Stoiber, 2002).

It is from the vantage of behavior management that childhood bullying problems can be addressed, because such issues often demand a significant portion of teachers' behavior modification efforts. Research has established a normative (i.e., routinely occurring) nature of bully–victim relationships in schools (Smith & Brain, 2000). Further, childhood bullying has increasingly been recognized as one of the most common and widespread forms of school violence occurring not only in the United States but in other countries as well. *Bullying* has been defined as repetitive instrumental aggression that results in an imbalance of power between perpetrator and victim (Smith & Brain, 2000), and it involves approximately 30% of U.S. students during their school careers (Nansel et al., 2001).

Victims of bullying behavior suffer from anxiety, depression, low self-esteem, physical and psychosomatic complaints, posttraumatic stress disorder, and suicidal ideation (Kaltiala-Heino, Rimpela, Marttunen, Rimpela, & Rantenan, 1999; McKenney, Pepler, Craig, & Connolly, 2002; Williams, Chambers, Logan, & Robinson, 1996). Perpetrators of bullying also experience negative effects, including an increased risk of mental health disorders, such as attention-deficit/hyperactivity disorder, depression, oppositional defiant disorder, and conduct disorder (Kumpulainen, Rasanen, & Puura, 2001). Children who bully also exhibit a greater likelihood of engaging in criminal behavior, domestic violence, and substance abuse as adults (Farrington, 1993) and are more likely to struggle with poor academic achievement and poor career performance in adulthood (Carney & Merrell, 2001). Finally, researchers have found that childhood bullies are often severely punitive with their own children, who are subsequently more likely to be aggressive with peers (Eron, Huesmann, Dubow, Romanoff, & Yarmel, 1987; Smokowski & Kopasz, 2005).

Much research has documented the prevalence and negative effects of bullying, yet some literature has also suggested that teachers sometimes contribute to or tolerate the problem. According to Olweus (1991), students often report that teachers do not intervene when a student is being bullied in school, and many times teachers are unaware of occurrences of bullying. This is particularly surprising because students frequently indicate that bullying occurs in the classroom while the teacher is present (Olweus, 1991). Olweus (1993) also explained that when teachers recognize that bullying is occurring, they often do relatively little to put a stop to the behavior and make only limited contact with students involved in the bullying to discuss the problem. This lack of intervention may be particularly dangerous because children who engage in bullying may interpret the resulting adult nonintervention as tacit approval of their behavior.

However, because of the incidence and negative effects on victims and perpetrators, school personnel are increasingly recognizing that bullying is a problem that must be addressed in the educational setting. For purposes of empowerment and a sense of control, it may be helpful for classroom teachers to view the problem of bullying as a behavior management issue, similar to off-task or other non–rule-governed behavior. Also, it may be easier to prevent childhood bullying problems rather than react to them, because responding to incidents of peer victimization can be difficult for such reasons as not directly observing the behavior or not being aware of the extent of the problem due to students not reporting bullying to adults (Crothers & Kolbert, 2004). Eight suggestions are offered to enable teachers to add to their toolkit of behavior management strategies, as well as to specifically address childhood bullying problems in their classrooms.

Assessment

Although teachers measure students' scholastic achievement on a daily basis in their classrooms, they often feel reluctant to use assessment methods to investigate nonacademic problems, believing that such domains are best handled by the training and skills demonstrated by school psychologists and counselors. However, engaging in assessment of bullying behavior is an important first step in addressing the problem. The best news about gathering data regarding childhood bullying is that it can be quite simple. Teachers can compile a list of their students' names and divide the children into three groups: *bullies, victims,* and *bystanders.* Similarly, educators can choose to identify which children match certain behavioral descriptors (e.g., aggressive, assertive, passive). After students have been identified as bullies or victims, they can be targeted for individual intervention efforts.

Some researchers have questioned the accuracy of teacher nomination of bullies and victims, believing that teachers may lack objectivity in identifying bullies and victims and may underestimate the amount of bullying that takes place in school (Smith & Ananiadou, 2003; Smith & Sharp, 1994). Also, teachers may be unable to discern between bullying and horseplay and may have biases regarding their students (Hazler, Carney, Green, Powell, & Jolly, 1997; Pellegrini & Bartini, 2000). However, teachers can minimize such problems by spending long periods of time observing their students in a variety of settings (e.g., classroom, playground, lunchroom) as well as engaging in periodic retraining in conducting accurate observations and reliability checks (e.g., comparing perceptions with another teacher). When possible, information provided through teacher assessment should be compared with students' perceptions of which students are bullying others or are frequently victimized; teachers' and students' shared experiences illuminate the problem (Pellegrini & Bartini, 2000).

Guidance Approaches

Whole-school anti-bullying programs typically use guidance lessons, such as drama (e.g., acting out scenarios), watching videos, and reading books as a means of addressing bullying in the classroom. The primary purpose of such activities can be viewed as sensitization to the problem of bullying. Drama, videos, books, and discussions about bullying can give children the language to identify and talk about the experience of bullying. Teachers of young children can act out bullying scenarios using puppets to play the roles of victim and bully. As children mature into adolescence, teachers can encourage children to develop scripts that depict bullying and use puppets to act out the scenarios.

Videos and books are also a helpful medium for educators to introduce awareness of bullying to their students. Children's literature that addresses bullying behavior, such as *Nobody Knew What to Do: A Story About Bullying* (McCain & Leonardo, 2001), can help children understand that bullying is a common problem by emphasizing the need to seek help from adults (Ralston, 2005). There are also nonfiction selections for students, such as *Bullies to Buddies: How to Turn Your Enemies Into Friends!* (Czarnecki, 2005; Kalman, 2004), which teaches children to avoid being victims of bullying by turning anger into humor, fear into courage, and enemies into friends through the use of verbal interactions and body language.

Videos and DVDs on bullying are also available, such as *Bullies Are a Pain in the Brain* (Comical Sense Company, 2005), in which the main character tries to develop solutions to make a bully leave him alone. Selections for older children, such as *End the Silence: Stop the Bullying* (Sunburst, 2004) are appropriate for Grades 7 through 12 and can model solution strategies for students, such as banding together and refusing to tolerate the behavior, as well as implementing a whole-school anti-bullying program. Teachers can use these materials and experiences as a catalyst for discussions about bullying in their classrooms.

Classroom Management Techniques

It may be helpful for teachers to consider classroom management as an aspect of instruction, curriculum, and school climate rather than one of control (Duke, 1982; Levin & Nolan, 2004). Effective instruction is probably the most powerful form of classroom management because children who are actively engaged in learning are less likely to have the time and inclination to engage in bullying. Curricula that encourage children to question their own assumptions and engage in critical thinking will reduce boredom and the opportunity to bully for entertainment purposes. Having activities overlap so that students are continuously busy with learning tasks can diminish the opportunity that children have to assert power over one another.

In conjunction with curriculum and effective teaching, consideration should be paid to creating a classroom climate that is inhospitable to bullying. Thus, one of the first strategies in addressing bullying is to establish rules prohibiting it. Teachers can provide students with information that instructs them on how they should handle bullying behavior (Batsche, 1997; Boulton & Underwood, 1992). As a part of a general classroom management strategy, teachers can also implement whole-class incentive systems that encourage children to control their aggressive behavior and concentrate on meeting behavioral goals. Programs such as *The Winning Ticket* (Floyd, 1985) are based on the notion that socially appropriate behaviors are skills that can be learned.

Another means of addressing bullying is teacher vigilance regarding student behavior in the classroom and throughout the school in general. Teachers need to be constantly aware of student conduct and activities, because bullying often occurs in the classroom without the teacher's knowledge. Behavior problems such as bullying are also as likely to occur during unstructured times, such as the transition from one class or activity to the next, in the gym, in the cafeteria, or on the bus. Consequently, adults responsible for supervising children during those times need to be aware of the signs of bullying behavior and be given the authority to intervene when they suspect bullying is occurring.

Cooperative Learning Activities

One way that teachers can increase student familiarity with and acceptance of others is to use cooperative learning activities in the classroom. Researchers have emphasized that such activities have been effective in improving attitudes and relationships among children in ethnically diverse and special education inclusion classrooms (Boulton & Underwood, 1992; Cowie, Smith, Boulton, & Laver, 1994; Johnson & Johnson, 1980). Classroom teachers can develop cooperative learning groups and offer group rewards to facilitate improved social integration that would not ordinarily occur (Hoover & Hazler, 1991; Johnson & Johnson, 1980). Teachers should strive to balance competitive activities, which focus on individual achievement, with cooperative goals that help emphasize group achievement (Hazler, 1996).

Boulton and Underwood (1992) suggested pairing older children with younger children through joint projects in the classroom or through peer tutoring. Cooperative learning activities encourage friendship, identification, and a sense of protectiveness between the older and younger students. Such feelings cause compassion in the children (Pink & Brownlee, 1988) and may help to lessen victimization. This was evidenced in a Japanese study, in which bullies' moral empathic perception and emotion toward victimization were positively related to the reduction of bullying (Honma, 2003).

Teachers should, however, consider power differentials between children when planning for group collaboration work in the classroom. Because bullying is associated with both implicit (i.e., wealth, attractiveness, and athletic competence) and explicit (i.e., physical and relational aggression) forms of power, educators need to make sure that groups are not vastly different in their power status (Vaillancourt, Hymel, & McDougall, 2003). Teachers may be naturally inclined to group bullies and victims together yet may instead consider forming groups with individuals who have only slight differences in social power. Alternately, because bullies tend to have high social status and power, educators can appeal to high-status non-bullies to intervene when victims are being bullied by peers. When assured that a high-status child would be amenable to advocate for another child, a teacher might then feel comfortable assembling these individuals together (Vaillancourt et al., 2003).

Assertiveness, Self-Esteem, and Social Skills Training for Victims of Bullying

Bullying prevention programs often include long-term interventions for victims of bullying to remedy deficits that are commonly found in this population. Social skills development appears to be an essential skill base because researchers have found that social isolation is a major risk factor for victimization (Boulton, Trueman, Chau, Whitehand, & Amataya, 1999), and perpetrators likely recognize the vulnerability of a student whom no peer will assist. Also, the development of friendships provides the unpopular student with a support network to ease the emotional pain of low social status. Teachers can promote victims' self-esteem by helping them identify their personal strengths that might attract peers as potential friends.

Furthermore, teachers can instruct students to replace negative statements about themselves with more positive or realistic ones, which is likely to increase the child's confidence as well as reduce his or her social anxiety. Victimized students are often realistically pessimistic about their chances of success in developing friendships, and research has suggested that the social status of victimized students is both negative and longstanding (Boulton & Smith, 1994; Salmivalli, Lappalainen, & Lagerspetz, 1998). Thus, victimized students often need encouragement to engage in such risk taking in an attempt to establish social connections. One helpful strategy is to encourage the victimized student to focus on his or her effort and performance to make friends, rather than the results of these efforts, which rarely bear immediate fruit.

Another common problem victimized students have as they pursue friendships is the lack of social intelligence, such as failing to understand the social status of other students. As a result, victimized students may attempt to befriend the most popular students, who are unlikely to reciprocate in a mutual desire for friendship. In such cases, the teacher can ask victimized students to think about who seems to want or need a friend, explaining that because popular students have many friends, they may not have enough time for another relationship.

An example of a long-term intervention to assist victimized students is Fox and Boulton's (2003) study of the effects of an eight-session social skills/assertiveness training program in which the curriculum was delivered in a group format to chronically victimized students. The social skills aspect of the program was used to teach students a variety of skills, including listening, having conversations, and asking to join in peer groups. The assertiveness component of the program was used to instruct students in the use of more confident body language, relaxation skills, positive thinking, and verbal strategies for dealing with bullying. Fox and Boulton found that the program led to a significant increase in victims' self-esteem, which was maintained at a 3-month follow-up but noted that the program did not have a significant impact upon victims' number of friends, peer acceptance, depression, or anxiety. Group interventions for victimized students may result in greater success when role-playing is used, with specific behaviors modeled for students and followed by supervised practice with peers.

Constructive Conversations with Victims of Bullying

When asked what teachers do to stop bullying behavior when it occurs, students are likely to report that teachers intervene in bullying scenarios less often than children would prefer (Crothers & Kolbert, 2004). In particular, victims of bullying may feel that bullies are actually receiving more teacher attention than do those who are being harassed by peers. Olweus (1992) has identified characteristics of those who are frequently victimized by bullying:

> Victims of bullying are more anxious and insecure than students in general. They are often cautious, sensitive, and quiet. When attacked by other students, they commonly react by crying (at least in the lower grades) and withdrawal. They have a negative view of themselves and their situation. They often look upon themselves as failures and feel stupid, ashamed, and unattractive. (p. 103)

Furthermore, Olweus (1993) noted that victims are often unpopular among their peers and lack even one identifiable friend. Because victims of bullying tend not to tease or display aggression toward peers, other students may assume that they will not retaliate when harassed.

Assisting the student who is frequently bullied may require both short- and long-term intervention. Short-term interventions address specific incidents of bullying, whereas long-term interventions involve skill building to increase confidence and avoid the probability of future victimization. Victims are unlikely to report bullying incidents because they fear exacerbation of the problem or retribution, so it is essential that teachers attempt to alleviate the anxiety of the victim during an investigation of bullying (Olweus, 1993). Educators should inform the child that whatever he or she decides to reveal will be held in confidence, while simultaneously building rapport and educating the victim in identifying what emotions he or she is likely to be experiencing. In addition, the teacher can instill hope in children by sharing that he or she has had success in dealing with such incidents in the past. Victims often internalize bullying, attributing the unwanted behaviors to characteristics within themselves. Thus, it is important to help the victim realize that he or she has done nothing to provoke the bullying behavior and that his or her anger regarding the experience is normal and justified.

Once information about the bullying behavior has been gathered, it is important to explain to the victim what the teacher will do with the information, which may include talking with witnesses and the alleged perpetrator, assigning a negative consequence to the perpetrator, and informing other teachers of the behavior so that they more closely observe the students who are involved. If the bullying incident is either severe or is indicative of an ongoing pattern, the teacher can gather additional data by interviewing other students who may have witnessed such incidents. Teachers can ask the victim to identify other students (who are not friends of the victim or the perpetrator) who may have observed such events, explaining to the victim that these witnesses will not be informed of how they were recognized as being involved. In many cases, the victimization has been occurring for several months and thus the victim can often readily identify other students who may have observed such events. Furthermore, victims should be encouraged to approach the teacher if bullying incidents reoccur.

Constructive Conversations with Students Who Frequently Bully

Research on students who frequently bully reveals some common characteristics. Perpetrators of bullying behavior tend to lack empathy (Olweus, 1993), misattribute their peers' actions as being the result of hostile intentions, demonstrate impulsivity, perceive aggression as an acceptable way to resolve conflict, and exhibit a high need for dominance (Graham & Juvonen, 1998; Olweus, 1993; Ross, 1996). Whereas students who are frequently victimized are generally unpopular with peers, perpetrators of bullying tend to have above-average popularity in primary grades and declining popularity in junior and senior high school.

When first meeting with a student who has been bullying peers, it is important to use a serious tone to convey an important message. The teacher should immediately indicate that he or she is speaking with the student because of his or her inappropriate behavior. To gain the trust of the bully, it is best to begin the conversation with the identification of the bullying behavior and the consequence for this behavior—a straightforward delivery ensures that the student will not be trapped in a lie by asking for his or her version of events. Thus, it is important that teachers collect evidence from other student witnesses prior to meeting with the perpetrator. The teacher should also inform the bully that other teachers and school staff will be made aware of the incident to prevent such behaviors from occurring in the future.

At this point, the teacher should shift into using more of a concerned and caring tone, as the objective is to enable the perpetrator to nondefensively evaluate whether his or her behavior is meeting his or her goals. A common misperception among adults is that students who bully have low self-esteem and thus are motivated to bully others in an attempt to feel better about themselves (Olweus, 1993). Rather than attempting to increase the self-esteem of the student who frequently bullies, teachers can affirm the student's strengths and popularity. Research has been suggestive of bullies' need for dominance, so a discussion of the student's high social status may be appealing to students who frequently bully (Graham & Juvonen, 1998; Olweus, 1993; Ross, 1996).

Ideally, this tactic will enable the student who frequently bullies to realize that victimizing peers is unnecessary to achieve his or her desire for social status. It also serves to help build the teacher–student relationship, which increases the likelihood that the student will engage in self-evaluative behavior. As the student begins to develop trust in the educator, the teacher can more assertively discuss the value of having concern for others, encouraging the student to consider what the victim was feeling and what restitution may be owed. It may be helpful to engage peer victimizers in middle/junior high school in discussions regarding the potential ramifications of bullying, such as the negative impact upon friendships in later grades, explaining that the popularity of students who use aggression typically decreases when they enter high school.

Parent–Teacher Collaboration

If students continue to bully after several months of intervention, the teacher may want to involve parents, although students who frequently bully are likely to receive parenting with little nurturance, along with discipline that is physical and severe (Olweus, 1993). Moreover, family members of child bullies often demonstrate a high need for power (Bowers, Smith, & Binney, 1994). Parents of children who bully others may not regard the behavior as a concern, possibly because such a strong power differential is demonstrated in their own family system. In other words, such behavior may appear to parents of bullies as normal and effective. Thus, it is important for teachers to recognize that parents of bullies may become emotionally reactive when attention and criticism is paid to their children's victimizing behavior.

A realistic objective in conferencing with the parents of perpetrators is to gain at least enough of their support so that they will not undermine teachers or administrators by directly or indirectly implying to their children that they do not need to adhere to the rules regarding bullying. In conferencing with parents of bullying students, teachers should use a no-nonsense, factual presentation and avoid engaging in questioning, long discussions, or using a tone that invites blame upon the parents of the bully. Similar to student perpetrators of bullying, it is not uncommon for parents to minimize or deny the bullying incident. For such situations, it is best that the school staff be prepared to offer concrete evidence of such behavior. Furthermore, the teacher may explain to the parents of the bully, in a respectful and non-emotional manner, the possible consequences if their child continues such behaviors, which may include further school sanctions and eventually decreased popularity among peers. Another effective technique is for the teacher to share with the parents some of their child's strengths and invite the parents to do so as well. Then ask the parents what they believe their child needs to learn at this point in his or her development.

Victims who require long-term intervention may also benefit from parental involvement. Research has suggested that students who are frequently bullied may be closely connected to their parents (Bowers et al., 1994; Olweus, 1993), which may actually impede the development of appropriate peer relations. Some parents react to knowledge that their child is being bullied through over-protection. For example, they may attempt to become their child's best friend, engaging in many social activities with the youngster that effectively fail to help the child develop positive peer relations. Teachers can help such parents develop a perspective of their child as competent, able to deal with bullying situations, and able to develop friendships with guided assistance.

Teachers may also encourage parents to think about how they might help to promote their child's social development, such as inviting friends to the home, role playing through social situations, and getting involved in social organizations that relate to their child's strengths. Encouraging non-athletic victimized children to become involved in team sports may lead to further social rejection, so parents of victims can also be encouraged to consider enhancing their child's physical development through supporting participation in individual sports such as karate, bicycling, swimming, and running.

Discussion

One reason that bullying has persisted throughout human history is that it has traditionally been treated as a socially acceptable means of establishing and securing social position as well as cementing power differences between people (Greene, 2003). Calling attention to the problem by encouraging teachers to tackle bullying as a common behavior management issue may help them effectively address peer victimization in the school environment. A variety of strategies have been presented that teachers can use to reduce child bullying. Educators are encouraged to use these techniques in conjunction with one another as researchers have suggested that bullying can be reduced most effectively through a comprehensive effort that addresses both individual incidents of bullying as well as modifying classroom and overall school environments that indirectly support bullying (e.g., Olweus, 1993).

Teachers are also encouraged to carefully consider the timing of implementing these techniques:

1. Assessment would logically precede guidance curricular approaches to both educate children about the nature of the problem and offer solutions for dealing with students who frequently bully.

2. Improving instruction and curriculum, modifying classroom management techniques, and initiating cooperative learning activities should occur alongside guidance lessons.

3. Constructive conversations with perpetrators and students who are frequently victimized should be reserved for when children have been educated about the new norms regarding this form of aggression.

4. Finally, parent–teacher collaboration is best used for the more entrenched cases of bullying problems given the time investment required of this technique.

Teachers have the power and the techniques available to them to make the classroom a socially just environment that is more hospitable to child development and learning. The techniques that have been identified are not complex, but they do require a significant effort on the part of the teacher. Still, such simple but clear efforts on the part of teachers to address the problem are likely to remove some of the tacit support that schools have historically provided to popular students' desire for dominance (Greene, 2003). The potential benefits seem well worth the effort and can be readily justified in the current educational environment given the negative impact bullying has on the social and emotional development and academic achievement of victims.

References

Batsche, G. M. (1997). Bullying. In G. G. Bear, K. M. Minke, & A. Thomas (Eds.), *Children's needs II: Development, problems, and alternatives* (pp. 171–179). Bethesda, MD: National Association of School Psychologists.

Boulton, M. J., & Smith, P. K. (1994). Bully/victim problems in middle school children: Stability, self-perceived competence, peer-perceptions and peer acceptance. *British Journal of Developmental Psychology, 12,* 315–329.

Boulton, M. J., Trueman, M., Chau, C., Whitehand, C., & Amataya, K. (1999). Concurrent and longitudinal links between friendship and peer victimization: Implications for befriending interventions. *Journal of Adolescence, 22,* 461–466.

Boulton, M. J., & Underwood, K. (1992). Bully/victim problems among middle school children. *British Journal of Educational Psychology, 62,* 73–87.

Bowers, L., Smith, P. K., & Binney, V. (1994). Perceived family relationships of bullies, victims, and bully/victims in middle childhood. *Journal of Social and Personal Relationships, 11,* 215–232.

Carney, A. G., & Merrell, K. W. (2001). Bullying in schools: Perspectives on understanding and preventing an international problem. *School Psychology International, 22*(3), 364–382.

The Comical Sense Company (Producer). (2005). *Bullies are a pain in the brain* [Motion picture]. (Available from the Comical Sense Company, http://www.trevorromain.com/Shop/item/?Videos/DVD00)

Cowie, H., Smith, P., Boulton, M., & Laver, R. (1994). *Cooperation in the multi-ethnic classroom.* London: David Fulton.

Crothers, L. M., & Kolbert, J. B. (2004). Comparing middle school teachers' and students' views on bullying and anti-bullying interventions. *Journal of School Violence, 3*(1), 17–32.

Czarnecki, K. (2005). Bullies to buddies: How to turn your enemies into friends! *School Library Journal, 51*(2), 148.

Discipline problems take a toll. (2004). *American Teacher,* 89(1), 7.

Dodge, K. A. (1993). The future of research on the treatment of conduct disorder. *Development and Psychopathology, 5,* 311–319.

Duke, D. L. (1982). *Helping teachers manage classrooms.* Alexandria, VA: Association for Supervision of Curriculum and Instruction.

Elliott, S. N., Witt, J. C., Kratochwill, T. R., & Stoiber, K. C. (2002). Selecting and evaluating classroom interventions. In M. A. Shinn, H. M. Walker, & G. Stoner (Eds.), *Interventions for academic and behavior problems II: Preventive and remedial approaches* (pp. 243–294). Bethesda, MD: National Association of School Psychologists.

Eron, L. D., Huesmann, R. L., Dubow, E., Romanoff, R., & Yarmel, P. W. (1987). Childhood aggression and its correlates over 22 years. In D. Crowell, I. M. Evans, & C. R. O'Donnell (Eds.), *Childhood aggression and violence* (pp. 249–262). New York: Plenum.

Farrington, D. P. (1993). Understanding and preventing bullying. In M. Tonry (Ed.), *Crime and justice: A review of research* (pp. 381–458). Chicago: University of Chicago Press.

Floyd, N. M. (1985). Pick on somebody your own size. *Pointer, 29,* 9–17.

Fox, C. L., & Boulton, M. J. (2003). Evaluating the effectiveness of a social skills training programme for victims of bullying. *Educational Research, 45*(3), 231–247.

Graham, S., & Juvonen, J. (1998). A social cognitive perspective on peer aggression and victimization. *Annals of Child Development, 12,* 21–66.

Greene, M. (2003). Counseling and climate change as treatment modalities for bullying in schools. *International Journal for the Advancement of Counselling, 25*(4), 293–302.

Hastings, R. P., & Bham, M. S. (2003). The relationship between student behaviour patterns and teacher burnout. *School Psychology International, 24*(1), 115–127.

Hazler, R. J. (1996). *Breaking the cycle of violence: Interventions for bullying and victimization.* Bristol, PA: Accelerated Development.

Hazler, R. J., Carney, J. V., Green, S., Powell, R., & Jolly, L. S. (1997). Areas of expert agreement on identification of school bullies and victims. *School Psychology International, 18*(1), 5–14.

Honma, T. (2003). Cessation of bullying and intervention with bullies: Junior high school students. *Japanese Journal of Educational Psychology, 51,* 390–400.

Hoover, J. H., & Hazler, R. J. (1991). Bullies and victims. *Elementary School Guidance and Counseling, 25,* 212–219.

Johnson, D. W., & Johnson, R. T. (1980). Integrating handicapped children into the mainstream. *Exceptional Children, 47*(2), 90–98.

Kalman, I. (2004). *Bullies to buddies: How to turn your enemies into friends.* Staten Island, NY: Wisdom Pages.

Kaltiala-Heino, R., Rimpela, M., Marttunen, M., Rimpela, A., & Rantenan, P. (1999). Bullying, depression, and suicidal ideation in Finnish adolescents: School survey. *British Medical Journal, 319*(7206), 348–351.

Kumpulainen, K., Rasanen, E., & Puura, K. (2001). Psychiatric disorders and the use of mental health services among children involved in bullying. *Aggressive Behavior, 27,* 102–110.

Levin, J., & Nolan, J. F. (2004). *Principles of classroom management: A professional decision-making model.* New York: Pearson.

McCain, B. R., & Leonardo, T. (2001). *Nobody knew what to do: A story about bullying.* Morton Grove, IL: Albert Whitman.

McKenney, K. S., Pepler, D. J., Craig, W. M., & Connolly, J. A. (2002). Psychosocial consequences of peer victimization in elementary and high school—An examination of posttraumatic stress disorder symptomatology. In K. A. Kendall-Tackett & S. M. Giacomoni (Eds.), *Child victimization: Maltreatment, bullying and dating violence, prevention and intervention* (pp. 15-1–15-17). Kingston, NJ: Civic Research Institute.

Nansel, T. R., Overpeck, M., Pilla, R. S., Ruan, W. J., Simons-Morton, B., & Scheidt, P. (2001). Bullying behaviors among US youth: Prevalence and association with psychosocial adjustment. *Journal of the American Medical Association, 285,* 2094–2100.

Olweus, D. (1991). Bully/victim problems among school children: Some basic facts and effects of a school-based intervention program. In D. Pepler & K. Rubin (Eds.), *The development and treatment of childhood aggression* (pp. 411–438). Hillsdale, NJ: Lawrence Erlbaum.

Olweus, D. (1992). Bullying among school children: Intervention and prevention. In R. Peters, J. McMahon, & V. I. Quinsley (Eds.), *Aggression and violence throughout the lifespan* (pp. 100–125). Newbury Park, CA: Sage.

Olweus, D. (1993). *Bullying at school: What we know and what we can do.* Cambridge, MA: Blackwell.

Pellegrini, A. D., & Bartini, M. (2000). An empirical comparison of methods of sampling aggression and victimization in school settings. *Journal of Educational Psychology, 92,* 360–366.

Pink, H., & Brownlee, L. (1988, March 4). Playground politics: Pairing off. *Times Educational Supplement,* p. 22a.

Ralston, J. (2005). Nobody knew what to do: A story about bullying. *School Library Journal, 51*(5), 50.

Ritter, D. R. (1989). Teachers' perceptions of problem behavior in general and special education. *Exceptional Children, 55*(6), 559–564.

Ross, D. (1996). *Childhood bullying and teasing.* Alexandria, VA: American Counseling Association.

Salmivalli, C., Lappalainen, M., & Lagerspetz, M. J. (1998). Stability and change of behavior in connection with bullying in schools: A two-year follow-up. *Aggressive Behavior, 24,* 205–218.

Smith, P. K., & Ananiadou, K. (2003). The nature of school bullying and the effectiveness of school-based interventions. *Journal of Applied Psychoanalytic Studies, 5*(2), 189–209.

Smith, P. K., & Brain, P. (2000). Bullying in school: Lessons from two decades of research. *Aggressive Behavior, 26,* 1–9.

Smith, P. K., & Sharp, S. (Eds.). (1994). *School bullying: Insights and perspectives.* London: Routledge.

Smokowski, P. R., & Kopasz, K. H. (2005). Bullying in school: An overview of types, effects, family characteristics, and intervention strategies. *Children and School, 27*(2), 101–110.

Sunburst (Producer). (2004). *End the silence: Stop the bullying* [Motion picture]. (Available from Sunburst, www.sunburstvm.com)

Vaillancourt, T., Hymel, S., & McDougall, P. (2003). Bullying is power: Implications for school-based intervention strategies. *Journal of Applied School Psychology, 19*(2), 157–176.

Williams, K., Chambers, M., Logan, S., & Robinson, D. (1996). Association of common health symptoms with bullying in primary school children. *British Medical Journal, 313,* 17–19.

Laura M. Crothers, DEd, is an assistant professor of school psychology in the Department of Counseling, Psychology, and Special Education at Duquesne University. Her current research interests include bullying of gay, lesbian, bisexual, and transgender children and adolescents and female adolescent relational aggression. Jered B. Kolbert, PhD, is an associate professor in the Department of Counseling and Development at Slippery Rock University and currently conducts research in bullying and the use of family therapy in responding to adolescent developmental adjustment problems.

Address: Laura M. Crothers, Duquesne University, 106 D Canevin Hall, Department of Counseling, Psychology, and Special Education, 600 Forbes Ave., Pittsburgh, PA, 15282; e-mail: crothersl@duq.edu

From *Intervention in School and Clinic,* January 2008, pp. 132–139. Copyright © 2008 by Pro-Ed, Inc. Reprinted by permission.

The Under-Appreciated Role of Humiliation in the Middle School

NANCY FREY AND DOUGLAS FISHER

In his book *The World Is Flat*, Friedman (2005) argued that we have under-appreciated the role that humiliation plays in terrorism. He notes that the reaction humans have when they are humiliated is significant and often severe. If it is true, that humiliation plays a role in terrorism, what role might this under-appreciated emotion play in middle school? If terrorists act, in part, based on humiliation, how do middle school students act when they experience this emotion?

To answer these questions, we interviewed 10 middle school teachers and 10 students. We asked them about times they (or their students or peers) were humiliated and what happened. In each case, they were surprised to be asked about this emotion. They said things like "It just happens; you gotta deal with it" and "You know how kids are, they can be mean." The responses from the teachers and students about the ways that students are humiliated clustered into three major areas: bullying, teacher behavior, and remedial reading. In addition, we searched the ERIC database for documentation about the impact humiliation has on middle school students. In this article, we will begin by discussing the findings from our interviews and surveys, then we will describe the effects of humiliation on middle school learners.

Types of Humiliation

The 10 teachers and 10 students we interviewed worked or attended one of three large urban middle schools in two southwestern states. These schools fit the profile of many schools across America—large (more than 1,000 students), located in major metropolitan communities, with diverse demographic profiles among students and teachers. None of the schools had a formal anti-bullying or character education program. We sought a representative sample of teachers based on experience, gender, and subject area. We chose students who represented different grade levels, genders, and achievement levels. The names of students and teachers are pseudonyms. We conducted individual interviews with each teacher and each student to ensure privacy and promote candor in their disclosures. Based on an analysis of their responses, we identified three themes.

Bullying

Student voices. The most common topic raised in the conversation for both teachers and students was bullying. Many students believed that bullying was part of life, something that was unavoidable. It need not be. "Being bullied is neither a 'part of growing up' nor a 'rite of passage'" (Barone, 1997, p. 80). Every student participant recounted a time in which he or she had been bullied or had witnessed it occurring with other students. Marcus, a sixth grader, described an incident that occurred earlier that school year.

> There're these older guys [eighth grade] who think they're the kings of the school. They talk loud, swear, shove people in the halls. I see them comin' and I bounce [leave]. My first month at this school, they walked behind me, talkin' loud about how I was a little faggot. I tried to ignore them, but they knocked my stuff out of my hand.

Marcus's experience is perhaps the most common type associated with bullying. There was an age and size differential between perpetrators and victim, accompanied by verbal abuse associated with sexual orientation, and some physical contact (Nishina & Juvonen, 2005; Olweus, 1993). This is also consistent with Bjorklund and Pellegrini's (2000) dominance theory of increased bullying directed at those entering a new social group.

Martha, a seventh grader, described a more subtle kind of bullying.

There's this girl, and she used to be our friend [named several girls] . . . but she's just so weird. What happened to her? We were all friends since second grade, but when she came back to school [entering middle school] she still dressed and talked like such a baby. It's embarrassing to be around her. So, we stopped talking to her.

Martha described relational bullying, memorably chronicled in a number of studies (Bjoerkqvist, Lagerspetz, & Kaukianen, 1992; Crick, Bigbee, & Howe, 1996; Simmons, 2002). Although Martha did not describe herself as a bully, she exhibited prevalent forms of female aggression: relational bullying and avoidance (Crick, Bigbee, & Howe, 1996). The transition from elementary to middle school appears to play a role as well. Pelligrini and Bartini's (2000) study of bullying across fifth and sixth grade noted that the move to larger, more impersonal school environments often interfered with the maintenance of peer affiliations.

We also sought students' perspectives on the reasons bullying exists. Their comments suggest that they accept bullying as a given, a common part of middle school life. "Everyone gets made fun of," remarked seventh grade student Juan. "If you can't take it . . . if you let anyone see it bothers you, you just get it even worse." Martha echoed this sentiment. "It's how girls are. One day you're friends, and the next day you're not. Better not be caught lookin' at someone else's man. That'll get you quicker than anything." Beliefs about the normative presence of bullying, verbal taunts, and teasing are prevalent among adolescents, who view these as *de facto* elements of the secondary school experience (Shakeshaft et al., 1997).

We also asked students about their reactions to being humiliated by their peers. Most described deep levels of shame and responses that could be categorized as either violent or avoidant. Students told us they "snapped," "pounded his face in," "blew," or "got my bitch on" to describe verbal or physical retaliation. In other cases, students described attempts to avoid a situation. Similar to Marcus's attempts to "bounce" when bullies were spotted, Al, an eighth grader, reported that he did not use certain restrooms or hallways, because he anticipated that his tormentor would be there. Adriana, an eighth grade student, poignantly recounted the following incident.

When I was in seventh, I made up a boyfriend to my friends. It was stupid. . . . Everyone had a boyfriend and I wanted one, too. I told them I had a boyfriend at [nearby middle school]. When Cindy found out that it wasn't true, she told everybody. They laughed at me, left notes . . . told some of the boys. I told my mom I was sick, and I didn't go to school for two weeks.

Adriana's avoidance of the situation is a common response to the humiliation resulting from bullying. According to the American Psychological Association and the National Education Association, 7% of eighth graders stay home from school at least once a month to avoid a bullying situation (cited in Vail, 1999). Other middle school students, like Marcus and Al, alter their paths in school to avoid encountering bullies (Wessler, 2003).

Teacher voices. The 10 teachers who participated in this study were conflicted about the role of bullying in middle school. All 10 participants expressed concern over the amount of bullying in their schools (i.e., responding positively to the queries, "Bullying occurs frequently at this school," and "Bullying negatively impacts the learning of students at this school"). All were aware of the deleterious effects of bullying on both the victims and the perpetrators. Mr. Lee, a seventh and eighth grade mathematics instructor, noted, "We have to worry about the kid who's doing the bullying as well as the one who's getting it. Those kids that are bullies now end up in trouble in school and in life." In addition, 8 of the 10 instructors reported that they "always" responded to incidents of bullying. Mr. Harper, a music teacher, said, "I had it happen last week. I was outside my class [during passing period] and saw a group of bigger students descend on this smaller boy. You could just see this kid brace himself for what was going to happen. It was like slow motion. . . . I stepped in and made the kids leave him alone." Five other teachers offered anecdotal reports of their personal responses to bullying incidents, although, in all cases, it was related to the threat of physical harm perpetrated by either boys or girls.

Verbal abuse did not prompt such swift responses. "I won't put up with profanity, name-calling. If I hear it, I stop it. I write a referral if I have to," stated Ms. Indria, a sixth grade social studies teacher. However, when probed, all 10 teachers stated that they did not get involved in "personal relationships, friendship stuff." Ms. Indria offered, "Girls just seem to treat each other badly. It's a part of adolescence. . . . I certainly remember doing it when I was that age." Seventh grade science teacher Ms. Anthony echoed a similar response. "I can't keep up with it. One week they're friends; the next week they aren't. Way too much drama. I find that when I have tried to mediate, it ends by consuming too much instructional time." Four other teachers made statements consistent with the belief that negotiating a verbally, or even physically, abusive landscape was a part of growing up. Physical education teacher Ms. Hartford noted,

> You really have to be careful when you choose to interfere. It [teacher involvement] can really make it worse. The kids will just pick more—"teacher's pet." If it looks like the kid is holding his own, I don't get directly involved. I keep an eye on it.

It is also likely that Ms. Hartford and the other teachers interviewed were not cognizant of their relationships with the aggressors. Elias and Zins (2003) found that bullies often hold high social capital with their teachers and are perceived positively, while victims are often perceived as less likable.

Statements like the one offered by the physical education and science teachers illuminate a commonly held belief among middle school educators—that the ability to "take it" is a necessary rite of adolescent passage. Computer instructor Ms. Andersen evoked her own junior high memories to defend this position.

> Face it, being able to dish it out and take it gets you ready for the real world. What's that old commercial? "Never let 'em see you sweat." Teenagers have to learn that you don't wear your emotions on your sleeve. People'll use it against you. I know, I went through it, but I survived. You have to toughen up.

When asked about the role of humiliation in bullying, she replied,

> Yeah, they're good at humiliating each other. I keep an ear on what's going on. But I have to say . . . a lot of times they use it to keep each other in line. In a funny way, they regulate each other's behavior.

Ms. Anderson's beliefs are not entirely misplaced. Tapper and Bolton (2005) used wireless recording equipment to analyze bullying interactions among 77 students. They found that direct aggression (without physical violence) often inspired peer support for the aggressor. The reaction of the victim is a factor in whether the bullying will continue. Perry, Williard, and Perry (1990) determined that displays of distress by the victim increased the likelihood that bullying would occur again. "Never let 'em see you sweat" appears to be accurate.

Teacher Behavior

Student voices. Students had strong feelings about the use of humiliation by teachers. Nine of the 10 student participants could recount times when a teacher had used sarcasm or humiliation to embarrass a student in front of the class. In some cases it was directed at them, while in others they had witnessed it in their classes.

> We had this one teacher in seventh grade; man, she was rough. She had a nickname for every kid in the class. Like, she called this one girl "Funeral," because she said she always looked like she was coming from one.

This story, told by Al, is admittedly an extreme example and not typical of the incidences that were shared by students. However, three students told of times when teachers had "busted someone" in front of the entire class for failing a quiz or test, using insulting language. "I don't know why they do it," said Gail, a sixth grader. "It's not like it makes a difference. Who wants to work harder for someone who embarrasses you that way?"

Other students admitted that the use of humiliation might have a positive effect, at least in the short term.

> My [seventh grade] math teacher reads everyone's quiz grades to the whole class. I failed one, and he said, "Spending too much time looking at girls?" It made me kinda mad . . . but I made sure I didn't fail another math quiz. (Juan, eighth grade)

Veronica, an eighth grade student, said,

> Ms._____ likes to catch you doing something wrong. Like, we were reading our social studies book out loud and I missed my turn. She goes, "Wake up, Veronica! We're all waiting," in this really stupid way she has [imitates a sarcastic tone]. Everyone laughed as though it never happened to them. I don't let her catch me.

Veronica then used profanity to describe her teacher, evidence of the anger she felt toward this adult and perhaps school in general.

When asked what they thought these teachers hoped to gain with the use of humiliation, their insights were surprising. "They want to be cool, like it's funny," remarked sixth grade student Marcus. Seventh grader Harlan responded similarly. "They don't treat you like little kids. My dad talks the same way. Making fun of kids in the class is just what they do."

The use of sarcasm and humiliation by teachers has been less well documented in the literature than the prevalence and effects of bullying. It is certainly long understood in the teaching profession, as evidenced by Briggs's (1928) article on the prevalence of the use of sarcasm by young secondary teachers. Martin's (1987) study of secondary students' perspectives on this phenomenon was derived from surveys of more than 20,000 Canadian students. Students reported that the use of sarcasm resulted in dislike for the teacher and even anger toward the teacher. Martin also reported that some students described "anticipatory embarrassment," the dread associated with the belief that the teacher would humiliate them again. In addition, this created learning problems, including decreased motivation to study and complete homework, increased cutting of classes, and thoughts of dropping out. Turner and associates (2002) studied the classroom learning environments of 65 sixth grade mathematics classrooms to study factors that promoted or reduced help-seeking behaviors and found that the teacher's classroom discourse, including use of sarcasm, influenced the likelihood that students would seek academic help when needed. Classrooms featuring more negative teacher talk, including sarcasm, were associated with high levels of avoidance in asking for assistance.

Teacher voices. Six of the 10 teachers in the study named colleagues who regularly used sarcasm and humiliation with students. Ms. Robertson, a seventh grade language arts teacher, described a colleague as "us[ing] words like a knife. He just cuts kids down to size." Mr. Lee, the math teacher, described an experience when he was a student teacher.

> [The master teacher] was just vicious with students. Everything was a big joke, but kind of mean-spirited, you know? He'd single out kids because of a quirk, like they talked funny, or they had a big nose, or they wore clothes that were kind of different. Kids would laugh, but I saw the cringes, too.

Five of the participating teachers discussed the fine line between humor and sarcasm. Ms. Andersen offered,

> You have to take into account that they're really very fragile, in spite of all their bluster. We all remember what it was like. Worried all the time about sticking out. They're already sensitive to the need for conformity. As teachers, we have to make sure that we don't make them feel different.

Ms. Hartford noted, "It's great to keep it light and fun, but not at someone else's expense." Sarcasm is typically used for three purposes: to soften a criticism, especially through feigned politeness; to mitigate verbal aggressiveness; or to create humor (Dews & Winner, 1995). However, the use of sarcasm in social discourse assumes an equal relationship between parties. This is never the case in the classroom, where the teacher holds the power in the relationship. Therefore, the student cannot respond with a sarcastic reply without consequences. The use of sarcasm with middle school students is ineffective as well, as evidenced by a study of 13-year-olds by the Harvard Zero Project. They found that 71% of the students studied

misinterpreted sarcasm as deception. In other words, the majority had not yet reached a linguistically sophisticated developmental level that would allow them to accurately discern the speaker's purpose, even when it was accompanied by a gestural cue (Demorest, Meyer, Phelps, Gardner, & Winner, 1984).

Remedial Reading and Mathematics

Bullying and sarcasm are age-old tools of humiliation, but a more recent (and inadvertent) tool is that of the remedial class created for students who fail to achieve in reading and mathematics. Commonly referred to as "double dosing," it is the practice of increasing the number of instructional hours spent in remediation, at the expense of electives or core classes such as science and social studies (Cavanaugh, 2006). Though well-intended, our student participants were vocal about the negative effects on the lives of adolescents.

Student voices. "Everyone knows who the dumb kids are," explained Martha, a seventh grade student. "All you have to do is look around at who's not on the wheel [elective class rotation]. They're all in reading mastery." At Martha's school, students who score below a cut point on the state language arts and mathematics examinations are automatically enrolled in another section of instruction. Jessika, an eighth grader, is one of those students. "I hate it. We're all the stupid kids. Everyone knows it." Carol, another eighth grade student, described her classmates this way:

> Nobody even tries in my [remedial] reading class. It's like, if you do, you're trying to make yourself look better than you really are. No offense, but it's "acting white." People just sleep in class. You know, pull their [sweatshirt] hood up. If you look like you're trying, you'll catch it from [classmates.]

Marcus and Al are also enrolled in similar classes for mathematics. When asked what others said to them and about them in regard to their participation in these courses, we heard, "retard," "SPED" [special education], "loser," "tard," "spaz," and "window licker." These labels are quite troubling for students with disabilities, because they suggest an accepted intolerance for students in need of academic supports.

Slavin's (1993) review of the literature on remedial classes in middle school found a zero effect size for academic gains. While it is too soon to gauge the long-term effectiveness of double-dosing academic achievement, the voices of middle school students provide a bellwether for assessing the social and emotional repercussions of such practices. In a few short years, these students will have reached an age at which they can voluntarily exit school. There is further evidence that low-achieving students are more likely to use so-called "self-handicapping strategies" such as giving up and refusing to study (Midgely & Urdan, 1995; Turner et al., 2002). In particular, they are more likely to associate with other negative-thinking students. The remediation classroom, it would seem, from Carol's and Jessika's comments, is a perfect environment for breeding this sort of attitude toward school and learning.

Teachers' voices. We were particularly interested in the views of Mr. Lee and Ms. Robertson, both of whom teach a section of remedial math or reading. "No one wants those classes," remarked Mr. Lee. "I got it because I'm new here. They stick the new teachers with these classes. Wouldn't you think that they should be taught by people with lots of experience?" he asked. Mrs. Robertson described her classroom learning environment. "I'm ashamed to say that I dread fourth [period] because of the students. I feel like all the energy gets sucked out of the room, and me. I can't seem to inspire them, and it affects the way I teach." When asked to elaborate, she said, "I know I'm stricter, and I feel like I can't even smile or make a joke. I'm grim, and it makes for a grim period."

Two other teachers explained that, while they saw the logic in double dosing, they worried about the detrimental effects on their students. Mr. Espinosa, a seventh grade social studies teacher, said,

> We're organized in houses here [a cohort model]. But every time we excuse students to go to another class, one that's different from everyone else, it chops away at the concept of a family of students and teachers. I can see the light go right out of their eyes when they have to pass up computer class to go for extra reading or math class.

Ms. Andersen, the computer teacher, expressed concern about the content students were missing. "If I'm not teaching literacy and math, then what am I doing? They'll just get further behind."

The Effects of Humiliation

In addition to the ways in which middle school students experience humiliation, we discussed the impact that humiliation has on young adolescents. Both students and teachers identified a number of outcomes from humiliation, including drug and alcohol use, attendance problems, dropping out of school, pregnancy, and suicide. Let us examine the perspectives of teachers and students on each of these issues.

Drug and Alcohol Use

Most educators recognize that experimentation with alcohol and drugs during adolescence is common. The Youth Risk Behavior Survey (www.cdc.gov/Healthy Youth/yrbs/index.htm) indicated that more than two-thirds of middle school students report ever having had a drink of alcohol and that 26% report ever having used marijuana. However, several students commented on the regular use of drugs and alcohol by students who feel humiliated at school. In the words of Marcus, "I know a kid who drinks every night. He hates school and says they make him feel stupid." One of the teachers noted that the rate of drug and alcohol use was highest for students who were enrolled in remedial reading classes. Mooney (Mooney & Cole, 2000), a student with a disability who subsequently graduated from an Ivy League college, discussed his use of drugs and alcohol to "turn off the shockers" at school.

Attendance Problems

Another outcome of humiliation that both students and teachers discussed was poor school attendance. Mr. Harper, the music teacher, put it eloquently—"They vote with their feet"— meaning that students tell us, by their physical presence in school, whether or not it is a comfortable place to be. Again, most educators acknowledge that there are patterns of problematic attendance, such as is typically seen in urban schools. More important, for our purpose here, is the difference of attendance patterns within the school. It is clear from an analysis of attendance patterns—both tardiness and absence—that students are communicating with which teachers they feel comfortable and with which they do not. While there are many reasons for students feeling comfortable with teachers, one reason is the climate that is created in class. Veronica reported, "Lots of us cut class with Mr._____ because he makes you feel bad when you try to answer."

Dropping Out

While calculating an accurate drop-out rate has been exceedingly difficult to do, it is important to note that in many states there is no mechanism for capturing middle school drop-outs. It seems that when the data systems were created, people assumed that middle school students either would not or could not drop out of school. Unfortunately, that is not the reality; middle school students are dropping out. In-grade retention (an indicator of either poor academic performance or poor attendance) is the single strongest school-related predictor of dropping out in middle school (Rumberger, 1995). As Ms. Indria reported, "There are students who just leave us. They don't find school fulfilling and are ashamed of their performance, and they stop coming. No one really knows where they go." Turner and associates' (2002) study on the relationship between classroom climate and help-seeking offers further evidence of the role of humiliation. There is also evidence that the overall school climate—the degree that students feel safe to learn and are not threatened by peers or teachers—is directly related to the drop-out problem (Wehlage, 1991). As Al indicated, "If I had to deal with the crap that Jeremy does, I'd just quit. I wouldn't come to this place."

School institutions related to humiliation play a factor as well. According to Goldschmidt and Wang (1999), "Two school policy and practice variables affect the middle school dropout rate significantly: the percentage of students held back one grade, and the percentage of students misbehaving" (p. 728). Here we see the snowballing effects of humiliation. Students retained in grade, attending remedial classes, surrounded by misbehavior (including bullying), with lower rates of attendance and less inclination to seek help from sarcastic teachers appear to be at great risk for dropping out, and humiliation plays a role in each.

Pregnancy

Another issue associated with humiliation, identified primarily by the teachers we interviewed, was teenage pregnancy. While less common at the middle school level than at the secondary level, teen pregnancy is still an issue with this age group. According to the Centers for Disease Control and Prevention, national data suggests that between six and seven of every 1,000 middle school girls become pregnant (Klien, 2005). While there are a number of theories about the causes of teenage pregnancy, including too much free time, poverty, access to alcohol, and physical maturity, Ms. Hartford had another take on the situation. She said, "In this community, pregnancy is one of the acceptable reasons to leave school. If school is a toxic environment for you, you can get pregnant and leave school. Nobody will question your decision."

Suicide

A final outcome of humiliation identified by the participants was suicide and suicidal thoughts. Public health officials have noted a significant increase in youth suicide—more than 300% since 1950 (Bloch, 1999). Suicide is now the third leading cause of death for youth ages 10 to 19 (following accidents and homicides) (Centers for Disease Control and Prevention, 2000). While the suicide rate for high school students has remained fairly stable over the past decade, the suicide rate for middle school students (ages 10 through 14), increased more than 100%

during the decade of the 1990s (Bloch, 1999). A haunting thought was shared by Adriana, who said, "Everybody I know has thought about suicide, but the one who did it was bothered all the time by other kids and no one did anything." As Fisher (2005) noted, teachers have to understand the signs and symptoms of suicide and ensure that students feel honored and respected at school. One of the teachers suggested, "I think that they're under a great deal of pressure to perform. If you add humiliation to that, they don't see a way out and might consider taking their own life."

Recommendations for Reducing Humiliation in Middle School

Some of the problems members of our profession discuss about the challenges to achievement in middle school might be explained by students' experiences with humiliation. When students experience humiliation, as these data suggest they do, a series of negative outcomes can be triggered. We recommend that educators make a commitment to reduce the needless opportunities for humiliation that creep into the daily experiences of their students.

Recommendation #1: Assess the School Climate

The first step to reducing humiliation is to recognize that it might, in fact, be present. Schools routinely administer annual school climate surveys, and this can provide an excellent starting point for analysis. For example, the California Healthy Kids Survey contains questions that can shed light on the issue of humiliation. The survey asks respondents to assess the extent to which adults "treat all students fairly" and "listen to what students have to say" and contains several queries about bullying and bully prevention programs (California Department of Education, 2005).

Recommendation #2: Observe and Analyze Curricular and Instructional Interactions

The middle school reform report entitled *Breaking Ranks in the Middle* (National Association of Secondary School Principals, 2006) strongly recommends heterogeneous grouping of students in small learning communities to improve achievement and personalize learning. This requires schools to abandon outdated ability grouping and tracking, which result in lowered expectations and missed opportunities for rigorous curriculum. Some schools cling to tracking and remedial classes because they do not possess the capacity to differentiate instruction for all learners. Building this capacity is not a matter of scattershot inservices, but rather targeted peer coaching, professional development, and administrative accountability. A first step toward realizing this goal is to conduct classroom observations for the purposes of data collection and analysis of needs. The Instructional Practices Inventory developed by the Middle Level Leadership Center is a useful tool for developing a school-wide profile of the instructional practices occurring at the school, including the amount of teacher-led instruction, student-led discussions, and levels of disengagement (www.mllc.org).[1] Classrooms with high levels of student disengagement should be targeted for further analysis to determine contributing factors, especially teacher behaviors and interaction styles. Teachers struggling with disengagement can participate in the Teacher Expectations and Student Achievement (TESA) professional development program developed by the Los Angeles County Office of Education (www.lacoe.edu/orgs/165/index.cfm). This is a five-month experience that involves peer observations and coaching focused on 15 specific instructional behaviors that increase positive student perceptions about learning. Other teachers who are having difficulty with curriculum design for heterogeneously grouped students can benefit from focused professional development and planning on differentiating instruction at the unit level. A beginning step may include the formation of book study groups using materials such as *Differentiation in Practice for Grades 5–9* (Tomlinson & Eidson, 2003). By collecting and sharing data to develop targeted professional development, teachers are able to move beyond "I've heard/read this before" to take specific action. This is further reinforced through administrative accountability and ongoing data collection to measure improvement at the curricular and instructional levels.

Recommendation #3: Make an Anti-bullying Curriculum Part of the School Culture

Much has been written in the past decade about anti-bullying curricula, especially in the wake of high-profile school shootings throughout the nation. Many fine programs exist, and the Olweus Bullying Prevention Program is among the most respected (www.clemson.edu/olweus/content.html). The multi-layered design of this program targets school-wide, classroom, and individual interventions for both bullies and victims. However, anti-bullying curricula are only effective if there is long-term commitment. Perhaps the most common mistake is that after a period of enthusiastic introduction and implementation, programs such as these fall to the wayside as other initiatives command attention. A multi-year plan that includes refreshers for existing staff as well as training for teachers new to the school is essential for sustainability. The anti-bullying program should be written into the school's accountability plan, the new teacher induction program, and as part of the curriculum for each grade level.

Conclusion

The recommendations made are all costly in terms of time, money, and resources. However, the unintended costs of humiliation are much higher for our students. It is time to take another look at the anti-bullying curricula being developed by groups across the country and how they can be sustained for more than one school year. It might also be time to notice our own behaviors and to have hard conversations with our colleagues about appropriate interactions with students—interactions that clearly demonstrate care, honesty, and high expectations. And finally, it may be time to reconsider the ways in which we group students and provide supplemental instructional interventions such that groups of students do not experience school as telling them they are stupid, incompetent, and not worthy. In doing so, we might just see increases in student achievement as well as youth who are more engaged in their educational experience.

Note

1. For a comprehensive assessment of middle school programs, procedures, and processes, readers might want to consider using the School Improvement Toolkit, available from National Middle School Association at www.nmsa.org/ProfessionalDevelopment/ SchoolImprovementToolkit/tabid/654/Default.aspx

References

Barone, F. J. (1997). Bullying in school. *Phi Delta Kappan, 79,* 80–82.

Bjoerkqvist, K., Lagerspetz, K. M. J., & Kaukianen, A. (1992). Do girls manipulate and boys fight? Developmental trends in regard to direct and indirect aggression. *Aggressive Behavior, 18,* 117–127.

Bjorklund, D. F., & Pellegrini, A. D. (2000). Child development and evolutionary psychology. *Child Development, 71,* 1687–1708.

Bloch, D. (1999). Adolescent suicide as a public health threat. *Journal of Child and Adolescent Psychiatric Nursing, 12,* 26–38.

Briggs, T. H. (1928). Sarcasm. *The School Review, 36*(9), 685–695.

California Department of Education. (2005). *California healthy kids school climate survey.* Retrieved February 18, 2007, from http://www.wested.org/chks/pdf/scs_05_alpha.pdf

Cavanaugh, S. (2006, June 14). Students double-dosing on reading and math: Schools aim to improve state test scores—and satisfy federal education laws. *Education Week.* Retrieved September 3, 2006, from http://www.all4ed.org/press/ EdWeek_061406_ StudentsDoubleDosingReadingMath.pdf

Centers for Disease Control and Prevention. (2000). *Youth risk behavior surveillance—United States, 1999.* In CDC surveillance summaries, June 9, 2000, MMRW. Atlanta, GA: Author.

Crick, N. R., Bigbee, M. A., & Howe, C. (1996). How do I hurt thee? Let me count the ways. *Child Development, 67,* 1003–1014.

Demorest, A., Meyer, C., Phelps, E., Gardner, H., & Winner, E. (1984). Words speak louder than actions: Understanding deliberately false remarks. *Child Development, 55,* 1527–1534.

Dews, S., & Winner, E. (1995). Muting the meaning: A social function of irony. *Metaphor and Symbolic Activity, 10,* 3–18.

Elias, M. J., & Zins, J. E. (2003). Bullying, other forms of peer harassment, and victimization in the schools: Issues for school psychology research and practice. In M. J. Elias & J. E. Zins (Eds.), *Bullying, peer harassment, and victimization in the schools: The next generation of prevention* (pp. 1–5). Binghamton, NY: Haworth.

Fisher, D. (2005). The literacy educator's role in suicide prevention. *Journal of Adolescent and Adult Literacy, 48,* 364–373.

Friedman, T. L. (2005). *The world is flat: A brief history of the twenty-first century.* New York: Farrar, Straus and Giroux.

Goldschmidt, P., & Wang, J. (1999). When can schools affect dropout behavior? A longitudinal multilevel analysis. *American Education Research Journal, 36,* 715–738.

Klein, J. D. (2005). Adolescent pregnancy: Current trends and issues. *Pediatrics, 116,* 281–286.

Martin, W. B. W. (1987). Students' perceptions of causes and consequences of embarrassment in the school. *Canadian Journal of Education, 12,* 277–293.

Midgely, C., & Urdan, T. (1995). Predictors of middle school students' use of self-handicapping strategies. *The Journal of Early Adolescence, 15,* 389–411.

Mooney, J., & Cole, D. (2000). *Learning outside the lines: Two Ivy League students with learning disabilities and ADHD give you the tools for academic success and educational revolution.* New York: Simon & Schuster.

National Association of Secondary School Principals. (2006). *Breaking ranks in the middle: Strategies for leading middle level reform.* Reston, VA: Author.

Nishina, A., & Juvonen, J. (2005). Daily reports of witnessing and experiencing peer harassment in middle school. *Child Development, 76,* 435–450.

Olweus, D. (1993). *Bullying at school: What we know and what we can do.* Oxford, UK: Blackwell.

Pellgrini, A. D., & Bartini, M. (2000). A longitudinal study of bullying, victimization, and peer affiliation during the transition from primary school to middle school. *American Educational Research Journal, 37,* 699–725.

Perry, D. G., Williard, J. C., & Perry, L. C. (1990). Peers' perceptions of the consequences that victimized children provide aggressors. *Child Development, 61,* 1310–1325.

Rumberger, R. W. (1995). Dropping out of middle school: A multilevel analysis of students and schools. *American Educational Research Journal, 32,* 583–625.

Shakcshaft, C., Mandel, L., Johnson, Y. M., Sawyer, J., Hergenrother, M. A., & Barber, E. (1997). Boys call me cow. *Educational Leadership, 55*(2), 22–25.

Simmons, R. (2002). Odd girl out: *The hidden culture of aggression in girls.* New York: Harcourt.

Slavin, R. E. (1993). Ability grouping in the middle grades: Achievement effects and alternatives. *The Elementary School Journal, 93,* 535–552.

Tapper, K., & Boulton, M. J. (2005). Victim and peer group responses to different forms of aggression among primary school children. *Aggressive Behavior, 31,* 238–253.

Tomlinson, C. A., & Eidson, C. C. (2003). *Differentiation in practice: A resource guide for differentiating curriculum grades 5–9.* Alexandria, VA: Association for Supervision and Curriculum Development.

Turner, J. C., Midgley, C., Meyer, D. K., Gheen, M., Anderman, E. M., Kang, Y., & Patrick, H. (2002). The classroom environment and students' reports of avoidance strategies in Mathematics: A multimethod study. *Journal of Educational Psychology, 94,* 88–106.

Vail, K., (1999). Words that wound. *American School Board Journal, 186*(9), 37–40.

Wehlage, G. (1991). School reform for at-risk students. *Equity and Excellence, 25,* 15–24.

Wessler, S. L. (2003). It's hard to learn when you're scared. *Educational Leadership, 61*(1), 40–43.

Vail, K., (1999). Words that wound. *American School Board Journal, 186*(9), 37–40.

Wehlage, G. (1991). School reform for at-risk students. *Equity and Excellence, 25,* 15–24.

Wessler, S. L. (2003). It's hard to learn when you're scared. *Educational Leadership, 61*(1), 40–43.

Nancy Frey is an associate professor of teacher education at San Diego State University, California. **Douglas Fisher** is a professor of teacher education at San Diego State University, California. Email: dfisher@mail.sdsu.edu

The Power of Our Words

Teacher language influences students' identities as learners. Five principles keep that influence positive.

PAULA DENTON

Think back to your childhood and recall the voices of your teachers. What kinds of words did they use? What tone of voice? Recall how you felt around those teachers. Safe and motivated to learn? Or self-doubting, insecure, even angry?

Teacher language—what we say to students and how we say it—is one of our most powerful teaching tools. It permeates every aspect of teaching. We cannot teach a lesson, welcome a student into the room, or handle a classroom conflict without using words. Our language can lift students to their highest potential or tear them down. It can help them build positive relationships or encourage discord and distrust. It shapes how students think and act and, ultimately, how they learn.

How Language Shapes Learners

From my 25 years of teaching and my research on language use, I've learned that language actually *shapes* thoughts, feelings, and experiences. (Vygotsky, 1978). Our words shape students as learners by

- *Affecting students' sense of identity.* Five-year-old Don loves to sing but isn't good at it—yet. His music teacher says, "Let's have you move to the back row and try just mouthing the words." Such language can lead Don to believe not only that he is a bad singer, but also that he will always be a bad singer. But suppose the teacher says, "Don, you really love to sing, don't you? Would you like to learn more about it? I have some ideas." Such words support Don's budding identity as one who loves to sing and is learning singing skills.
- *Helping students understand how they work and play.* For example, an educator might comment on a student's writing by saying, "These juicy adjectives here give me a wonderful sense of how your character looks and feels." Naming a specific attribute—the use of adjectives—alerts the writer to an important strength in her writing and encourages her to build on that strength.
- *Influencing our relationships with students.* To a student who—once again—argued with classmates at recess, we

might say either "Emory, if you don't stop it, no more recess!" or "Emory, I saw you arguing with Douglas and Stephen. Can you help me understand what happened from your point of view?" The former would reinforce a teacher-student relationship based on teacher threats and student defensiveness, whereas the latter would begin to build a teacher-student relationship based on trust.

Five Guiding Principles for Positive Language

How can we ensure that our language supports students' learning and helps create a positive, respectful community? During the 20 years I've been involved with the Responsive Classroom, 1 have found this approach to be a good base for using language powerfully. The Responsive Classroom approach, developed by Northeast Foundation for Children, offers language strategies that enable elementary teachers to help students succeed academically and socially. Strategies range from asking open-ended questions that stretch students' thinking to redirecting students when behavior goes off-track. These strategies are based on the following five general principles.

1. Be Direct

When we say what we mean and use a kind, straightforward tone, students learn that they can trust us. They feel respected and safe, a necessary condition for developing self-discipline and taking the risks required for learning.

It's easy to slip into using indirect language as a way to win compliance. For example, as a new teacher, I tried to get students to do what I wanted by pointing out what I liked about other students' behavior. "I like the way May and Justine are paying attention," I would cheerfully announce while impatiently eyeing Dave and Marta fooling around in the corner.

When this strategy worked, it was because students mimicked the desired behavior so that they, too, would win praise from me, not because I had helped them develop self-control or internal motivation. And often, when I pointed out how I liked certain learners' behavior, the rest of the class ignored me. If I liked the way May and Justine were paying attention, that was nice for the three of us, but it had nothing to do with the rest of the class, who had more compelling things to do at the moment.

Moreover, comparative language can damage students' relationships. By holding May and Justine up as exemplars, I implied that the other class members were less commendable. This can drive a wedge between students.

Later in my career, I learned to speak directly. To call the students to a meeting, for example, I rang a chime to gain their attention (a signal we practiced regularly), then said firmly, "Come to the meeting rug and take a seat now." To Dave and Marta in the previous example, I'd say, "It's time to listen now." The difference in students' response was remarkable.

Sarcasm, another form of indirect language, is also common—and damaging—in the classroom. Sometimes teachers use sarcasm because we think it will provide comic relief; other times we're just tired, and it slips in without our even knowing it. If a teacher says, "John, what part of 'Put your phone away' don't you understand?" students will likely laugh, and the teacher may think she has shown that she's hip and has a sense of humor. But John will feel embarrassed, and his trust in this teacher will diminish. The position of this teacher may shift in the other students' eyes as well: They no longer see her as an authority who protects their emotional safety but as someone who freely uses the currency of insult. Much better to simply say, "John, put your phone away." If he doesn't, try another strategy, such as a logical consequence.

2. Convey Faith in Students' Abilities and Intentions

When our words and tone convey faith in students' desire and ability to do well, students are more likely to live up to our expectations of them.

"When everyone is ready, I'll show you how to plant the seeds." "You can look at the chart to remind yourself of our ideas for good story writing." "Show me how you will follow the rules in the hall." These teacher words, spoken in a calm voice, communicate a belief that students want to—and know how to—listen, cooperate, and do good work. This increases the chance that students will see themselves as respectful listeners, cooperative people, and competent workers, and behave accordingly.

Take the time to notice and comment on positive behavior, being quite specific: "You're trying lots of different ideas for solving that problem. That takes persistence." Such observations give students hard evidence for why they should believe in themselves.

3. Focus on Actions, Not Abstractions

Because elementary-age children tend to be concrete thinkers, teachers can communicate most successfully with them by detailing specific actions that will lead to a positive environment. For example, rather than saying, "Be respectful," it's more helpful to state, "When someone is speaking during a discussion,

the rest of us will listen carefully and wait until the speaker is finished before raising our hands to add a comment."

Sometimes it's effective to prompt students to name concrete positive behaviors themselves. To a student who has trouble focusing during writing time, a teacher might say matter-of-factly, "What will help you think of good ideas for your story and concentrate on writing them down?" The student might then respond, "I can find a quiet place to write, away from my friends."

There is a place, of course, for such abstract terms as *respectful* and responsible, but we must give students plenty of opportunities to associate those words with concrete actions. Classroom expectations such as "treat one another with kindness" will be more meaningful to students if we help them picture and practice what those expectations look like in different situations.

Focusing on action also means pointing to the desired *behavior* rather than labeling the learner's character or attitude. I had a student who chronically did poor work when he could do better. In a moment of frustration, I said to him, "I don't think you even care!" This allowed me to vent, but it did nothing to help the student change. His energy went toward defending himself against my negative judgment, not toward examining and changing his behavior. Worse, such language can lead students to accept our judgment and believe that they indeed don't care.

It's more helpful in such situations to issue a positive challenge that names the behavior we want: "Your job today is to record five observations of our crickets. Think about what you'll need to do before you start." This moves the focus to what the student can do.

4. Keep It Brief

It's hard for many young children to follow long strings of words like this:

> When you go out to recess today, be sure to remember what we said about including everyone in games, because yesterday some kids had an issue with not being included in kickball and four square, and we've talked about this. You were doing really well for a while there, but lately it seems like you're getting kind of careless, and that's got to change or . . .

By the end of this spiel, many students would be thinking about other things. Few could follow the entire explanation. Students understand more when we speak less. Simply asking, "Who can tell us one way to include everyone at recess?" gives them an opportunity to remind themselves of positive behaviors. If you have taught and led students in practicing the class's expectations for recess, students will make good use of such a reminder.

5. Know When to Be Silent

The skillful use of silence can be just as powerful as the skillful use of words. When teachers use silence, we open a space for students to think, rehearse what to say, and sometimes gather the courage to speak at all.

We can see the benefit of silence if, after asking a question, we pause before taking responses from students. Researchers have found that when teachers wait three to five seconds, more students respond, and those responses show higher-level thinking (Swift & Gooding, 1983; Tobin, 1980).

Three to five seconds can feel uncomfortably long at first. But if we stick to it—and model thoughtful pausing by waiting a few seconds ourselves to respond to students' comments—we'll set a pace for the entire classroom that will soon feel natural. Our reward will be classroom conversations of higher quality.

Remaining silent allows us to listen to students and requires us to resist the impulse to jump in and correct students' words or finish their thoughts. A true listener tries to understand a speaker's message before formulating a response. When we allow students to speak uninterrupted and unhurried, we help them learn because speaking is an important means of consolidating knowledge.

In my current role teaching educators Responsive Classroom strategies, I watch teachers incorporate these five principles of language into their daily communications with students, and I see them build classrooms where students feel safe, respected, and engaged. By paying attention to our language, we can use it to open the doors of possibility for students.

References

Swift, J. N., & Gooding, T. (1983). Interaction of wait time feedback and questioning instruction on middle school science teaching. *Journal of Research in Science Teaching, 20*(8), 721–730.

Tobin, K. G. (1980). The effect of an extended teacher wait-time on science achievement. *Journal of Research in Science Teaching, 17,* 469–475.

Vygotsky, L. (1978). *Mind in society.* Cambridge, MA: Harvard University Press.

PAULA DENTON is Director of Program Development and Delivery for Northeast Foundation for Children, developer of the Responsive Classroom approach; www.responsiveclassroom.org; paula@responsiveclassroom.org. She is the author of *The Power of Our Words: Teacher Language that Helps Children Learn* (Northeast Foundation for Children, 2007).

Author's note—A 2006 study by Sara Rimm-Kaufman and colleagues at the University of Virginia showed that Responsive Classroom practices were associated with students having higher reading and math test scores, better social skills, and more positive feelings about school. The U.S. Department of Education's Institute of Education Sciences has awarded Rimm-Kaufman a $2.9 million grant to further investigate how Responsive Classroom practices contribute to gains in students' math achievement.

Marketing Civility

How can you improve communication so high school students feel safe and secure?

MICHAEL STILES AND BEN TYSON

Some students rise each morning anticipating another fulfilling and challenging day of high school. Others view their educational experiences differently.

Do these students perceive that the communication that takes place between them is filled with putdowns? Do they want a school climate that allows them to feel more comfortable about being themselves without fear of being judged?

The teen years are difficult for many and too difficult for some. Suicide is the third leading cause of death for people ages 15 to 24, according to a 2006 report from the Centers for Disease Control and Prevention. A 2005 survey conducted by Indiana University stated that 45 percent of students do not feel safe at school. And reports by the National School Boards Association link, at least anecdotally, the relationship between school climate and student achievement in the upper grades.

One's lack of feeling safe can even aggravate asthma. In 2003, research analyzing the connections between victimization and absenteeism found that students who felt unsafe were more likely to experience an asthma episode.

If you look more closely at studies and research over the past decade, it appears that a lack of civility in schools is reaching epidemic proportions. As students observe their peers engaging in uncivil behavior, often with little or no consequences, the behavior is then perceived to be socially acceptable, causing the behavior to be exhibited by more students.

So what can be done? Schools have implemented civility promotion programs and initiatives that promote positive behavior support. And, at least initially, these program interventions have had good results.

What We Learned

For our study, we looked at a high school in Connecticut to determine how students perceived the communication climate on campus and to get guidance on how improvements might be instituted. Even though we examined only one school, we believe our findings provide some strong suggestions that school districts should consider.

Seventy-six percent of the school's student population (563 of 738) completed the survey. Of those who responded, 47 percent were female and 53 percent were male.

Here are some of our findings:

- More than 75 percent of the students claim they "have witnessed students intimidating other students."
- Nearly 70 percent recognize "name-calling" as a common form of intimidation.
- One-third of the students reported that they have "been bullied or made to feel afraid while in school."
- Only 6 percent of the students surveyed either disagreed or strongly disagreed with the statement, "I do not like it when students bully other students."
- Two-thirds said they would like to go to a school where students do not intimidate or bully other students. However, strong feelings against bullying do not translate into taking action against bullying. Only 5 percent believed that students report bullying when they witness it, although the majority say they wish they would report bullying incidents.
- Student perceptions of how teachers and administrators handle bullying are somewhat negative. For example, only 31 percent feel that teachers properly deal with students who bully, and only 34 percent believe the administration properly addresses the problem. And 63 percent agree or strongly agree that teachers are unaware of conflicts that occur between students.
- What are the ramifications of teasing, bullying, rumors, conflicts, or otherwise uncivil behavior? Forty-two percent of students feel their academic performance is affected, and 60 percent feel verbal arguments have a negative impact on the school environment. Seventy-three percent believe rumors contribute to a negative school environment. And nearly 80 percent agree or strongly agree that "most students who are teased feel hurt, even though they may not let it show."
- How do students perceive their school's overall social environment? Only 37 percent feel the environment is

supportive. In terms of emotional and physical safety, 51 percent say they feel emotionally safe at school, and 69 percent say they feel physically safe. That means that significant proportions of students are either unsure or feel unsafe while in school.

What We Recommended

Based on our survey findings, we made several recommendations to improve the communication climate at the school. You might find that these recommendations will help at your schools as well.

Inform your staff: Keep your staff informed, from the time you decide to conduct the survey until after you receive the results. Use the results to raise staff awareness and initiate conversations about how bullying should be addressed.

Utilize students: Not surprisingly, our study found that students are influenced much more by their peers rather than adults. So how do you reach your students? Utilize student organizations within the school to a greater extent to promote your civility message. Your school's peer mediation program should continue to function as an intervention resource to take advantage of the students' ability to help their classmates work through conflicts.

Improve supervision: Better supervision by staff, especially in the hallways, will reduce bullying. Common areas where bullying takes place, according to students, are: hallways, cafeterias, locker rooms, bathrooms, and study halls. All staff should make a greater effort to be visible in the halls between classes. Also, as one student told us, "Teachers should intervene when they see bullying behavior and not ignore the problem."

Share actual "norms": Often the perception of peer behavior, rather than the actual behavior, is the accepted norm. By clarifying misperceptions of norms, students may be more apt to behave in ways that are more in line with their personal values. Student organizations such as peer mediators, peer advocates, members of student council, or a combination of these could plan a campaign to share the actual student norms with the school population. The actual norm is a desire for more civility and less acceptance of bullying.

Clarify discipline reports: At the start of this study, the high school discipline data was viewed with regard to the frequency and type of disciplinary infractions that occurred in the past year. It was difficult to put infractions into distinct categories. Improving the clarity and specificity of the categories will make it easier for the administration to track uncivil behavior.

Monitor and evaluate: Periodic evaluation is necessary to monitor progress and determine the effectiveness of any interventions you choose to make. This helps program leaders recognize progress or setbacks and adjust strategies as necessary. Administer your schoolwide survey each year to examine student perceptions of the school's communication climate. Also, records involving discipline issues should be compared from year to year as a means of tracking your progress.

Consider offering an annual survey to all staff members to determine their perceptions of the school's communication climate. Most important, ask how each staff member feels he or she can work to improve the climate. After all, the perception of your staff is just as important as the perception of your students. And for things to improve, the commitment to a positive and respectful climate will take everyone.

Michael Stiles is a physical and health education instructor in Connecticut. **Ben Tyson** (tysonc@ccsu.edu) is a professor in the Department of Communication at Central Connecticut State University.

From *American School Board Journal*, March 2008, pp. 36–37. Copyright © 2008 by National School Board Association. Reprinted by permission.

Classwide Interventions
Effective Instruction Makes a Difference

MAUREEN A. CONROY ET AL.

Whether leaching in a general education classroom or in a specialized program for students with special needs, teachers face a variety of classroom behaviors that can detract from the learning process. At limes, they may spend so much time with a few students who exhibit disruptive and off-task behaviors that they are less available for academic instruction with all students.

The research literature provides numerous examples of effective teaching strategies that can help teachers address problem behavior in their classrooms. These strategies include manipulating *antecedents* (i.e., environ-mental factors that are likely to increase a behavior), such as increasing opportunities to respond to academic requests (OTRs), and manipulating *consequences* (i.e., environmental factors that maintain behaviors), such as providing contingent praise. Unfortunately, some teachers are not skilled at employing these effective teaching tools in their classrooms. Consider the case scenarios "A Classroom That Works" and "A Classroom With Challenges. "

Creating a Positive Climate Through Classwide Interventions

Classrooms are dynamic environments in which teachers and students engage in ongoing reciprocal interactions throughout the school day. As indicated in both case scenarios, classes that include classwide effective intervention practices are likely to have positive teacher-student interactions and to promote student learning and engagement while minimizing problem behaviors. However, when classwide interventions are missing from a classroom, teacher-student interactions are likely to become reactively negative [and perhaps even coercive). Such interactions interfere with learning and create a chaotic and aversive classroom atmosphere.

Classwide interventions are a group of research-based effective teaching strategies used positively and preventively to promote and reinforce social and behavioral competence in students while minimizing problem behaviors (Farmer et al., 2006). Classwide interventions do not represent a single type of intervention; instead, they include a combination of effective behavior management practices that have a long history in our field, such as using contingent and frequent *praise,* providing *OTRs,* and applying *classroom rules.*

Classwide Interventions: Universal Classroom Tools for Effective Instruction

Teachers should consider the following classwide interventions when implementing positive behavior supports:

- Using close supervision and monitoring.
- Establishing and teaching classroom rules.
- Increasing OTRs.
- Increasing contingent praise.
- Providing feedback and error correction and monitoring progress.
- Implementing the good behavior game (GBG).

Close Supervision and Monitoring

Close supervision and monitoring generally means that the teacher has active, frequent, and regular engagement with students. These engagements may include placing students close to the teacher, scanning and moving frequently, initiating and reciprocating purposeful interactions, and providing opportunities for direct instruction and feedback (Colvin, Sugai, & Patching, 1993). When teachers are in proximity to students and monitor students' learning and behavior, they can prevent problem behaviors before they occur and can redirect them before they escalate. For example, when a teacher is near a student who is becoming frustrated and is struggling with a task, the teacher can intervene quickly and provide academic and behavior supports before a problem behavior occurs.

Case Scenario: A Classroom That Works

Collaboration between special and general education teachers in the classroom can be beneficial to students with and without special needs, especially when the collaboration works seamlessly. Ms. Harman and Ms. Easley teach in an urban elementary school. At the beginning of the school year, they worked collaboratively with their students to develop classroom rules that both special and general education students could follow and to identify specific procedures, such as turning in homework and lining up to go to lunch, for regular classroom activities. In addition, they spent a significant amount of time praising their students not just for work done correctly but also for good attempts.

Ms. Harman and Ms. Easley, who continuously sought ways to improve their teaching and help their students learn, took part in an applied research project that facilitated positive changes in their instructional language and methods. They incorporated a group behavior management system called *the good behavior game (GBG:* Barrish, Saunders, & Wolfe, 1969) into their instructional time.

Ms. Harman and Ms. Easley audiotaped an instructional lesson and graphed the numbers of opportunities to respond (OTRs) that they provided, as well as the number of times that they praised their students during the lesson. Through this self-evaluation of their instructional language, they developed a greater awareness of the frequency with which they provided their students with OTRs to instructional requests and of the frequency of their praise statements. Using these self-management procedures enabled Ms. Harman and Ms. Easley to increase the number of OTRs from only 10 per 15 minutes to almost 6 per minute, approximating the recommendations of the Council for Exceptional Children (1987). This change in the OTR rate encouraged student engagement and led to decreased undesirable behavior. In addition, the teachers increased their rate of praise from only 2 per 15 minutes to almost 1 per minute, resulting in further improvements in the behavior of the students. Making small changes in the ways that they instructed their students and rewarding their students more often for work attempted resulted in an improved positive classroom atmosphere and an increase in students' effort.

Implementing close supervision and monitoring may require developing a plan in collaboration with other adults or paraprofessionals in the classroom. For example, a classroom teacher may implement a zone-monitoring and supervision plan during an instructional time when many students need assistance and engage in problem behaviors. With a zone-monitoring plan, adults in the classroom are at strategic locations throughout the classroom, and each of them monitors a small number of students. This system enables adults to closely supervise and monitor students and facilitates students' access to teacher assistance.

Considerable evidence supports the use of close supervision and monitoring as a classwide intervention. For example, research has documented that close supervision and monitoring result in decreases in disruptive behavior across various educational settings, including classroom instruction (DePry & Sugai, 2002); recess (Lewis, Powers, Kelk, & Newcomer, 2002); and transition time (Colvin, Sugai, Good, & Lee, 1997).

Classroom Rules

The development and implementation of classroom rules is another universal classwide intervention that influences the learning environment for all students. Classroom rules serve as behavioral expectations that create an organized and productive learning environment for students and teachers by promoting appropriate classroom behaviors. Without classroom rules, such problem behaviors as aggression and disruption are more likely (Walker, Colvin, & Ramsey, 1995). Research has indicated that effective teachers do the following:

- Establish rules for expected behavior at the beginning of the year.
- Systematically teach the rules to the students.
- Monitor and reward students' compliance with the rules.
- Consistently apply consequences to rule violations (Anderson, Evertson, & Emmer, 1980; Evertson & Emmer, 1982).

Classroom rules serve as behavioral expectations that create an organized and productive learning environment for students and teachers by promoting appropriate classroom behaviors.

Opportunities to Respond (OTRs)

Increasing instructional pacing through OTRs is a questioning, prompting, or cueing technique that begins a learning trial (e.g.. "What number comes after 10?"). This technique helps increase the number of active child responses, which in turn can result in increases in correct responses and engagement of all students in the classroom (Greenwood, Delquadri, & Hall, 1984). Although OTRs vary in type and characteristics (e.g., choral responses, individual responses, and visual or auditory cuing), all types of OTRs generally include the following components:

- Increasing rates of teacher instructional talk that includes repeated verbal, visual, or verbal and visual types of prompts for responding.
- Presenting information in a manner that increases student correct responding (e.g., "This is an *A*. What letter Is this?").
- Implementing individualized instructional modifications appropriate for the students' level of functioning, along with frequent checks for understanding and accuracy.
- Using repeated instructional prompting that incorporates wait time to allow students to respond.
- Providing corrective feedback, error correction, and progress monitoring (Stichter & Lewis, 2006).

When researchers increase rates of OTR, they have found increases in on-task student behavior and in correct responses, as well as fewer disruptive behaviors by students (Brophy & Good, 1986; Carnine, 1976; Greenwood et al., 1984; Sutherland, Gunter, & Alder, 2003). Students who are engaged in learning are less likely to demonstrate problem behaviors (Sutherland et al.) and more likely to engage in active and correct responses (Sutherland & Snyder, 2007).

Contingent Praise

"Catch 'em being good" is a familiar strategy to most teachers. Although many teachers are aware of the powerful effects of praise, they often underuse it. Fortunately, training can help teachers learn to use praise as a reinforcer. Praise is a generalized reinforcer and has a rich research base that demonstrates its effectiveness in increasing social and behavioral competence in students (Alber, Heward, & Hippler, 1999; Sutherland, 2000). *Effective* praise is specific and contingent (Sutherland). *Specific* praise occurs when the teacher specifies the target behavior reinforced within the praise statement (e.g., "Good, you stayed in your seat during the entire reading session"). Praise is *contingent* when it is a consequence for a specific expected behavior, such as completing an assigned task, following a teacher's instruction, or engaging in appropriate social behavior.

Researchers have found that when teachers increase their use of specific and contingent praise, improvement occurs in the number of correct responses by students, task engagement, words read correctly per minute, problems completed, and student engagement (Kirby & Shields, 1972; Luiselli & Downing, 1980; Sutherland, Wehby, & Copeland, 2000). In general, teachers should offer praise statements more often than corrective statements. For example. Good and Grouws (1977) recommend that teachers strive to achieve and maintain a ratio of 4 or 5 positive statements to corrective statement.

Case Scenario: A Classroom with Challenges

Ms. Walters taught 12 students, whose grade levels ranged from second grade to fifth grade, in an urban elementary school. The students had a variety of disabilities—for example, emotional disorders (ED), learning disabilities (LD), and attention deficit hyperactivity disorder (ADHD).

As a group, these students presented many classroom challenges. Each day, Ms. Walters greeted her students by saying "Good morning, class," only to be confronted by disruptive student talk, papers flying at her, and students who were not in their assigned seats. Along with her paraprofessional, Ms. Johnson, Ms. Walters spent the first 45 minutes of every day just trying to get her students to sit down, hand in their homework, and attend to language arts, the first lesson of the day. She had very few doable procedures in place for daily tasks, and most of the students regularly ignored classroom rules. Ms. Walters had assigned students to small groups on the basis of their skill levels; however, she spent a tremendous amount of time correcting disruptive students, who would provoke others. Needless to say, she was frustrated and often raised her voice at her students in an effort to persuade them to pay attention to her. She knew that what she was doing was not working, but she and her students were caught in a negative, coercive interaction cycle.

Discouraged and ready to quit before she had even finished her first year, Ms. Walters agreed to have a behavioral consultant come into her classroom to help her with classroom management. The consultant worked with Ms. Walters to arrange her classroom so that all students could see her and the blackboard. The consultant and Ms. Walters developed procedures for entering the classroom in the morning (e.g., routines for putting away backpacks and homework), and Ms. Walters distributed students with disruptive behavior across the small groups in the classroom. As a reward for good behavior, she assigned a "daily leader" to each group for the next day.

The consultant also trained the paraprofessional to step in when Ms. Walters was having difficulty with a particular student and engage other students in small-group or individualized work so that Ms. Walters was not responsible for the whole class. After Ms. Walters received this support, her teaching strategies improved, and she felt and looked more competent and effective in her ability to manage her students' behavior and promote their learning. Students responded to her effective teaching practices; and as a result, they were more engaged. Although more growth was necessary, the classwide atmosphere improved, and everyone had hope for a better school year.

Feedback, Error Correction, and Progress Monitoring

Providing students with feedback relative to their behavior and performance level is another important classwide intervention. When used effectively, feedback should

- Help students learn the correct response in a timely way.
- Be specific to students' skill and knowledge levels.
- Occur following a student error (i.e., error correction).

Error correction procedures begin with the teacher's providing a corrective model (e.g., "Remember that to determine the area of a square or rec-tangle, multiply length times width"). This corrective model precedes the student's correct response, which the student should base on the teacher's model (e.g., "if the length of a rectangle is 5 feet and its width is 4 feet, I multiply length by width to obtain a result of 20 square feet."). Corrective feedback should accompany continuous monitoring of the student's academic and/or social behavior performance (e.g., curriculum-based measurement), as well as accurate and consistently presented instruction and interventions (i.e., fidelity of implementation).

Effective feedback can take many forms (e.g., answering questions, checking seatwork, and responding directly), and researchers have linked it positively to student engagement and achievement (Fisher et al., 1980). Similarly, when teachers use error correction, increases occur in academic performance (Barbetta, Heron, & Heward, 1993; Barbetta & Heward, 1993) and correct responses (Bangert-Downs, Kulik, Kulik, & Morgan, 1991).

Good Behavior Game (GBG)

The GBG is a group contingency designed to

- Improve the teacher's ability to define tasks, set rules, and discipline students.
- Reduce disruptive, aggressive, off-task, and shy behaviors in elementary-age children.
- Promote good behavior by rewarding teams that do not exceed mal-adaptive behavior standards.

The teacher begins the GBG by assigning each student in the class to a team and selecting team leaders. The teacher and students read and review the class-room rules, and the teacher informs students that each rule violation results immediately in a check mark on the blackboard next to the team's name. In addition, the teacher tells the students that he or she will state the rule that a student has violated, identify the student who has violated the rule, and praise the other teams for adhering to the rules. At the end of an instructional session, the teacher and students review the number of check marks per team, repeat the preset criteria for winning the game, and announce the winning team or teams. Team leaders then hand out rewards to winning team members (e.g., stamps, stickers, or "I did it" badges), and the nonwinning teams must stay in their seats and continue to engage in their lesson. Because teams try to beat the preset limit, more than one—or even all—teams can win.

Researchers initially associated the GBG with reduced rates of out-of-seat and talking-out behaviors of fourth-grade students (Barrish et al., 1969). Over the next 35 years, this finding led to a line of research that has documented the effectiveness of the GBG with students of varying ages and disabilities across many different settings. For example, Dolan and colleagues (1993) examined the effect of the GBG on first graders' disruptive classroom behaviors and found that teacher ratings of aggressive and shy behavior were significantly lower in the spring of the first grade than in the fall. In sum, the GBG is a good example of a classwide intervention that can have an effect on the behavior—and ultimately, on the learning—of many students.

Where Do You Begin? Steps for Creating a Positive Classroom Atmosphere

Creating a positive classroom environment through implementing classwide interventions does not solve all classroom problem behaviors overnight. As illustrated in the classroom of Ms. Harman and Ms. Easley in "Case Scenario: A Classroom That Works," implementing these effective teaching practices requires up-front planning and ongoing problem solving. In addition, teachers must implement these practices efficiently and correctly (i.e., with fidelity) and individualize the practices to make them appropriate for unique aspects of their classrooms. For example, classroom rules may vary from classroom to classroom, depending on the expectations and ability levels of the students. Similarly, the teacher may implement close supervision and monitoring differently depending on the classroom size and layout. Like other behavior support strategies, implementing classwide interventions requires ongoing monitoring and evaluation of the use and effectiveness of these strategies. Thus, teachers will want to monitor their implementation of targeted classwide strategies and student outcomes. Ms. Harman and Ms. Easley demonstrated that collecting data on their own teaching behaviors helped them improve their skills. Additionally, by collecting data on their students' behavior, they obtained enough evidence to know that the practices were working.

Finally, as illustrated by the example of Ms. Walters in "Case Scenario: A Classroom With Challenges," teachers sometimes need a person outside their classroom to teach them classwide interventions and help them discover how to implement these strategies in their classrooms. Teachers

Table 1 Universal Classwide Interventions

Classwide Interventions	What Are You Currently Doing?	What Do You Want to Change to Improve Your Instruction?
Close supervision and monitoring	Are students in proximity to you?	During which instructional time will you implement closer supervision and monitoring?
	Can you visually monitor all the students in your classroom?	
	Do you actively engage with your students?	What staff will you involve in close supervision and monitoring?
	Do students in your classroom have quick and efficient access to teacher assistance?	How will you implement close supervision and monitoring?
	Is the adult-student ratio sufficient to provide close supervision and monitoring?	How will you monitor the effectiveness of close supervision and monitoring?
Classroom rules	Do you have classroom rules?	Do you and your students implement the classroom rules effectively?
	Did you develop your classroom rules in collaboration with your students?	Do you need to rewrite or adapt your classroom rules?
	Do your students know the classroom rules, and are they able to perform them?	How will you communicate your classroom rules to your students?
	Do you communicate classroom rules to your students in an effective and efficient manner?	How will you monitor whether the rules are working?
	Do adults in the classroom contingently and regularly provide reinforcement to students for adhering to the rules?	How will you provide positive reinforcement to students for complying with the rules?
	Do you apply consequences consistently when students break classroom rules?	What will you do if students do not comply?
Opportunities to respond (OTRs)	Do you use various types of OTRs in your classroom [e.g., choral, individual]?	Can you increase the number of OTRs for your students?
	Do you provide students with an adequate rate of OTRs?	Can you "switch up" the delivery method you use to offer more OTRs?
	What type of instructional delivery model do you use (direct, whole group, small group, etc.)?	How can you use more direct instruction?
Contingent praise	Do you regularly praise students for answering correctly?	Can you increase your positive interactions with your students?
	Do you praise students for an attempt to answer, even if it is not correct?	Can you increase your use of specific praise statements?
	Are you specific about what you are praising a student for (rather than simply "good girl" or "good boy")?	Can you increase your use of contingent praise?
	Do you praise students for desirable social behavior?	Can you find reasons to praise all students in your class more frequently than you reprimand them?

may want to begin by assessing their current use of classwide interventions (see Table 1) and systematically identifying and targeting specific classwide interventions for classroom application.

Final Thoughts

When teachers systematically implement classwide interventions, teacher–student interactions become more positive, students are more engaged, and teachers are able to focus on teaching appropriate behaviors—all these result in a positive classroom environment that promotes student learning and engagement.

> When teachers systematically implement classwide interventions, teacher–student interactions become more positive, students are more engaged, and teachers are able to focus on teaching appropriate behaviors.

References

Alber. S. R., Heward, W. L., & Hippler, B. J. (1999). Teaching middle school students with learning disabilities to recruit positive teacher attention. *Exceptional Children, 65,* 253–270.

Anderson, L., Evertson, C., & Emmer, E. (1980). Dimensions in classroom management derived from recent research. *Journal of Curriculum Studies, 12,* 343–356.

Bangert-Downs, R. L., Kulik, C. C., Kulik, J. A., & Morgan. M. (1991). The instructional effects of feedback in test-like events. *Review of Educational Research, 61,* 213–238.

Barbetta, P. M., Heron, T. E., & Heward, W. L. (1993). Effects of active student response during error correction on the acquisition, maintenance, and generalization of sight words by students with developmental disabilities. *Journal of Applied Behavior Analysis, 26,* 111–119.

Barbetta, P. M., & Heward, W. L. (1993). Effects of active student response during error correction on the acquisition and maintenance of geography facts by elementary students with learning disabilities. *Journal of Behavioral Education, 3,* 217–233.

Barrish, H., Saunders. M., & Wolfe, M. (1969). Good behavior game: Effects of individual contingencies for group consequences on disruptive behavior in a classroom. *Journal of Applied Behavior Analysis, 2,* 119–124.

Brophy, J. H., & Good, T. (1986). Teacher behavior and student achievement. In M. C. Wittrock (Ed.), *Handbook of research in teaching* (3rd ed.; pp. 328–375). New York: Macmillan.

Carnine, D. W. (1976). Effects of two teacher-presentation rates on off-task behavior, answering correctly, and participation. *Journal of Applied Behavior Analysis, 9,* 199–206.

Colvin, G., Sugai, G., Good, R. H., & Lee, Y. (1997). Using active supervision and pre-correction to improve transition behaviors in an elementary school. *School Psychology Quarterly, 12,* 344–363.

Colvin, G. Sugai, G., & Patching, W. (1993). Precorrection: An instructional approach for managing predictable problem behaviors. *Intervention in School and Clinic, 28,* 143–150.

Council for Exceptional Children. (1987). *Academy for effective instruction: Working with mildly handicapped students.* Reston, VA: Author.

DePry, R. L., & Sugai, G. (2002). The effect of active supervision and pre-correction on minor behavioral incidents in a sixth grade general education classroom. *Journal of Behavioral Education, 11,* 255–267.

Dolan. L. J., Kellam, S. G., Brown, C. H., Werthamer-Larson, L., Rebok, G. W., Mayer, L. S., et al. (1993). The short-term impact of two classroom-based preventive interventions on aggressive and shy behaviors and poor achievement, *Journal of Applied Developmental Psychology, 14,* 317–345.

Evertson, C., & Emmer, E. (1982). Effective management at the beginning of the year in junior high classes. *Journal of Educational Psychology, 74,* 485–498.

Farmer, T. W., Goforth, J., Hives. J., Aaron, A., Hunter, F., & Sgmatto, A. (2006). Competence enhancement behavior management. *Preventing School Failure, 50,* 39–44.

Fisher, C. W., Berliner, D. C., Filby, N. N., Marliave, R., Cahen, L. S., & Dishaw, M. M. (1980). Teaching behaviors, academic learning time, and student achievement: An overview. In C. Denham & A. Lieberman (Eds.), *Time to learn* (pp. 7–32). Washington, DC: U.S. Department of Education, National Institute of Education.

Good, T., & Grouws, D. (1977). Teaching effects: A process-product study in fourth grade mathematics classrooms. *Journal of Teacher Education, 28,* 49–54.

Greenwood, C. R., Delquadri, J. C., & Hall, R. V. (1984). Opportunity to respond and student academic performance. In W. L. Heward, T. E. Heron, D. S. Hill, & J. Trap-Porter (Eds.), *Focus on behavior analysis in education* (pp. 58–88). Columbus, OH: Charles E. Merrill.

Kirby, F. D., & Shields, F. (1972). Modification of arithmetic response rate and attending behavior in a seventh-grade student. *Journal of Applied Behavior Analysis, 5,* 79–84.

Lewis, T. J., Powers, L. J., Kelk, M. J., & Newcomer, L. L. (2002). Reducing problem behaviors on the playground: An investigation of the application of school-wide positive behavior and supports. *Psychology in the Schools, 39,* 181–190.

Luiselli, J. K., & Downing, J. N. (1980). Improving a student's arithmetic performance using feedback and reinforcement procedures. *Education and Treatment of Children, 3,* 45–49.

Stichter, J., & Lewis, T. J. (2006). Classroom assessment: Targeting variables to improve instruction through a multi-level eco-behavioral model. In M. Hersen (Ed.), *Clinician's handbook of child behavioral assessment* (pp. 569–586). Burlington, MA: Elsevier.

Sutherland, K. S., (2000). Promoting positive interactions between teachers and students with emotional/behavioral disorders. *Preventing School Failure, 44,* 110–115.

Sutherland, K. S., Gunter. P. L., & Alder, N. (2003). The effect of varying rates of OTR on the classroom behavior of students with EBD. *Journal of Emotional and Behavioral Disorders, 11,* 239–248.

Sutherland, K. S., & Snyder. A. (2007). Effects of reciprocal peer tutoring and self-graphing on reading fluency and classroom behavior of middle school students with emotional or behavioral disorders. *Journal of Emotional and Behavioral Disorders, 15,* 103–118.

Sutherland, K. S., Wehby, J. H., & Copeland, S. R. (2000). Effect of varying rates of behavior-specific praise on the on-task behavior of students with emotional and behavioral disorders. *Journal of Emotional and Behavioral Disorders, 8,* 2–8, 26.

Walker, H., Colvin, G., & Ramsey, E. (1995). *Antisocial behavior in school: Strategies and best practices.* New York: Brooks/Cole.

MAUREEN A. CONROY (CEC VA Federation). Professor; **KEVIN S. SUTHERLAND** (CEC VA Federation). Associate Professor: **ANGELA L. SNYDER** (CEC VA Federation), Collateral Assistant Professor; and **SAMANTHA MARSH** (CEC VA Federation), Doctoral Student, Department of Special Education and Disability Policy, Virginia Commonwealth University, Richmond.

Address correspondence to Maureen A. Conroy, Department of Special Education and Disability Policy, Virginia Commonwealth University, 1015 W. Main Street, P.O. Box 842020, Richmond, VA 23284 (e-mail: maconroy@vcu.edu).

Developing Effective Behavior Intervention Plans

Suggestions for School Personnel

With federal mandates to develop and implement programs for students with disabilities who have behavior problems that impede their educational performance, school personnel are faced with increasing responsibility for developing individualized interventions. Developing interventions that appropriately, effectively, and efficiently address the relationship between learning and behavior problems is a complex task that requires a host of essential elements and procedures. For intervention team members who lead and design the functional behavior assessment and behavior intervention plans, specific issues to consider in developing and monitoring these plans are discussed.

KIM KILLU

Behavioral difficulties that interfere with a student's school performance have long been a challenge for educators. To address this issue, the 1997 reauthorization of the Individuals with Disabilities Education Act (IDEA) required educators to develop and implement behavior intervention plans (BIPs). When IDEA 1997 was reauthorized in 2004 as the Individuals with Disabilities Education Improvement Act (IDEIA), BIPs were included again. These plans consider the relationship between student learning and behavior problems that impede classroom performance. Behavior intervention plans outline strategies and tactics for dealing with the problem behavior along with the role that educators must play in improving student learning and behavior. Although many students respond positively to conventional classroom behavior management strategies (e.g., establishing classroom rules, redirection) many others require specially designed interventions to address the relationship between learning and behavior (Morgan & Jenson, 1988). Educators are increasingly placed in a position to develop specialized interventions, yet developing an intervention plan that appropriately and effectively addresses the relationship between student learning and the problem behavior is a complex task. Despite good faith efforts to develop a plan that best meets a student's behavioral needs, educators may find that

their plans do not achieve desired results. This article examines specific issues that must be considered and addressed by school personnel who design and monitor the BIP process to enhance the effectiveness of BIPs.

Functional Behavior Assessment

With IDEIA 2004, a functional behavior assessment (FBA) is required prior to the development of a BIP for students with disabilities who have behavioral challenges that impede functioning in the educational environment. Practitioners have sought to analyze the factors involved in student behavior, and fortunately for educators, a behavioral technology for the assessment of challenging behavior exists. Functional behavior assessment involves using several methods to determine the causal and maintaining factors for a behavior that lead to the development of intervention strategies to meet the individualized and unique needs of the student. The FBA mandate in IDEIA continues to reflect a change in practice from one-dimensional approaches that simply seek to increase desired responses or eliminate problem behavior, to a multifaceted process that focuses on examining the contextual variables that set the occasion for problem behavior, linking assessment results to intervention planning, and seeking to develop positive instructional or behavioral strategies and supports to address more appropriate and functional skills.

Discussions and examples of FBA methodology are abundant in the literature. Several comprehensive resources on the design and execution of FBAs, and the relationship between the outcomes of an FBA and the subsequent development and execution of BIPs, are available for practitioners (Crone & Horner, 2003; Crone, Horner, & Hawken, 2004; Florida Department of Education, 1999; O'Neill et al., 1997). The underlying theme to the FBA is that all behavior has a function and occurs for a reason. Determining this function is achieved through a process that usually involves a wide variety of strategies. The primary outcome of the FBA that summarizes these findings is a hypothesis statement that describes the problem and the variables correlated with its occurrence and nonoccurrence (Sugai, Lewis-Palmer, & Hagan-Burke, 1999–2000). Developing this hypothesis is achieved through the following:

1. consensus on the problem behavior,
2. a precise definition of the target behavior (Alberto & Troutman, 2006),
3. a review of the student's records and past interventions,
4. interviews with the student or all relevant parties (O'Neill et al., 1997),
5. team discussion,
6. assessment scales (e.g., Durand, 1988),
7. direct observation and measurement of the target behavior,
8. scatterplot data (Touchette, MacDonald, & Langer, 1985),
9. assessment of antecedents to and consequences of the target behavior,
10. identification of reinforcers (DeLeon & Iwata, 1996; Fisher et al., 1992; Holmes, Cautela, Simpson, Motes, & Gold, 1998; Pace, Ivancic, Edwards, Iwata, & Page, 1985),
11. examination of the ecological context to the problem behavior (Greenwood, Carta, & Atwater, 1991), and
12. analog experimentation of the proposed hypothesis (O'Neill et al., 1997).

It should be stressed that conducting an FBA is a comprehensive *process* supported by data and not simply a matter of those involved with a student achieving consensus on the problem and speculated causes. This process may involve multiple sources (teachers, parents, peers) and multiple environments and contexts (e.g., group activities vs. independent activities, different classrooms, classroom vs. playground or lunchroom). Due to the necessity of examining all of these variables, a team-based approach is essential (Todd, Horner, Sugai, & Colvin, 1999). Once the function or reason for the behavior is determined, appropriate intervention strategies can be developed and implemented. The relationship between developing interventions based on assessment information has been established, for example, in the Curriculum Based Measures (CBM) literature where student assessment is linked to instruction (Deno, 1985). Research indicates that using CBM results in more effective instructional plans (Deno, Marston, & Tindal, 1986). Similarly, an established body of research indicates that successful interventions depend on identifying the environmental correlates of problem behavior (e.g., Dunlap et al., 1993) and that identifying function serves to improve the effectiveness and efficiency of behavioral intervention (Lalli, Browder, Mace, & Brown, 1993; Umbreit, 1995).

Mandating FBAs within IDEIA improves the overall effectiveness of behavioral interventions. Failure to conduct a comprehensive FBA may result in programming that is insufficient to deal with the target behavior. Functional behavior assessments provide information on factors such as the most appropriate course of intervention, strategies and support systems, whether there are multiple functions to the target behavior, the conditions under which the behavior occurs, and the most effective reinforcer. Lack of attention to these variables affects the integrity of the plan. The intervention developed may work to change the target behavior, but the strategy developed may not be comprehensive enough to be most efficient, effective, and relevant. For example, often an FBA is conducted and a plan is developed to be used in multiple environments. However, the same behavior may serve different functions in different environments (e.g., different classrooms). Interventions developed within a plan should ensure that the setting events and function are addressed, appropriate and effective supports are designed and made available, and the occurrence or non-occurrence of the behavior results in consequences that alter the future probability of the behavior. Similarly, the same behavior may also serve multiple functions within the *same* environment. It is context that dictates function, not type or form of the behavior. Conducting the FBA process *across* environments is the most effective means to determine this.

Assess Antecedent Variables and Setting Events

Traditionally, assessment of problem behavior involved examination of antecedents that trigger the occurrence of the target behavior and consequences that serve to maintain it. Subsequent intervention focused on manipulating the antecedent and consequent events to increase the occurrence of a desirable behavior or decrease the occurrence of an undesirable behavior. More recently, however, greater emphasis has been placed on examining behavior within its context (Horner, 1994; O'Neill et al., 1997; Sugai, Horner, & Sprague, 1999; Sugai, Lewis-Palmer, & Hagan, 1998). This emphasis has intensified with the emergence of the philosophy and practices of positive behavioral support. Within the framework of the traditional three-term contingency (i.e., Antecedent-Behavior-Consequence [A-B-C]), events and conditions that are more distant to the target behavior's direct and immediate antecedent (Smith & Iwata, 1997) are a focus of investigation. These conditions or events, referred to as *setting events*, serve to temporarily change the effectiveness of reinforcers and punishers, thus altering a student's response to environmental events and situations. For example, a student's argument with a peer earlier in the morning may serve to affect his or her on-task behavior later in the afternoon, despite modifications made to the curriculum and instructional strategies to facilitate greater on-task behavior. A poor night's sleep resulting in fatigue may serve to make a student more argumentative with peers, despite programming in place designed to promote more prosocial behavior. Setting events may occur just prior to a target behavior, or even days before. They may involve environmental factors (e.g., method and delivery of instruction, curriculum, the physical setting, number of people in the environment), physiological factors (e.g., illness, medical conditions, side effects of meds) or social factors (e.g., family circumstances, interactions with peers on the school bus; Jolivette, Wehby, & Hirsch, 1999; Kern, Childs, Dunlap, Clarke, & Falk, 1994). Assessing for, examining, and evaluating the presence (or absence) of setting events, referred to as a *structural analysis* (see Stichter & Conroy, 2005), is similar to the FBA process with the focus shifted to antecedent and contextual factors rather than maintaining variables.

The implications of examining the setting and contextual factors on the development of an efficient, effective, and relevant BIP cannot be underestimated. Interventions may focus on manipulating setting events (e.g., preventing the occurrence of a setting event, removing a setting event, minimizing/maximizing the effects of a setting event) so as to set the occasion for the occurrence of more desired behavior. Programming may also focus on manipulating other antecedents when setting events are in effect (e.g., modifying events so they are less aversive). Although school personnel may not have access to setting events outside of the school environment (or even be aware of them), operating within the contingencies and context that one does have access to and can control can make a significant difference in the effectiveness of an intervention.

Establish the Validity of Reinforcers

Many intervention plans focus on using rewards, contingent upon the occurrence of desired behavior. By using these rewards, teachers apply the principle of positive reinforcement, where a response is followed by the presentation of a stimulus (i.e., the reward), thereby increasing the future probability of that response (Cooper, Heron, & Heward, 2007). Yet a serious flaw may result from the simple delivery of a reward. Unless the future occurrence of the behavior increases after the reward is presented, reinforcement has not occurred. A common programming strategy is using a reinforcement system or token system where a student receives a reward for desired behaviors. Rewards may not necessarily serve as reinforcers (Maag, 2001). As many intervention plans rely on this strategy for developing or increasing the occurrence of target behaviors, plans may be abandoned or may be seen as ineffective or unsuccessful when there is no resulting increase in behavior. Without a corresponding increase in a target behavior, the presentation of a reinforcer is not reinforcement. An often underutilized strategy in programming is using negative reinforcement (see Cooper et al., 2007). Like positive reinforcement, negative reinforcement results in an increase in the future probability of a response. The difference, however, is that the response is followed by the termination or reduction of a stimulus.

For example, a teacher develops a system in which students receive one homework pass for every 10 consecutive days that homework is submitted. Assuming a student's homework submission rate increases, the process of negative reinforcement has been in operation. The function of the behavior under the negative reinforcement paradigm is to escape or avoid an aversive stimulus. Improving behavior is neither a simple nor a quick fix, but educators have strategies at their disposal to determine what reinforcers (positive or negative) may be more effective under the circumstances (DeLeon & Iwata, 1996; Fisher et al., 1992; Holmes et al., 1998; Northup, George, Jones, Broussard, & Vollmer, 1996; Pace et al., 1985).

The same argument holds true for using punishment in an attempt to discipline a student. The overriding, desired effect is to decrease the future occurrence of the inappropriate behavior. If the behavior did not decrease, then punishment has not occurred. A frequent disciplinary strategy is to send a student to the principal's office when misbehavior occurs. It is assumed that the effect of this action will punish the student and result in a decrease in the future occurrence of the misbehavior. However, if the target behavior did not decrease in frequency, punishment has not occurred. In fact, the strategy may have served to negatively reinforce the target behavior instead. The important consideration for reinforcement and punishment is that they are not *things*, but rather *effects* (Maag, 2001) and these effects impact the occurrence/nonoccurrence of desirable *and* undesirable behaviors. Reinforcement and punishment are not events but a process that results in the increase or decrease of a behavior; reinforcers and punishers must function as such rather than *look like* such.

Describe and Specify Target Behaviors and Intervention Strategies

Oftentimes, several individuals will note problem behavior with a student. The different perspectives and vocabulary of these individuals can lead to a variety of terms used to describe the problem behavior. These terms may be general or specific, but the resulting consensus can have an impact on the effectiveness of a BIP. For example, a student may be described as "aggressive." Such broad descriptors can have different meanings for different people. Does the student hit others, destroy property, or verbally threaten others? Achieving consensus on the target behavior among all of those implementing the BIP ensures that the plan is implemented consistently, under appropriate conditions. A description of a target behavior should be so specific that an individual unfamiliar with the student should be able to identify the student and the target behavior when it occurs. The term *operational definition* (Alberto & Troutman, 2006) has been used to describe the precision with which target behaviors should be identified. To minimize the differing interpretations of the same target behavior, a clear description of the observable and measurable characteristics of the target response is essential. Without a clear definition of the BIP's focus, it is very likely that a plan will be inconsistently implemented, thereby minimizing its overall effectiveness and relevance.

When establishing definitions of target behaviors, the notion of response class (i.e., a set of behaviors that have a similar function but vary in their basic elements or topography) must be considered. For example, a student's attempt to avoid difficult classroom work may take many forms. She or he may verbally refuse to comply with instructions, engage in tantrum behaviors, or slam the book shut. The similarity between all of these responses is that they serve to avoid work. One must not assume, however, that the same response classes will serve the same function in a different environment, or even in the same environment with a different context. Function dictates the type of intervention, not the setting, definition or types of behavior.

Occasionally, generic, nonspecific BIPs are developed and designed to improve a student's behavior without operationally defining the behavior or focusing on specific target behaviors. For example, a student will receive reinforcement or a reward for the absence of any problem behavior in a given period of time (e.g., if the student is good for the entire class period, he or she will receive a reward). These generic approaches may not provide the specificity and results that a more direct focus provides (e.g., providing a student with a reinforcer if 80% of math problems are completed correctly within a class session). Furthermore, as the consequence is not provided for a specific response, such interventions may have minimal impact on the acquisition or development of new target responses. Along similar lines, a lack of specificity in the BIP itself is another cause for concern. Just as target behaviors must be specifically described, the intervention itself must be clearly outlined. For example, designing a BIP that states a teacher will modify the way she or he interacts with a student gives very little information as to how those interactions are modified. Should the teacher modify the delivery of instruction and if so, how? Should the teacher provide more verbal praise or corrective feedback? In addition to delineating the strategies to use, a BIP must indicate the necessary resources and support along with the expectations of those carrying out the outlined procedures. Those implementing the BIP must know what to do and what not to do when the target behavior occurs (or does not occur). Specifically outlining procedures ensures that the plan is implemented as intended with little room for interpretation.

Consistently Collect Data

Although the process of measuring student performance is not new to teachers, the practice is generally limited to measuring academic response by recording students' grades on tests or other measures of work performance. Many teachers see little value in measuring and recording the occurrence of other student behavior in the classroom (Alberto & Troutman, 2006), and behavioral interventions are often developed with little consistency and attention to necessary details such as monitoring and evaluation (Buck, Polloway, Kirkpatrick, Patton, & Fad, 2000). If a student's behavior warrants implementing a BIP, it stands to reason that steps must be taken to evaluate the effectiveness of the plan in changing that behavior. Just as teachers use different

strategies to measure students' academic performance in the classroom to evaluate the effectiveness of their instruction, a measurement of student behavior allows for evaluation of student performance and the effectiveness of the plan. Data should reflect progress toward the intervention's goal.

As previously discussed, contributing to the success of a BIP involves developing specific definitions of the target behavior. To effectively evaluate these behaviors, planned observation and measurement of their occurrence is essential. Without observation and measurement, there is no standard, objective method for determining the effectiveness of a BIP. A BIP may be prematurely modified or discontinued, or an ineffective plan may continue and prolong the student's exposure to ineffective strategies. To evaluate the effectiveness of a BIP, the student's behavior should be observed, measured, and recorded before, during, and after implementing the BIP, and the occurrence or nonoccurrence of the target behavior should be continuously assessed. Continuous measurement of student behavior reduces the likelihood of error in the intervention process (Cooper et al., 2007). Without data to represent student performance, the teacher is forced to rely on perception and opinion to assess the effectiveness of a BIP. A myriad of factors can cloud the accuracy of one's perception and opinion. The chance of error in evaluation of performance is much less when direct and objective measures are used.

Without data, no objective basis exists for judging improvement or decline in performance. Furthermore, continuous assessment of student performance and data collection improves the quality and efficiency of the decision-making process (Horner, Sugai, & Todd, 2001). That is, if an intervention is found to be unsuccessful, continuous evaluation allows for the teacher to change the intervention. Data must be used to assist with understanding, analysis, intervention, evaluation, and decision making (Sugai & Horner, 2005). Researchers have suggested that teachers who frequently and continuously collect data are better decision makers than teachers who do not (Fuchs & Fuchs, 1986; Fuchs, Fuchs, & Stecker, 1989).

Maag (2003) outlined several reasons for measuring and recording behavior. First, to accurately evaluate the effectiveness of the intervention, a precount, or baseline, is necessary. Without baseline data, no standard of comparison exists between pre- and postintervention occurrences of behavior, and there is no objective means of determining whether the intervention was effective. Second, measurement of the behavior allows the practitioner to determine whether the behavior targeted for measurement is the problem behavior (Levitt & Rutherford, 1978). Oftentimes, behaviors targeted for measurement may not be the problem. Behaviors targeted for measurement should be those that are the true problem or those targeted for intervention. For example, disruptive behavior is often the focus of intervention. Though disruptive behavior may certainly be a concern, it may also consist of several other responses such as roaming the room, talking with peers, or playing with objects. The true problem, however, is that the student does not complete work or attend to task. By collecting data on one response, other information is indirectly obtained on other related responses (Maag, 2003). As these other responses are better suited for intervention, it is more appropriate to measure their occurrence. Third, measurement of behavior assists with determining the severity of the problem. Because perceptions may be biased, data allow for an objective assessment of the degree to which the behavior occurs and its severity, relative to the occurrence of other students in the classroom. Data collection may reveal that the degree to which the behavior occurred was not as severe as perceived to be.

Implement Plan Accurately and Consistently

Central to the effectiveness of a BIP is the fidelity of the plan's implementation and several issues may contribute to the BIP's integrity. *Procedural integrity* (also referred to as treatment fidelity) refers to the accuracy and consistency of implementation (Baer, Wolf, & Risley, 1968; Gable, Quinn, Rutherford, Howell, & Hoffman, 2000; Peterson, Homer, & Wonderlich, 1982) and can result from factors such as a poorly defined target behavior or a poorly developed plan. As previously discussed, a poorly defined target behavior may affect accurate implementation of the plan. A poorly developed plan, at best, results in inconsistent implementation, and at worst, incorrect implementation; yet both are likely to negatively impact the effectiveness of the intervention. As Gresham, MacMillan, Beebe-Frankenberger, and Bocian (2000) indicated, the degree of treatment fidelity is directly related to the effectiveness of the plan; that is, a more accurately and consistently implemented plan increases the likelihood of producing positive behavior changes. Intervention is effective only to the degree to which it is reliably implemented. Furthermore, if a plan is poorly understood, difficult to implement, or inefficient, and thus poorly implemented, it is unlikely that appropriate decisions regarding the plan and a student's progress can be made. Just as data should be taken on student performance, data on program implementation provides team members with a measure of accountability. With increased emphasis on accountable systems, it would behoove educators and researchers to develop more practical and direct methods of ensuring and monitoring treatment integrity.

A second, and often overlooked reason for poor procedural integrity, is the social validity of the plan. Social validity is defined as an intervention's acceptance by its consumers; those who implement the plan or benefit from its implementation. Gunter and Denny (1996) noted that acceptability is based upon the judgment of those implementing the plan. The complexity of the plan, the perceived effectiveness of the plan, the teacher's knowledge of the plan's implementation, the willingness and ability of school personnel to execute the plan, and the social context of the plan all impact acceptance (Gresham et al. 2000; Gunter & Denny, 1996; Quinn, 2000; Scott et al., 2004; & Sugai & Horner, 2002; Wilson, Gutkin, Hagen, & Oates, 1998). Plans viewed as demanding, ineffective, or those that go against the philosophical beliefs of those who implement them are less likely to be implemented correctly or consistently and may even be abandoned. Furthermore, with a greater focus on accountability being placed on the educational system, treatment integrity is strongly related to treatment effectiveness. It benefits educators to develop and maintain collaborative relationships with all involved in the intervention process and discuss concerns about the intervention process that may impact its utility and acceptance in the classroom. Teachers have indicated that they are better able to solve behavioral problems when collaboration among team members occurs (Giangreco, Cloninger, Dennis, & Edelman, 2000).

Address Student Skill Deficits

Maladaptive behaviors that serve as the focus of BIPs undoubtedly interfere with a student's ability to effectively interact with the environment, yet the reduction of these target behaviors does not necessarily result in a functional improvement in the classroom (Ferritor, Buckholdt, Hamblin, & Smith, 1972). Ferritor et al. (1972) found that reducing disruptive classroom behavior does not always result in a corresponding improvement in academic performance. As important as reducing inappropriate behavior is, it is equally important for BIPs to address instruction in constructive and productive social and classroom behaviors. Knowledge of the inappropriate behavior's function is particularly important here, as knowing the function is critical for identifying relevant replacement behaviors that serve the same function as the target response. Many inappropriate behaviors are the result of a *skill* deficit rather than a *performance* deficit. Simply addressing the removal of an inappropriate behavior fails to address a possible skill deficit because the student has not learned an alternative, appropriate response. Particularly relevant to the classroom is the lack of academic skills that may impede classroom performance and the behavioral problems that often accompany these skill deficits (e.g., a student's off-task behavior during silent reading time is not due to his or her refusal to follow directions but rather to poor reading skills). Rather than developing a plan only to eliminate the undesired behavior, intervention must also focus on remediating the academic deficiencies correlated with the target behavior, the nature of which may be more appropriately addressed in an individualized education program (IEP). Generally the function of a given behavior, though the focus of intervention, is not usually a cause for concern, but rather the behavior used to achieve that function is. A plan that focuses on teaching a functional, alternative replacement behavior (e.g., teaching a student to recruit teacher reinforcement rather than calling out in class) allows the student to receive the same outcomes as the targeted undesirable behavior but by emitting a more desirable and adaptive functional response. A concurrent focus of intervention can address the acquisition of an alternative behavior that serves the same function as the target behavior.

Program for Generalization and Maintenance

The ultimate expectation of a BIP is that the intervention will result in lasting behavior change across a variety of environments that the student is expected to encounter.

Unfortunately, simply implementing a BIP and successfully modifying behavior does not guarantee sustained and generalized behavior change. The desired change resulting from the implementation of a BIP may be short-lived, or the target behavior may not extend into other environments. Two types of outcomes are most often the concern with behavioral programming: stimulus generalization and response maintenance.

Stimulus generalization refers to the occurrence of a behavior in a different setting or under different conditions than in which it was trained (Alberto & Troutman, 2006; Cooper et al., 2007). For example, if the focus of a BIP is to teach a student to raise his or her hand rather than call out answers in the classroom, stimulus generalization has occurred when the student raises a hand, rather than calling out answers, in classrooms other than the classroom in which the BIP was in effect. The student also participates in a variety of questions and situations.

The second type of outcome is *response maintenance*, when a learned behavior continues long after the programmed contingencies in a BIP have been removed (Cooper et al., 2007). For example, as in the same situation just discussed, response maintenance would occur if the student continued to raise a hand, rather than call out answers, throughout her or his educational career. Generalization and maintenance rarely occur without specific programming for their occurrence. Unfortunately, a "train and hope" (Stokes & Baer, 1977) approach is often used with BIPs, where the student is taught a skill and those implementing it hope that it remains in the student's repertoire across settings and time. Although a technology for generalization and maintenance is established in the literature (Alberto & Troutman, 2006; Cooper et al., 2007; Stokes & Baer, 1977; Stokes & Osnes, 1988), these strategies are not often addressed in behavioral programming. Addressing generalization and maintenance issues in a BIP has an impact on programming design. When generalization and maintenance are addressed in programming, programming objectives change as generalization and maintenance objectives differ from typical programming objectives that focus on acquisition of behavior (Haring & Liberty, 1990). For example, the conditions under which the behavior occurs, materials used, schedule of reinforcement, or other performance criteria, differ when considering generalization and maintenance. Consequently, the BIP should be designed to reflect the conditions that the student will encounter in the real world environment.

Students may also need to be taught self-monitoring and self-management strategies to maximize generalization and maintenance (see Todd, Horner, Vanater, & Schneider, [1997] for an example of integrating self-management into the BIP process). Within generalization objectives, conditions reflecting the natural environment are addressed rather than objectives that address the successful acquisition of the skill. Thus, the criteria for successful performance differ. Because the criteria are not the same, it stands to reason that the design and execution of a BIP must also differ if these criteria are to be addressed.

Focus on Demonstrated Behavior Change, Not "Just Talk"

The intent of behavioral planning is to change specific student behavior. As such, programming must focus on the student actually emitting a desired response. Rather than focusing on a specified response, a plan may simply focus on the student verbally reporting what the appropriate response should have been. For example, when a student responds to the teacher's request to begin working by throwing the book across the room and tipping over the desk, a BIP may indicate that she or he talks with the school social worker about more appropriate ways to handle anger. Unfortunately, simply focusing on verbalizations as a behavior change strategy is not likely sufficient enough to establish a desired behavior change.

Correspondence training involves individuals making verbal statements about future behavior. Correspondence is established through programming that reinforces the individual's stated intention (Baer, Williams, Osnes, & Stokes, 1984; Guevremont, Osnes, & Stokes, 1986a, 1986b; Stokes, Osnes, & Guevremont, 1987). However, follow-through to the actual emission of the desired response is essential, especially for the acquisition of new behaviors. Without the follow-through established with correspondence training, it is likely the programming will only serve to establish verbal reports of a desired response rather than the actual desired response.

Provide Sufficient Time, Staffing, Resources, and Supports

Despite good faith efforts to ameliorate a student's problem behavior, barriers may exist that prohibit effective implementation. First, time is an important factor to consider. Time refers not only to the time to implement the plan but also time to allow progress to be made. Second, sufficient personnel must be on board to implement the plan, especially if the plan is implemented across multiple environments (e.g., different classrooms, home and community). Some individuals may think that time and resources are insufficient to implement the program while still addressing the needs of other students, but resources are a key factor in the development and execution of BIPs. These may include materials to implement programming, ongoing consultation, or training. Support is not limited to school personnel but to the supports students require to facilitate their social and learning outcomes, to prevent problem behaviors, and to promote positive, appropriate, and functional behavior change (Carr et al., 2002; Horner, Albin, Sprague, & Todd, 1999). Rather than focusing on means to eliminate undesirable behavior, positive behavioral support strategies seek to promote student achievement through understanding of the unique factors involved in a student's behavior, individualizing interventions, and providing the necessary supports to achieve desired and sustained outcomes (see Crone & Horner, 2003; Florida Department of Education, 1999; Sugai & Horner, 2002). Effective practices require sustained support (Sugai & Horner, 2005). Resources may even

✓	Essential BIP Elements
	Functional Behavior Assessment
	• Consensus on problem
	• Review of records & past interventions
	• Interviews with all relevant parties
	• Team discussion
	• Assessment scales
	• Direct observation & measurement of the target behavior across settings & context
	• Scatterplot
	• A-B-C analysis
	• Reinforcer preference assessment
	• Ecological analysis
	• Hypothesized statement of the behavior's function
	• Analog experimentation of proposed hypothesis
	Antecedent Variables & Setting Events
	• A-B-C analysis
	• Determine the presence or absence of setting events
	• Contextual factors
	• Environmental factors
	• Physiological factors
	• Social factors
	Validity of Reinforcers
	• Reinforcer preference assessment
	• Corresponding increase in the target behavior when reinforcement is used
	• Corresponding decrease in the target behavior when punishment is used
	• Data to verify change in target behavior
	Clear Description of Target Behavior & Intervention Strategies
	• Observable, measurable, definable, & precise definition of the target behavior
	• Examination of similarities & differences between multiple target responses
	• Intervention focuses on a specific response or class of responses
	• Clear outline of BIP's procedures, specifying what one should/should not do when the behavior does/does not occur
	• Specific resources & support necessary to execute the plan
	Consistent Data Collection
	• Data collection system for continuous measurement of the target behavior is established
	• Data & student performance is continuously evaluated
	• BIP is modified, if necessary, based upon evaluation of the data
	Accurate & Consistent Implementation
	• BIP is accurately implemented
	• BIP is consistently implemented
	• Data is collected on BIP implementation
	• Social validity of the plan is established
	• Collaborative process is maintained
	Student Skill Deficits Addressed
	• Skill vs. performance deficits are determined
	• Skill deficits are remediated within a BIP or IEP
	• Establish a functional & adaptive replacement behavior
	Generalization & Maintenance Programming
	• Long-term outcomes for the target behavior are established (environmentally, contextually)

Figure 1   Checklist for designing, implementing, and evaluating effective behavior intervention plans.

Note. BIP = behavior intervention plan; IEP = individualized education program.

include feedback on a teacher's performance of the plan's implementation. Codding, Feinberg, Dunn, and Pace (2005) found that providing performance feedback to teachers improved treatment integrity of the plan in the classroom. Moreover, teachers rated performance feedback as valuable to the intervention process (Codding et al., 2005; Noell, Duhon, Gatti, & Connell, 2002). It would be inappropriate and naïve to assume that programming can be adopted and accurately implemented without adequate resources, training, or support.

Conclusion

As the practice of intervention planning grows within the educational arena and educators become more comfortable with its development and practice, the necessary and essential requirements inherent in an appropriately developed and effective plan will become more mainstream. Figure 1 provides a summary checklist for designing more effective BIPs. Although this discussion has focused on the development of individual plans, practitioners should be aware that to provide effective interventions, not only must BIPs address issues specific to an individual student, but specific systems inherent to the school that also serve as contextual factors and that may contribute to the occurrence of undesirable behaviors (Todd, Horner, Sugai, & Sprague, 1999). Effective interventions are not developed in isolation, but rather are the product of individual and cumulative efforts and global and specific assessment strategies. Future resources should be directed toward training educators on more effective practices to improve the quality of intervention programming to most effectively meet the educational needs of students with behavior problems in the classroom and other school settings.

References

Alberto, P. A., & Troutman, A. C. (2006). *Applied behavior analysis for teachers* (7th ed.). Upper Saddle River, NJ: Merrill/Prentice Hall.

Baer, D. M., Wolf, M. M., & Risley, T. R. (1968). Some current dimensions of applied behavior analysis. *Journal of Applied Behavior Analysis, 1,* 91–97.

Baer, R. A., Williams, J. A., Osnes, P. G., & Stokes, T. F. (1984). Delayed reinforcement as an indiscriminable contingency in verbal/ nonverbal correspondence training. *Journal of Applied Behavior Analysis, 17,* 429–440.

Buck, G. H., Polloway, E. A., Kirkpatrick, M. A., Patton, J. R., & Fad, K. M. (2000). Developing behavioral intervention plans: A sequential approach. *Intervention in School and Clinic, 36,* 3–9.

Carr, E. G., Dunlap, G., Horner, R. H., Koegel, R. L., Turnbull, A. P., Sailor, W., et al. (2002). Positive behavior support: Evolution of an applied science. *Journal of Positive Behavior Interventions, 4,* 4–16.

Codding, R. S., Feinberg, A. B., Dunn, E. K., & Pace, S. M. (2005). Effects of immediate performance feedback on implementation of behavior support plans. *Journal of Applied Behavior Analysis, 38,* 205–219.

Cooper, J. O., Heron, T. E., & Heward, W. L. (2007). *Applied behavior analysis* (2nd ed). Upper Saddle River, NJ: Pearson/ Prentice Hall.

Crone, D. A., & Horner, R. H. (2003). *Building positive behavior support systems in schools: Functional behavioral assessment.* New York: Guilford.

Crone, D. A., Horner, R. H., & Hawken, L. S. (2004). *Responding to problem behavior in schools: The behavior education program.* New York: Guilford.

DeLeon, I., & Iwata, B. (1996). Evaluation of a multiple-stimulus presentation format for assessing reinforcer preferences. *Journal of Applied Behavior Analysis, 29,* 519–533.

Deno, S. L. (1985). Curriculum-based measurement: The emerging alternative. *Exceptional Children, 52,* 219–232.

Deno, S. L., Marston, D., & Tindal, G. (1986). Direct and frequent curriculum-based measurement: An alternative for educational decision making. *Special Services in the Schools, 2,* 5–27.

Dunlap, G., Kern, L., dePerezel, M., Clarke, S., Williams, D., Childs, K., et al. (1993). Functional assessment of classroom variables for students with emotional/behavioral disorders. *Behavioral Disorders, 18,* 275–291.

Durand, V. M. (1988). The motivation assessment scale. In M. Hersen & A. S. Bellack (Eds.), *Dictionary of behavioral assessment techniques* (pp. 309–310). Elmsford, NY: Pergamon.

Ferritor, D. E., Buckholdt, D., Hamblin, R. L., & Smith, L. (1972). The noneffects of contingent reinforcement for attending behavior on work accomplished. *Journal of Applied Behavior Analysis, 5,* 7–17.

Fisher, W., Piazza, C., Bowman, L., Hagopian, L., Owens, J., & Slevin, I. (1992). A comparison of two approaches for identifying reinforcers for persons with severe and profound disabilities. *Journal of Applied Behavior Analysis, 25,* 491–498.

Florida Department of Education (1999, November). *Facilitator's guide: Positive behavioral support.* Tampa, FL: Bureau of Instructional Support and Community Services.

Fuchs, L. S., & Fuchs, D. (1986). Effects of systematic formative evaluation: A meta-analysis. *Exceptional Children, 53,* 199–208.

Fuchs, L. S., Fuchs, D., & Stecker, P. M. (1989). The effects of curriculum-based measurement on teachers instructional planning. *Journal of Learning Disabilities, 22,* 51–59.

Gable, R. A., Quinn, M. M., Rutherford, R. G., Howell, K. W., & Hoffman, C. C. (2000). *Addressing student problem behavior: Part III: Creating positive behavioral intervention plans and supports.* Washington, DC: Center for Effective Collaboration and Practice.

Giangreco, M. F., Cloninger, C. J., Dennis, R. E., & Edelman, S. W. (2000). Problem solving methods to facilitate inclusive education. In R. A. Villa & J. S. Thousand (Eds.), *Restructuring for caring and effective education: Piecing the puzzle together* (2nd ed., pp. 293–327). Baltimore: Brookes.

Greenwood, C. R., Carta, J. J., & Atwater, J. (1991). Ecobehavioral analysis in the classroom: Review and implications. *Journal of Behavioral Education, 1,* 59–77.

Gresham, F., MacMillan, D. L., Beebe-Frankenberger, M. B., & Bocian, K. M. (2000). Treatment integrity in learning disabilities intervention research: Do we really know how treatments are implemented? *Learning Disabilities Research and Practice, 15,* 198–205.

Guevremont, D. C., Osnes, P. G., & Stokes, T. F. (1986a). Programming maintenance after correspondence training interventions with children. *Journal of Applied Behavior Analysis, 19,* 215–219.

Guevremont, D. C., Osnes, P. G., & Stokes, T. F. (1986b). Preparation for effective self-regulation: The development of generalized verbal control. *Journal of Applied Behavior Analysis, 19,* 99–104.

Gunter, P., & Denny, K. (1996). Research issues and needs regarding teacher use of classroom management strategies. *Behavioral Disorders, 22,* 15–20.

Haring, N. G., & Liberty, K. A. (1990). Matching strategies with performance in facilitating generalization. *Focus on Exceptional Children, 22,* 1–16.

Holmes, G., Cautela, J., Simpson, M., Motes, P., & Gold, J. (1998). Factor structure of the school reinforcement survey schedule: School is more than grades. *Journal of Behavioral Education, 8,* 131–140.

Horner, R. H. (1994). Functional assessment: Contributions and future directions. *Journal of Applied Behavior Analysis, 27,* 401–404.

Horner, R. H., Albin, R. W., Sprague, J. R., & Todd, A. W. (1999). Positive behavior support for students with severe disabilities. In M. E. Snell & F. Brown (Eds.), *Instruction of students with severe disabilities* (5th ed., pp. 207–243). Upper Saddle River, NJ: Merrill/ Prentice Hall.

Horner, R. H., Sugai, G., & Todd, A. W. (2001). Data need not be a four-letter word: Using data to improve school-wide discipline. *Beyond Behavior, 11,* 20–22.

Jolivette, K., Wehby, J. H., & Hirsch, L. (1999). Academic strategy identification for students exhibiting inappropriate classroom behaviors. *Behavioral Disorders, 24,* 210–221.

Kern, L., Childs, K., Dunlap, G., Clarke, S., & Falk, G. D. (1994). Using assessment-based curricular intervention to improve the classroom behavior of a student with emotional and behavioral challenges. *Journal of Applied Behavior Analysis, 27,* 7–19.

Lalli, J. S., Browder, D. M., Mace, F. C., & Brown, D. K. (1993). Teacher use of descriptive analysis data to implement interventions to decrease students' problem behaviors. *Journal of Applied Behavior Analysis, 26,* 227–238.

Levitt, L. K., & Rutherford, R. B. (1978). *Strategies for handling the disruptive student.* Tempe: Arizona State University, College of Education.

Maag, J. W. (2001). Rewarded by punishment: Reflections on the disuse of positive reinforcement in schools. *Exceptional Children, 67,* 173–186.

Maag, J. W. (2003). Targeting behaviors and methods for recording their occurrences. In M. J. Breen & C. R. Fiedler (Eds.), *Behavioral approach to assessment of youth with emotional/ behavioral disorders: A handbook for school-based practitioners* (2nd ed., pp. 297–333). Austin, TX: PRO-ED.

Morgan, D., & Jenson, W. R. (1988). *Teaching behaviorally disordered students: Preferred practices.* Columbus, OH: Merrill.

Noell, G. H., Duhon, G. J., Gatti, S. L., & Connell, J. R. (2002). Consultation, follow-up, and implementation of behavior management interventions in general education. *School Psychology Review, 31,* 217–234.

Northup, J., George, T., Jones, K., Broussard, C., & Vollmer, T. (1996). A comparison of reinforcer assessment methods: The utility of verbal and pictorial choice procedures. *Journal of Applied Behavior Analysis, 29,* 201–212.

O'Neill, R. E., Horner, R. H., Albin, R. W., Sprague, J. R., Storey, K., & Newton, J. S. (1997). *Functional assessment for problem behavior: A practical handbook* (2nd ed.). Pacific Grove, CA: Brookes/Cole.

Pace, G., Ivancic, M., Edwards, G., Iwata, B., & Page, T. (1985). Assessment of stimulus preference and reinforcer value with profoundly retarded individuals. *Journal of Applied Behavior Analysis, 18,* 249–255.

Peterson, L., Homer, A. L., & Wonderlich, S. A. (1982). The integrity of independent variables in behavior analysis. *Journal of Applied Behavior Analysis, 15,* 477–492.

Quinn, M. M. (2000). Creating safe, effective, and nurturing schools: New opportunities and new challenges for serving all students. In L. M. Bullock & R. A. Gable (Eds.), *Positive academic and behavioral supports: Creating safe, effective, and nurturing schools for all students* (pp. 1–5). Reston, VA: Council for Children with Behavioral Disorders.

Scott, T. M., Bucalos, A., Liaupsin, C., Nelson, C. M., Jolivette, K., & DeShea, L. (2004). Using functional behavior assessment in general education settings: Making a case for effectiveness and efficiency. *Behavioral Disorders, 29*(2), 189–201.

Smith, R. G., & Iwata, B. A. (1997). Antecedent influences on behavior disorders. *Journal of Applied Behavior Analysis, 30,* 343–375.

Stichter, J., & Conroy, M. (2005). Using structural analysis in natural settings: A responsive functional assessment strategy. *Journal of Behavioral Education, 14,* 19–34.

Stokes, T. F., & Baer, D. M. (1977). An implicit technology of generalization. *Journal of Applied Behavior Analysis, 10,* 349–367.

Stokes, T. F., & Osnes, P. G. (1988). The developing applied technology of generalization and maintenance. In R. H. Horner, G. Dunlap, & R. L. Koegel (Eds.), *Generalization and maintenance* (pp. 5–19). Baltimore: Brookes.

Stokes, T. F., Osnes, P. G., & Guevremont, D. C. (1987). Saying and doing: A commentary on a contingency-space analysis. *Journal of Applied Behavior Analysis, 20,* 161–164.

Sugai, G., & Horner, R. H. (Eds.). (2002). Introduction to the special series on positive behavior support in schools. *Journal of Emotional and Behavioral Disorders, 10(3),* 130–136.

Sugai, G., & Horner, R. H. (2005). Schoolwide positive behavior supports: Achieving and sustaining effective learning environments for all students. In W. L. Heward, T. E. Heron, N. A. Neef, S. M. Peterson, D. M. Sainato, G. Cartledge, et al. (Eds.), *Focus on behavior analysis in education: Achievements, challenges, and opportunities* (pp. 90–102). Upper Saddle River, NJ: Pearson.

Sugai, G., Horner, R. H., & Sprague, J. (1999). Functional assessment-based behavior support planning: Research-to-practice-to-research. *Behavioral Disorders, 24,* 223–227.

Sugai, G., Lewis-Palmer, T., & Hagan, S. (1998). Using functional assessments to develop behavior support plans. *Preventing School Failure, 43*(1), 6–13.

Sugai, G., Lewis-Palmer, T., & Hagan-Burke, S. (1999–2000). Overview of the functional behavior assessment process. *Exceptionality, 8*(3), 149–160.

Todd, A. W., Horner, R. H., Sugai, G., & Colvin, G. (1999). Individualizing school-wide discipline for students with chronic problem behaviors: A team approach. *Effective School Practices, 17*(4), 72–82.

Todd, A. W., Horner, R. H., Sugai, G., & Sprague, J. R. (1999). Effective behavior support: Strengthening school-wide systems through a team-based approach. *Effective School Practices, 17*(4), 23–27.

Todd, A. W., Horner, R. H. Vanater, S. M., & Schneider, C. F. (1997). Working together to make change: An example of positive behavioral support for a student with traumatic brain injury. *Education and Treatment of Children, 20,* 425–440.

Touchette, P. E., MacDonald, R. F., & Langer, S. N. (1985). A scatterplot for identifying stimulus control of problem behavior. *Journal of Applied Behavior Analysis, 18,* 343–351.

Umbreit, J. (1995). Functional assessment and intervention in a regular classroom setting for the disruptive behavior of a student with attention-deficit hyperactivity disorder. *Behavioral Disorders, 20,* 267–278.

Wilson, P. C., Gutkin, T. B., Hagen, K. M., & Oates, R. G. (1998). General education teacher's knowledge and self-reported use of classroom interventions for working with difficult-to-teach students: Implications for consultation, prereferral intervention and inclusive services. *School Psychology Quarterly, 13,* 45–62.

KIM KILLU, PhD, is an associate professor of special education at the University of Michigan–Dearborn. Her current interests include applied behavior analysis, the assessment and treatment of severe behavior disorders, and functional behavior assessment/behavior intervention planning policy and practice.

Address: Kim Killu, University of Michigan–Dearborn, School of Education, 19000 Hubbard Dr., Dearborn, MI, 48126; e-mail: kimkillu@umd.umich.edu

UNIT 7

Creating Caring Communities of Learners

Unit Selections

35. **Becoming Citizens of the World,** Vivien Stewart
36. **Democracy and Education: Empowering Students to Make Sense of Their World,** William H. Garrison
37. **Thinking about Patriotism,** Joel Westheimer
38. **What Is Personalization?,** James W. Keefe
39. **Cultivating Optimism in the Classroom,** Richard Sagor

Key Points to Consider

- Are there certain values about which most of us can agree? Should they be taught in schools? Why, or why not?

- What can teachers do to help students become caring, morally responsible persons?

- Do you agree that patriotism should be taught in the schools? Explain why.

- Consider that cultivating optimism might be a deterrent against bullying. Would you agree or disagree? Explain your answer.

Student Website
www.mhcls.com

Internet References

Association for Supervision and Curriculum Development (ASCD)
http://www.ascd.org
Educators for Social Responsibility International (ESR)
http://www.esrnational.org
Coalition of Essential Schools
http://www.essentialschools.org
The Forum for Education and Democracy
http://www.forumforeducation.org/index.php
Institute for Democracy in Education
http://www.ohiou.edu/ide/index.htm

All of us are situated in social, political, and economic circumstances that inform and develop our values. Our values usually derive from principles of conduct that we learn in each of our histories of interacting with ourselves (as they form) and in interaction with others. This is to say that societal values develop in a cultural context. Teachers cannot hide all of their moral preferences. They can, however, learn to conduct just and open discussions of moral topics without succumbing to the temptation to indoctrinate students with their own views. In democratic societies, such as the United States, alternative sets of values and morals co-exist.

What teachers perceive to be worthwhile and defensible behavior informs our reflections on what we as educators should teach. We are conscious immediately of some of the values that affect our behavior, but we may not be as aware of what informs our preferences. Values that we hold without being conscious of them are referred to as tacit values; values derived indirectly after reasoned reflection on our thoughts about teaching and learning. Much of our knowledge about teaching is tacit knowledge, which we need to bring into conscious cognition by analyzing the concepts that drive our practice. We need to acknowledge how all our values inform, and influence, our thoughts about teaching. Teachers grapple with the dilemma of their own values versus the values of their students. Is it ethical to try to change character, values, and beliefs of our students? In this unit of this book, we are focusing on character education, becoming altruistic (displaying selfless or self-sacrificial behavior), living as citizens of the world, the idea of active participation in a democratic society, and the responsibilities of being patriotic. Here we will explore what it means to be teachers and students in a democratic society.

Students need to develop a sense of genuine caring both for themselves and others. They need to learn alternatives to violence and human exploitation. Teachers need to be examples of responsible and caring persons who use reason and compassion in solving problems in school. Teachers need to help students develop within themselves a sense of critical social consciousness and a genuine concern for social justice. Insight into the nature of moral decision making should be taught in the context of real current and past social problems and should lead students to develop their own skills in social analysis relating to the ethical dilemmas of human beings. Thus promoting altruism in our classrooms will help students develop the purest form of caring that is selfless and noncontingent upon reward.

One of the most compelling responsibilities of schools is that of preparing young people for their moral duties as free citizens of free nations. Governments have always wanted schools to teach the principles of civic morality based on their respective constitutional traditions. Indeed, when the public school movement began in the 1830s and 1840s, the concept of universal public schooling as a mechanism for instilling a sense of national identity, and civic morality was supported. In every nation, school curricula have certain value preferences embedded in them. However, as the United States becomes more multiethnic, multicultural, and multilingual, should we also be teaching our students to be citizens of the world? Our world and country are changing and are fundamentally different from the world in which many teachers grew up. How will our students manage such a world if we do not prepare them for it? These are the questions and issues addressed in the article by Stewart.

Teaching students to respect all people, to revere the sanctity of life, to uphold the right of every citizen to dissent, to believe in the equality of all people before the law, to cherish freedom to learn, and to respect the right of all people to their own convictions—these are principles of democracy and ideals worthy

© Image Source/Alamy

of being cherished. An understanding of the processes of ethical decision making is needed by the citizens of a democratic nation; thus, this process of learning to live in a democracy should be taught in a free nation's schools. Some believe that as teachers we must allow students to assume the freedom and responsibility to make choices that might include directing their own learning experiences.

Since 9/11 and during the wars in Iraq and Afghanistan, we have heard much about patriotism. What is a patriot? Why are patriots important? This topic is a hot button issue and highly contested territory. It seems to contradict our notion of being citizens in a multicultural world. Is patriotism blind loyalty to an ideal, political party, or government leaders, or is it a commitment to democratic ideals such as equality, compassion, and justice in a democratic society? Still others see it as acts we perform when we are at war or during time of national crisis, such as after 9/11 or Hurricane Katrina. The article by Westheimer examines way to provide students with opportunities to discuss the notion of patriotism and to think deeply about issues of public importance.

As teachers work to build communities of caring, Keefe suggests we should engage in personalization of educational experiences. As he notes, this is not a new idea, in fact we often see similar ideas under the heading of learner-centered teaching. He provides a research base for his ideas and clear explanation of how to implement the concept of personalized teaching. Another concept that is essential to building a caring community is a student that believes her efforts will make a difference and that the future holds promise for her life. These are the important aspects of Sagor's article on cultivating optimism. He asks us to consider why some students are motivated to do well and others are not. His answer is optimism. Motivated students believe in the future. These students believe that investing in today will bring a positive payoff in the future. His examples from popular movies about teachers to personal examples of his own children illustrate how we might cultivate optimism in our students.

For whom do the schools exist? Is a teacher's primary responsibility to his or her client, the student, or to the student's parents? Do secondary school students have the right to study and to inquire into subjects not in officially sanctioned curricula? What ethical questions are raised by arbitrarily withholding information regarding alternative viewpoints on controversial topics? We present this group of articles to help teachers answer the questions in the paragraph above and to support their efforts.

Becoming Citizens of the World

The future is here. It's multiethnic, multicultural, and multilingual. But are students ready for it?

VIVIEN STEWART

The world into which today's high school students will graduate is fundamentally different from the one in which many of us grew up. We're increasingly living in a globalized society that has a whole new set of challenges. Four trends have brought us here.

The first trend is economic. The globalization of economies and the rise of Asia are central facts of the early 21st century. Since 1990, 3 billion people in China, India, and the former Soviet Union have moved from closed economies into a global one. The economies of China, India, and Japan, which represented 18 percent of the world's gross domestic product (GDP) in 2004, are expected to represent 50 percent of the world's GDP within 30 years (Wilson, 2005). One in five U.S. jobs is now tied to international trade, a proportion that will continue to increase (U.S. Census Bureau, 2004). Moreover, most U.S. companies expect the majority of their growth to be in overseas markets, which means they will increasingly require a workforce with international competence. According to the Committee for Economic Development (2006),

> To compete successfully in the global marketplace, both U.S.-based multinational corporations as well as small businesses increasingly need employees with knowledge of foreign languages and cultures to market products to customers around the globe and to work effectively with foreign employees and partners in other countries.

Science and technology are changing the world and represent a second trend. *In The World Is Flat,* Thomas Friedman (2005) describes how the "wiring of the world" and the digitization of production since 1998 are making it possible for people to do increasing amounts of work anywhere and anytime. Global production teams are becoming commonplace in business. In addition, scientific research, a key driver of innovation, will increasingly be conducted by international teams as other countries ramp-up their scientific capacity.

The third trend involves health and security matters. Every major issue that people face—from environmental degradation and global warming, to pandemic diseases, to energy and water shortages, to terrorism and weapons proliferation—has

an international dimension. Solving these problems will require international cooperation among governments, professional organizations, and corporations. Also, as the line between domestic and international affairs blurs, U.S. citizens will increasingly vote and act on issues—such as alternative energy sources or security measures linked to terrorism—that require a greater knowledge of the world. In response to this need, a 2006 report from the National Association of State Boards of Education recommends infusing classroom instruction with a strong global perspective and incorporating discussions of current local, national, and international issues and events.

The fourth trend is changing demographics. Globalization has accelerated international migration. New immigrants from such regions as Asia and Central and South America are generating a diversity in U.S. communities that mirrors the diversity of the world. Knowledge of other cultures will help students understand and respect classmates from different countries and will promote effective leadership abroad.

In short, U.S. high school graduates will

- Sell to the world.
- Buy from the world.
- Work for international companies.
- Manage employees from other cultures and countries.
- Collaborate with people all over the world in joint ventures.
- Compete with people on the other side of the world for jobs and markets.
- Tackle global problems, such as AIDS, avian flu, pollution, and disaster recovery (Center for International Understanding, 2005).

However, U.S. schools are not adequately preparing students for these challenges. Surveys conducted by the Asia Society (2002) and National Geographic-Roper (2002) indicated that, compared with students in nine other industrialized countries, U.S. students lack knowledge of world geography, history, and current events. And shockingly few U.S. students learn languages that large numbers of people speak, such as Chinese (1.3 billion speakers) and Arabic (246 million speakers).

Many countries in Europe and Asia are preparing their students for the global age by raising their levels of education attainment; emphasizing international knowledge, skills, and language acquisition; and fostering respect for other cultures. The United States must create its own education response to globalization, which should include raising standards, increasing high school and college graduation rates, and modernizing and internationalizing the curriculum.

What Global Competence Looks Like

The new skill set that students will need goes well beyond the United States' current focus on the basics and on math, science, and technology. These skills are necessary, of course, but to be successful global citizens, workers, and leaders, students will need to be knowledgeable about the world, be able to communicate in languages other than English, and be informed and active citizens.

World Knowledge

Teaching about the rest of the world in U.S. schools has often focused on the superficial: food, fun, and festivals. Today, we need deeper knowledge, such as understanding significant global trends in science and technology, how regions and cultures have developed and how they interconnect, and how international trade and the global economy work. For example, students might consider how increasing the supply of fresh water or changing forms of energy use in one country could have major effects on another country.

In a world in which knowledge is changing rapidly and technology is providing access to vast amounts of information, our challenge is not merely to give students more facts about geography, customs, or particular conflicts. Rather, our challenge is to hone students' critical-thinking skills and to familiarize students with key concepts that they can apply to new situations. In this way, they can make sense of the explosion of information from different sources around the world and put factual information into perspective and context. Only then can this information become meaningful.

Teaching students about the world is not a subject in itself, separate from other content areas, but should be an integral part of *all* subjects taught. We need to open global gateways and inspire students to explore beyond their national borders. Programs like iLEARN and Global Learning and Observations to Benefit the Environment (GLOBE) make it possible for students to work collaboratively with peers in other countries. School-to-school partnerships enable both real and virtual exchanges.

U.S. students are global teenagers, similar in many ways to their technology-enabled peers around the world. Adding an international dimension to subjects and encouraging students to reach out to peers in other countries are powerful ways to make the curriculum relevant and engaging to today's youth.

Language Skills

Only about one-half of U.S. high school students study a foreign language. The majority never go beyond the introductory level, and 70 percent study Spanish (Draper & Hicks, 2002). This results in a serious lack of capacity in such languages as Arabic and Chinese, both of which are crucial to the prosperity and security of the United States.

The United States should do as other industrialized countries in Europe and Asia do—start offering foreign languages in the elementary grades, where research has shown that language learning is most effective (Pufahl, Rhodes, & Christian, 2001), and continue the emphasis in secondary school to create pipelines of proficient language speakers. U.S. students need opportunities to learn a broader range of languages, as in Australia, where 25 percent of students now learn an Asian language (Asia Society, 2002). Heritage communities in the United States—communities in which a non-English language is spoken at home, such as Spanish or Navajo—provide rich sources of teachers, students, and cultural experiences (National Language Conference, 2005). Specific practices, such as immersion experiences, can greatly enhance language proficiency.

> As the line between domestic and international affairs blurs, U.S. citizens will increasingly vote and act on issues that require a greater knowledge of the world.

The growing interest in learning Chinese, as shown by the fact that 2,400 U.S. high schools expressed interest in offering the new advanced placement course in Mandarin, suggests that parents and teachers are realizing the importance of communication skills in a multilingual, multicultural world (see www.AskAsia.org/Chinese). Even if graduates don't use a second language at work, quite possibly they will work in cross-cultural teams and environments.

Civic Values

U.S. students need to extend traditional American values into the global arena. These include a concern for human rights and respect for cultures that differ from the United States. By learning to understand other perspectives, students can develop critical-thinking skills and enhance their creativity.

Students should focus on becoming active and engaged citizens in both their local and global environments. Schools can promote civic engagement by weaving discussions of current events throughout the school day and through participatory forms of education, such as Model UN or the Capitol Forum on America's Future, in which high school students voice their opinions on current international issues. Schools should use technology to connect students directly to peers in other parts of the world and promote service learning projects on issues that students can address at both the local and international levels, such as alleviating hunger, providing education support to students in poverty, and improving the environment.

What Schools Can Do

Across the United States, many schools already define their mission as producing students who are prepared for work, citizenship, and leadership in the global era. These schools have found that internationalizing the curriculum creates a more exciting environment for students and teachers alike (Bell-Rose & Desai, 2005). Several approaches have proven successful.

Have a large vision of what you want to achieve, but start slowly, one course or grade level at a time.

Introducing an international studies requirement for graduation. More than a decade ago, the school board of Evanston Township, Illinois, introduced an international studies requirement for graduation and asked the high school's teachers to develop the necessary courses. Now, every sophomore in this diverse Chicago suburb must complete the one-year international studies requirement. Students choose from a series of in-depth humanities courses on the history, literature, and art of Asia, Africa, Latin America, and the Middle East. Simulations and participatory projects are central to instruction, and partnerships with local universities ensure that teachers have ongoing professional development in international affairs.

Creating an elementary school immersion program. After surveying parents and local businesses about the future needs of the community—they cited skills in English, Spanish, and Japanese as important—Seattle public schools created the John Stanford International School, a public elementary bilingual immersion school. Students spend half the day studying math, science, culture, and literacy in either Japanese or Spanish; they spend the other half of the day learning reading, writing, and social studies in English. The school also offers English as a second language courses for immigrant students and after-school courses for their parents. As a result of the school's success, the city of Seattle has recently decided to open 10 more internationally oriented schools.

Developing international schools-within-schools. The Eugene International High School is a school-within-a-school on four high school campuses in Eugene, Oregon. The school is open to all interested students. The four-year sequence of courses centers thematically on culture, history, and the political, economic, and belief systems of different world regions, such as Asia, Africa, the Middle East, and Latin America. The school also emphasizes independent research courses to give students the tools to address global issues. An extended essay and a community-service requirement in 11th and 12th grade both have an international focus. For example, one student wrote a 4,000-word research essay on hydrogen cars and their place in the world economy. Students volunteer at such places as Centro Latino Americano, University of Oregon International Education and Exchange, and Holt International Children's Services. Finally, students have the option of pursuing the International Baccalaureate.

Teaching crucial language skills to prepare for the global economy. With strong support from Mayor Richard M. Daley, whose goal is to make Chicago a hub for international trade, the city has created the largest Chinese-language program in the United States. Twenty public schools teach Mandarin, from an all-black school on the West Side to a nearly all-Hispanic school on the South Side to more diverse schools throughout the city. For many of these students, Chinese is their third language after English and Spanish. The program resulted from partnerships among political, business, school, and community leaders and the Chinese Ministry of Education, which provides Chinese teachers and organizes a summer cultural program for Chicago educators in China.

Redesigning urban secondary schools with an international focus. Using the International High School of the Americas in San Antonio, Texas, and the Metropolitan Learning Center in Hartford, Connecticut, as anchor schools, the Asia Society has created a network of small, internationally themed secondary schools across the United States (see www.international studiesschools.org/). The mission of each school is to prepare low-income students for college and to promote their knowledge of world regions and international issues. Each public or charter school incorporates international content across the curriculum, offers both Asian and European languages, provides international exchange opportunities, and provides links to international organizations and community-service opportunities. To date, 10 schools have opened in New York City; Los Angeles; Charlotte, North Carolina; Denver, Colorado; and Houston, Texas. Additional schools are slated to open in other locations, such as Mathis and Austin, Texas, and Philadelphia, Pennsylvania.

Using student-faculty exchanges to promote curriculum change. Two public high schools in Newton, Massachusetts—Newton North and Newton South—run an exchange program with the Jingshan School in Beijing, China. Created by two teachers in 1979, the exchange enables U.S. and Chinese teachers and students to spend time in one another's schools every year. The program has served as a catalyst for districtwide curriculum change, bringing the study of Asian cultures into various academic disciplines, from social studies to science, and adding Chinese to the district's broad array of language options. The leaders of this exchange now help schools around the United States develop exchange programs with China as a way to internationalize their curriculums.

Using a K–12 foreign language sequence to promote excellence. The Glastonbury School District in Connecticut has long promoted language study, beginning with a K–8 language requirement. Ninety-three percent of students study at least one foreign language, and 30 percent study more than one. The foreign language curriculum is thematic and interdisciplinary, integrating both foreign language and world history standards. All high school students take a one-semester history course on a non-Western geographic/cultural region and a civics/current issues course that includes international content. The school district's reputation for languages and international studies is a major draw for families moving to the area.

These and other pioneering schools offer models that all schools can replicate. What are the lessons learned? Have a large vision of what you want to achieve, but start slowly, one course or grade level at a time. Involve parents as well as business and community leaders in planning and supporting international education and world languages. Focus on professional development for teachers, including partnerships with local colleges, so teachers can broaden and deepen their international knowledge. Include a focus on mastery of languages, including nontraditional languages, and start at the lowest grade levels possible. Use international exchanges, both real and virtual, to enable students to gain firsthand knowledge of the culture they are studying. If it is unfeasible for students to travel, try technology-based alternatives, such as classroom-to-classroom linkages, global science projects, and videoconferences (Sachar, 2004).

What Policymakers Can Do

Recognizing that future economic development and jobs in their states will be linked to success in the global economy, many states are developing innovations to promote international knowledge and skills. Nineteen states have been working together through the Asia Society's States Network on International Education in the Schools. States have developed commissions (North Carolina, Vermont); statewide summits (Delaware, Indiana, Massachusetts, Washington); and reports to assess the status of international education in their state (North Carolina, New Jersey, Wisconsin, West Virginia). They have created mechanisms, such as International or Global Education Councils (Ohio, Indiana, Wisconsin), and appointed International Education Coordinators to develop new policies and action plans (Delaware, Indiana, Ohio, New Jersey, Wisconsin). They are revising standards (Delaware, Idaho) or high school graduation requirements (New Mexico, Virginia) to incorporate international content. Some states are offering professional development (Oklahoma); initiating new language programs (Connecticut, Delaware, Illinois, Minnesota, Wisconsin, Wyoming); engaging in school exchanges with China (Connecticut, Massachusetts); adding crucial foreign language courses to their virtual high schools (Kentucky); and adding an international dimension to science, technology, engineering, and math (STEM) schools (Ohio, Texas). Finally, some (Arizona, Massachusetts, North Carolina, Washington) have introduced state legislation to provide additional funds to incorporate a global dimension into their schools (see http://Internationaled.org/states).

Many states recognize that future economic development and jobs in their states will be linked to success in the global economy.

In 2006, the National Governors Association held a session on International Education at its annual meeting. In addition, the Council of Chief State School Officers recently adopted a new policy statement on global education (2007). These state efforts are a good start, but the United States has yet to make international knowledge and skills a policy priority on the federal level and develop the systems and supports necessary to get high-quality international content into U.S. classrooms.

States need to pursue four policy goals to make this happen. They should

- Redesign high schools and create new graduation requirements to motivate higher achievement and promote important international knowledge and key skills.
- Expand teacher training to deliver rigorous study in world history and cultures, economics, world regions, and global challenges.
- Develop world language pipelines from primary school to college that focus on crucial languages, such as Chinese, and that address the acute shortage of language teachers.
- Use technology in innovative ways to expand the availability of international courses and ensure that every school in the United States has an ongoing virtual link to schools in other countries.

For almost 50 years, the U.S. government has played a crucial role in fostering foreign languages and international education in *higher* education. We need to extend this commitment to K–12 education and make it an urgent priority. By doing so, we can improve students' international knowledge and skills and increase both the competitive edge and security of the United States.

In his 2006 report, *The Economics of Knowledge: Why Education Is Key for Europe's Success*, Andreas Schleicher from the Organisation for Economic Cooperation and Development wrote,

The world is indifferent to tradition and past reputations, unforgiving of frailty and ignorant of custom or practice. Success will go to those individuals and countries which are swift to adapt, slow to complain, and open to change.

Part of the great strength of the United States is its adaptability. U.S. schools adapted to the agrarian age, then to the industrial age. It's time to open to change once more and adapt to the global age.

References

Asia Society. (2002). *States institute on international education in the schools: Institute report, November 20–22, 2002.* New York: Author.

Bell-Rose, S., & Desai, V. N. (2005). *Educating leaders for a global society.* New York: Goldman Sachs Foundation.

Center for International Understanding. (2005). *North Carolina in the world: A plan to increase student knowledge and skills about the world.* Raleigh, NC: Author.

Committee for Economic Development. (2006). *Education for global leadership: The importance of international studies and foreign language education for U.S. economic and national security.* Washington, DC: Author. Available: www.ced.org/docs/report/report_foreignlanguages.pdf

Council of Chief State School Officers. (2007). *Global education policy statement.* Washington, DC: Author. Available: www.ccsso.org/projects/International_Education/Global_Education_Policy_Statement/

Draper, J. B., & Hicks, J. H. (2002). *Foreign language enrollments in secondary schools, fall 2000.* Washington, DC: American Council on the Teaching of Foreign Languages. Available: http://actfl.org/files/public/Enroll2000.pdf

Friedman, T. L. (2005). *The world is flat: A brief history of the twenty-first century.* New York: Farrar, Straus, and Giroux.

National Association of State Boards of Education. (2006). *Citizens for the 21st century: Revitalizing the civic mission of schools.* Alexandria, VA: Author. Available: www.nasbe.org/publications/Civic_Ed/civic_ed.html

National Geographic-Roper. (2002). *2002 global geographic literacy survey.* Washington, DC: Author.

National Language Conference. (2005). *A call to action for national foreign language capabilities.* Washington, DC: Author. Available: www.nlconference.org/docs/White_Paper.pdf

Pufahl, I., Rhodes, N. C., & Christian, N. (2001). *What we can learn from foreign language teaching in other countries.* Washington, DC: Center for Applied Linguistics.

Sachar, E. (2004). *Schools for the global age: Promising practices in international education.* New York: Asia Society.

Schleicher, A. (2006). *The economics of knowledge: Why education is key for Europe's success.* Brussels: Lisbon Council. Available: www.oecd.org/dataoecd/43/11/36278531.pdf

U.S. Census Bureau. (2004). Table 2. In *Exports from manufacturing establishments: 2001* (p. 8). Washington, DC: U.S. Department of Commerce.

Wilson, W. T. (2005). *The dawn of the India century: Why India is poised to challenge China and the United States for global economic hegemony in the 21st century.* Chicago: Keystone India. Available: www.keystone-india.com/pdfs/The%20India%20Century.pdf

Vivien Stewart is Vice President, Education, at the Asia Society, 725 Park Ave., New York, New York, 10021; vstewart@asiasoc.org.

From *Educational Leadership,* April 2007, pp. 9–14. Copyright © 2007 by ASCD. Reprinted by permission. The Association for Supervision and Curriculum Development is a worldwide community of educators advocating sound policies and sharing best practices to achieve the success of each learner. To learn more, visit ASCD at www.ascd.org

Democracy and Education

Empowering Students to Make Sense of Their World

WILLIAM H. GARRISON

Ever wonder why democratic societies are unrivaled in expanding knowledge and creativity? There is a simple yet vital link between democracy and education, and it is found in how we learn best. If you have studied educational psychology or learning theory, you probably have insight into the causes of this phenomenon. If your instructional practices include such things as self-directed learning, self-reflection, or action research, you are probably well aware of the practical mechanism underlying this productivity even if you don't know it by name.

It is a fundamental belief under our system of governance that education is necessary for democracy. Less recognized is the equally important principle that democracy is necessary for education. Looking closely at the relationship between democracy and education reveals a common foundation in a learning mechanism that is as important for classroom practice as it is for a democratic society.

In *Democracy and Education*, Dewey defines education as the "reconstruction or reorganization of experience which adds to the meaning of experience and which increases the ability to direct the course of subsequent experience."[1] Education, like democracy, is fundamentally empowerment. Both provide the participants with the means to shape and direct their experiences.

The educational process in a democratic society, even in the most autocratic of classrooms and institutions, is grounded in basic freedoms. These freedoms exist beyond the particular classroom and institution, if not within them. From a learning perspective, the most important of these freedoms is the freedom to choose, to act on that choice, and to experience the results of those actions. Instructional practices that include self-reflection and action research are based on the idea that we learn by following our thoughts and actions and examining their consequences. By choosing a course of action and experiencing the results, our beliefs and understandings about the world, how it works, and how we fit into it are reinforced or modified.

In describing "intelligence," Jean Piaget echoes this fundamental play between thinking, acting, and learning: "The essential functions of intelligence consist in understanding and in inventing, in other words in building up structures by struc-turing reality."[2] We learn by constructing meaning from our experiences. We reconstruct, reorganize, and direct our experiences as we attempt to make sense of our world. Our understanding of the world is constructed through what we make of our experiences, how we interpret them, and how these interpretations are integrated into our knowledge and beliefs. These learnings provide the mental structures and dispositions that influence and direct subsequent experience.

We continually make choices in all of our thoughts and actions. Ulric Neisser wrote about the "perceptual cycle" of learning: of all the possibilities presented in our environment, our thought processes or mental structures guide our perceptual awareness, which samples the available information. As we choose to focus our attention, what we experience serves to modify or reinforce these structures, which guide further perceptual exploration and experience.[3]

This fundamental learning mechanism underlies the rich and productive relationship between democracy and education. Learning is the process of constructing meaning or structuring reality. It is necessarily a self-directed process contingent on individual choice and action.

The critical connection between democracy and education is that democratic social institutions are produced and sustained by the same progressive mechanism: the freedom to learn from experience, to build on experience, and to use this knowledge to direct the course of subsequent experience. Learning, individually or as a democratic society, is fundamentally contingent on freedom and self-governance: the ability to make choices and to take action, to formulate understandings and to test those understandings in actual experience.[4]

Formal education, as a system by which society transfers its knowledge and customs from generation to generation, generally does a poor job of teaching students how to learn, specifically a poor job of helping students to develop as self-directed learners, which is so critical in a rapidly changing world. The motivation we provide in school for learning is mostly external and driven by the belief that today's curriculum is essentially preparation for what comes next in the curriculum. But the curriculum is actually the total learning environment that we as educators create. For the future of each student's education, this environment is responsible for what he or she learns about learning. Cultivating the desire to learn is the single most important objective for any instructional strategy.

An often-quoted analysis of a major international study of science and mathematics education criticized the United States for a curriculum that is "a mile wide and an inch deep."[5] Nowhere is this more apparent than in our secondary schools, in which college preparation, including grades and test scores, is too often the only rationale for what and how we teach. In a curriculum that is always focused on what's next, there is little time to connect the subject matter and concepts to student experience. But it is precisely these connections that motivate and engage students and promote the joy of learning that feeds the desire to learn more.

The interests that teachers inspire often arise from their efforts to make the subject matter relevant. Schooling should focus on the connectedness of the subject matter to the student's life and world. The curriculum, as Dewey and others have argued, needs to connect in a meaningful way to the world in which our students live rather than rationalize its pace and content as necessary for the course and sequence ahead.

The primary mission of schooling should not be to prepare for the next grade level but to help students understand, to make sense of, and to be successful in their world today and tomorrow. The skills our students need now and in the future are acquired only through learning. It is learning that needs to be cultivated.

It is really that simple: the best curriculum is structured around helping students make sense of their world. This is a natural drive, a survival instinct that we all share. This does not require a radical change in today's curriculum, just a different mindset.

And the best learning happens under a democratic system, as our ever-maturing students increasingly assume the freedom and responsibility to make choices and direct their learning experiences. As teachers in a democratic society, we should cultivate a learning curriculum by empowering students to make sense of their world.

Notes

1. John Dewey, *Democracy and Education* (New York: Macmillan, 1916; reprint, 1944), p. 76.

2. Jean Piaget, *Science and the Psychology of the Child* (New York: Orion Press, 1970), p. 27.

3. Ulric Neisser, *Cognition and Reality* (San Francisco: W. H. Freeman, 1976).

4. William H. Garrison, "Democracy, Experience, and Education: Promoting a Continued Capacity for Growth," *Phi Delta Kappan*, March 2003, pp. 525–29.

5. A phrase employed by William Schmidt, director of the U.S. National Research Center for the Third International Mathematics and Science Study (TIMSS).

WILLIAM H. GARRISON is director of assessment and evaluation for the Palo Alto Unified School District, Palo Alto, Calif.

From *Phi Delta Kappan*, January 2008, pp. 347–348. Copyright © 2008 by Phi Delta Kappan. Reprinted by permission of the publisher and William Garrison.

Thinking about Patriotism

To prepare students to participate in civic life, we must teach them the skills of analysis and exploration, free political expression, and independent thought.

JOEL WESTHEIMER

Nine of 10 Americans agree with the statement "I am very patriotic" (Doherty, 2007). More than seven of 10 U.S. high school seniors report that they would be offended by someone carrying on a conversation while the national anthem was being played (Hamilton College, 2003). Statistics like these suggest that Americans are in harmony about the idea of patriotism.

But patriotism is never simple. Although many people describe themselves as patriotic, the easy consensus disappears when we ask them what the term means. Some believe that patriotism requires near-absolute loyalty to government leaders and policies. Others see patriotism as commitment not to the government, but rather to such democratic ideals as equality, compassion, and justice. Still others advocate a healthy skepticism toward governmental actions in general, but prefer to close the ranks during times of war or national crisis. Indeed, there are as many ways to express our commitment to country as there are ways to show our commitment to loved ones or friends.

Nowhere are the debates around the various visions of patriotism more pointed, more protracted, and more consequential than in our schools. In Madison, Wisconsin, the parent community erupted in fierce debate over a new law requiring schools to post American flags in each classroom and to lead students in either pledging allegiance or listening to the national anthem each day (Ladson-Billings, 2006). In Detroit, Michigan, a student was repeatedly suspended, first for wearing a T-shirt with an upside-down American flag and then for wearing a sweatshirt with an antiwar quotation by Albert Einstein, before the American Civil Liberties Union (ACLU) filed a civil liberties suit resulting in the student's reinstatement (ACLU, 2004). And in Virginia, House Bill 1912, which would have required schools to notify parents any time a student declined to recite or stand for the Pledge of Allegiance, passed the House of Delegates with a 93–4 vote before being defeated in the State Senate (Virginia Legislative Assembly, 2005).

As these and many other stories make clear, patriotism is highly contested territory, especially when it comes to the daily activities of school-children. Yet public schools in a democratic society have a particular obligation to provide students with opportunities to think deeply about issues of public importance. So it seems fitting to ask, What and how should we teach students about patriotism? How can we best prepare them to participate in the civic life of their community and nation?

Two Kinds of Patriotism

If you stepped into a school at a moment of patriotic expression, how could you tell whether you were in a totalitarian nation or a democratic one? Both the totalitarian nation and the democratic one might have students sing a national anthem. You might hear a hip-hip-hooray kind of cheer for our land emanating from the assembly hall of either school. Flags and symbols of national pride might be front and center in each school. And the students of each school might observe a moment of silence for members of their country's armed forces who had been killed in combat.

But how would the lessons on patriotism in the democratic nation be unique? What should schools in the United States ask students to consider that schools in China, North Korea, or Iran would not?

Social theorists differentiate between *authoritarian patriotism* and *democratic patriotism* (Lummis, 1996; Westheimer, 2007). Although either might employ familiar rituals to foster a sense of belonging and attachment, authoritarian patriotism demands unquestioning loyalty to a centralized leader or leading group. We would not be surprised to learn, for example, that North Korean children are taught to abide by an "official history" handed down by President Kim Jong-il and his single-party regime. Political scientist Douglas Lummis (1996) notes that authoritarian patriotism represents "a resigning of one's will, right of choice, and need to understand to the authority; its emotional base is gratitude for having been liberated from the burden of democratic responsibility" (p. 37). A school curriculum that teaches one unified, unquestioned version of "truth" is one of the hallmarks of a totalitarian society.

One would reasonably expect to see a different picture in U.S. schools. Democratic patriotism entails commitment not necessarily to government institutions, but rather to the people, principles, and values that underlie democracy—such as political participation, free speech, civil liberties, and social equality. Schools might develop students' democratic patriotism, at least in part, through lessons in analysis and exploration, free political expression, and independent thought. And U.S. schools often support democratic dispositions in just such ways.

But patriotism in U.S. classrooms does not always conform to democratic goals and ideals. Tensions abound, and in recent years independent thinking has increasingly come under attack. If being a good U.S. citizen requires thinking critically about important social assumptions, then that foundation of citizenship is at odds with recent trends in education policy.

No Child Left Thinking

In the past five years, dozens of school boards, districts, states, and the federal government have enacted policies that seek to restrict critical analysis of historical and contemporary events in the school curriculum. In June 2006, Florida passed a law that included language specifying that "American history shall be viewed as factual, not as constructed, shall be viewed as knowable, teachable, and testable." Other provisions in the bill mandate "flag education, including proper flag display and flag salute" and require educators to stress the importance of free enterprise to the U.S. economy. But I am most concerned that the bill's designers view historical literacy as the teaching of facts. For example, the bill requires that only facts be taught when it comes to discussing the "period of discovery" and the early American colonies. Florida is perhaps the first state to ban historical interpretation in public schools, thereby effectively outlawing critical thinking.

Of course, historians almost universally regard history as *exactly* a matter of interpretation. Indeed, the competing interpretations are what make history so interesting. Historians and educators alike have widely derided the mandated adherence to an "official story" embodied in the Florida legislation (Craig, 2006; Zimmerman, 2006). But the effect of such mandates should not be underestimated—especially because Florida is not alone.

The drive to engage schools in reinforcing a unilateral understanding of U.S. history and policy—reflecting a "my country right or wrong" stance—shows no sign of abating. For example, Nebraska's state board of education specified that the high school social studies curriculum should include "instruction in . . . the benefits and advantages of our government, the dangers of communism and similar ideologies" as well as "exploits and deeds of American heroes, singing patriotic songs, memorizing 'The Star Spangled Banner' and 'America,' and reverence for the flag" (Westheimer & Kahne, 2003).

The federal role in discouraging critical analysis of historical events has been significant as well. In 2002, the U.S. Department of Education announced a new set of history and civic education initiatives that President George W. Bush said was designed to teach our children that "America is a force for good in the world, bringing hope and freedom to other people" (Bush, 2002). Similarly, in 2004, Senator Lamar Alexander (former U.S. secretary of education) warned that students should not be exposed to competing ideologies in historical texts but should be instructed that the United States represents one true ideology. Alexander sponsored his American History and Civics Education Act to put civics back in its "rightful place in our schools, so our children can grow up learning what it means to be an American" (Alexander, 2003).

I focus on history teaching here, but the trend is not limited to social studies. In many states, virtually every subject area is under scrutiny for any deviation from one single narrative based on knowable, testable, and purportedly uncontested facts. An English teacher in a recent study undertaken by my colleagues and myself told us that even novel reading was now prescriptive in her states rubric with meanings predetermined, vocabulary words preselected, and essay topics predigested. A science teacher put it this way: "The only part of the science curriculum now being critically analyzed is evolution."

As many people have observed, the high-stakes testing mandated by No Child Left Behind (NCLB) has further pushed to the margins education efforts to challenge students to grapple with tough questions about society and the world. In a recent study by the Center on Education Policy (Rentner et al., 2006), 71 percent of districts reported cutting back time for other subjects—social studies in particular—to make more space for reading and math instruction. Last June, historian David McCullough told a U.S. Senate committee that because of NCLB, "history is being put on the back burner or taken off the stove altogether in many or most schools" (Dillon, 2006). An increasing number of students are getting little to no education about how government works, the Constitution, the Bill of Rights, the evolution of social movements, and U.S. and world history. As Peter Campbell (2006), Missouri state coordinator for FairTest, noted,

> The sociopolitical implications of poor black and Hispanic children not learning about the Civil Rights movement, not learning about women's suffrage, not learning about the U.S. Civil War, and not learning about any historical or contemporary instance of civil disobedience is more than just chilling. It smacks of an Orwellian attempt not merely to rewrite history, but to get rid of it.

The implications Campbell describes are not limited to poor black and Hispanic students. Any student being denied knowledge about historical events and social movements misses out on important opportunities to link his or her patriotic attachments with quintessentially American experiences of struggles for a better society for all.

Let's Talk Facts

The most common criticism of educators who seek to teach students to think and interpret information is that they have no respect for facts, rigor, and standards. Somehow, critics have become convinced that those who say they want students to think for themselves do not care whether students can read, write, or perform addition or subtraction. This is nonsense. But many educators do want students to know more than facts and formulas. They want the knowledge that students acquire to be embedded in the service of something bigger. It is not enough for students to learn how to read; they also need to learn to decide what is worth reading and why. In other words, they need to learn how to think.

Proponents of "factual" history also rapidly lose interest in facts when those facts call into question the "one true story." As an example, we can look at the history of the United States' most revered patriotic symbols and rituals. Although millions of schoolchildren recite the Pledge of Allegiance every day, few know many facts about its author. Francis Bellamy, author of the original 1892 pledge (which did not contain any reference to God), was highly critical of many trends of late 19th-century American life, most notably unrestrained capitalism and growing individualism. He wanted the United States to reflect basic democratic values, such as equality of opportunity, and he worked openly to have his country live up to its democratic ideals.

Katharine Lee Bates, an English professor and poet at Wellesley College, wrote the lyrics to "America the Beautiful," including the words "America! America! God mend thine every flaw!" Bellamy,

Bates, and many like-minded reformers throughout U.S. history asserted their patriotism by strongly proclaiming their belief in democratic values, such as free speech, civil liberties, greater participation in politics, and social and economic equality (Dreier & Flacks, 2007).

Yet schools have become increasingly oriented away from the kinds of thinking these historical figures advocated and toward pedagogical models of efficiency that discourage deeper consideration of important ideas. The relentless focus on testing means that time for in-depth critical analysis of ideas is diminished. Social studies scholar Stephen Thornton (2005) notes that by "critical thinking," school officials too often mean that students should passively absorb as "truth" the thinking already completed by someone else. Current school reform policies and classroom practices often reduce teaching and learning to the kind of mindless rule-following that leaves students unable to make principled stands that have long been associated with being American. The hidden curriculum of post-NCLB schooling is how to please authority and pass the tests, not how to develop convictions and stand up for them.

Teaching about Patriotism

There are many varied and powerful ways to teach a democratic form of patriotism aimed at improving people's lives (see "Online Resources for Teaching Democratic Patriotism"). Longtime teacher Brian Schultz's inspiring efforts with his 5th grade class in Chicago's Cabrini-Green housing project area included having his students conduct research on improving conditions in their own neighborhood, especially with regard to broken promises to build a new school. His students studied historical approaches to change and, rejecting passivity, demonstrated a deep attachment to their community and neighbors (Schultz, 2007).

Bob Peterson, a one-time Wisconsin Elementary Teacher of the Year, worked with his students at La Escuela Fratney in Madison to examine the full spectrum of ideological positions that emerged following the September 11, 2001, terrorist attacks. Instead of avoiding the challenging questions his 5th grade students posed, Peterson encouraged them, placing a notebook prominently at the front of the classroom labeled "Questions That We Have." As the students discussed their questions and the unfolding current events, Peterson repeatedly asked students to consider their responsibilities to one another, to their communities, and to the world. Through poetry (Langston Hughes's "Let America Be America Again"); historical readings (the Declaration of Independence, the U.S. Constitution, the 1918 Sedition Act); and current events (photographs of September 11 memorial gatherings, protests in the United States and abroad, newspaper editorials), Peterson allowed students to explore political events surrounding the September 11 attacks and their effect on American patriotism and democracy (Peterson, 2007; Westheimer, 2007).

El Puente Academy in the Williamsburg neighborhood of Brooklyn, New York, ties the entire school curriculum to students' and teachers' concerns about the community. Named a New York City School of Excellence, El Puente boasts a 90 percent graduation rate in an area where schools usually see only 50 percent of their students graduate in four years. El Puente principal Héctor Calderón attributes the school's success to a curriculum that engages students in efforts to realize American ideals of justice and equality, reverse the cycle of poverty and violence, and work toward change in their own neighborhood. Students study environmental hazards in the area, not only because they care about the health of the natural environment, but also because these hazards directly affect the health of the community to which they are deeply committed.

In one unit, students surveyed the community to chart levels of asthma and identify families affected by the disease. Their report became the first by a community organization to be published in a medical journal. Students and teachers also successfully fought a 55-story incinerator that was proposed for their neighborhood (Gonzales, 1995; North Central Regional Educational Laboratory, 2000; Westheimer, 2005).

These approaches to teaching about patriotism share several characteristics. First, teachers encourage students to ask questions rather than absorb pat answers—to think about their attachments and commitments to their local, national, and global communities. Second, teachers provide students with the information (including competing narratives) they need to think about patriotism in substantive ways. Third, they root instruction in local contexts, working within their own specific surroundings and circumstances because we cannot teach democratic patriotism without paying attention to the environment in which we are teaching it. This last point makes standardized testing difficult to reconcile with in-depth thinking about patriotism.

An Invitation to Action

To return to my earlier question, what makes a classroom in the United States or any democratic country different from one in an authoritarian state? For democratic patriotism to properly flourish, educators must convey to students that they have important contributions to make. In a democracy, patriotism is not a spectator sport.

The exit of the Canadian War Museum bears the following inscription:

History is yours to make. It is not owned or written by someone else for you to learn . . . . History is not just the story you read. It is the one you write. It is the one you remember or denounce or relate to others. It is not predetermined. Every action, every decision, however small, is relevant to its course. History is filled with horror and replete with hope. You shape the balance.

I suspect many readers could imagine teaching students to think about patriotism by beginning a discussion with just such a quotation.

References

Alexander, L. (2003). Remarks of Senator Lamar Alexander on the introduction of his bill: The American History and Civics Education Act, March 4, 2003. Available: www.congresslink. org/print_expert_amhist.htm

American Civil Liberties Union. (2004). Michigan school reverses suspension of student for wearing "anarchy" T-shirt [online press release]. New York: Author. Available: www.aclu.org/StudentsRights/StudentsRights.cfm?ID=15672&c=159

Bush, G. W. (2002). *President introduces history and civic education initiatives* [online press release]. Washington, DC: The White House. Available: www.whitehouse.gov/news/releases/2002/09/20020917-1.html

Campbell, P. (2006, October 18). Ballot initiatives, democracy, and NCLB. *Transform Education* [blog]. Available: http://transformeducation.blogspot.com/2006_10_01_archive.html

Craig, B. (2006). The coalition column: History defined in Florida legislature. *Perspectives, 44*(6), 16. Available: www.historians.org/Perspectives/issues/2006/0609/0609nch1.cfm

Dillon, S. (2006, March 26). Schools cut back subjects to push reading and math. *New York Times,* p. A1.

Doherty, C. (2007). *Who files the flag? Not always who you might think: A closer look at patriotism.* Washington, DC: Pew Research Center. Available: http://pewresearch.org/pubs/525/who-flies-the-flag-not-always-who-you-might-think

Dreier, R, & Flacks, D. (2007). Patriotism's secret history. In J. Westheimer (Ed.), *Pledging allegiance: The politics of patriotism in America's schools* (pp. 165–169). New York: Teachers College Press.

Gonzales, D. (1995, May 23). Alternative schools: A bridge from hope to social action. *New York Times*, p. B2.

Hamilton College. (2003). *Hamilton College patriotism poll.* Clinton, NY: Author. Available: www.hamilton.edu/Levitt/surveys/patriotism

Ladson-Billings, G. (2006). Once upon a time when patriotism was something you did. *Phi Delta Kappan, 87*(8), 585–588.

Lummis, C. D. (1996). *Radical democracy.* Ithaca, NY: Cornell University Press.

North Central Regional Educational Laboratory. (2000). *Viewpoints: Vol. 7: Small by design—Resizing America's high schools.* Naperville, IL: Learning Points Associates.

Peterson, B. (2007). La Escuela Fratney: A journey toward democracy. In M. Apple & J. Beane (Eds.), *Democratic schools: Lessons in powerful education* (pp. 30–61). Portsmouth, NH: Heinemann.

Rentner, D. S., Scott, C., Kober, N., Chudowsky N., Chudowsky, V., Joftus, S., et al. (2006). *From the capital to the classroom: Year 4 of the No Child Left Behind Act.* Washington, DC: Center on Education Policy.

Schultz, B. D. (2007). Not satisfied with stupid band-aids: A portrait of a justice-oriented, democratic curriculum serving a disadvantaged neighborhood. *Equity and Excellence in Education, 40*(2), 166–176.

Thornton, S. (2005). Incorporating internationalism in the social studies curriculum. In N. Noddings (Ed.), *Educating citizens for global awareness* (pp. 81–92). New York: Teachers College Press.

Virginia Legislative Assembly. (2005). Pledge of Allegiance HB 1912. Available: http://legl.state.va.us/cgi-bin/legp504.exe?ses=051&typ=bil&rval=hbl912

Westheimer, J. (2005). *Real world learning: El Puente Academy and educational change* (Democratic Dialogue occasional paper series). Ottawa, Ontario: Democratic Dialogue.com.

Westheimer J. (2007). (Ed.). *Pledging allegiance: The politics, of patriotism in America's schools.* New York: Teachers College Press.

Westheimer J., & Kahne, J. (2003). Reconnecting education to democracy: Democratic dialogues. *Phi Delta Kappan Online.* Available: www.pdkintl.org/kappan/k0309wes.htm

Zimmerman J. (2006, June 7). Revisionists, get out of Florida. *Los Angeles Times,* p. B13.

JOEL WESTHEIMER is University Research Chair and Professor of Education, University of Ottawa, Ontario, Canada; joelw@uottawa.ca. He is the editor of *Pledging Allegiance: The Politics of Patriotism in America's Schools* (Teachers College Press, 2007).

Author's Note: Sharon Cook, Barbara Leckie, and Kristina Llewellyn contributed helpful comments on this article.

What Is Personalization?

Perhaps more than ever, today's schools need to produce lifelong learners who can adapt to a rapidly changing world. Mr. Keefe offers an idea that has been with us for decades that just might satisfy that need.

JAMES W. KEEFE

In the long history of formal education, schooling has rarely been personalized. It would be easy to compile a long list of famous individuals from the past who have been expelled from schools for their purported inability to learn. It is interesting to speculate whether such notably creative people as Charles Darwin, Patrick Henry, James Russell Lowell, Sir Isaac Newton, Louis Pasteur, Sir Walter Scott, and Daniel Webster were actually advantaged by being pushed out of the schools of their time. In more recent years, Madame Curie, Orville Wright, Albert Einstein, and Marlon Brando shared their fate.

But a truly personalized school would be able to recognize such budding genius. Indeed, it would be able to diagnose and support the whole range of human talents. A personalized school is one in which each individual person, whether student or teacher, matters a great deal and has a program that is good for him or her.

It was probably excusable for educators of Horace Mann's time to structure their schools on the assumption that all students learn in the same way and need precisely the same content. However, we are now faced with the enormous task of educating for a post-technological age. Today's schools must increasingly produce adaptable individuals who are lifelong learners and able to keep pace with the era of rapid change in which we will continue to live. The task of creating, maintaining, and improving the conditions for learning is thus the most basic challenge facing educators today. The outmoded structures that have encumbered schools for over a century must be replaced with more personalized ways of educating students and categorizing subject matter.

Human knowledge is expanding at an alarming rate. Technology and computerization have drastically altered the ways in which we earn a living. Social, political, and economic problems of unprecedented complexity face everyone on the planet. Schools can no longer be satisfied with organizing themselves primarily for administrative convenience. They must become schools for learning rather than schools for teaching and testing.

The conventional age-graded school system is a product of another century and initially of another culture. It was devised by the Prussians to prepare young people for a militaristic society, one in which authoritarianism was the dominant style. The system was imported into the U.S. at the Quincy Grammar School in Boston in 1848 and grew as population increases necessitated accommodating larger numbers of students. It has endured principally because it is easy to administer and neatly categorizes students and curriculum by age and subject.

We are faced with an equally large transition today from arbitrary grouping patterns to personalized learning alternatives. Unfortunately, we are also currently blessed with policy makers who believe they can solve all educational problems by testing. What we require are new models for a new kind of schooling. And we need to avoid the pitfalls of earlier decades when we successively concentrated on new curricula utilizing old teaching techniques or old content using new structures.

The Personalization Premise

Contemporary schools must acknowledge the validity of the personalization premise. They must accept the biological truth that no two organisms are alike, and that includes learners. Every learner has a unique experiential background and a unique set of innate talents and personal interests. No two learners exhibit the same behavioral patterns or possess the same goals or levels of aspiration. No two learners solve problems in the same way or are motivated by the same incentives. No two learners are ready to learn at the same time or to the same degree. Learning for each individual is, at least to some extent, unique.

The personalization of teaching and learning refers to any effort on the part of a school to suit its program to its student body. Ideally, each school should tailor the learning process to each student's needs and capacities. In practice, however, personalization can take on many forms, limited only by the human, institutional, and instructional resources of a given school. There is no one best way to personalize.

Admittedly, personalization is one of those concepts that take on many meanings depending on the experience and point of view of the observer. To some, it means individualization;

to others, it suggests a personal touch in dealing with students or a supportive school or classroom climate; to still others, it means an effort to empower individual students personally, psychologically, and instructionally. Differences in approaches to personalization over the past several decades have caused some confusion. However, I believe that we can be fairly precise in describing personalization. Indeed, if the pedagogy of personalization is to grow and exert a real influence on educational practice, we must be more specific.

Personalized instruction might well trace itself to the days when Mark Hopkins sat on one end of a log and his student James Garfield sat on the other. Surely no one can quarrel with that student/teacher ratio, but even tutoring can fall far short of personalization if the teacher is not aware of the student's previous knowledge and interests, cannot sufficiently relate to the student, or lacks sufficient pedagogical skills to help the student.

Antecedents of personalization have been known in the past under different names: nongraded education, continuous progress education, individualized instruction, individually guided or prescribed education, adaptive instruction, and so forth. Each of these concepts is concerned with personalization but in a limited way. Personalization is more focused on individual student needs and interests and is more authentic in its goals and strategies.

Personalization was cultivated in the Model Schools Project (MSP), sponsored from 1969 through 1974 by the National Association of Secondary School Principals (NASSP). It was adopted as the modus operandi by the special education movement. It was nurtured in the Learning Environments Consortium (LEC) International—a follow-up to MSP—and in the Coalition of Essential Schools.

The earliest formal use of the term "personalized" can be found in the Personalized System of Instruction (PSI) introduced for college students in 1962 by Fred Keller and his colleagues at the University of Brasilia. PSI is distinguished by student self-pacing, a mastery requirement for advancing to new material, the use of lectures and demonstrations as vehicles of motivation rather than information, stress on the written word in teacher/student communication, and the use of proctors to facilitate testing, tutoring, and social interaction.[1] The MSP relied on a variation of PSI as its preferred instructional model.

In the mid-1970s, University of Denver special educator Anne Welch Carroll proposed a new look at the relationship between general and special education. Her solution was personalized education, "an attempt to achieve a balance between the characteristics of the learner and the learning environment." Carroll recommended three basic elements for a personalized approach to education: the learner must be actively involved, the teacher must be a learning facilitator, and a student's program must be success-oriented.[2] Carroll's approach is still very much representative of best practice in special education today.

Also in the mid-1970s, I formulated a systematic model of personalization for LEC International that fleshed out the diagnosis/prescription/instruction/evaluation model employed by the Model Schools Project. I defined personalized education as "a systematic effort on the part of a school to take into account individual student characteristics and effective instructional practices in organizing the learning environment."[3] This personalized model is still employed by LEC International (with some refinements) and is used in self-directed Canadian schools.

In 1996, in *Breaking Ranks: Changing an American Institution,* NASSP proposed that American high schools commit themselves to substantive renewal, guided by six main themes and 13 interrelated sets of recommendations. First among the report's main themes, with many elements derived from MSP and LEC models, is personalization.[4] NASSP followed this report in 2004 with *Breaking Ranks II: Strategies for Leading High School Reform,* in collaboration with the Education Alliance at Brown University and its Center for Secondary School Design.[5] This second NASSP report included John Clarke's more elaborate definition of personalization, characterizing it as "a learning process in which schools help students assess their own talents and aspirations, plan a pathway toward their own purposes, work cooperatively with others on challenging tasks, maintain a record of their explorations, and demonstrate their learning against clear standards in a wide variety of media, all with the close support of adult mentors and guides."[6]

LEC International also updated its personalized education model in 2000, focusing specifically on the instructional component. In *Personalized Instruction: Changing Classroom Practice,* John Jenkins and I proposed six basic elements of personalized instruction that we believe constitute the *culture* and *context* of personalized instruction. The cultural components are a dual teacher role as facilitator and adviser, diagnosis of student learning characteristics, and a school culture of collegiality. The contextual factors are an interactive learning environment, flexible scheduling and pacing, and authentic assessment.[7]

Making Sense of Personalization

So personalization is not a new idea. It has been around for a long time—at least 40 years. Most educators, of course, have not given it a real try. Many don't know much about it or consider it too much trouble. Some see it as just another in the long line of innovations that have come and just as quickly gone. But personalization is not gone. It has grown in reputation and influence over the past decade.

Operationally, personalization consists in providing a program as nearly appropriate for each learner as is educationally and financially feasible. Personalization can be classroom-based or schoolwide. It can encompass older techniques, such as contract learning, project-based learning, and cooperative learning, or newer strategies, such as cognitive apprenticeships, guided practice, topic study, and differentiated instruction. But whatever the techniques, personalization starts and ends with the student.

It is apparent from even a cursory review of recent highly publicized school reform initiatives that personalization has not been a high priority in many of these designs. In our book on personalization, Jenkins and I judge the *quality* of personalization in terms of the *degree* of interaction and thoughtfulness that the design brings to the school learning environment. But neither interaction nor thoughtfulness is apparent in a number of contemporary school reform projects. Consider how little personalization is evident in the American Diploma Project (ADP), created in 1996 by the nation's governors and business leaders, and sponsored by Achieve, Inc. The ADP would mandate a college-prep curriculum for all students. It argues that recent research suggests that the skills that colleges require of incoming freshmen are very similar to those needed for "good" white-collar and blue-collar jobs. The ADP urges a kind of "default" curriculum for all students, which would "align high school standards and assessments with the knowledge and skills required for success after high school" and "require all high school graduates to take challenging courses that actually prepare them for life after high school."[8]

While this research may well be valid, and the goal is certainly worthwhile, this strategy is unfortunately closer to begging the question than finding the answer to America's school achievement problem. Not all students have the interest or even the academic skills to complete a college-prep curriculum. Nor could some of them even attempt such a program unless it were paired with a highly responsive and personalized instructional delivery system. And that's not a part of *any* of these one-size-fits-all proposals. For many students, this curriculum would mean adding months or years to their schooling—certainly acceptable educationally, but very expensive and hardly motivating to the recipients. If the ADP "core curriculum" were the "essential learnings" of the NASSP Model Schools Project, LEC International, and the Coalition of Essential Schools, then the goal would be more readily achievable. (Essential learnings in these projects are what every student should basically know and be able to do.) And of course, there remains the question of what constitutes a "good" job, which still lies very much in the eye of the beholder.

In 1999, a coalition of educational associations (including administrators' associations and teacher unions) published a review of 24 existing school renewal efforts. Of these, about one-third exhibit strong elements of personalization, while another third utilize some personalized features, and a final third use none at all.[9] The New American Schools project, a national initiative to develop replicable, schoolwide reform programs, and its successor, the Coalition for Comprehensive School Improvement, recommend several school designs that favor personalization. These include the Accelerated Schools Project (building on teacher and student strengths and collaborative inquiry), ATLAS Learning Communities (respect for individual differences, authentic assessment, student exhibitions, and school climate improvement), and Expeditionary Learning Schools Outward Bound (multidisciplinary projects and a school culture of collaboration).[10]

Several other independent school renewal initiatives also encompass elements of personalization. The Foxfire Fund "Core Practices," developed in 1966 by Eliot Wigginton, incorporate student choice and design, teacher as collaborator and facilitator, active learning, smallgroup work, peer teaching, community as learning laboratory, and reflection as a component of learning. The High/Scope K-3 model was also developed in the 1960s to include active and hands-on learning, students' planning and evaluation of their own learning activities, small-group

"experience" workshops, and "activity centers" where students work together. The Coalition of Essential Schools embodies in its "Common Principles" the concepts of essential knowledge and skills, personalized teaching and learning, teacher as coach, a supportive school "ethos," and authentic assessment.[11]

The Bill & Melinda Gates Foundation approach also incorporates some elements of personalization. The Gates initiative focuses on increasing U.S. graduation and college-readiness rates. The foundation envisions "High Schools for the New Millennium," in which "all students in the United States can and must graduate from high school, and they must leave with the skills necessary for college, work, and citizenship."

The Gates program advocates a new 3 R's: rigor, relevance, and relationships. Rigor implies a challenging and coherent curriculum that emphasizes depth over coverage, encourages analytic thinking, and focuses on "fewer topics and grappling with the subtleties." Relevance presumes real-world application, where "students are given the time to explore important topics and apply their learning to new problems in a variety of settings." Relationships envision a supportive school environment and small school size (no more than 400 students), with counselors taking an enhanced role in advising no more than 80 students each. Teachers serve as coaches and lead students to take responsibility for their own learning. The Gates view is a compromise between college-prep for all and a personalized vision for the curricular and instructional environment of the school.[12]

So What Is Personalization?

Students of personalization might very well disagree on a precise conceptual definition for the process, but I believe that we can formulate a *descriptive profile* of personalization by bringing together the concepts that most of the pioneers, practitioners, and scholars of personalization might include in such a description. Personalization from this perspective is a systematic process for organizing a school for success. It is an attempt to achieve a balance between the characteristics of the learner and those of the learning environment, between what is challenging and productive and what is beyond the student's present capabilities. It is a systematic effort on the part of a school to take into account individual student characteristics and effective instructional practices in organizing the learning environment. It is a learning process in which schools help students assess their own talents and aspirations, plan a pathway to meet their own purposes, work cooperatively with others on challenging tasks, maintain a record of their explorations, and demonstrate their learning against clear standards in a wide variety of media, all with the close support of adult mentors and guides.[13]

The *philosophy* of personalization is learner-centered—the learner must be actively involved. Personalization builds on the learner's strengths and employs real skill development that reduces cognitive deficiencies so that the learner can experience satisfaction and success. Emphasis is placed on the uniqueness of the individual student, the tenets of self-direction, and the need for student responsibility.

Personalization requires interactive *learning environments* designed to foster collaboration and reflective conversation. The personalized learning environment is child-centered, with a values orientation, a measure of creativity, and constructive learning activities. It builds on the child's natural ways of learning, with a unity of thought, action, activities, and experiences. An essential ingredient of personalization is a school culture of collaboration in which teachers, students, parents, and other community members work together in a cooperative social environment to develop meaningful learning activities for all students.

No single pattern of horizontal or vertical *school organization* is normative in a personalized school. The school is structured as a knowledge-work organization, with students as active workers and learning apprentices; with teachers as designers of high-quality work, learning facilitators, and performance coaches; and with both students and teachers as collaborative decision makers. Educational space is organized into learning centers, laboratories, or seminar areas where students can pursue personal research, work with self-paced learning materials, fulfill educational contracts, and participate in small-group projects.

Advisement is integral to personalization. Advisement is a process that brings the student continuously into contact with persons, places, and actions that facilitate development of the student's talents and interests. The "teacher adviser" or "personal adult advocate" is the key person in this process. Each student has a teacher adviser who acts as an academic adviser and personal advocate. Students select or are assigned a teacher adviser who meets with them on a regular basis, usually daily, to help them establish a personal plan for progress (i.e., an individualized educational plan), to check their attendance, and to make adjustments in their schedules. The foundation of advisement is a diagnostic profile developed for each student, identifying the learner's personal characteristics, attitudes, knowledge, skills, and learning styles.

The *curriculum* of a personalized school connects to real life whenever possible, helping students to connect their education to the future. Each secondary school identifies a set of essential learnings—in literature and language, writing, mathematics, social studies, science, and the arts—in which students must demonstrate achievement in order to graduate. The academic program extends beyond the secondary school campus to take advantage of learning opportunities outside the four walls of the building.

In personalization, no attempt is made to impose one model of *instruction* or *learning* on all teachers and students. Personalization demands that the teacher assume a dual role—subject-matter coach and teacher adviser—for small groups of students. Teachers as instructors are primarily facilitators, guides, and consultants rather than presenters of information. The teacher focuses on student development, motivation, and success, starting with a diagnostic profile and meaningful learning activities for each student and culminating in an instructional process and a learning environment that support authentic student performance. Instruction is authentic, reflecting construction (rather than reproduction) of knowledge, disciplined

inquiry, and value beyond school. Teachers have primary input into the selection of subject matter, the actual instruction, and the day-to-day administration of the school. They also develop self-paced instructional materials and small-group activities to enable students to progress at their own pace and according to their own individual needs. Thus students may work for longer or shorter periods of time on some activities without being tied to the teacher's schedule.

The personalized *school schedule* provides both flexibility and adequate structure for learning activities. Personalized scheduling may use blocks of time or continuous progress arrangements or may be entirely open, but the schedule is always flexible and serves the perceived needs of students. Thus the schedule departs from the traditional arrangement of six to eight separate subjects and a school day divided into related and virtually equal units of time.

Personalized *assessment* begins with the diagnosis of individual students' knowledge and skills (formative assessment). Teachers integrate assessment into instruction so that it not only rates student performance but becomes part of the learning process. Students are judged in terms of performance criteria and personal achievement, rather than according to relative standing within a group. Personalization places the emphasis on performance rather than on time. Personalization typically employs a mastery requirement that allows students to advance to new material only after demonstrating mastery of what preceded it. Students complete end-of-unit tests when they are ready, rather than when an arbitrary class schedule dictates. Personalized assessment includes such activities as demonstrations, oral and written presentations, performances, contests, projects, and problem-solving activities.

> **Personalized assessment includes such activities as demonstrations, oral and written presentations, performances, contests, projects, and problem-solving activities.**

Schools rate the *academic progress* of students in a variety of ways so that a clear and valid picture emerges of what students know and are able to do. If grades are given, they are assigned on an absolute basis and certify what a student has or has not learned, not where the student stands in relation to classmates.

Conclusion

The recent motion picture *Freedom Writers* graphically illustrates how challenging and yet how variable personalized education can be. The film is based on the experiences of a new freshman English teacher, Erin Gruwell, who accepts a position in a Long Beach, California, high school shortly after the 1992 Rodney King riots in Los Angeles. The 23-year-old Gruwell has no idea how to relate to, much less teach, her predominantly minority students in this integrated and gang-ridden inner-city school. She tries a number of unsuccessful strategies and then begins to think outside the box. She knows that she must connect with her students first and break down cultural and generational barriers before she can begin to teach them anything.

Gruwell tells the students about the Holocaust, and they read Anne Frank's diary in paperbacks that she personally buys for them. The students can relate to Anne, and they begin to open up. Gruwell has found a strategy to allow her students to begin where they are and to work with their personal identities. She asks them to keep a journal of their thoughts and experiences, like Anne Frank's, to write in it whatever they feel is important to them, and to keep it confidential—even from her, unless they want her to read it.

Of course, the students recognize an opportunity to express their most personal thoughts and aspirations, without even knowing that they are writing, communicating, and demonstrating many of the skills that most English teachers would die for. And of course, they want their teacher to read their journals. (The compilation was eventually published.)

In a keynote address to the 2006 PDK Summit on Public Education, John Goodlad cautioned that our schools are becoming more like "training centers." He commented that "academic test scores do not correlate with any of the virtues to which our democracy aspires. None. . . . Good education provides a sense of community, personal identity, inner strength, purpose, meaning, and belonging."[14] Erin Gruwell found a way to bring that sense of personal identity, purpose, and belonging to her students. That "good education" about which Goodlad speaks is precisely what personalization hopes to bring to all students.

Benjamin Disraeli once said that "the goal of politicians is to get in front of the inevitable." I believe that personalization is the inevitable design and fabric of schooling. Today's politicians, policy makers, and educators should get in front of the inevitable. It is high time that we acknowledge that all human learning is personal. No one can learn for anyone else, nor can anybody teach anyone anything unless the learner wants to know it. Personalizing instruction and learning is education's only valid response to these facts of human nature.

In programs committed to personalization, students are expected to take a greater share of the responsibility for the success of their own education. Initially, many students find this difficult because they have been "trained" to be highly dependent on others for their learning. Indeed, many students come from a background that includes a large measure of teacher spoonfeeding. Hence, the whole learning environment must be restructured to help students become more self-directed. No social promotions, no merciful D's. Everyone has to work. There will certainly need to be a period of reorganization and redesign of our current bureaucratic model of schooling. What happens next depends on the knowledge and skills of school principals, school leadership teams, teaching staffs, and parents and community support groups. All of these stakeholders must work together and keep clearly in mind that personalization simply means humanizing the learning process and placing the learner first.

References

1. Fred S. Keller, "Goodbye, Teacher . . . ," *Journal of Applied Behavior Analysis,* vol. 1, 1968, pp. 79–89.
2. Anne Welch Carroll, *Personalized Education in the Classroom* (Denver: Love Publishing, 1975), pp. 19–25.
3. James W. Keefe, "Personalized Education," in Herbert J. Walberg and John J. Lane, eds., *Organizing for Learning: Toward the 21st Century* (Reston, Va.: National Association of Secondary School Principals, 1989), pp. 74–78.
4. *Breaking Ranks: Changing an American Institution* (Reston, Va.: NASSP, 1996), p. 5.
5. *Breaking Ranks II: Strategies for Leading High School Reform* (Reston, Va.: NASSP, 2004), p. 67.
6. John H. Clarke, *Changing Systems to Personalize Learning: Introduction to the Personalization Workshop* (Providence: Brown University, Education Alliance, 2003), p. 15.
7. James W. Keefe and John M. Jenkins, *Personalized Instruction: Changing Classroom Practice* (Larchmont, N.Y.: Eye on Education, 2000), pp. 35–93.
8. Achieve, Inc., "How States Are Closing the Expectations Gap," available at www.achieve.org/node/477; or see American Diploma Project, *Ready or Not: Creating a High School Diploma That Counts* (Washington, D.C.: Achieve, 2004), available at www.achieve.org/node/552.
9. *An Educator's Guide to Schoolwide Reform* (Arlington, Va.: Educational Research Service, 1999), available at www.aasa .org. Search on the title.
10. The Coalition for Comprehensive School Improvement, available at www.improvingschools.org/accomplishments/ index.html.
11. See *An Educator's Guide to School Reform.*
12. Bill & Melinda Gates Foundation, "High Schools for the New Millennium: Imagine the New Possibilities," pp. 6–10, available at www.gatesfoundation.org/nr/downloads/ed/edwhitepaper.pdf.
13. This definition is derived from Keller, op. cit.; Carroll, op. cit.; Keefe, op. cit; *Breaking Ranks* and *Breaking Ranks II;* Keefe and Jenkins, op. cit.; and Clarke, op. cit.
14. John Goodlad, "What Schools Are For," keynote address to the 2006 PDK Summit on Public Education, quoted in *PDK Connection,* Winter 2007, p. 1.

JAMES W. KEEFE, a former Model Schools Project high school principal, is retired director of research for the National Association of Secondary School Principals and current president of LEC International. His most recent book, co-authored with John Jenkins, is *Personalized Instruction: Key to Student Achievement,* available in February 2008 from Rowman & Littlefield. He lives in Reston, Va.

Cultivating Optimism in the Classroom

Students are motivated to put forth their best effort when they have faith in the future and themselves.

RICHARD SAGOR

There's a proverb, "The best predictor of the future is the past." This notion isn't lost on Hollywood and helps explain the attractiveness of such movies as *Stand and Deliver* and *Freedom Writers,* which turn it on its head. *Stand and Deliver* tells the story of math teacher Jaime Escalante, whose previously underachieving students went on in great numbers to pass the advanced placement (AP) test in calculus; and *Freedom Writers* tells the story of Erin Gruwell, who inspired her inner-city students to transform their lives through journal writing. Audiences are captivated by seeing poor, alienated teenagers who are well behind their peers in basic skills and have a near total disdain for the education process unexpectedly emerge a few years later with top AP scores, published books, and a desire for a college education.

Unfortunately, what makes this storyline so compelling is that it's so rare. A more familiar scene is this: angry, low-income teenagers with a history of school failure wandering the school hallways with little apparent interest in academics, the curriculum, or their teachers. For too many of them, gangs are more attractive than school activities, drugs are more valuable than learning, and the streets are more appealing than school.

We know the facts. Nearly 50 percent of Latino, black, and American Indian youth leave school before graduating (Orfield, Losen, Wald, & Swanson, 2004). The academic performance of students in low-income communities lags well behind that of students living in more privileged enclaves. The message most often taken from movies like *Stand and Deliver* is that these students' success was the result of the magical powers of a few special, charismatic teachers.

Hollywood wants us to think that Escalante and Gruwell are superheroes, but I'd rather think of them as colleagues who have demonstrated an important lesson regarding what it takes to motivate all our diverse students to strive for the best.

Building Optimism

Whenever we face a choice, we intuitively make a calculation. Typically, we assess the potential costs and benefits—both short- and long-term—of doing one thing instead of another. On the basis of that assessment, we act.

As parents, we are delighted when we see our children defer immediate gratification to achieve a more important long-range goal. At school, we often deliberately teach the merit of investing now for returns in the future. For example, teenage athletes learn the relationship between hard work at practices and success at the game on Friday night. Other students elect to do well in school out of a firm belief that getting good grades will lead to admission to a selective college, which will lead to a happy adult life.

We might wonder why this calculation isn't convincing for all students. Why aren't they buying in? The reason is simple: Investing today for a payoff tomorrow requires believing in your future. Put succinctly, motivation requires optimism.

Investing today for a payoff tomorrow requires believing in your future.

Sometimes it appears that optimism—a positive belief in the future—is a genetic trait. This is one explanation for why children of successful people tend to be successful themselves. And, conversely, it helps explain why children from families that must continually struggle to just get by often find themselves engaged in similar struggles on reaching adulthood.

But the good news, dramatically demonstrated by teachers like Jaime Escalante and Erin Gruwell, is that optimism can be taught and learned. Two key variables are the building blocks of optimism: faith and efficacy.

Building Block 1: Faith in the Future

For me to invest time and energy today for a benefit I won't realize until tomorrow, I need to have a good reason to believe that my investment will pay off. Clearly, it's much easier to acquire that faith when one's immediate environment regularly shows concrete evidence of return on investment. John Ogbu (1991) has written extensively about how children tend to look to the experience of adults in their communities and extended families to predict what lies ahead for them.

If children see despair around them, it's likely that they will fear that this represents their destiny. Many children simply have no good reason to expect tomorrow to be any better than today. There are many legitimate reasons for despair: the impact of poverty, chemical dependency, bigotry, family break-ups, and so on.

If the picture is rosier, however, children have a better chance of being optimistic about their futures. One powerful demonstration of the positive influence of faith in the future was the experience of philanthropist Eugene Lang (White, 1987), the founder of the "I Have a Dream" Foundation. In an impromptu speech, Lang promised a free college education to 61 6th graders at a New York public school if they stayed in school and graduated. Although statistics showed that 75 percent of the students wouldn't go on to graduate from high school, more than 90 percent of Lang's dreamers graduated, with more than two-thirds attending college. What these students had lacked was sufficient reason to believe in their futures. Once they had a justification for faith, they did what it took to realize success.

Efficacy is a deep-seated belief in our own capabilities. It explains the phenomenon of success breeding success.

Building Block 2: Personal Efficacy

In general, it takes more than faith to commit to a difficult pursuit. Optimistic people have the fortitude to persevere with complex tasks because they are confident that if they work long and hard enough and apply enough creativity, they will, in fact, succeed.

Efficacy is a deep-seated belief in our own capabilities. It explains the phenomenon of success breeding success. Every time people attack a problem and succeed, they have authentic evidence of their capability. The more data I have about my capabilities, the more confident I will be of my potential to achieve future success.

Early in my teaching career, I decided to expect every student to produce work deserving of an *A* or *B*; otherwise, his or her grade would be *NYE*—not yet excellent. Occasionally it took extra time, but every student was ultimately able to leave my class with evidence of his or her capability.

There's a reason why so many parents love the story of The Little Engine That Could. We all know that if someone keeps hearing a credible inner voice repeating, "I think I can, I think I can, I think I can," that person will start believing it.

Building Faith and Efficacy in School

Empowered Preschoolers

My daughters went to the Montessori preschool in the local Catholic church. They loved it, as did all their classmates, and they happily got up each morning to go to school. Donna

Hargraeves was their teacher, and in her classroom, the children had continual opportunities to explore and learn. She directed the students to activities at a level at which, with effort, they could achieve success.

I can still vividly recall the first open house we attended. I was expecting to hear a teacher presentation, receive handouts, or engage in a conference with the teacher. It was nothing like that. As I entered the room, it looked no different from when I dropped Ellisa off each morning. An aide greeted my daughter and handed her a 3 × 5 index card that listed all the lessons she had mastered. She was then invited to show us what she could do.

For the next 40 minutes, Ellisa led us around the room and treated us to demonstrations of things she had learned. Her pride in her accomplishments was palpable, and as I looked around, I saw the same scene repeated child after child. It was clear to me that the teacher was developing optimism in that room every day with every child.

This was my first experience with student-led parent-teacher conferences, this one brilliantly directed by a 4-year-old. In 40 minutes, I learned more about what my daughter could do, what she had accomplished, and what she was still working on than I ever could have gotten from a traditional conference. But, most important, I witnessed the development of a powerful sense of efficacy on Ellisa's part. She was sharing *her* accomplishments, which were the result of *her* efforts, and she was deservedly beaming with pride and confidence.

Now a junior in college, Ellisa takes on any challenge placed in front of her. There is no doubt in my mind that those crucial early experiences in Donna Hargraeves's classroom empowered her with the conviction that when she sets her mind to something, she can do it.

Sixth Grade Astronauts

Every May at Liberty Middle School in Camas, Washington, approximately 125 6th graders spend a long 10-hour day in space. This extraordinary simulation is a collaborative project that has evolved over several years.

Each space station crew includes five specialists—a mission commander, a life sciences specialist, a health and nutrition specialist, a robotics specialist, and a communications officer. Immediately after spring break, students must prepare written applications for at least two different positions. The teachers then select students for the five crews, and over the next 10 weeks, the students prepare for the mission. At times, all the students who have the same position work with one another in a group—all the mission commanders meet, all the life sciences specialists meet, and so on. At other times, students work with their crewmates, training for the work required during their day in space.

When parents bring their kids to school on the morning of the mission, the gymnasium is a sight to behold. In one corner is mission control, a bank of computers, monitors, and microphones from which the teachers and mission control officers (older students who have been through the program) monitor the astronauts' work. Most of the gym is filled with the space station, which is made up of six connected modules. Soon the students don their spacesuits and gather for the preflight briefing from their teacher. Then, like clockwork, every five minutes another crew enters the space shuttle for the short flight to the International Space Station. For the next 10 hours, the only people each crew will interact with are fellow crew members and mission control.

The five crews rotate through the different modules and carry out their work without ever seeing or interacting with one another. They prepare and eat food in the galley, manipulate objects outside the spacecraft with robotic equipment, conduct experiments on plants and animals, observe rest periods, and even follow exercise routines to keep fit.

The day in space ends with a press conference conducted from the space station. Parents and guests get to see their children on the monitors and listen as the "astronauts" describe what transpired and what they learned on their long and grueling mission. After the press conference, the astronauts board the shuttle and return to earth.

The teachers have structured this 10-week experience in a manner that enhances the academic program rather than detracts from it. Each crew member must do a great deal of reading, writing, math, science, and social studies to prepare for the mission; and this intensive training pays off. Invariably, the mission succeeds, and the crews do their work well. Most important, each crew member possesses concrete evidence of his or her success as a leader, learner, and teacher, engendering a powerful sense of optimism. This optimism lasts quite a while; several former 6th grade astronauts are now in college studying aerospace.

Middle School Reformers

At a large middle school in Southern California that serves a racially, economically, and ethnically diverse community, an English teacher and a doctoral student invited interested students to join them as coresearchers in an investigation of the obstacles to learning at their school (SooHoo, 1993). Twelve students agreed to meet for regular lunchtime discussions. The student researchers were mostly a diverse group of immigrant and minority students, with several English language learners among them. These students weren't particularly comfortable with their place in society or school. Armed with cameras and sketch pads, the students set out to record areas of concern and discuss them at their lunch meetings.

After a few months of deliberation, the student researchers began to see a pattern in their data. Some aspects of the school program weren't working as well as they should. Students had ideas about changing the school's discipline and reward policy as well as the physical education program. They began developing ideas for program improvement.

They soon realized that they lacked power to bring about the desired changes. Together with their adult mentors, the students requested the opportunity to present their research to the faculty. In a faculty meeting at which they served cookies, cupcakes, and soft drinks, the students presented their research. Later that spring on a scheduled professional development day, the 12 students were invited to work side by side with their teachers in making plans for the new school year. On the basis of the students' input, the school revised the discipline and reward process and redesigned the physical education program.

I met these students a few years later when they presented their research to an audience of university professors at the annual American Educational Research Association conference. The students—now high school sophomores—were articulate, confident, and absolutely certain they were headed to college and professional careers. After they learned as middle school students that they had powerful voices and were capable of persuading adult professionals with their arguments, nothing could stop them from achieving their goals.

After they learned as middle school students that they had powerful voices, nothing could stop them from achieving their goals.

An Environmental Advocate

A high school student named Sam recently became interested in the movement to design and build environmentally sound "green" buildings. He was not a good student academically, had few friends and little status, and didn't fit in with or have much respect for the social activities that defined the traditional high school experience.

But he didn't lack confidence. He went to the high school administrators with an elaborate written proposal describing an independent study he wanted to do on the potential conversion of a recently built public building to meet green building standards. He worked hard on his proposal and was excited about pursuing this work. Unfortunately, the school didn't see it the same way. As a result, Sam decided to leave to attend a nearby alternative school in the hope that its community-based learning model might be a better fit.

The teachers' reaction to his proposal at the alternative school was markedly different. The school made arrangements for Sam to intern at one of the largest and most prestigious architectural firms in the region. One day in a meeting with several of the firm's top architects, a lead architect commented that the constraints of school construction limited possible energy efficiencies.

Sam spoke up. His research had revealed that six buildings recently built in Los Angeles now operated completely off the grid. Impressed, the architects asked Sam to do more research. The next day Sam presented this "new information" to some of the leaders in the field.

Sam has now graduated and is making plans to attend college. Although he readily admits that he is the proverbial square peg that people try to push through a round hole, he has no doubt about his ability to accomplish whatever he sets his mind to.

Great Expectations

It is naive to think there could be an easy answer to all our student motivation problems. But one thing is clear: Young people are more likely to invest their energy in pursuit of what they view to be an achievable dream than in what they sense is futility.

That's why students need continuous encouragement and hope from schools—so they can believe in their futures and themselves. Every day as students leave our classrooms we need to ask ourselves two questions: As a result of todays experience, will these students be more or less confident that their futures are bright? Will students walk out of the classroom feeling more capable than when they walked in?

Will students walk out of the classroom feeling more capable than when they walked in?

Every morning an alarm clock goes off, a student awakes, and thoughts begin to form. What should the student expect from the upcoming day? If he or she were lucky enough to have had a teacher like Jaime Escalante or Erin Gruwell, or had been promised a college education by Eugene Lang, that student may well be looking forward to a bright future. But optimism shouldn't depend on having a superhero as a teacher or on receiving help from a philanthropist. We teachers can

nurture optimism in all our students by creating routine education experiences in which hard work leads to success and a world of possibilities.

References

Ogbu, J. U. (1991). Immigrant and involuntary minorities in comparative perspective. In M. A. Gibson & J. U. Ogbu (Eds.), *Minority status and schooling: A comparative study of immigrant and involuntary minorities* (pp. 3–33). New York: Garland.

Orfield, G., Losen, D., Wald, J., & Swanson, C. B. (2004). *Losing our future: How minority youth are being left behind by the graduation rate crisis.* Cambridge, MA: The Civil Rights Project at Harvard University. Available: www.urban.org/uploadedPDF/410936_LosingOurFuture.pdf

SooHoo, S. (1993). Students as partners in research and restructuring schools. *The Educational Forum, 57*(4), 386–393.

White, J. (1987). Eugene Lang: Dream-maker to the kids of Harlem. *AGB Reports, 29*(3), 10–17.

RICHARD SAGOR is Professor and Director of the Educational Leadership Program at Lewis and Clark College, Portland, Oregon; sagor@lclark.edu.

Test-Your-Knowledge Form

We encourage you to photocopy and use this page as a tool to assess how the articles in *Annual Editions* expand on the information in your textbook. By reflecting on the articles you will gain enhanced text information. You can also access this useful form on a product's book support website at *http://www.mhcls.com*.

NAME: DATE:

_____

TITLE AND NUMBER OF ARTICLE:

_____

BRIEFLY STATE THE MAIN IDEA OF THIS ARTICLE:

_____

LIST THREE IMPORTANT FACTS THAT THE AUTHOR USES TO SUPPORT THE MAIN IDEA:

_____

WHAT INFORMATION OR IDEAS DISCUSSED IN THIS ARTICLE ARE ALSO DISCUSSED IN YOUR TEXTBOOK OR OTHER READINGS THAT YOU HAVE DONE? LIST THE TEXTBOOK CHAPTERS AND PAGE NUMBERS:

_____

LIST ANY EXAMPLES OF BIAS OR FAULTY REASONING THAT YOU FOUND IN THE ARTICLE:

_____

LIST ANY NEW TERMS/CONCEPTS THAT WERE DISCUSSED IN THE ARTICLE, AND WRITE A SHORT DEFINITION:

We Want Your Advice

ANNUAL EDITIONS revisions depend on two major opinion sources: one is our Advisory Board, listed in the front of this volume, which works with us in scanning the thousands of articles published in the public press each year; the other is you—the person actually using the book. Please help us and the users of the next edition by completing the prepaid article rating form on this page and returning it to us. Thank you for your help!

ANNUAL EDITIONS: Education 10/11

ARTICLE RATING FORM

Here is an opportunity for you to have direct input into the next revision of this volume.
We would like you to rate each of the articles listed below, using the following scale:

1. **Excellent: should definitely be retained**
2. **Above average: should probably be retained**
3. **Below average: should probably be deleted**
4. **Poor: should definitely be deleted**

Your ratings will play a vital part in the next revision.
Please mail this prepaid form to us as soon as possible.
Thanks for your help!

RATING	ARTICLE	RATING	ARTICLE
	1. Where Have All the Strong Poets Gone?		21. Why Teacher Networks (Can) Work
	2. Proficiency for All?		22. Response to Intervention (RTI): What Teachers of Reading Need to Know
	3. Bridging the Gap between Research and Practice: What's Good, What's Bad, and How Can One Be Sure?		23. You Should Read This Book!
	4. Learning to Love Assessment		24. Getting Children In2Books : Engagement in Authentic Reading, Writing, and Thinking
	5. The Case for and against Homework		25. Using Literature Circles with English Language Learners at the Middle Level
	6. Assessing Applied Skills		26. Losing the Fear of Sharing Control: Starting a Reading Workshop
	7. From the Mouths of Middle-Schoolers: Important Changes for High School and College		27. Nine Ways to Catch Kids Up
	8. Industrial Arts: Call It What You Want, the Need Still Exists		28. The Classroom That Math Built: Encouraging Young Mathematicians to Pose Problems
	9. High Schools Have Got It Bad for Higher Ed— And That Ain't Good		29. Tackling a Problematic Behavior Management Issue: Teachers' Intervention in Childhood Bullying Problems
	10. All Our Students Thinking		30. The Under-Appreciated Role of Humiliation in the Middle School
	11. As Diversity Grows, So Must We		31. The Power of Our Words
	12. African American Parents: Improving Connections with Their Child's Educational Environment		32. Marketing Civility
	13. The Myth of the "Culture of Poverty"		33. Classwide Interventions: Effective Instruction Makes a Difference
	14. Becoming Adept at Code-Switching		34. Developing Effective Behavior Intervention Plans : Suggestions for School Personnel
	15. Overcoming Lethargy in Gifted and Talented Education with Contract Activity Packages: I'm Choosing to Learn!		35. Becoming Citizens of the World
	16. Mother Goose Teaches on the Wild Side: Motivating At-Risk Mexican and Chicano Youngsters via a Multicultural Curriculum		36. Democracy and Education: Empowering Students to Make Sense of Their World
	17. Celebrating Diversity through Explorations of Arab Children's Literature		37. Thinking about Patriotism
	18. Books That Portray Characters with Disabilities: A Top 25 List for Children and Young Adults		38. What Is Personalization?
	19. Reluctant Teachers, Reluctant Learners		39. Cultivating Optimism in the Classroom
	20. Musing: A Way to Inform and Inspire Pedagogy through Self-Reflection		

ABOUT YOU

Name   Date

Are you a teacher? ❏ A student? ❏
Your school's name

Department

Address   City   State   Zip

School telephone #

YOUR COMMENTS ARE IMPORTANT TO US!

Please fill in the following information:
For which course did you use this book?

Did you use a text with this ANNUAL EDITION? ❏ yes ❏ no
What was the title of the text?

What are your general reactions to the Annual Editions concept?

Have you read any pertinent articles recently that you think should be included in the next edition? Explain.

Are there any articles that you feel should be replaced in the next edition? Why?

Are there any World Wide Websites that you feel should be included in the next edition? Please annotate.

May we contact you for editorial input? ❏ yes ❏ no
May we quote your comments? ❏ yes ❏ no